Debates and Issues in
Feminist Research and Pedagogy

Debates and Issues in Feminist Research and Pedagogy

This Reader is part of an Open University Course (E826) Gender Issues in Education: Equality and Difference, forming one module in the MA in Education programme. The selection is related to other material available to students. Opinions expressed in individual articles are not necessarily those of the course team or of the University.

Other volumes published as part of this course by Multilingual Matters Ltd in association with The Open University:

Identity and Diversity: Gender and the Experience of Education
    M. BLAIR and J. HOLLAND, with S. SHELDON (eds)
Equality and Inequality in Education Policy
    L. DAWTREY, J. HOLLAND and M. HAMMER, with S. SHELDON (eds)

For information about books of related interest, please contact:
Multilingual Matters Ltd,
Frankfurt Lodge, Clevedon Hall, Victoria Road,
Clevedon, Avon BS21 7SJ, England

Gender Issues in Education: Equality and Difference

Debates and Issues in Feminist Research and Pedagogy

A Reader edited by
Janet Holland and Maud Blair,
with Sue Sheldon
at The Open University

MULTILINGUAL MATTERS LTD
Clevedon • Philadelphia • Adelaide
in association with
THE OPEN UNIVERSITY

Library of Congress Cataloging in Publication Data

Debates and Issues in Feminist Research and Pedagogy: A Reader/Edited by Janet Holland and Maud Blair with Sue Sheldon.
(Equality and Difference)
1. Feminism and education. 2. Feminism and education–Research. 3. Sex differences in education. 4. Education–Research–Methodology. I. Holland, Janet. II.
Blair, Maud. III. Sheldon, Sue. IV. Series.
LC197.D42   1995
370.19'345–dc20   94-29844

British Library Cataloguing in Publication Data

A CIP catalogue record for this book is available from the British Library.

ISBN 1-85359-252-8 (hbk)
ISBN 1-85359-251-X (pbk)

Multilingual Matters Ltd

UK: Frankfurt Lodge, Clevedon Hall, Victoria Road, Clevedon, Avon BS21 7SJ.
USA: 1900 Frost Road, Suite 101, Bristol, PA 19007, USA.
Australia: P.O. Box 6025, 83 Gilles Street, Adelaide, SA 5000, Australia.

Selection, editorial matter and commissioned items (Articles 10 and 11)
copyright © 1995 The Open University.

Cover design by Bob Jones Associates.
Index by Meg Davies (Society of Indexers).
Typeset by Action Typesetting, Gloucester.
Printed and bound in Great Britain by WBC Ltd, Bridgend.

CONTENTS

PART 3: RESEARCH

PREFACE

This Reader is the third in a set of three volumes that have been prepared for the course E826, *Gender Issues in Education: Equality and Difference*, a module in the Open University's taught MA in Education. In addition to the two companion Readers, *Identity and Diversity: Gender and the Experience of Education* and *Equality and Inequality in Education Policy*, the course materials include a Study Guide and two audio-cassettes.

In this Reader the focus is on practical issues concerned with teaching and research, class, gender, 'race' and sexuality. Several of the authors consider the possibilities and practicalities of transformative feminist pedagogies, and also deal with the ongoing and lively debate on feminist methodology and epistemology, indicating the variety of approaches and positions that are being adopted in this area. A wide range of perspectives are covered within these articles, and the opinions expressed are not necessarily those of the course writers or of The Open University. The Reader should be of particular interest to teachers who want to translate explanations for gender relations into transformative action in the classroom.

Further information about the course can be obtained by writing to: Central Enquiry Service, PO Box 200, The Open University, Milton Keynes MK7 6YZ.

SOURCES

We would like to thank the authors and publishers concerned for kindly granting permission to reproduce copyright material in this Reader. Every effort has been made to trace the correct copyright owners, both authors and publishers, as listed by article below.

1. **S. Taylor** Feminist Classroom Practice and Cultural Politics: 'Girl Number Twenty' and Ideology
   From: *Journal for Theoretical Studies: Media and Cultures*, Vol. 11 (2), 1991. Bloomington: Indiana University Press.
2. **K. Weiler** Freire and a Feminist Pedagogy of Difference
   From: *Harvard Educational Review*, Vol. 61 (4), pp. 499–74, 1991. Copyright by the President and Fellows of Harvard College. All rights reserved.
3. **B. Davies and C. Banks** The Gender Trap: A Feminist Poststructuralist Analysis of Primary School Children's Talk About Gender
   From: *Journal of Curriculum Studies*, Vol. 24 (1), pp. 1–25, 1992. Basingstoke: Taylor and Francis.
4. **H.E. Longino and E. Hammonds** Conflicts and Tensions in the Feminist Study of Gender and Science
   From: Hirsch, M. and Fox-Keller, E. (1990) *Conflicts in Feminism* (pp. 164–83). London: Routledge.
5. **S. Scraton** Gender and Girls' Physical Education: Future Policy, Future Directions
   From: Scraton, S. (1992) *Shaping up to Womanhood: Gender and Girls' Physical Education* (pp. 112–136). Buckingham: Open University Press.
6. **H.S. Mirza** Life in the Classroom
   From: Mirza, H.S. (1992) *Young, Female and Black* (pp. 1–3, 54–83). London: Routledge.
7. **D. Attar** Boys: From Sea-cooks to Catering Managers
   From: Attar, D. (1992) *Wasting Girls' Time: The History and Politics of Home Economics* (pp. 114–35). London: Virago.
8. **N. Browne** 'Girls' Stuff, Boys' Stuff': Young Children Talking and Playing
   From: Browne, N. (ed.) (1991) *Science and Technology in the Early Years: An Equal Opportunities Approach* (pp. 37–51). Buckingham: Open University Press.
9. **G. Moss** Rewriting Reading
   From: Kimberly, K., Meek, M. and Miller, J. (eds) (1992) *New Readings: Contributions to an Understanding of Literacy* (pp. 183–93). London: A. & C. Black.
10. **P. Connolly** Boys will be Boys? Racism, Sexuality and the Construction of Masculine Identities Amongst Infant Boys
    Commissioned article.
11. **S. Prendergast** With Gender on my Mind: Menstruation and Embodiment at Adolescence
    Commissioned article.
12. **J.E. Jayaratne and A. J. Stewart** Quantitative and Qualitative Methods in the Social Sciences: Feminist Issues and Practical Strategies
    From: Fonow, M.M. and Cook, J.A. (1991) *Beyond Methodology: Feminist Scholarship as Lived Research*. Bloomington: Indiana University Press.

13. **L. Kelly, L. Regan and S. Burton**   Defending the Indefensible? Quantitative Methods and Feminist Research
    From: Hinds, H., Phoenix, A. and Stacey, J. (eds) (1992) *Working Out: New Directions for Women's Studies* (pp. 149–60). London: Falmer Press.
14. **M. Blair**   Race, Class and Gender in School Research
    This article is based on a paper first presented at a conference on ethnographic research in education in Barcelona, October 1993.
15. **J. Morris**   Personal and Political: A Feminist Perspective on Researching Physical Disability
    From: *Disability, Handicap and Society,* Vol. 7 (2), pp. 157–66, 1992. Abingdon: Carfax Publishing Company, P.O. Box 25, Abingdon, Oxfordshire, OX14 3UE.
16. **J. Holland and C. Ramazanoglu**   Accounting for Sexuality, Living Sexual Politics: Can Feminist Research be Valid?
    This article is abridged from a paper given at the British Sociological Association Conference on Research Imaginations, April 1993.
17. **P. Lather**   Feminist Perspectives on Empowering Research Methodologies
    From: *Women's Studies International Forum,* Vol. 11 (6), pp. 569–81, 1988. Oxford: Elsevier Science Ltd., Pergamon imprint.

INTRODUCTION

We are going through a period of profound change in the way that gender and education are theorized. This presents a major challenge to feminist teachers who want to translate explanations for gender relations into transformative action in the classroom.

The postmodern and poststructuralist critiques of theory and epistemology require feminists to rethink gender relations in education, without losing sight of their goals of social justice, or the insights that have emerged from feminist theory and educational practice in the past. In this Reader the opening articles by Taylor, Weiler, and Davies and Banks suggest ways of developing a feminist pedagogy that takes up the opportunities occurring in the classroom at all levels of education, whereby different understandings of the world can be introduced—opportunities that constitute the 'pedagogical moments' (Lewis, 1992).

A feminist pedagogy needs to take into account the complex interactions of a wide range of factors. These factors include the different subject positionings of students, the fact that students are not just passive recipients but active participants in constructing their own identities through the contradictions of their experiences, the complexity of the forms of resistance adopted by children and young people, and the dangers of ideological imposition. Thus, in her article, Weiler suggests that feminist pedagogy should build upon Freire's liberatory pedagogy, but with Friere's concept re-envisioned to take account of the complex processes suggested above so that the focus is on subject positions, experience and diversity.

The situational factors that can guide pedagogy—the factors relating to students' lives, experiences, and their understanding of those experiences—are neatly encapsulated by the recommendation 'Start where students are at'. Taylor, for example, points to the fact that young girls' experience of popular cultural representations of femininity is a crucial part of their identity formation and must be accepted and worked with, rather than denied or repressed by teachers. Davies and Banks on the one hand, and Browne and Ross on the other, coming from different perspectives, draw attention to the importance of the frames of reference that young children bring to new experience and knowledge. Davies and Banks found that children, in reading texts that attempt to subvert traditional gender relations and behaviour, will cling to traditional narrative structures, seeming to seek continuity in the meanings that they confer on the text. Similarly, Browne and Ross found that young children felt more secure in their own gender domain and resisted any adult attempt to impose a different order on their activities.

Feminist pedagogy has to be sufficiently sensitive to recognize and build on the possibility that an assertion of gender domain could represent an acceptance of gender-appropriate behaviour or a resistance to attempts to control and dictate forms of behaviour (Lewis, 1992; Walkerdine, 1981). Grasping the pedagogical moment can enable children/students to recognize, reflect upon and deconstruct the contradictions of their own lives, with these insights being linked to the broader social context. Moss describes how pupils themselves can provide the catalyst which generates the pedagogical moment, as she experienced in a discussion of male and female perceptions of male and female talk in a mixed classroom.

Challenging gender divisions is no easy task, however. If we take science and scientific knowledge—the defining masculine domain—as an example, the work of Browne and Ross demonstrates that, from a very early age, children have a clear idea of science as masculine and of the scientific and technical incapacity of women, even if they are not too certain what scientists do. This socially constructed and deep-laid perspective is a clear challenge for feminist teachers who wish to disrupt or transform this domain. Kelly (1985) has argued that the principles of scientific knowledge could be taught entirely through domestic science. Attar's study demonstrates why this cannot happen: it is not merely that home economics is defined as a female sphere, but that it is denied as a science. Teaching home economics as a science would disrupt the normative understanding of what science is. You cannot create female knowledge within a framework of male knowledge; as Lorde (1984, p. 112) says, 'The master's tools will never dismantle the master's house'.

The difficulties are exemplified by women who engage with and in science in different ways. Longino and Hammond discuss four feminist scientists who each take a different perspective on 'the science question', from reform to radical transformation. They also consider how women scientists who have been incorporated into the male knowledge base of science and its social manifestations resist all feminist critiques and, through this resistance, perpetuate and reproduce science as a male arena. In the same way that these women scientists do not recognize, and even seem to embrace, their incorporation into a masculine domain, so too, teachers (including feminist teachers) may be unaware of the contradictions in their practices.

Schools are not neutral environments, and teachers, despite their professional intentions to create an equal learning context for all, continue to produce and reproduce differential educational experiences for students. Thus children are treated differently by teachers when they should be treated as the same, and they are treated as the same when they should be treated differently. Prendergast, for example, demonstrates that schools are often neglectful of the psychological, emotional and material needs of young women who are reaching puberty and 'handling' menstruation. Mirza, focusing on 'race', gives examples of the different ways in which teachers respond to the needs of black girls. In the schools she studied, black girls experienced overt racism, patronizing religiosity, impositional ideology, condescending liberal chauvinism and, luckily in this sorry catalogue, empathetic understanding from different types of teachers.

Class and sexuality are, of course, integral to the school environment, like 'race' and gender, as Mirza and Connolly both demonstrate. Mirza describes how white teachers' relations with black girls are often informed by stereotypes of black working-class girls' sexuality. Connolly describes the processes through which children as young as six acquire masculine sexualities. He argues that the whole school environment (and all the players in it) actively construct racialized, class-based and sexualized identities.

We can see from the results of these recent studies that class, 'race' and gender differentiation still exist across the entire school curriculum, and particularly, as Scraton's work in relation to gender shows, in the area of physical education.

The studies we have discussed so far have employed qualitative methods— often regarded as the quintessential feminist mode of research. Harding (1987) distinguishes between three elements in the research process which are often conflated—methods, methodology, and epistemology. Methods are techniques for gathering evidence; methodology is the theoretical framework employed in research; and epistemology is the theory of knowledge which underlies the theoretical framework, providing a philosophical basis for deciding what kinds of knowledge are possible and for ensuring that the knowledge is both adequate and legitimate (Stanley and Wise, 1990). There are a variety of feminist theories which provide the methodology for research, but feminists are divided about the appropriate methods and even about the necessity of prescribing methods at all. While there is a general tendency towards the use of qualitative methods, this is not universal. For example, Kelly, Regan and Burton defend the use of quantitative methods in a particularly sensitive area of feminist research, child abuse. Others, like Jayaratne and Stewart, argue that the question being researched will dictate the appropriate methods, which can and should be drawn from the entire armoury of research techniques. In fact, Jayaratne and Stewart provide a practical guide for feminist research, and stress that it is important for feminists to be able to engage with quantitative research.

There are other areas of debate in feminist research. To what extent does the actual practice of research fulfil the requirements of feminism in realizing the experience and world view of women and in recognizing the different subject positions and power relations of researcher and researched? Morris asks these questions directly with regard to disability research. Is this research emancipatory and empowering? Does it explore the power relations within the research process between non-disabled and disabled, both as researcher and researched?

Blair examines the type of analyses which feminists have made of the research process, through the experience of the black researcher. She describes both the power and powerlessness of the researcher in that process and points out that the feminist researcher does not always have the authority or capacity to empower the researched. She questions whether feminist standpoint theory can capture the complexity of the interrelationship between class, gender and 'race' as integral parts of the researcher's identity.

Holland and Ramazanoglu carry the discussion into the thorny area of validity. Can feminist conclusions be valid? Indeed, can any conclusions drawn in social research be valid? They suggest that 'this problem is not solved, but rather is with us at the start of every research project and must be resolved at the point of interpretation in that project'. Holland and Ramazanoglu elaborate on the hypothetico-deductive model of research in order to incorporate the experience and subjectivity of researcher and researched, and to treat the research itself as a social process. They argue that reality cannot be accessed through correct technique as in the positivist model, and that there are no general rules of validation which can impose an abstract order on the confusion and complexity of daily life, but that openly reflexive interpretation is essential if there is to be any claim to validity.

Finally, Lather brings together the various strands that have been introduced in this Reader. She describes the approach she employed in researching resistance to a feminist pedagogy in the university classroom. Her concerns are with student resistance to a liberatory curriculum, with the creation of empowering pedagogy, and with the conduct of empirical research in a postpositivist/post-modern era. She argues that feminist research is multiparadigmatic, but that the main objective should be to maximize the research process as a change-enhancing, reciprocally educative encounter. And from here we can make the link back through this collection of articles, from research paradigm, through education research in practice, to a feminist pedagogy.

References

Harding, S. (1987) (ed.) *Feminism and Methodology.* Bloomington: Indiana University Press.

Kelly, A. (1985) Changing schools and changing society: some reflections on the Girls Into Science and Technology project. In M. Arnot (ed.) *Race and Gender: Equal Opportunities Policies in Education.* Oxford: Pergamon Press.

Lewis, (1990) Interrupting patriarchy: politics, resistance and transformation in the feminist classroom. *Harvard Educational Review* 60(4), 467–88.

Lorde, A. (1984) *Sister Outsider.* Trumansburg, NY: The Crossing Press.

Stanley, L. and Wise, S. (1990) Methodology and epistemology in feminist research processes. In L. Stanley (ed.) *Feminist Praxis: Research, Theory and Epistemology in Feminist Sociology.* London: Routledge.

Walkerdine, V. (1981) Sex, power and pedagogy. *Screen Education* 38, 14–24.

Note

The articles in this book have been edited: significant wording additions are shown in square brackets, and substantive deletions of text are indicated by ellipses (three points); however, minor changes are not flagged.

Part 1: Approaches to Pedagogy

1 FEMINIST CLASSROOM PRACTICE AND CULTURAL POLITICS: 'GIRL NUMBER TWENTY' AND IDEOLOGY

SANDRA TAYLOR

It is now around fifteen years since girls were defined as an educationally disadvantaged group and policy initiatives were first developed to address issues concerning the education of girls. [...] Policy initiatives have to some extent reflected theoretical understandings about gender and education. Over the years, schooling has been viewed both as an important site for the reproduction of gender relations and as a site for intervention and change. Different aspects of the schooling process have been highlighted—for example, subject choices, curriculum, resources, classroom interaction—and targeted for attention. [...] Despite these official policies, change is very slow and recent statistics show that education and training experiences are still sex differentiated and that gender-based inequalities in the labour market persist (NSW Ministry of Education and Youth Affairs, 1988). Consequently, there has been some questioning of how much real progress has been made in the education of girls, particularly given the influence of 'economic rationalism' (Kenway, 1989; Henry and Taylor, 1989).

It seems that many of the policies and curriculum approaches which have developed over the last decade or so fail to take account of the complexities involved in gender relations. It is easy enough to talk about 'widening options' and 'raising awareness' of girls and young women, but to do so not only involves providing opportunities in the labour market, it also means changing prevailing notions of femininity and masculinity at a personal level.

Two recent Australian research studies, interestingly both conducted in primary schools, highlight the complexities of gender relations, the pervasiveness of the 'gender agenda' and the difficulties of change. Terry Evans (1989, p. 74) defines the 'gender agenda' as the ways in which knowledge, meaning, interpretation and discourse are structured in the 'classroom of life'. Evans' (1988) research showed the ways in which the children in the primary schools he studied were presented with 'living curricula' through the everyday lives of their parents and teachers with respect to men's breadwinning roles and women's domestic and parenting roles. Similarly, Margaret Clark concludes from the evidence of her study that:

Source: Abridged from 'Feminist classroom practice and cultural politics: some further thoughts about 'Girl Number Twenty' and ideology. *Journal of Theoretical Studies: Media and Cultures* (1991), 11(2), 22–46.

even among teachers who have the best intentions, many unwittingly contribute to a narrow construction of femininity and masculinity through the daily practices which make up classroom life and through the absences of other practices that could make a difference.

(Clark, 1989, p. 90)

[...]

In a review of theory on gender and education, Bronwyn Davies (1989) writes:

As children learn the discursive practices of their society, they learn to correctly position themselves as male or female, since that is what is required of them to have a recognizable identity ... We need to recognize the extent to which it is a gendered world that students are required to make sense of. That sense is not just a cognitive sense. It is as well, apprehended bodily, each person's body takes on the knowledge of maleness or femaleness through its practices. (Davies, 1989, pp. 5–6)

These writers focus on the importance of cultural processes and the role of discourses and ideologies in the re-production of gender relations, and their analyses place issues concerning the construction of femininity and masculinity at the heart of the matter.

In this article I want to develop a theoretical base for a feminist classroom practice which focuses on cultural processes, and to explore the possibilities for radical change through the cultural politics of the classroom. A feminist pedagogy needs to take account of the complexities involved in the construction of femininity if it is to be effective. Thus it needs to draw on theoretical understandings about subjectivity and change, on research on girls' subcultures, and also on research on popular cultural texts and femininity.

It is now some time since Judith Williamson's (1981/2) landmark paper, 'Girl number twenty', in *Screen Education* about the difficulties which are involved in helping teenage girls and young women to develop a critical awareness about gender ideologies in their own lives. This article is still relevant in the context of current discussions about feminist pedagogy, and has useful insights for thinking about a feminist classroom practice.

In reviewing relevant research, I will draw on my own research on teenage girls' cultural perspectives and on the role of popular cultural texts in teenage girls' lives (Taylor, 1989a, b). My focus is on the teenage period, which is a crucial time in relation to educational and life choices, but the construction of femininity is not confined to this period, and an exploration of the processes involved can illustrate the cultural construction of femininity more generally.

An adequate theoretical base for this task needs to link cultural processes with broader power relations: cultural processes are integrally related to the social structure and to power relations, and are important in maintaining gender-based inequalities. It is also necessary to take account of agency and the shift from 'reproduction theories' to 'theories of production' (Weiler, 1988). I use the term 're-production', with a hypen, following Wendy Hollway (1984), to emphasize agency in the social processes involved, and therefore the potential for change. The focus in this article will be on the cultural construction of femininity and on 'the cultural framework within which individuals find a sense of themselves' (MacDonald, 1981, p. 163)—particularly on the role of cultural texts—within a re-production theory framework. [...]

THEORIZING CULTURE

My approach is interdisciplinary—using sociology, feminist theory, and media studies. My conceptualization of culture draws on John Fiske as follows:

> Culture is concerned with meanings and pleasures: our culture consists of the meanings we make of our social experience and of our social relations, and therefore the sense we have of our 'selves'. It also situates those meanings within the social system, for a social system can only be held in place by the meanings that people make of it. Culture is deeply inscribed in the differential distribution of power within a society, for power relations can only be stabilized or destabilized by the meanings that people make of them. Culture is a struggle for meanings as society is a struggle for power. (Fiske, 1987, p. 20)

The definition captures nicely the relationship between culture and social structure, and between meanings and power relations for meanings and their circulation are 'part and parcel of [the] social structure' (Fiske, 1987, p. 1). It also emphasizes the dynamic nature of cultural processes where people as agents are involved in shaping the social structure. [...]

I am interested in the generation and circulation of meanings, in this case meanings relating to gender, and how these meanings are implicated in the construction of femininity in girls and young women. Such meanings are organized at a number of interrelated levels within a dynamic ideological system. In relation to the construction of femininity, I will refer to *discourse* about gender as 'a language or system of representation that has developed socially in order to make and circulate a coherent set of meanings about an important topic area' (Fiske, 1987, p. 14). At a broader level such coherent sets of meanings may be referred to as *ideologies*, although both discourses and ideologies operate in a dynamic ideological field: ideologies 'do not operate through single ideas; they operate in discursive chains, in clusters, in semantic fields, in discursive formations' (Hall, 1985).

Within this framework, cultural texts are part of a network of meanings which constitute the social world and which may be viewed as a series of sites of struggle over meaning. Following Leslie Roman and Linda Christian-Smith

(1988), my definition of *cultural text* includes both representational forms (for example, a video clip or a teen magazine) and lived social relations (for example, of a specific group such as Greek girls in a high school). Although these two types of cultural text are separable analytically, they are closely interrelated in everyday social practice.

Another term which needs to be defined is *popular culture*. There is a need for an alternative position to the 'cultural populism' and 'pessimism' approaches to popular culture; an alternative position which recognizes that structural positions set limits on the resistance which can be exerted by consumers to popular cultural forms. Such conditions may prevent oppositional intentions from becoming politically effective, constraining them to passive forms of dissent (Roman and Christian-Smith, 1988).

This general approach to culture and meaning, culture and power relations, and to popular culture, can now be related to a specific consideration of gender issues.

GENDER RELATIONS

An understanding of the re-production of gender relations needs to take account of the links between personal lives and social structures, to consider how everyday social practices constitute social structures. Bob Connell's (1986, 1987) practice-based theory provides a useful basis for a conceptualization of gender relations in that it takes account of structural dimensions and historical change in gender relations. Connell uses the concept 'gender order' which he defines as 'a historically constructed pattern of power relations between men and women' (1987, p. 99). Within this broad framework of the gender order we can view various institutional settings, such as schools, families and the workplace, where social practices are gender structured. Connell refers to the state of play in such settings as the 'gender regime' (1987, p. 120). Cultural texts of all kinds are a part of the gender regime in various institutional settings. For example, in a school setting, as well as in the family or in the street, there will be a network of interrelating cultural texts, both representational and 'lived'.

Also associated with everyday gendered practices are appropriate definitions of femininity and masculinity which help to maintain, and in turn are shaped by, the patriarchal gender order. These understandings of what it means to be female or male, which are implicated in all aspects of social life, develop in relation to each other in particular historical and social situations. Societies where the gender order is patriarchal, such as contemporary Western societies, are characterized by 'emphasized femininity' and 'hegemonic masculinity' (Connell, 1987, p. 183). Hegemonic masculinity is heterosexual and tends to be characterized by power, authority, aggression and technical competence (p. 187). Emphasized femininity, the form of femininity which complements hegemonic masculinity, is characterized by compliance with subordination and is oriented to accommodating the interests and desires of men. Associated with emphasized femininity are qualities of sociability, sexual passivity and acceptance of domesticity and motherhood (p. 187).

A number of versions of femininity and masculinity are constructed in everyday social practices within institutions, but at a broad cultural level the dominant versions promoted provide the basis for women's subordination. Thus we see emphasized femininity and hegemonic masculinity represented at the symbolic level in the mass media as the cultural ideals, though as Connell (1987, p. 186) observes, 'the ideological representations of femininity draw on, but do not necessarily correspond to, actual femininities as they are lived'.

Schooling is a site where gender ideologies are transmitted via the gender regime, and recent research suggests that this hidden curriculum is both powerful and pervasive and makes the task of changing gender relations very difficult.

Popular culture and femininity

Gender ideologies are crucial in sustaining the patriarchal gender order and cultural texts play an important role in promoting the dominant forms of femininity and masculinity at a symbolic level. I am particularly interested in the images of femininity represented in the popular cultural texts that are part of the everyday world of teenage girls. Such texts can be viewed as *representational cultural texts* and play an important part in the struggle over meaning in the popular cultural field.

The increasing sexualization of women's bodies in representational cultural texts from the 1920s and through the post-war period has been discussed by Rosemary Pringle (1983). Pringle suggests that sexuality was restructured in relation to consumption such that consumption came to be seen as a way of completing the ideal feminine identity. For older women that ideal identity centres on the domestic sphere and on being the perfect wife and mother. For young women, however, the focus is on appearance and on being the perfect sex object. In the construction of sexuality under consumer capitalism femininity has come to be associated with passive sexuality, with being touched and being looked at; masculinity is defined actively, and involves touching and looking (Game and Pringle, 1979, p. 11). As a result, women are constantly aware of being on view. [. . .]

This focus on appearance and sexuality is significant in relation to the construction of femininity in young women and girls and the emphasis on women's looks 'becomes a crucial way in which society exercizes control over women's sexuality' (Coward, 1984, p. 77). Coward argues that the camera in contemporary media can be seen as an extension of the male gaze on women, with the result that the development of female identity is fraught with anxiety and enmeshed with judgements about desirability.

The emphasis on women's looks is most apparent in women's magazines, in advertizing material and on television, where visual representations of women are central. [. . .] In relation to girls and young women the overall message in representational cultural texts is that sexuality confers power—though in relation to the social and economic contexts this power, derived from appearance and attractiveness, is extremely limited.

The role which cultural texts play in the construction of femininity is complex. [. . .] Although dominant ideologies may be pervasive, media texts reflect a range of contradictory and conflicting ideologies, some of which may be oppositional. In addition, we need to be cautious about too readily assuming 'effects' from readings of texts. Representational cultural texts need to be considered in the context of *lived social tests*: everyday subcultural social relations.

Girls' subcultures To understand the framework within which girls make sense of themselves, it is necessary to take account of their cultural perspectives. A number of studies of teenage girls' subcultures, particularly those of working-class girls, provide useful insights about the contradictions teenage girls experience and the concerns they express. This research is important not only for understanding the construction of femininity, but also for considering appropriate ways for feminist educators to work with teenage girls.

Research on 'cultures of femininity' shows that teenage girls experience a number of conflicts resulting from the contradictory messages they receive about how they should behave, and it is possible to group these conflicts into three sets of interrelated contradictory discourses (Taylor, 1989a). I have identified these three conflicts as follows: the domesticity/paid work conflict in relation to their futures, the 'slags or drags' conflict relating to sexuality, and the adolescence/femininity conflict relating to maturity. I have suggested that these three related sources of conflict work together to define and construct femininity in particular ways and that they do so within the private, domestic sphere. For teenage girls, relationships are still usually seen in terms of marriage and motherhood, and sexual behaviour as only being appropriate within a context of love and/or marriage. Such sexual codes create pressures on teenagers to get and keep a steady boyfriend (McRobbie, 1978; Cowie and Lees, 1984, Lees, 1986; Kostash, 1987) and, because of these pressures, 'romance' emerges as a central theme in studies of the lives of teenage girls.

These powerful pressures are experienced at a critical time, a time when girls could be thinking and planning for the future. Consequently, girls and young women often experience a conflict between their preoccupation with issues relating to femininity, and their awareness of educational concerns. Research studies of teenage girls' subcultures suggest that they often are aware of their likely futures and their need to earn a living, but find themselves trapped between the sexual, marriage and labour markets (Griffin, 1984).

During the eighties, a number of studies which have attempted to explore issues relating to gender and education in their wider cultural context have investigated the lived experiences of girls within and outside school, highlighting the diversity and complexity of these experiences. For example, Claire Thomas (1980) has explored the complexities of class and gender, while Alison Jones (1988) has documented ethnic differences in girls' school experiences. In general, such studies have been concerned with 'the ways in which girls, both individually and collectively, make sense of and try to negotiate oppressive social relationships and structures in order to gain more control over their own lives' (Weiler, 1988, pp. 45–6). These studies have utilized concepts of resistance and accommodation in attempting to understand how girls and women actively respond to oppression rather than passively internalize dominant ideologies. Recent work clearly demonstrates both the awareness girls have of their social situation and their ability to make rational choices about their lives. For example, Johanna Wyn comments on the fact that working-class girls place a continuing priority on friendships and domestic concerns:

> . . . the evidence in these studies suggests that the young women approach their futures positively and hopefully as they face the difficult task of balancing the demands of school and home in anticipation of conflicting demands of private and public life in their futures.
>
> These young women are not compliant, or victims, making 'wrong' choices. The choices they do make are based on their knowledge and experience of life around them, in a context in which class and gender politics are experienced daily.   (Wyn, 1988, p. 125)

Gender ideologies are not passively internalized but actively negotiated and resisted by girls and women, and a number of feminist research studies have documented how working-class girls in particular resist the official gender ideology of the school (e.g. Samuel, 1983). It is likely that, as with working-class boys, opposition to school leads working-class girls to a traditional working-class future. Willis's (1977) 'lads', in opposing school values, qualified themselves for futures as manual workers. However, for them manual work confirmed their masculinity and thereby gave them status. But in the case of working-class girls, status is not achieved from the kinds of jobs available to them, and in the long run they see few alternatives to motherhood and child-rearing, whether they be with or without love, romance and marriage.

As well as this growing body of research concerned with girls' subcultures there has also been an interest in exploring the ways in which popular cultural texts relate to girls' lives (McRobbie, 1978, 1984; Frith, 1985; Willinsky and Hunniford, 1986; Taylor, 1989a, b). This work has usefully highlighted the nature of the inter-relationship between the images of femininity in representational cultural texts, and the lived social relations of adolescent girls. For example, popular cultural texts such as teenage magazines are viewed as active in the production and circulation of new meanings for young women. As MacDonald comments:

> The problem, therefore, is not one of trying to fit these representations of women to the realities of their lives but rather to recognize the ideological 'work' carried out by these texts in the *reconstruction* rather than the reproduction of gender definitions and relations.
>
> (MacDonald, 1981, p. 173)

Many studies show 'romance' to be a central theme in the popular cultural texts which are part of girls' everyday lives. For example, teen romance novels are the most popular genre of literature read by teenage girls in the USA, Canada and the UK, as well as in Australia. Similarly, romance is a central theme in other popular cultural texts like magazines, soap operas and contemporary music. Clearly 'romance' plays a major and complex role in the processes involved in the construction of femininity, and it is a central theme in both representational cultural texts and girls' subcultures. Through romance, girls can reverse the contradictory messages and anxieties they experience in their real lives, in their fantasy worlds, and in the blurred margins between them.

Construction of feminine subjectivity

[...]

Recent theorists interested in the relationship between the individual and social structure have tended to replace the notion of 'the individual' with that of 'the subject' (Beechey and Donald, 1985; Henriques *et al.*, 1984). The distinction between these two concepts is relevant to the notion of 'sense of self'. While 'the individual' is viewed as being essentially biological, the notion of 'the subject' highlights the 'constructed sense of the individual in a network of social relations' (Fiske, 1987, p. 48). Thus, from this perspective a sense of identity which is socially constructed is referred to as *subjectivity*, in contrast to *individuality*, which is the product of nature or biology. [...]

This approach to subjectivity is particularly useful in exploring constructions of femininity, because it explains the contradictory ways in which gender ideologies are experienced. For example, for teenage girls there may be a contradiction between their intellectual awareness about trends in society, and their personal dreams for themselves (Baker, 1985). Similarly, there may be a contradiction about having children:

> It is neither a question of free choice, nor of false consciousness. For example, women can recognize child-rearing as restrictive and oppressive and yet still want to bear children.   (Henriques *et al.*, 1984, p. 220)

However, while it is important to acknowledge the way in which gender ideologies work at an unconscious level through the structuring of desires, it is also important to understand that these desires are produced and are therefore potentially changeable.

While it is clear that gender ideologies are not passively internalized, those mediated through schooling, along with those circulated in other arenas, become part of a repertoire of ways of thinking about what it means to 'be female'. Consequently, it is this range of available discourses which is crucial in providing the framework within which the construction of femininity takes place.

Despite the possibility of oppositional readings, popular cultural texts relate in complex ways to girls' everyday lives, girls' experiences and subjectivities are always already structured by patriarchal gender relations and often oppositional readings will merely be a diversion, a way of coping, and not lead to any real change in gender relations. Popular cultural texts legitimate gender relations as much by the way they enter into the politics of girls' and women's everyday lives as through the ideological messages they transmit.

Teen romance novels appear to offer some resolution to the 'problem' of becoming feminine, by presenting a possible solution to some of the contradictions in teenage girls' lives (Taylor, 1989a). And despite some claims that the 'escape' which romance reading offers has progressive elements (Radway, 1984), the discourse of romance is a patriarchal discourse which locks women into passivity and dependency. Girls' writing tends to reflect this narrow range of discourses about gender which is available to them and shows the difficulties they encounter in writing 'against the grain', that is, in writing outside of patriarchal conventions (Gilbert, 1988b).

In the case of soap opera viewing (Taylor, 1989b), teenage girls already show well-established feminine patterns in the way they use television in their lives, both in terms of viewing patterns and in the way in which the programmes are used to rehearse problems and contradictions in their own lives. The appeal of soap operas for this group lies in the focus of the genre on feelings and relationships, and in the opportunities they offer for 'time out' from the 'real world'. Some writers have expressed the view that soap operas offer the potential for oppositional and resistive readings because they are polysemic and because they tend to 'play' with the myths of patriarchy and allow them to be questioned by their audiences (Brown, 1987). For example, in soaps the perfect, happy, stable family is presented as an ideal which is never achieved. However, despite these apparently progressive possibilities offered by soap opera texts, the range of discourses they present to teenage girls is narrow and limiting (Gilbert and Taylor, 1991) and opportunities to offer alternative versions of femininity through soap opera viewing are relatively restricted.

In both teen romance novels and soap operas we see what Coward terms 'the lure of pleasure'. She writes:

Subtly, in complicated ways, recognizing some conflict and problems,
discourses on female desire nevertheless work inexorably towards closure,
towards putting the lid on love, desire and especially on change.

(Coward, 1984, p. 16)

Given that schools and classrooms are important sites for intervention
in the construction of femininity, we need to think carefully through
the implications of research on girls and popular culture. In developing
approaches for the classroom we need to ask, firstly, what is the significance
of popular cultural texts in girls' lives and how do we take account of this
in the curriculum? And secondly, how do we use popular cultural texts in
the classroom to challenge traditional versions of femininity and develop
new and alternative versions? In other words, what possibilities are there
for constructing femininity in new ways?

SUBJECTIVITY AND CHANGE

There are some general implications for working with teenage girls which
arise out of a consideration of the issues discussed in the first part of the
article. Firstly, there is a need to take account of the research on the lived
experiences and cultural perspectives of teenage girls, and here it is important
to recognize that these will vary with class and ethnic differences. Often it
has been assumed that all that is necessary is to provide 'alternative models'
for girls, with the result that teenage girls and young women, particularly
those from working-class backgrounds, have become alienated from feminists
and feminism. An understanding of the complexities of the construction of
femininity shows why such approaches are unlikely to be successful.

The challenge for feminist educators is to work *with* girls and young women
and help them to reflect critically on their own lives and futures. As Judith
Williamson (1981/2) has argued, we cannot *teach* ideologies—or even *teach
about* ideologies. We can only try to bring students to an understanding,
from their own experiences, of the way that we are all caught up in ideological
processes in our everyday lives. Unless students can make sense of the issues in
terms of their own lives and experiences they are likely to become alienated
or resistant, and educational programmes will be counter-productive.

It is important that teachers and others working with girls and young
women take account of the conflicts and concerns which this group express,
and that girls are encouraged to explore and to discuss the contradictions and
pressures they face with each other. These concerns centre on girls' futures
(both in the workforce and as mothers), on sexuality, and on issues related to
age and maturity. They should not be dismissed as unimportant and irrelevant
because of an educational preoccupation with 'career planning'. Rather, they
need to be taken up in work education programmes which include studies
of women's work from an historical perspective, and also discussions about
childbearing/childrearing and combining paid work with parenting.

I have highlighted the complexities of the construction of femininity and have shown that the power of gender ideologies lies in the fact that they work at an unconscious level, through the structuring of desires, as well as at a conscious or rational level. The construction of a gendered subjectivity is crucial to the re-production of patriarchal gender relations. Subjectivity is not acquired in a unified or coherent way, rather it is struggled over and imperfectly held because different discourses offer different subject positions or points of view, many of which are contradictory and incompatible. I have argued that the acceptance of a particular subject position inevitably means the acceptance of a gendered subjectivity: 'Everything we do signifies compliance or resistance to dominant norms of what it means to be a woman' (Weedon, 1987, pp. 86–7).

Although it is essential to begin with students' experiences, this is in fact problematic. It is personally threatening for many students to place their lives under scrutiny as their very sense of themselves is at stake (Williamson 1981/2, 1985). Williamson comments:

> If we mean what we write about the formation of the subject through social discourses, and so on, and then direct the thrust of our teaching *at* social discourse, we ought to *know* that we are thereby hacking at the very roots of those formed subjects.   (Williamson, 1981/2, p. 85)

She discusses how traumatic it can be to first 'see' that social reality is ideological. The other important insight she offers is that students learn about ideologies when they actually have to confront them in a practical situation. In Williamson's view, students can never understand these issues purely intellectually; they need to bump up against ideologies in the course of practical, productive work (1981/2). For these reasons reconstructing femininity in new ways will be difficult and challenging, because it will involve deconstructing dominant ideologies and changing subjectivities.

Furthermore, it will be even more difficult because of the 'lure of pleasure' (Coward, 1984). Various definitions of female desire are offered to women in their everyday lives—through 'feminine pleasures' such as cooking, fashion, soap operas and romantic fiction—and these work to sustain the patriarchal gender order through the production of female pleasure and desire:

> ... our subjectivity and identity are formed in the definitions of desire which encircle us. These are the experiences which make change such a difficult and daunting task, for female desire is constantly lured by discourses which sustain male privilege.   (Coward, 1984, p. 16)

[...]

Cultural politics and change

Recent work on critical pedagogy emphasizes the importance of cultural politics and places education in its wider cultural context. For example, in the collection of articles entitled *Critical Pedagogy and Cultural Power* (Livingstone, 1987), there is 'an attempt to understand how forms of subjectivity are regulated and transformed through the structured character of such social forms as language, ideologies, myths, significations, and narratives' (p. xv). Cultural politics have also been seen as an important arena for radical change in relation to social issues. In this context, Williamson's insights about the use of media studies as a way of connecting issues of personal identity with cultural activity have been significant, and she views such activity as politically important:

> ... It is only as familiar structures of meaning are shaken and taken apart that new ones can form. And looking at things differently makes it possible to act differently.   (Williamson, 1989, p. 6).

[...]

Towards a feminist critical pedagogy

While aspects of critical educational theory can be utilized in the construction of a feminist pedagogy, Patty Lather (1984) has argued that the critical theorists have failed to recognize that women's studies is, in fact, an example of what they themselves are attempting to develop: transformative practice. Lather describes women's studies as 'intellectual consciousness raising', which she suggests can be conceptualized as counter-hegemonic work. Consequently, she argues that critical theory and women's studies 'would each benefit from an attempt to explore the 'practical political activity' that is women's studies' (Lather, 1984, p. 30). [...] Many feminists have used 'consciousness raising' as an important approach in teaching (Weiler, 1988). As Sue Middleton (1987) points out, activist pedagogies are based on the assumption that people learn best by critically reflecting on and theorizing their own actions in the social world. She documents the use of life-history analysis as a teaching technique in a women's studies course in an attempt to help students learn to link 'biography, history and social structure'. Such an approach gives students the opportunity to interpret their own experiences in a way which reveals how these experiences have been shaped and influenced by the dominant culture.

Giroux (1981) argues that subjective awareness becomes the first step in transforming those experiences, and elsewhere he acknowledges that a radical pedagogy must take seriously the task of providing the conditions for changing subjectivity as well as changing broad political, economic and social structures. He writes: 'In short, an essential aspect of radical pedagogy centres around the need for students to interrogate critically their inner histories and experiences' (Giroux, 1984, p. 319).

However, it is important that the focus on the personal is a critical focus, and there are dangers in humanistic approaches which end up divorcing the social relations of the classroom from a viable political perspective. It is important when working with other oppressed groups, for example with Aborigines, to develop and encourage a sense of cultural and collective identity. Similarly the key to empowerment for young women seems to lie in the development of a sense of *social* or *collective identity* as girls or young women—rather than merely in the development of a sense of identity as an *individual*. (Gilbert (1988a) uses the term 'gender esteem'.) In this way, by an exploration of the personal experiences and life histories of women, girls and young women can develop a strong sense of identity of themselves as women. A crucial aspect of all this is to illuminate the interaction of the social and the personal on one hand and of history and private experience on the other.

However, subjectivities are constructed at an unconscious as well as a conscious level and the role of pleasure and desire, and fantasy, must be considered in the development of a feminist pedagogy. In the final section of the article I will consider aspects of such a pedagogy by offering practical suggestions for working with girls and young women. [...] The issues being addressed are complex, and the development of appropriate and effective classroom approaches is not a simple matter. However, the following suggestions seem to offer possibilities for practice.

RECONSTRUCTING FEMINITY

A cultural studies approach

A cultural studies perspective [...] is useful in developing activities to encourage girls to reflect on their own experiences, and on the experiences of women in their own families, and ultimately on their own futures. [...]

Andrew Dewdney and Martin Lister (1986) claim that the cultural studies approach allows ways of basing general educational practice on young people's views and experience, and emphasize that 'Without conscious and active engagement with the content of young people's resistance, teaching is bound to reproduce more than it transforms' (p. 31). Photography is central, though not indispensable to this approach, as it is a particularly useful means of representing and reconstructing everyday experiences and, through these activities, reflecting on them. The value of family photographs to help girls explore women's experience within the family, has been well demonstrated by an interesting project documented by Adrian Chappell (1984) involving a young unemployed working-class woman.

This kind of approach was attempted as part of action research on the 'gender inclusive curriculum', in an inner city girls' school in Melbourne with a large proportion of girls from non-English speaking families, and is reported in detail elsewhere (Taylor, 1989a). I worked with a class of year 9 girls, together with one teacher, for three hours a week over nine weeks.

Together we were attempting to develop activities which would help the girls to think about their futures, initially by encouraging them to reflect on their own futures and on the experiences of the women in their own families. The students were given the choice of doing photographic work, either using family photographs or doing photographic work themselves, or of interviewing their mothers or grandmothers about their lives.

We also developed a unit on teen romances—once again to help the girls to explore issues concerning their own lives and futures. We discussed romance stories and the reasons for their popularity with teenage girls, and followed this with work on the romance genre. This kind of analytical work can be followed by activities which allow students to play with the generic conventions and produce their own alternative texts which articulate their experiences. It would also be useful to construct a research project around an investigation of the teen romance market. Such research could help to develop a critical awareness of the social and historical production and marketing of such cultural texts.

Popular cultural texts like the soap opera can also be a focal point for critical reflection. The initial phase of such work might involve helping students to reach an understanding of the characteristics of the genre and of a successful soap opera, including aspects of production and marketing. Given the polysemic nature of soap operas, teachers also have a particularly important role in highlighting the resistant or oppositional readings which can be made of soap operas when analytical work is being undertaken.

In implementing a unit on soap operas in a mixed year 10 English class in Brisbane, the prime time soap opera *Home and Away* was chosen for study and compared with the daytime soap *Days of our Lives*. The students then followed this by group work which involved developing new soap opera texts using their understandings of the genre. In this way they were able to become involved in the construction of alternative texts which better articulated their interests and experiences. Depending on the available time, students could actually make a video tape of an episode of their soap opera, write scripts, or construct promotional material about the new soap opera. This last approach would involve research of marketing and promotional aspects of popular cultural texts, as well as consideration of the conventions of the setting, plots, characters and casting. It seems desirable that students go beyond critical analysis and become involved in this kind of cultural production, which allows students to explore the issues through fantasy as well as through more conventional analytical approaches. However, the process of making an alternative text becomes a richer re-fashioning activity if students have acquired some understanding of the roots of the generic conventions they work with, and an understanding of the way in which such roots are ideologically constructed.

It is also necessary to think about widening the range of discourses available to girls and young women, thereby extending the repertoire on which they draw in the construction of femininity. In particular, this means carefully considering the cultural texts which are used in the classroom, and which are so often 'a discourse not intended for her' (Rich, 1980, p. 243), and instead offering access to discourses *intended* for her. This is also a necessary base for critical reflection.

Discourses intended for her

In this article I have argued that young women need to have access to alternative discourses that position them differently in terms of adolescent femininity, but I have also argued that this alternative positioning will not be an easy task for educators. In general terms, popular cultural texts often serve to perpetuate dominant ideologies, and the space available for resistance and reconstruction of these popular cultural texts is slight. This space needs always to be explored and extended, and alternative textual practices might go some way towards this exploration and extension. In general terms we need to make alternative discourses available to young women, and we can facilitate this through the textual *materials* that schools work with, and through the textual *practices* schools adopt to work with such materials.

It is clear that popular cultural texts like soap operas and romance fiction are extremely attractive to young women. The way in which these texts connect with lived experiences of growing up as a woman in contemporary society gives them a particular potency and appeal, and it would seem that schools' efforts to have students 'see through' the ideology of such texts have been fraught with danger. For example, Williamson's (1981/2) discussion of a mixed-sex group working on magazine stereotyping indicated how easy it was for the lesson to deride and devalue women's worth. The introduction of contemporary romance novels into the classroom as set textual matter may not be appreciated by many young women, and for committed romance readers, it might well represent school colonization—and subsequent devaluation—of a central aspect of girls' culture. For non-committed romance readers, it might well represent further pedagogical reinforcement of the need for 'academic' girls to separate themselves from female sub-cultures and learn to read, write and talk like men.

The same could be said about the study of television texts in the classroom. Valerie Walkerdine (1986), for instance, argues that the analysis of popular television programmes in media studies courses in schools can present great difficulty for many students:

> What concerns me is how these ... children ... are being asked to deal with their previous enjoyment of such things—a pleasure shared with family, friends and their general social and cultural environment. It seems that they are being left little room for any response other than feeling stupid, or despising those who are still enjoying these 'perverse' pleasures. (Walkerdine, 1986, p. 196)

Contemporary approaches to reading and language study in the classroom have made the introduction of popular cultural texts into classrooms a much more likely event than in the past. The very popularity of such texts appears to guarantee their relevance to children. This does, of course, pose some problems for classroom use of romance texts, and it is interesting to note the resistance of teachers to the use of such texts (Altus, 1984; Christian-Smith, 1988). Romantic fiction is particularly devalued, and this seems to be a variant of the more general devaluing of women's experiences and women's texts across the curriculum. Romance fiction is devalued as a literary genre because it is formulaic, ritualistic and closed. It is also devalued as a subject area because it focuses on a set of supposedly women's preoccupations—love, emotions and relationships. On a more general scale, while male stories of war, death and the search for identity become the stories of universal value, female stories of love, birth, and nurturing become marginalized 'women's' stories.

This inequality in the treatment of popular cultural texts would be significantly addressed if the approach to studying texts was different. If texts were dealt with in terms of their construction and production, then the speaking positions and the subject positions that particular texts rely upon could be more readily associated with broader power relations.

Why and how books are selected for school study have long been of interest to educators, but there seems little doubt that a consideration of the ideological content of material is not an issue that many teachers regard as significant (Gilbert with Rowe, 1989). In early literacy classrooms, in the junior school, and in secondary schools and colleges, book selections seldom acknowledge the need to have material written by and about women, or to have material which addressed women's lived experiences (Gilbert, 1983). On the contrary, many of the book selections that are made present images of girls and women which are stereotypical and limiting. The 'great tradition' which most girls will work with in schools will be essentially a male tradition, and the reading practices that most girls will learn in schools will be male reading practices. Students will learn to read the 'great tradition' as men have learnt to read it, and by so doing, they learn to devalue women's experiences and worth, and to regard male activity, male need, and male images of women as universal images (Gilbert with Rowe, 1989).

There are two ways to work against these traditions. One is to develop a critical approach to the naturalistic and personalist emphases in language study (Gilbert, 1988a), and to engage instead in textual study which explores the construction and production of texts as social, cultural practice. The other is to make texts and alternative reading positions available to young women, so that discourses that are intended for them do reach them.

Alternative texts are much more accessible now than they have been in the past. Non-sexist picture book lists are available, as are guides for adolescent literature, and general guides for children's books. [. . .]

While texts like these are crucial in providing access to alternative discourses for young women—discourses which offer alternative reading positions and alternative subject positions for women—girls may need to learn alternative reading practices so that they can read these texts 'differently'. In her analysis of the way in which young girls are prepared for adolescent sexuality through pre-teen comics, Valerie Walkerdine (1984) warns of the difficulties associated with introducing young girls to alternative views and images through texts. She suggests that the 'simple realism' of much anti-sexist literature may fail, because it assumes a 'rationalist' reader who will change as a result of receiving the correct information 'about how things *really* are'. Instead she argues for the power of fantasy to understand the way in which some literature—notably preparatory romance literature—works more powerfully on the 'psychic organization of desire'.

The argument put by Walkerdine is that the constitution of femininity (and masculinity) is not fixed or appropriated, but 'struggled over in a complex relational dynamic' (1984, pp. 183–4). Cultural texts are obviously crucial in this struggle, and Walkerdine's concern is with the different ways in which such texts might operate:

> What we need to ask is how much texts operate at the level of fantasy. For some girls they might well provide the vehicle for an alternative vision, while for others they might, by stressing the one as alternative to the other, feed or fuel a resistance to the feminist alternative.
>
> (Walkerdine, 1984, p. 183)

Given this, it would seem important for a feminist pedagogy to be concerned both with the social construction of female desire—and with the way in which cultural texts differently position women in relation to such desire—and also with the role that cultural texts might play in constructing such desire differently.

This will necessitate not only alternative texts for young women—texts which move beyond simple realistic options of role models—but alternative textual strategies for the classroom, which move beyond simple realistic readings of the 'world' of the fiction. Texts can also be played with, and writing and reading practice can become the focus of classroom language work. Women's experiences and concerns are, as I have argued, too often devalued. Learning to read and write 'against the grain'

> ... is therefore about learning to read and write against conventions that construct women in ways that are demeaning and restricting. It is ... about learning to read and write in ways that offer constructions of female subjectivity that are not fixed and static, but are dynamic and shifting. It is about learning to understand the discursive construction of subjectivity and the potential spaces for resistance and rewriting.
>
> (Gilbert and Taylor, 1991, p. 150)

I have argued in this article that restructuring femininity can play a crucial role in transforming patriarchal gender relations, and wish to emphasize my earlier argument that, though strategies are needed to address broad structural inequalities, changes in the cultural sphere are of equal importance. In particular, I have argued that a critical awareness of the social construction of femininity is an essential first stage for a change in gender relations. My aim in this work has been to explore the spaces that are available for such reconstruction in the classroom, and to suggest ways in which popular cultural texts might be read and re-written so that femininity may be reconstructed in alternative ways. Classroom possibilities do exist to offer girls alternative subject positions from which they might read and write differently, from which they might differently position themselves in relation to dominant patriarchal discourse, and from which they might fashion their own versions of femininity.

References

Altus, M. (1984) Sugar-coated pills. *Orana* 20 (2) 70–90.

Baker, M. (1985) *What will Tomorrow Bring? A Study of the Aspirations of Adolescent Women.* Ottawa: Canadian Advisory Council on the Status of Women.

Beechey, V. and Donald, J. (eds) (1985) *Subjectivity and Social Relations.* Milton Keynes: Open University Press.

Brown, M.E. (1987) The politics of soaps: Pleasure and feminine empowerment. *Australian Journal of Cultural Studies* 4 (2), 1–25.

Chappell, A. (1984) Family fortunes: A practical photography project. In A. McRobbie and M. Nava (eds) *Gender and Generation* (pp. 112–29). Basingstoke: Macmillan.

Christian-Smith, L. (1988) Romancing the girl: Adolescent romance novels and the construction of femininity. In L. Roman and L. Christian-Smith (eds) *Becoming Feminine: The Politics of Popular Culture* (pp. 76–101). London: Falmer Press.

Clark, M. (1989) *The Great Divide. The Construction of Gender in the Primary School.* Canberra: Curriculum Development Centre.

Connell, R.W. (1986) Theorizing gender. In N. Grieve and A. Burns (eds) *Australian Women. New Feminist Perspectives* (pp. 342–57). Melbourne: Oxford University Press.

— (1987) *Gender and Power. Society, the Person and Sexual Politics.* Sydney: Allen and Unwin.

Coward, R. (1984) *Female Desire.* London: Paladin Books.

Cowie, C. and Lees, S (1981) Slags or drags. *Feminist Review* 9 (October) 17–31.

Davies, B. (1989) Education for sexism: A theoretical analysis of the sex/gender bias in education. *Educational Philosophy and Theory* 21 (1) 1–19.

Dewdney, A. and Lister, M. (1986) Photography, school and youth: The Cockpit Arts project. In S. Bezencenet and P. Corrigan (eds) *Photographic Practices: Towards a Different Image* (pp. 29–52). London: Comedia.

Evans, T. (1988) *A Gender Agenda.* Sydney: Allen and Unwin.

— (1989) Living curricula. In G. Leder and S. Sampson (eds) *Educating Girls: Practice and Research* (pp. 73–83). Sydney: Allen and Unwin.

Fiske, J. (1987) *Television Culture.* London: Methuen.

Frith, G. (1985) 'The time of your life': The meaning of the school story. In C. Steedman, C. Urwin and V. Walkerdine (eds) *Language, Gender and Childhood* (pp. 113–36). London: Routledge and Kegan Paul.

Game, A. and Pringle, R. (1979) Sexuality and the suburban dream. *Australian and New Zealand Journal of Sociology* 15 (2), 4–15.

Gilbert, P. (1983) Down among the women: Girls as readers and writers. *English in Australia* June, 26–7.

— (1988a) Personal growth or critical resistance? Self esteem in the English classroom. In J. Kenway and S. Willis (eds) *Hearts and Minds: Self Esteem and the Schooling of Girls* (pp. 167–83). Canberra: Department of Education, Employment and Training.

— (1988b) Stoning the romance: girls as resistant readers and writers. *Curriculum Perspectives* 8 (2) 13–19.

Gilbert, P., with Rowe, K. (1989) *Gender, Literacy and the Classroom.* Melbourne: Australian Reading Association.

Gilbert, P. and Taylor, S. (1991) *Fashioning the Feminine: Girls, Popular Culture, and Schooling.* Sydney: Allen & Unwin.

Giroux, H. (1981) *Ideology, Culture and the Process of Schooling.* London: Falmer Press.

Giroux, H. (1984) Ideology, agency and the process of schooling. In L. Barton and S. Walker (eds) *Social Crisis and Educational Research* (pp. 306–334). London: Croom Helm.

Griffin, C. (1984) *Typical Girls.* London: Routledge & Kegan Paul.

Hall, S. (1985) Signification, representation, ideology: Althusser and the post-structuralist debates. *Critical Studies in Mass Communications* 2 (2), 91–114.

Henriques, J., Hollway, W., Urwin, C., Venn, C. and Walkerdine, V. (1984) *Changing the Subject.* London: Methuen.

Henry, M. and Taylor, S. (1989) On the agenda at last? Recent developments in educational policy relating to women and girls. In S. Taylor and M. Henry (eds) *Battlers and Blue Stockings: Women's Place in Australian Education* (pp. 101–9). Canberra: Australian College of Education.

Hollway, W. (1984) Gender difference and the production of subjectivity. In J. Henriques *et al.* (eds) *Changing the Subject* (pp. 227–63) London: Methuen.

Jones, A. (1988) Which girls are 'learning to lose'? In S. Middleton (ed) *Women and Education in Aotearoa* (pp. 143–52). Wellington: Allen and Unwin/Port Nicholson Press.

Kenway, J. (1989) After the applause. *Education Links* 36, 24–6.

Kostash, M. (1987) *No Kidding. Inside the World of Teenage Girls.* Toronto: McClelland and Stewart.

Lather, P. (1984) Critical theory, curricular transformation and feminist mainstreaming. *Journal of Education* 166 (1), 49–62.

Lees, S. (1986) *Losing Out. Sexuality and Adolescent Girls.* London: Hutchinson.

Livingstone, D. (ed) (1987) *Critical Pedagogy and Cultural Power.* London: Macmillan.

MacDonald, M. (1981) Schooling and the reproduction of class and gender relations. In R. Dale *et al.* (eds) *Politics, Patriarchy and Practice* (pp. 159–77). Lewes: Falmer/Open University Press.

McRobbie, A. (1978) Working-class girls and the culture of femininity. In Women's Studies Group (ed.) *Women Take Issue* (pp. 96–108). London: Hutchinson.

— (1984) Dance and social fantasy. In A. McRobbie and M. Nava (eds) *Gender and Generation* (pp. 130–61). Basingstoke: Macmillan.

Middleton, S. (1987) Feminist educators in a university setting: A case study in the politics of 'educational' knowledge. *Discourse* 8 (1) 25–47.

NSW Ministry of Education and Youth Affairs (1988) *National Data Base on the Education of Girls in Australian Schools.* Sydney: Southwood Press.

Pringle, R. (1983) Women and consumer capitalism. In C.V. Baldock and B. Cass (eds)

Women, Social Welfare and the State (pp. 85–103). Sydney: Allen and Unwin.

Radway, J. (1984) *Reading the Romance: Women, Patriarchy and Popular Literature.* Chapel Hill: North Carolina University Press.

Rich, A. (1980) *On Lies, Secrets and Silence.* London: Virago.

Roman, L. and Christian-Smith, L. (1988) *Becoming Feminine: The Politics of Popular Culture.* London: Falmer Press.

Samuel, L. (1983) The making of a school resister. In R.K. Browne and L.E. Foster (eds) *Sociology of Education* (pp. 367–75). Melbourne: Macmillan.

Taylor, S. (1989a) Empowering girls and young women: The challenge of the gender inclusive curriculum. *Journal of Curriculum Studies* 21 (5), 441–56.

— (1989b) Days of their lives?: Popular culture, femininity and education. *Continuum* 2 (2), 43–62.

Thomas, C. (1980) Girls and counter school culture. In D. McCallum and U. Ozolins (eds) *Melbourne Working Papers* (pp. 125–56). Sociology Research Group in Cultural and Educational Studies, University of Melbourne.

Walkerdine, V. (1984) Some day my prince will come: young girls and the preparation for adolescent sexuality. In A. McRobbie and M. Nava (eds) *Gender and Generation* (pp. 162–184). Basingstoke: Macmillian.

Walkerdine, D. (1986) Video replay: Families, films and fantasy. In V. Burgin *et al.* (eds) *Formations of Fantasy* (pp. 166–99). London: Methuen.

Weedon, C. (1987) *Feminist Practice and Post Structuralist Theory.* Oxford: Basil Blackwell.

Weiler, K. (1988) *Women Teaching for Change, Gender, Class and Power.* Massachusetts: Bergin & Garvey.

Williamson, J. (1981/2) How does girl number twenty understand ideology? *Screen Education* 40 (Autumn-Winter), 80–7.

— (1985) Is there anyone here from a classroom? And other questions of education. *Screen* 26 (1), 90–5.

Williamson, J. (1989) AIDS and perceptions of the Grim Reaper. *Metro* 80 (Spring), 2–6.

Willinsky, J. and Hunniford, R.M. (1986) Reading the romance younger. The mirrors and fears of a preparatory literature. *Reading-Canada-Lecture* 4 (1), 16–31.

Willis, P. (1977) *Shaping Futures: Youth Action for Livelihood.* Sydney: Allen and Unwin.

Wyn, J. (1988) Working class girls and educational outcomes: Is self esteem an issue? In J. Kenway and S. Willis (eds) *Hearts and Minds: Self Esteem and the Schooling of Girls* (pp. 116–27). Canberra: Department of Education, Employment and Training.

2 FREIRE AND A FEMINIST PEDAGOGY OF DIFFERENCE

KATHLEEN WEILER

We are living in a period of profound challenges to traditional Western epistemology and political theory. These challenges, couched in the language of postmodernist theory and in postcolonialist critiques, reflect the rapid transformation of the economic and political structure of the world order: the impact of transnational capital; the ever more comprehensive integration of resources, labor, and markets; the pervasiveness of media and consumer images. This interdependent world system is based on the exploitation of oppressed groups, but the system at the same time calls forth oppositional cultural forms that give voice to the conditions of these groups. White male bourgeois dominance is being challenged by people of color, women, and other oppressed groups, who assert the validity of their own knowledge and demand social justice and equality in numerous political and cultural struggles. In the intellectual sphere, this shifting world system has led to a shattering of Western metanarratives and to the variety of stances of postmodernist and cultural-identity theory. A major theoretical challenge to traditional Western knowledge systems is emerging from feminist theory, which has been increasingly influenced by both postmodernist and cultural-identity theory. Feminist theory, like other contemporary approaches, validates difference, challenges universal claims to truth, and seeks to create social transformation in a world of shifting and uncertain meanings.

In education, these profound shifts are evident on two levels: first, at the level of practice, as excluded and formerly silenced groups challenge dominant approaches to learning and to definitions of knowledge; and second, at the level of theory, as modernist claims to universal truth are called into question (see as representative Giroux, 1991; Cherryholmes, 1988; Giroux and Simon, 1989; Britzman, 1991; Lather, 1991). These challenges to accepted truths have been raised not only to the institutions and theories that defend the status quo, but also to the critical or liberatory pedagogies that emerged in the 1960s and 1970s. Feminist educational critics, like other theorists influenced by postmodernism and theories of difference, want to retain the vision of social justice and transformation that underlies liberatory pedagogies, but they find that their claims to universal truths and their assumptions of a

Source: Abridged from *Harvard Educational Review* (1991), 61 (4), 449–74.

collective experience of oppression do not adequately address the realities of their own confusing and often tension-filled classrooms. This consciousness of the inadequacy of classical liberatory pedagogies has been particularly true for feminist educators, who are acutely aware of the continuing force of sexism and patriarchal structures and of the power of race, sexual preference, physical ability, and age to divide teachers from students and students from one another.

Paulo Freire is without question the most influential theorist of critical or liberatory education. His theories have profoundly influenced literacy programs throughout the world and what has come to be called critical pedagogy in the United States. His theoretical works, particularly *Pedagogy of the Oppressed*, provide classic statements of liberatory or critical pedagogy based on universal claims of truth (Freire, 1971, p. 28). Feminist pedagogy as it has developed in the United States provides a historically situated example of a critical pedagogy in practice. Feminist conceptions of education are similar to Freire's pedagogy in a variety of ways, and feminist educators often cite Freire as the educational theorist who comes closest to the approach and goals for feminist pedagogy (see Culley and Portuges, 1985: Introduction for comparisons of Freirean and feminist pedagogy; see also Maher, 1985, 1987). Both feminist pedagogy as it is usually defined and Freirean pedagogy rest upon visions of social transformation; underlying both are certain common assumptions concerning oppression, consciousness, and historical change. Both pedagogies assert the existence of oppression in people's material conditions of existence and as a part of consciousness; both rest on a view of consciousness as more than a sum of dominating discourses, but as containing within it a critical capacity—what Antonio Gramsci (1971) called 'good sense'; and both thus see human beings as subjects and actors in history and hold a strong commitment to justice and a vision of a better world and of the potential for liberation. These ideals have powerfully influenced teachers and students in a wide range of educational settings, both formal and informal.

But in action, the goals of liberation or opposition to oppression have not always been easy to understand or achieve. As universal goals, these ideals do not address the specificity of people's lives; they do not directly analyze the contradictions between conflicting oppressed groups or the ways in which a single individual can experience oppression in one sphere while being privileged or oppressive in another. Feminist and Freirean teachers are in many ways engaged in what Teresa deLauretis (1984, p. 178) has called 'shifting the ground of signs', challenging accepted meanings and relationships that occur at what she calls 'political or more often micropolitical' levels, groupings that 'produce no texts as such, but by shifting the "ground" of a given sign . . . effectively intervene upon codes of perception as well as ideological codes.' But in attempting to challenge dominant values and to 'shift the ground of signs,' feminist and Freirean teachers raise conflicts for themselves and for their students, who also are historically situated and whose own subjectivities are often contradictory and in process. These conflicts have become increasingly clear as both Freirean and feminist pedagogies are put into practice. Attempting to implement these pedagogies without acknowledging the conflict not only of divided consciousness—what Audre Lorde (1984) calls 'the oppressor within us'—but also the conflicts among groups trying to work together to name and struggle against oppression—among teachers and students in classrooms, or among political groups working for change in very specific areas—can lead to anger, frustration, and a retreat to safer or more traditional approaches. The numerous accounts of the tensions of trying to put liberatory pedagogies into practice demonstrate the need to re-examine the assumptions of the classic texts of liberatory pedagogy and to consider the various issues that have arisen in attempts at critical and liberatory classroom practice (see, for example, Ellsworth, 1989; Berlak, 1989; Britzman, 1992).

[...]

THE PEDAGOGY OF PAULO FREIRE

Freire's pedagogy developed in particular historical and political circumstances of neocolonialism and imperialism. As is well known, Freire's methods developed originally from his work with peasants in Brazil and later in Chile and Guinea-Bissau.[1] Freire's thought thus needs to be understood in the context of the political and economic situation of the developing world. In Freire's initial formulation, oppression was conceived in class terms and education was viewed in the context of peasants' and working people's revolutionary struggles. Equally influential in Freire's thought and pedagogy were the influence of radical Christian thought and the revolutionary role of liberation theology in Latin America. As is true for other radical Christians in Latin America, Freire's personal knowledge of extreme poverty and suffering challenged his deeply felt Christian faith grounded in the ethical teachings of Jesus in the Gospels. Freire's pedagogy is thus founded on a moral imperative to side with the oppressed that emerges from both his Christian faith and his knowledge and experience of suffering in the society in which he grew up and lived. Freire has repeatedly stated that his pedagogical method cannot simply be transferred to other settings, but that each historical site requires the development of a pedagogy appropriate to that setting (see, for example, Freire, 1985; Freire and Macedo, 1987; Freire and Shor, 1987). In his most recent work, he has also addressed sexism and racism as systems of oppression that must be considered as seriously as class oppression (Horton and Freire, 1990). Nonetheless, Freire is frequently read without consideration for the context of the specific settings in which his work developed and without these qualifications in mind. His most commonly read text still is his first book to be published in English, *Pedagogy of the Oppressed* (1971). In this classic text, Freire presents the epistemological basis for his pedagogy and discusses the concepts of oppression, conscientization, and dialogue that are at the heart of his pedagogical project, both as he enacted it in settings in the developing world and as it has been appropriated by radical teachers in other settings.

Freire organizes his approach to liberatory pedagogy in terms of a dualism between the oppressed and the oppressors and between humanization and dehumanization. This organization of thought in terms of opposing forces reflects Freire's own experiences of literacy work with the poor in Brazil, a situation in which the lines between oppressor and oppressed were clear. For Freire, humanization is the goal of liberation; it has not yet been achieved, nor can it be achieved so long as the oppressors oppress the oppressed. That is, liberation and humanization will not occur if the roles of oppressor and oppressed are simply reversed. If humanization is to be realized, new relationships among human beings must be created.

> Because it is a distortion of being more fully human, sooner or later being less human leads the oppressed to struggle against those who made them so. In order for this struggle to have meaning, the oppressed must not, in seeking to regain their humanity (which is a way to create it), become in turn oppressors of the oppressors, but rather restorers of the humanity of both.   (Freire, 1971, p. 28)

The struggle against oppression leading to humanization is thus utopian and visionary. As Freire (1985, p. 57) says elsewhere: 'To be utopian is not to be merely idealistic or impractical but rather to engage in denunciation and annunciation.' By denunciation, Freire refers to the naming and analysis of existing structures of oppression; by annunciation, he means the creation of new forms of relationships and being in the world as a result of mutual struggle against oppression. Thus Freire presents a theoretical justification for a pedagogy that aims to critique existing forms of oppression and to transform the world, thereby creating new ways of being, or humanization.

Radical educators throughout the world have used *Pedagogy of the Oppressed* as the theoretical justification for their work. As an eloquent and impassioned statement of the need for and possibility of change through reading the world and the word, there is no comparable contemporary text (Freire and Macedo, 1987). But when we look at *Pedagogy of the Oppressed* from the perspective of recent feminist theory and pedagogy, certain problems arise that may reflect the difficulties that have sometimes arisen when Freire's ideas are enacted in specific settings. The challenges of recent feminist theory do not imply the rejection of Freire's goals for what he calls a pedagogy for liberation; feminists certainly share Freire's emphasis on seeing human beings as the subjects and not the objects of history. A critical feminist rereading of Freire, however, points to ways in which the project of Freirean pedagogy, like that of feminist pedagogy, may be enriched and re-envisioned.

From a feminist perspective, *Pedagogy of the Oppressed* is striking in its use of the male referent, a usage that was universal in the 1960s, when this book was written.[2] Much more troublesome, however, is the abstract quality of terms such as humanization, which do not address the particular meanings imbued by men and women, Black and White, or other groups. The assumption of *Pedagogy of the Oppressed* is that in struggling against oppression, the oppressed will move toward true humanity. But this leaves unaddressed the forms of oppression experienced by different actors, the possibility of struggles among people oppressed differently by different groups—what Cameron McCarthy (1988) calls 'nonsynchrony of oppression.' This assumption also presents humanization as a universal, without considering the various definitions this term may bring forth from people of different groups. When Freire speaks of the oppressed needing to fight the tendency to become 'sub-oppressors', he means that the oppressed have only the pattern of oppression before them as a way of being in a position other than the one they are in. As Freire (1971, p. 30) writes: 'Their ideal is to be men; but for them, to be men is to be oppressors. This is their model of humanity.' What is troubling here is not that 'men' is used for human beings, but that the model of oppressor implied here is based on the immediate oppressor of men—in this case, bosses over peasants or workers. What is not addressed is the possibility of simultaneous contradictory positions of oppression and dominance: the man oppressed by his boss could at the same time oppress his wife, for example, or the White woman oppressed by sexism could exploit the Black woman. By framing his discussion in such abstract terms, Freire slides over the contradictions and tensions within social settings in which overlapping forms of oppression exist.

This usage of 'the oppressed' in the abstract also raises difficulties in Freire's use of experience as the means of acquiring a radical literacy, 'reading the world and the word.' At the heart of Freire's pedagogy is the insistence that all people are subjects and knowers of the world. Their political literacy will emerge from their reading of the world—that is, their own experience. This reading will lead to collective knowledge and action. But what if that experience is divided? What if different truths are discovered in reading the world from different positions? For Freire, education as the practice of freedom 'denies that men are abstract, isolated, independent, and unattached to the world ... Authentic reflection considers neither abstract man nor the world without men, but men in their relations with the world' (Freire, 1971, p. 69). But implicit in this vision is the assumption that, when the oppressed perceive themselves in relation to the world, they will act together collectively to transform the world and to move toward their own humanization. The nature of their perception of the world and their oppression is implicitly assumed to be uniform for all the oppressed. The possibility of contradictory experience of oppression among the oppressed is absent. [...]

Central to Freire's pedagogy is the practice of conscientization; that is, coming to a consciousness of oppression and a commitment to end that oppression. Conscientization is based on this common experience of oppression. Through this reading of the world, the oppressed will come to knowledge. The role of the teacher in this process is to instigate a dialogue between teacher and student, based on their common ability to know the world and to act as subjects in the world. But the question of the authority and power of the teacher, particularly those forms of power based on the teacher's subject position as raced, classed, gendered, and so on, is not addressed by Freire. There is, again, the assumption that the teacher is 'on the same side' as the oppressed, and that as teachers and students engage together in a dialogue about the world, they will uncover together the same reality, the same oppression, and the same liberation. In *Pedagogy of the Oppressed,* the teacher is presented as a generic man whose interests will be with the oppressed as they mutually discover the mechanisms of oppression. [...] In fact, of course, teachers are not abstract: they are women or men of particular races, classes, ages, abilities, and so on. The teacher will be seen and heard by students not as an abstraction, but as a particular person with a certain defined history and relationship to the world. [...] Without recognizing more clearly the implicit power and limitations of the position of teachers, calls for a collective liberation or for opposition to oppression slide over the surface of the tensions that may emerge among teachers and students as subjects with conflicting interests and histories and with different kinds of knowledge and power. A number of questions are thus left unaddressed in *Pedagogy of the Oppressed:* How are we to situate ourselves in relation to the struggles of others? How are we to address our own contradictory positions as oppressors and oppressed? Where are we to look for liberation when our collective 'reading of the world' reveals contradictory and conflicting experiences and struggles? The Freirean vision of the oppressed as undifferentiated and as the source of unitary political action, the transparency of the subjectivity of the Freirean teacher, and the claims of universal goals of liberation and social transformation fail to provide the answers to these questions.

Calling into question the universal and abstract claims of *Pedagogy of the Oppressed* is certainly not to argue that Freire's pedagogy should be rejected or discarded. The ethical stance of Freire in terms of praxis and his articulation of people's worth and ability to know and change the world are an essential basis for radical pedagogies in opposition to oppression. Freire's thought illuminates the central question of political action in a world increasingly without universals. Freire postitions himself on the side of the oppressed; he claims the moral imperative to act in the world. [...] But in order better to seek the affirmation of our own humanity and to seek to end suffering and oppression, I am arguing for a more situated theory of oppression and subjectivity, and for the need to consider the contradictions of such universal claims of truth or process.

Like Freirean pedagogy, feminist pedagogy is based on assumptions of the power of consciousness raising, the existence of oppression and the possibility of ending it, and the desire for social transformation. But in its historical development, feminist pedagogy has revealed the shortcomings that emerge in the attempt to enact a pedagogy that assumes a universal experience and abstract goals. In the attempt of feminist pedagogy to address these issues, a more complex vision of a liberatory pedagogy is being developed and explored.

FEMINIST PEDAGOGY, CONSCIOUSNESS RAISING, AND WOMEN'S LIBERATION

[. . .]

The pedagogy of feminist teachers is based on certain assumptions about knowledge, power, and political action that can be traced beyond the academy to the political activism of the women's movement in the 1960s. This same commitment to social change through the transformative potential of education underlay Freire's pedagogy in Brazil during the same period. Women's studies at the university level have since come to encompass a wide variety of political stances and theoretical approaches. Socialist feminism, liberal feminism, radical feminism, and postmodern feminism all view issues from their different perspectives. Nonetheless, feminist pedagogy continues to echo the struggles of its origins and to retain a vision of social activism. [. . .] Thus, like Freirean pedagogy, feminist pedagogy is grounded in a vision of social change. And, like Freirean pedagogy, feminist pedagogy rests on truth claims of the primacy of experience and consciousness that are grounded in historically situated social change movements. Key to understanding the methods and epistemological claims of feminist pedagogy is an understanding of its origins in more grassroots political activity, particularly in the consciousness-raising groups of the women's liberation movement of the late 1960s and 1970s.

[. . .] Early consciousness-raising groups, based on friendship and common political commitments, focused on the discussion of shared experiences of sexuality, work, family, and participation in the male-dominated left political movement. Consciousness raising focused on collective political change rather than on individual therapy. [. . .]

A second fundamental aspect of consciousness raising is the reliance on experience and feeling. According to Kathie Sarachild (1975), the focus on examining women's own experience came from a profound distrust of accepted authority and truth. These claims about what was valuable and true tended to be accepting of existing assumptions about women's 'inherent nature' and 'proper place.' In order to call those truths into question (truths we might now call hegemonic and that Foucault, for example, would tie to structures of power), women had nowhere to turn except to their own experience. Sarachild describes the process in her group.

> In the end the group decided to raise its consciousness by studying women's lives by topics like childhood, jobs, motherhood, etc. We'd do any outside reading we wanted to and thought was important. But

our starting point for discussion, as well as our test of the accuracy of what any of the books said, would be the actual experience we had in these areas.   (Sarachild, 1975, p. 145)

The last aspect of consciousness raising was a common sharing of experience in a collective, leaderless group. [. . .] The assumption underlying this sharing of stories was the existence of commonality among women; as Sarachild puts it, 'we made the assumption, an assumption basic to consciousness raising, that most women were like ourselves—not different' (Sarachild, 1975, p. 147).

Consciousness raising shared the assumptions of earlier revolutionary traditions: that understanding and theoretical analysis were the first steps to revolutionary change, and that neither was adequate alone: theory and practice were intertwined as praxis. As Sarachild (1975, p. 147) puts it, 'Consciousness raising was seen as both a method for arriving at the truth and a means for action and organizing.' What was original in consciousness raising, however, was its emphasis on experience and feeling as the guide to theoretical understanding, an approach that reflected the realities of women's socially defined subjectivities and the conditions of their lives. Irene Peslikis, another member of Redstockings, wrote, 'When we think of what it is that politicizes people it is not so much books or ideas but experience' (Peslikis, 1970, p. 339).

While early feminists influenced by a left political tradition explored the creation of theory grounded in women's feelings and experiences, they never lost the commitment to social transformation. In their subsequent history, however, consciousness raising and feminist pedagogy did not always retain this political commitment to action. As the women's movement expanded to reach wider groups of women, consciousness raising tended to lose its commitment to revolutionary change. This trend seems to have been particularly true as the women's movement affected women with a less radical perspective and with little previous political involvement. Without a vision of collective action and social transformation, consciousness raising held the possibility of what Berenice Fisher (1980) calls 'a diversion of energies into an exploration of feelings and "private" concerns to the detriment of political activism' (see also bel hooks 'on self-recovery', 1989). The lack of structure and the local nature of consciousness-raising groups only reinforced these tendencies toward a focus on individual rather than collective change. The one site in which the tradition of consciousness raising did find institutional expression was in academia, in the growth of women's studies courses and programs stimulated by the new scholarship on women. The founders of these early courses and programs tended to be politically committed feminists who themselves had experienced consciousness raising and who, like Freire, assumed that education could and should be a means of social change.

[...] The growth of women's studies programs and feminist scholarship provided an institutional framework and theoretical underpinning for feminist pedagogy, the attempt to express feminist values and goals in the classroom. But while feminist scholarship has presented fundamental challenges to traditional androcentric knowledge, the attempt to create a new pedagogy modeled on consciousness raising has not been as successful or coherent a project. Serious challenges to the goal of political transformation through the experience of feminist learning have been raised in the attempt to create a feminist pedagogy in the academy. The difficulties and contradictions that have emerged in the attempt to create a feminist pedagogy in traditional institutions like universities raise serious questions for all liberatory pedagogies and echo some of the problems raised by the unitary and universal approach of *Pedagogy of the Oppressed*. But in engaging these questions, feminist pedagogy suggests new directions that can enrich Freirean pedagogies of liberation.

Feminist pedagogy has raised three areas of concern that are particularly useful in considering the ways in which Freirean and other liberatory pedagogies can be enriched and expanded. The first of these concerns the role and authority of the teacher; the second addresses the epistemological question of the source of the claims for knowledge and truth in personal experience and feeling; the last, emerging from challenges by women of color and postmodernist feminist theorists, raises the question of difference. Their challenges have led to a shattering of the unproblematic and unitary category 'woman,' as well as of an assumption of the inevitable unity of 'women.' Instead, feminist theorists have increasingly emphasized the importance of recognizing difference as a central category of feminist pedagogy. The unstated assumption of a universal experience of 'being a woman' was exploded by the critiques of postmodern feminists and by the growing assertion of lesbians and women of color that the universal category 'woman' in fact meant 'White, heterosexual, middle-class woman,' even when used by White, heterosexual, socialist feminists, or women veterans of the civil rights movement who were committed to class or race struggles (see, for example, Fuss, 1989; hooks, 1989; Britzman, 1992). These theoretical challenges to the unity of both 'woman' and 'women' have in turn called into question the authority of women as teachers and students in the classroom, the epistemological value of both feeling and experience, and the nature of political strategies for enacting feminist goals of social change. I turn next to an exploration of these key issues of authority, experience, feeling and difference within feminist pedagogy and theory.

The role and authority of the teacher

In many respects, the feminist vision of the teacher's authority echoes the Freirean image of the teacher who is a joint learner with students and who holds authority by virtue of greater knowledge and experience. But as we have seen, Freire fails to address the various forms of power held by teachers depending on their race, gender, and the historical and institutional settings in which they work. In the Freirean account, they are in this sense 'transparent.' In the actual practice of feminist pedagogy, the central issues of difference, positionality, and the need to recognize the implications of subjectivity or identity for teachers and students have become central. Moreover, the question of authority in institutional settings makes problematic the possibility of achieving the collective and nonhierarchical vision of early consciousness-raising groups within university classrooms. The basic elements of early consciousness-raising groups—an emphasis on feeling, experience, and sharing, and a suspicion of hierarchy and authority—continue to influence feminist pedagogy in academic settings. But the institutionalized nature of women's studies in the hierarchical and bureaucratic structure of academia creates tensions that run counter to the original commitment to praxis in consciousness-raising groups. Early consciousness-raising groups were homogeneous, antagonistic to authority, and had a commitment to political change that had directly emerged from civil rights and new left movements. Feminist pedagogy within academic classrooms addresses heterogeneous groups of students within a competitive and individualistic culture in which the teacher holds institutional power and responsibility (even if she may want to reject that power) (Friedman, 1985). As bell hooks (1989, p. 29) comments, 'The academic setting, the academic discourse (we) work in, is not a known site for truthtelling.' The very success of feminist scholarship has meant the development of a rich theoretical tradition with deep divisions and opposing goals and methods. (For an excellent discussion of these perspectives see Jagger, 1983.) Thus the source of the teacher's authority as a 'woman' who can call upon a 'common woman's knowledge' is called into question; at the same time the feminist teacher is 'given' authority by virtue of her role within the hierarchiacal structure of the university.

The question of authority in feminist pedagogy seems to be centered around two different conceptions. The first refers to the institutionally imposed authority of the teacher within a hierarchical university structure. The teacher in this role must give grades, is evaluated by administrators and colleagues in terms of expertise in a body of knowledge, and is expected to take responsibility for meeting the goals of an academic course as it is understood within the wider university. This hierarchical structure is clearly in opposition to the collective goals of a common women's movement and is miles from the early structureless consciousness-raising groups in which each woman was an expert on her own life. Not only does the university structure impose this model of institutional authority, but students themselves expect it. As Barbara Hillyer Davis (1983, p. 91) comments: 'The institutional pressure to (impart knowledge) is reinforced by the students' well-socialized behavior. If I will tell them "what I want," they will deliver it. They are exasperated with my efforts to depart from the role of dispenser of wisdom.' Feminist educators have attempted to address this tension between their ideals of collective education and the demands of the university by a variety of expedients: group assignments and grades, contracts for grades, pass/fail courses, and such techniques as self-revelation and the articulation of the dynamics of the classroom (see, for example, Beck, 1983).

Another aspect of institutionalized authority, however, is the need for women to *claim* authority in a society that denies it to them. As Culley and Portuges have pointed out, the authority and power of the woman feminist teacher is already in question from many of her students precisely because she is a woman.

> As women, our own position is precarious, and the power we are supposed to exercise is given grudgingly, if at all. For our own students, for ourselves, and for our superiors, we are not clearly 'us' for 'them.' The facts of class, of race, of ethnicity, of sexual preference—as well as gender—may cut across the neat divisions of teacher/student.
> (Culley and Portuges, 1985, p. 12; see also Culley, 1985)

Thus the issue of institutional authority raises the contradictions of trying to achieve a democratic and collective ideal in a hierarchical institution, but it also raises the question of the meaning of authority for feminist teachers, whose right to speak or to hold power is itself under attack in a patriarchal (and racist, homophobic, classist, and so on) society. The question of asserting authority and power is a central concern to feminists precisely because as women they have been taught that taking power is inappropriate. From this perspective, the feminist teacher's acceptance of authority becomes in itself liberating to her and to her students. It becomes a claim to authority in terms of her own value as a scholar and a teacher in a patriarchal society that structurally denies or questions that authority as it is manifest in the organization and bureaucracy of the university. Women students, after all, are socialized to be deferential, and both men and women students are taught to accept male authority. It is instructive for students to see women assert authority. But this use of authority will lead to positive social change only if those teachers are working also to empower students in a Freirean sense. (For a thoughtful discussion of the contradictory pressures on the feminist teacher both to nurture and challenge women students, see Davis, 1983.) As Susan Stanford Friedman argues:

> What I and other women have needed is a theory of feminist pedagogy consistent with our needs as women operating at the fringes of patriarchal

space. As we attempt to move on to academic turf culturally defined as male, we need a theory that first recognizes the androcentric denial of *all* authority to women and, second, points out a way for us to speak with an authentic voice not based on tyranny. (Friedman, 1985, p. 207)

These concerns lead to a conception of authority and power in a positive sense, both in terms of women asserting authority as women, and in terms of valuing intellectual work and the creation of theory as a means of understanding and, thus, of changing the world.

The authority of the intellectual raises issues for feminists in the academy that are similar to those faced by other democratic and collective political movements, such as those described by Freire. There is a contradiction between the idea of a women's movement including all women and a group of what Berenice Fisher (1980, p. 22) calls 'advanced women.' Feminists who question the whole tradition of androcentric thought are deeply suspicious of women who take a position of 'experts' who can translate and interpret other women's experiences. [. . .]

In terms of feminist pedagogy, the authority of the feminist teacher as intellectual and theorist finds expression in the goal of making students themselves theorists of their own lives by interrogating and analyzing their own experience. In an approach very similar to Freire's concept of conscientization, this strategy moves beyond the naming or sharing of experience to the creation of a critical understanding of the forces that have shaped that experience. This theorizing is antithetical to traditional views of women. As Bunch points out, traditionally

women are supposed to worry about mundane survival problems, to brood about fate, and to fantasize in a personal manner. We are not meant to think analytically about society, to question the way things are, to consider how things could be different. Such thinking involves an active, not a passive, relationship to the world.   (Bunch, 1983, p. 156)

Thus feminist educators like Fisher and Bunch accept their authority as intellectuals and theorists, but they consciously attempt to construct their pedagogy to recognize and encourage the capacity of their students to theorize and to recognize their own power. (For a thoughtful discussion of the difficulties of retaining an activist stance for feminists in the academy, see Fisher, 1982.) This is a conception of authority not in the institutional terms of a bureaucratized university system, but rather an attempt to claim the authority of theorist and guide for students who are themselves potential theorists.

Feminist concerns about the authority of the feminist teacher address questions of classroom practice and theory ignored by Freire—in his formulation of the teacher and student as two 'knowers' of the world, and in his assertion that the liberatory teacher should acknowledge and claim authority but not authoritarianism. The feminist exploration of authority is much richer and addresses more directly the contradictions between goals of collectivity and hierarchies of knowledge. Feminist teachers are much more conscious of the power of various subject positions than is represented in Freire's 'transparent' liberatory teacher. An acknowledgment of the realities of conflict and tensions based on contradictory political goals, as well as of the meaning of historically experienced oppression for both teachers and students leads to a pedagogy that respects difference not just as significant for students, but for teachers as well.

Personal experience as a source of knowledge and truth

[...] Basic to the Freirean method of conscientization is the belief in the ability of all people to be knowers and to read both the word and the world. In Freirean pedagogy, it is through the interrogation of their own experiences that the oppressed will come to an understanding of their own power as knowers and creators of the world; this knowledge will contribute to the transformation of their world. In consciousness-raising groups and in feminist pedagogy in the university, a similar reliance on experience and feeling has been fundamental to the development of a feminist knowledge of the world that can be the basis for social change. Underlying both Freirean and early feminist pedagogy is an assumption of a common experience as the basis for political analysis and action. [...]

In many ways, feeling or emotion has been seen traditionally as a source of women's knowledge about the world. In the early consciousness-raising groups, feelings were looked to as the source of a 'true' knowledge of the world for women living in a society that denied the value of their perceptions. Feelings or emotions were seen as a way of testing accepted claims of what is universally true about human nature or, specifically, about women. [...] However, as feminist educators have explored the uses of feeling or emotion as a source of knowledge, several difficulties have become clear. First of all, there is a danger that the expression of strong emotion can simply be cathartic and can deflect the need for action to address the underlying causes of that emotion. Moreover, it is not clear how to distinguish among a wide range of emotions as the source of political action. At a more theoretical level, there are contradictions involved in claiming that the emotions are a source for knowledge and at the same time arguing that they are manipulated and shaped by dominant discourses. Both consciousness-raising groups and feminist theorists have asserted the social construction of feelings and their manipulation by the dominant culture; at the same time, they look to feelings as a source of truth. Berenice Fisher points to the contradiction implicit in these claims:

> In theoretical terms, we cannot simultaneously claim that all feelings are socially conditioned and that some feelings are 'true.' We would be more consistent to acknowledge that society only partly shapes our emotions, leaving an opening where we can challenge and change the responses to

which we have been socialized. That opening enables the consciousness-raising process to take place and gives us the space in which to reflect on the new emotional responses that our process evokes. (Fisher, 1987)

In this formulation, Fisher seems to be arguing for a kind of Gramscian 'good sense,' a locus of knowing in the self that is grounded in feeling as a guide to theoretical understanding. Feelings thus are viewed as a kind of cognition—a source of knowledge.

Perhaps the most eloquent for feelings as a source of oppositional knowledge is found in the work of Audre Lorde. Lorde, a Black lesbian feminist theorist and poet, writes from the specificity of her own socially defined and shaped life. For her, feeling is the source of poetry, a means of knowing that challenges White, Western, androcentric epistemologies. She specifically ties her own feelings as a Black woman to a non-Western way of knowing.

[...]

Lorde is acutely aware of the ways in which the dominant society shapes our sense of who we are and what we feel. As she points out, 'Within living structures defined by profit, by linear power, by institutional de-humanization, our feelings were not meant to survive (Lorde, 1984, p. 34). Moreover, Lorde is conscious of the oppressor within us: 'For we have, built into all of us, old blueprints of expectation and response, old structures of oppression, and these must be altered at the same time as we alter the living conditions which are the result of those structures' (Lorde, 1984, p. 123). But although Lorde does not deny what she calls 'the oppressor within,' she retains a belief in the power of deeper feeling to challenge the dominant definitions of truth and to point the way to an analysis that can lead to an alternative vision.

[...]

Both Freire and Lorde retain a Utopian faith in the possibility that human beings can create new ways of being in the world out of collective struggle and a human capacity to feel. Lorde terms this the power of the erotic; she speaks of the erotic as 'a measure between the beginnings of our sense of self and the chaos of our strongest feelings,' a resource 'firmly rooted in the power of our unexpressed or unrecognized feeling' (Lorde, 1984, p. 53). Because the erotic can challenge the dominant, it has been denied as a source of power and knowledge. But for Lorde, the power of the erotic provides the basis for visionary social change.

[...]

Lorde's discussion of feeling and the erotic as a source of power and knowledge is based on the assumption that human beings have the capacity to feel and know, and can engage in self-critique; people are not completely shaped by dominant discourse. The oppressor may be within us, but Lorde insists that we also have the capacity to challenge our own ways of feeling and knowing. When tied to a recognition of positionality, this validation of feeling can be used to develop powerful sources of politically focused feminist education.

For Lorde and Fisher, this kind of knowing through an exploration of feeling and emotion requires collective inquiry and constant re-evaluation. It is a contingent and positioned claim to truth. Similar complexities arise in the use of experience as the basis for feminist political action. Looking to experience as the source of knowledge and the focus of feminist learning is perhaps the most fundamental tenet of feminist pedagogy. This is similar to the Freirean call to 'read the world' to seek the generative themes that codify power relationships and social structures. [...] As became clear quite early in the women's movement, claims about experience as a source of women's knowledge rested on certain assumptions about commonalities in women's lives. Women were conceived as a unitary and relatively undifferentiated group. [...] Underlying this approach was the assumption of a common woman's experience, one reflecting the world of the White, middle-class, heterosexual women of the early feminist movement. But as the critiques of lesbians, women of color, and postmodernist feminist theorists have made clear, there is no single woman's experience to be revealed. Both experience and feeling thus have been called into question as the source of an unproblematic knowledge of the world that will lead to praxis. As Diana Fuss (1989, p. 114) comments: ' "female experience" is never as unified, as knowable, as universal, and as stable as we presume it to be.'

Challenges to the concept of a unitary women's experience by both women of color and by postmodern critics has not meant the abandonment of experience as a source of knowledge for feminist teachers. Of course experience, like feeling, is socially constructed in the sense that we can only understand it and speak about it in ideas and terms that are part of an existing ideology and language. But feminist teachers have explored the ways in which women have experienced the material world through their bodies. This self-examination of lived experience is then used as a source of knowledge that can illuminate the social processes and ideology that shape us. As Fuss (1989, p. 118) suggests: 'Such a position permits the introduction of narratives of lived experience into the classroom while at the same time challenging us to examine collectively the central role social and historical practices play in shaping and producing these narratives.' [...]

The question of difference

Both women of color writing from a perspective of cultural feminism and postmodernist feminist theorists converge in their critique of the concept of a universal 'women's experience.' While the idea of a unitary and universal category 'woman' has been challenged by women of color for its racist assumptions, it has also been challenged by recent analyses of feminist theorists influenced by postmodernism, who point to the social construction of subjectivity and who emphasize the 'unstable' nature of the self. Postmodernist feminist critics such as Chris Weedon (1887, p. 33) have argued that socially given identities such as 'woman' are 'precarious, contradictory, and in process, constantly being reconstituted in discourse each time we speak.' This kind of analysis considers the ways in which 'the subject' is not an object; that is, not fixed in a static social structure, but constantly being created, actively creating the self, and struggling for new ways of being in the world through new forms of discourse or new forms of social relationships. Such analysis calls for a recognition of the positionality of each person in any discussion of what can be known from experience. [...] If we view individual selves as being constructed and negotiated, then we can begin to consider what exactly those forces are in which individuals shape themselves and by which they are shaped. The category of 'woman' is itself challenged as it is seen more and more as a part of a symbolic system of ideology. [...]

Both women of color and lesbian critics have pointed to the complexity of socially given identities. Black women and other women of color raise challenges to the assumption that the sharing of experience will create solidarity and a theoretical understanding based upon a common women's standpoint. Lesbian feminists, both White and of color, point to the destructive nature of homophobia and what Adrienne Rich has called compulsory heterosexuality. As is true of White, heterosexual, feminist educators, these theorists base their analysis upon their own experiences, but those experiences reveal not only the workings of sexism, but of racism, homophobia, and class oppression as well. This complex perspective underlies the Combahee River Collective Statement, a position paper written by a group of African-American feminists in Boston in the 1970s. This statement makes clear what a grounded theory of experience means for women whose value is denied by the dominant society in numerous ways. The women in the Combahee River Collective (1983, p. 275) argue that 'the most profound and potentially most radical politics come directly out of our own identity, as opposed to working to end somebody else's oppression.' For African-American women, an investigation of the shaping of their own identities reveals the ways in which sexism and racism are interlocking forms of oppression:

> As children we realized that we were different from boys and that we were treated differently. For example, we were told in the same breath to be quiet both for the sake of being 'ladylike' and to make us less objectionable in the eyes of white people. As we grew older, we became aware of the threat of physical and sexual abuse from men. However, we had

no way of conceptualizing what was so apparent to us, what we *knew* was really happening.

(Combahee River Collective, 1983, p. 274)

When African-American teachers like Michele Russell or Barbara Omolade describe their feminist pedagogy, they ground that pedagogy in an investigation of experience in material terms. As Russell (1983, p. 155) describes her teaching of an introductory Black Studies class for women at Wayne County Community College in Detroit: 'We have an hour together ... The first topic of conversation—among themselves and with me—is what they went through just to make it in the door, on time. That, in itself becomes a lesson.' And Omolade points out in her discussion of her teaching at Medgar Evers College in New York, a college whose students are largely African-American women:

> No one can teach students to 'see,' but an instructor is responsible for providing the coherent ordering of information and content. The classroom process is one of information-sharing in which students learn to generalize their particular life experiences within a community of fellow intellectuals.

(Omolade, 1987, p. 39)

Thus the pedagogy of Russell and Omolade is grounded in experience as a source of knowledge in a particularly materialistic way; the knowledge generated reveals the overlapping forms of oppression lived by women of color in this society.

The investigation of the experiences of women of color, lesbian women, women whose very being challenges existing racial, sexual, heterosexual, and class dominance leads to a knowledge of the world that both acknowledges differences and points to the need for an 'integrated analysis and practice based upon the fact that the major systems of oppression are interlocking' (Combahee River Collective, 1983, p. 272). The turning to experience thus reveals not a universal and common women's essence, but, rather, deep divisions in what different women have experienced, and in the kinds of knowledge they discover when they examine their own experience. The recognition of the differences among women raises serious challenges to feminist pedagogy by calling into question the authority of the teacher/theorist, raising feelings of guilt and shame, and revealing tensions among students as well as between teacher and students. In classes of African-American women taught by African-American teachers, the sharing of experience can lead to the same sense of commonality and sharing that was true of early consciousness-raising groups. But in settings in which students come from differing positions of privilege or oppression, the sharing of experience raises conflicts rather than building solidarity. In these circumstances, the collective exploration of experience leads not to a common knowledge and solidarity based on sameness, but to the tensions of an articulation of difference. Such exploration raises again the problems left unaddressed by Freirean pedagogy: the overlapping and multiple forms of oppression revealed in 'reading the world' of experience.

CONCLUSION

Both Freirean and feminist pedagogies are based on political commitment and identification with subordinate and oppressed groups; both seek justice and empowerment. Freire sets out these goals of liberation and social and political transformation as universal claims, without exploring his own privileged position or existing conflicts among oppressed groups themselves. Writing from within a tradition of Western modernism, his theory rests on a belief of transcendent and universal truth. But feminist theory influenced by postmodernist thought and by the writings of women of color challenges the underlying assumptions of these universal claims. Feminist theorists in particular argue that it is essential to recognize, as Juliet Mitchell (1984) comments, that we cannot 'live as human subjects without in some sense taking on a history.' The recognition of our own histories means the necessity of articulating our own subjectivities and our own interests as we try to interpret and critique the social world. This stance rejects the universalizing tendency of much 'malestream' thought, and insists on recognizing the power and privilege of who we are. [...]

Fundamental to recent feminist theory is a questioning of the concept of a coherent subject moving through history with a single essential identity. Instead, feminist theorists are developing a concept of the constant creation and negotiation of selves within structures of ideology and material constraints. (See, for example, Flax, 1987; Harding, 1986; Smith, 1987; Haraway, 1987; Hartsock, 1983; O'Brien, 1981; Diamond and Quinby, 1988; Alcoff, 1988; *Feminist Studies*, 1988; Butler, 1990; Nicholson, 1990.) This line of theoretical analysis calls into question assumptions of the common interests of the oppressed, whether conceived of as women or peasants; it challenges the use of such universal terms as oppression and liberation without locating these claims in a concrete historical or social context. The challenges of recent feminist theory and, in particular, the writings of feminists of color point to the need to articulate and claim a particular historical and social identity, to locate ourselves, and to build coalitions from a recognition of the partial knowledges of our own constructed identities. Recognizing the standpoint of subjects as shaped by their experience of class, race, gender, or other socially defined identities has powerful implications for pedagogy, in that it emphasizes the need to make conscious the subject positions not only of students but of teachers as well. These lines of theoretical analysis have implications for the ways in which we can understand pedagogy as contested, as a site of discourse among subjects, teachers and students whose identities are, as Weedon puts it, contradictory and in process. The theoretical formulation of the 'unstable self,' the complexity of subjectivities, what Giroux calls 'multi-layered subjects,' and the need to position ourselves in relation to our own histories raise important issues for liberatory pedagogies. If all people's identities are recognized in their full historical and social complexity as subject positions that are in process, based on knowledges that are partial and that reflect deep and conflicting differences, how can we theorize what a liberatory pedagogy actively struggling against different forms of oppression may look like? How can we build upon the rich and complex analysis of feminist theory and pedagogy to work toward a Freirean vision of social justice and liberation?

In the complexity of issues raised by feminist pedagogy, we can begin to acknowledge the reality of tensions that result from different histories, from privilege, oppression, and power as they are lived by teachers and students in classrooms. To recognize these tensions and differences does not mean abondonment of the goals of social justice and empowerment, but it does make clear the need to recognize contingent and situated claims and to acknowledge our own histories and selves in process. One significant area of feminist work has been grounded in the collective analysis of experience and emotion, as exemplified by the work of Haug and her group in Germany or by the Jamaican women's theater group, Sistren. In many respects, these projects look back to consciousness raising, but with a more developed theory of ideology and an acute consciousness of difference. As Berenice Fisher (1987, p. 49) argues, a collective inquiry 'requires the slow unfolding of layers of experience, both the contradictory experiences of a given woman and the conflicting experiences of different women.' Another approach builds on what Bernice Reagon calls the need for coalition building, a recognition and validation of difference. This is similar to what has come to be known as identity politics, exemplified in what Minnie Bruce Pratt (1984) is seeking in her discussion of trying to come to terms with her own identity as a privileged Southern White woman. Martin and Mohanty (1986) speak of this as a sense of 'home,' a recognition of the difficulties of coming to terms with privilege or oppression, of the benefits of being an oppressor, or the rage of being oppressed. This is a validation of both difference and conflict, but also an attempt to build coalitions around common goals rather than a denial of differences. It is clear that this kind of pedagogy and exploration of experiences in a society in which privilege and oppression are lived is risky and filled with pain. Such a pedagogy suggests a more complex realization of the Freirean vision of the collective conscientization and struggle against oppression, one which acknowledges difference and conflict, but which, like Freire's vision, rests on a belief in the human capacity to feel, to know, and to change.

Notes

1. Freire's method of codifications and generative themes have been discussed frequently. Perhaps the best introduction to these concrete methods can be found in Freire (1973).
2. See Simone de Beauvoir (1953), for a more striking use of the male referent.
3. See, for example, Kathy McAfee and Myra Wood (1970) for an early socialist feminist analysis of the need to connect the women's movement with the class struggle.

References

Alcoff, L. (1988) Cultural feminism versus post structuralism: The identity crisis in feminist theory. *Signs* 13, 405–37.

Beck, E. T. (1983) Self-disclosure and the commitment to social change. *Women's Studies International Forum* 6, 159–64.

Berlak, A. (1989) Teaching for outrage and empathy in the liberal arts. *Educational Foundations* 3 (2), 69–94.

Britzman, D. (1991) *Practice Makes Practice.* Albany: State University of New York Press.

—(1992) Decentering discourses in teacher education: Or, the unleashing of unpopular things. In C. Mitchell and K. Weiler (eds) *What Schools Can Do: Critical Pedagogy and Practice.* Albany: State University of New York Press.

Bunch, C. (1983) Not by degrees: Feminist theory and education. In C. Bunch and S. Pollack (eds) *Learning Our Way.* Trumansburg, NY: The Crossing Press.

Butler, J. (1990) *Gender Trouble.* New York: Routledge.

Cherryholmes, C. (1988) *Power and Criticism: Poststructural Investigations in Education.* New York: Teachers College Press.

Combahee River Collective (1983) Combahee River Collective River Statement. In B. Smith (ed.) *Home Girls.* New York: Kitchen Table/Women of Color Press.

Culley, M. (1985) Anger and authority in the introductory women's studies classroom. In M. Culley and C. Portuges (eds) *Gendered Subjects* (pp. 209–17). Boston, MA: Routledge & Kegan Paul.

Culley, M. and Portuges, C. (1985) *Gendered Subjects.* Boston, MA: Routledge and Kegan Paul.

Davis, B. H. (1983) Teaching the feminist minority. In C. Bunch and S. Pollack (eds) *Learning Our Way.* Trumansburg, NY: The Crossing Press.

de Beauvoir, S. (1953) *The Second Sex.* New York: Knopf.

deLauretis, T. (1984) *Alice Doesn't: Feminism, Semiotics, Cinema.* Bloomington: Indiana University Press.

Diamond, I. and Quinby, L. (1988) *Feminism and Foucault.* Boston, MA: Northeastern University Press.

Ellsworth, E. (1989) Why doesn't this feel empowering? Working through the repressive myths of critical pedagogy. *Harvard Educational Review* 59, 297–324.

Feminist Studies (1988) Special issue on feminism and deconstruction. *Feminist Studies* 14 (1).

Fisher, B. (1980) What is feminist pedagogy? *Radical Teacher* 18, 20–25.

—(1982) Professing feminism: Feminist academics and the women's movement. *Psychology of Women Quarterly* 7, 55–69.

—(1987) The heart has its reasons: Feeling, thinking, and community building in feminist education. *Women's Studies Quarterly* 15 (3–4), 48.

Flax, J. (1987) Postmodernism and gender relations in feminist theory. *Signs* 12, 621–43.

Freire, P. (1971) *Pedagogy of the Oppressed.* New York: Herder & Herder.

—(1973) *Education for Critical Consciousness.* New York: Seabury Press.

—(1985) *The Politics of Education.* Westport, CT: Bergin and Garvey.

Freire, P. and Macedo, D. (1987) *Literacy: Reading the Word and the World.* Westport, CT: Bergin and Garvey.

Freire, P. and Shor, I. (1987) *A Pedagogy for Liberation.* London: Macmillan.

Friedman, S. S. (1985) Authority in the feminist classroom: A contradiction in terms? In M. Culley and C. Portuges (eds) *Gendered Subjects* (pp. 203–8). Boston, MA: Routledge and Kegan Paul

Fuss, D. (1989) *Essentially Speaking.* New York: Routledge.

Giroux, H. (ed.) (1991) *Postmodernism, Feminism and Cultural Politics.* Albany: State University of New York Press.

Giroux, H. and Simon, R. (eds) (1989) *Popular Culture, Schooling and Everyday Life.* Westport, CT: Bergin and Garvey.

Gramsci, A. (1971) *Selections from the Prison Notebooks.* New York: International Publishers.

Haraway, D. (1985) A manifesto for cyborgs. *Socialist Review* 80, 64–107.

Harding, S. (1986) *The Science Question in Feminism.* Ithaca: University of Cornell Press.

Hartsock, N. (1983) *Money, Sex and Power.* New York: Longman.

hooks, b. (1989) *Talking Back, Thinking Feminism, Thinking Black.* Boston, MA: South End Press.

Horton, M. and Freire, P. (1990) *We Make the Road by Walking: Conversations on Education and Social Change.* Edited by B. Bell, J. Gaventa and J. Peters. Philadelphia: Temple University Press.

Jagger, A. (1983) *Feminist Politics and Human Nature.* Sussex: The Harvester Press.

Lather, P. (1991) *Getting Smart: Feminist Research and Pedagogy With/in the Postmodern.* New York: Routledge.

Lorde, A. (1984) *Sister Outsider.* Trumansburg, NY: The Crossing Press.

McAfee, K. and Wood, M. (1970) Bread and roses. In L. Tanner (ed.) *Voices from Women's Liberation.* New York: New American Library.

McCarthy, C. (1988) Rethinking liberal and radical perspectives on racial inequality in schooling: Making the case for nonsynchrony. *Harvard Educational Review* 58, 265–80.

Maher, F. (1985) Classroom pedagogy and the new scholarship on women. In M. Culley and C. Portuges (eds) *Gendered Subjects* (pp. 29–48). Boston, MA: Routledge and Kegan Paul.

—(1987) Toward a richer theory of feminist pedagogy: A comparison of 'liberation' and 'gender' models for teaching and learning. *Journal of Education* 169 (3), 91–100.

Martin, B. and Mohanty, C. (1986) Feminist politics: What's home got to do with it? In T. deLauretis (ed.) *Feminist Studies/Critical Studies.* Bloomington: University of Indiana Press.

Mitchell, J. (1984) *Women: The Longest Revolution.* New York: Pantheon Books.

Nicholson, L. (ed.) (1990) *Feminism/Postmodernism.* New York: Routledge.

O'Brien, M. (1981) *The Politics of Reproduction.* Boston, MA: Routledge and Kegan Paul.

Omolade, B. (1987) A black feminist pedagogy. *Women's Studies Quarterly* 15 (3–4), 32–40.

Peslikis, I. (1970) Resistances to consciousness. In R. Morgan (ed.) *Sisterhood is Powerful.* New York: Vintage Press.

Pratt, M. B. (1984) Identity: Skin blood heart. In E. Bulkin, M. B. Pratt and B. Smith (eds) *Yours in Struggle.* Brooklyn, NY: Long Hard Press.

Reagon, B. (1983) Coalition politics: Turning the century. In B. Smith (ed.) *Home Girls* (pp. 356–69). New York: Kitchen Table/Women of Color Press.

Russell, M. (1983) Black-eyed blues connection: From the inside out. In C. Bunch and S. Pollack (eds) *Learning Our Way* (pp. 272–84). Trumansburg, NY: The Crossing Press.

Sarachild, K. (1975) Consciousness raising: A radical weapon. In Redstockings (ed.) *Feminist Revolution.* New York: Random House.

Smith, D. (1987) *The Everyday World as Problematic.* Boston, MA: Northeastern University Press.

Weedon, C. (1987) *Feminist Practice and Poststructuralist Theory.* Oxford: Basil Blackwell.

3 THE GENDER TRAP: A FEMINIST POSTSTRUCTURALIST ANALYSIS OF PRIMARY SCHOOL CHILDREN'S TALK ABOUT GENDER

BRONWYN DAVIES AND CHAS BANKS

This study of primary school children and gender was inspired by an earlier study of preschool children published as *Frogs and Snails and Feminist Tales: Preschool Children and Gender* (Davies, 1989a). The original study, conducted four years ago, involved a feminist poststructuralist analysis of the ways in which sex/gender is constituted through discursive practices (cf. Weedon 1987; Walkerdine, 1981). It looked in particular at storylines or narratives and the ways in which gendered identities are implicated in preschool children's understandings of the dominant cultural storylines made available to them (cf. Walkerdine, 1984). It was observed that children could not necessarily understand feminist stories because their hearings were informed by dominant discourses of gender. It is the power of those dominant discourses to trap children within conventional meanings and modes of being that is a central concern of the follow-up study.

[...] This study is concerned, therefore, with the political implications of the ways in which children are constrained by the dominant discourses on gender and is oriented towards means by which they might be liberated from that constraint.

The children in this follow-up study are now in primary school. In this paper, we analyse how these children's understandings have shifted, especially their interpretations of lived and told narratives. We compare the children's current thinking with their thinking of four years ago, looking both for continuities and discontinuities in their discourses on gender and in the storylines they use to interpret both text and their own lived experience.

Frogs and Snails looked, in particular, at the ways in which preschool children made sense of feminist fairy-tales, and how that sense-making related to their understanding of what it means to be male or female in the everyday world. What we found in this earlier study was that many of these four- and five-year-old children tended to hear the feminist stories not as feminist stories, but as traditional stories in which the counter-stereotypical princess had somehow 'got things wrong'. On the other hand, children who could hear the stories as ones in which the female character was the central

Source: Abridged from *Journal of Curriculum Studies* (1992), 24 (1), 1–25.

protagonist, for example, brought with them to that hearing a discourse that allowed an interpretation of maleness and femaleness as other than dualistic, antithetical opposites. But for the majority of children in *Frogs and Snails* it was argued (Davies, 1989a, p. x) that:

> Children learn to take up their maleness and femaleness as if it were an incorrigible element of their personal selves, and they do so through learning the discursive practices in which all people are positioned as either male or female. By basing our interactions with children on the presumption that they are in some unitary and bipolar sense male or female, we teach them the discursive practices through which they can constitute themselves in that way.

The aim of this larger and more recent primary school study, of which the longitudinal data reported here are one part, is to undertake similar work with primary school children, and thus to extend this work into an examination of older children and of gender discourses made available to and used by them in formal school settings (Davies, 1989b). We will examine the particular interpretations of maleness and femaleness that the children make in their talk and their interactions as well as the narrative structures that inform those interpretations.

The longitudinal data consist of follow-up interviews with seven of the children in the preschool study. We compare their talk now with their actions when they were in preschool. Our purpose in extending the earlier data, and with the same children, is to gain access to the subjectivity of the children as it is manifested in their reading/hearing of text. By 'subjectivity' we mean here the particular ways in which a person gives meaning to themselves, others, and the world. Subjectivity is largely the product of discursive networks which organize and systematize social and cultural practice.

FEMINIST POSTSTRUCTURALIST THEORY

[...]

We are interested in exploring the ways in which individuals take up as their own aspects of a traditional and coercive gender order such that it is difficult to undo the patterns of desire that hold them into that order. While we realize that there must always be a social order of *some* kind, we adopt a feminist poststructuralist position in relation to the current gender order, that is, we see the current gender order as problematic and locate the problem in its dualistic and hierarchical nature. Until such time as the current order has broken down, children (and adults) need to understand precisely how the current order is held in place and how their identity is organized in terms of it, if they are to resist it. We suggest that individuals who understand the processes through which they are made subject are better positioned to resist particular forms of subjectivity rather than to cling to them through a mistaken belief that they are their own—that they signal who they are (Davies, 1992a).

[...] It is thus to the detailed examination of *subjectivity* that we turn to try to understand how old patterns are held in place and how they might be let go. We explore the way in which texts become part of the children's subjectivity, become something of their own to be struggled over in the process of developing a critical awareness which can inform identity and everyday practice.

In order to examine this process we look at the discourses about gender that appeared in the children's talk and at the narratives or storylines that make each discourse a lived reality (Davies, 1990c). We also look at the way in which each child conceives of themselves as a person. We do this not just in terms of gender relations, but also in terms of adult–child relations. We also look at the patterns of desire implicated in their preferred storylines. It is through these storylines that they understand and live out the discourses of gender that they have taken up as their own and through which they constitute themselves as the particular person that they take themselves to be (Davies, 1990b; Davies, 1992b).

The connection between agency and desire in the children's talk was of particular importance. Their interpretations of themselves as agentic and their beliefs about agency are based to a large extent on a sense of themselves as having desires or 'wants' that stem from and signal who they are. The fulfilment of their wants or desires is seen as a confirmation of this self. This connection is modified to some extent by Sebastian (one of the children in the study) who several times states that his desires or wants should be subordinated either to his own reason or to parental desire. That their desires might be discursively constituted or might result from the influences of others is not thinkable within these children's interpretive frameworks.

In using the term desire here, we are not invoking a psychoanalytic model of desire (as some poststructuralist writers do), but seeing desire as implicated in storyline. Because story provides a substantial and detailed manifestation of the culture, it is through story that children can learn the patterns of desire appropriate for their gender. Walkerdine (1984) shows, for example, that girls, in reading pre-teen comics, are interpellated into the romantic storyline thus taking on as their own the feminine desire to be passive and beautiful. Children discover from lived and told stories what positions are available to members of their sex and how to live the detail of those positionings. Most importantly, for our purposes here, they come to understand and take up as their own the particular patterns of desire relevant to their gender.

One of the observations made in *Frogs and Snails* was that there were many different ways of being male and female and that in an ideal world we would all have access to many or all of these possible ways of being. In the current social order, it was observed, there are limitations not just in terms of gender and of what is thought proper to each sex/gender, but also limitations inherent in the humanist version of the person, which is the current dominant discourse about what it means to be a person. Humanist discourse constrains each person to constitute themselves as unitary and non-contradictory (Henriques *et al*, 1984; Walkerdine, 1981; Weedon, 1987). These constraints were evident in the children's talk about themselves and their gender. The interpretive strategies that they had taken up as their own severely limited their ways of being male or female. One reason for conducting the longitudinal aspect of the study reported here is to see how stable those interpretive strategies are. If children invest their identity in specific positionings in specific discourses then there will inevitably be considerable continuity in their interpretations of themselves then and themselves now.

At the same time, because there are inevitably contradictions in the discourses in which they have invested themselves and because some of them will have been exposed to new positionings and new discursive practices, there may well be interesting shifts and developments in their interpretations of their own and others' genderedness.

THE FOLLOW-UP STUDY

[. . .] In the analysis that follows we have grouped the children who were interviewed into four 'positions' which are based on their theories about, or interpretative strategies in relation to, the gender order and their place within it (Davies and Harre, 1989). These positions were as follows:

(1)   The fact that there is a profound difference between females and males is incontestable but of little interest and not worth discussing. My own gender, however, is well accomplished in action and in patterns of desire (Sebastian, Tony).

(2)   Differences between females and males is of some small interest but it is impossible to say whether there really is any observable difference. On balance any differences are probably very superficial. My own patterns of desire, however, are very much in line with my sex/gender (Catherine, Robbie).

(3)   Difference between females and males is important. I value and want to do the things that are thought proper for the other sex. My strategy is to become exceptionally competent in the activities of the other sex rather than to philosophize about or to deny the differences (Joanne).

(4)   Essentially there is (or should be) no difference between females and males and I can be both. The social order is in error if it divides people according to the sex they happen to have been assigned. This is a much thought-through position (Mark, Anika).
       [. . .]

Position 1:

The fact that there is a profound difference between males and females is incontestable but of little interest and not worth discussing. My own gender is well accomplished in action and in patterns of desire.

Sebastian:

In the original study, Sebastian indicated a strong support for establishing and maintaining himself as male and for doing so inside a dualistic gender order. At the age of five he, along with many other children, saw this as what his parents would want and in keeping with a properly deferential attitude to their authority. In a discussion about *Oliver Button is a Sissy* (De Paola, 1981), for example, in which Oliver wants to do things that are understood as 'girls things', Sebastian commented:

S: My Dad's a boy.
BD: Would your dad say go out and do things boys do and play ball?
S: Yes and I would do that.
BD: You would? If you were wanting to dress up and play with paper dolls and your dad said 'Sebastian, go outside and do what boys do and play with the cricket bat and football'?
S: I would do that.

(Davies, 1989a, p. 50)

His unquestioning attitude to parental authority at the age of five was such that his stated desire was to be just what he imagined his parents wanted him to be, not wanting ever to be bad, not wanting to escape from parental authority in order to have fun.

The readings of *The Paper Bag Princess* (Munsch and Marchenko, 1980) were a major source of insight in the preschool study. This is an amusing story about a princess called Elizabeth who goes to incredible lengths to save her prince (Ronald) from a fierce dragon. Sebastian's hearing of this story at the age of five was one in which Elizabeth was seen as totally in the wrong. Ronald was constituted as a hero by Sebastian even when he was sailing through the air, held by the dragon by the seat of his pants. His version of the story was as follows:

> 'I'm glad he held onto his tennis racquet to hard. When you've done that, well, you just have to hold onto your racquet tight and the dragon holds you up.' Elizabeth 'tricks' the dragon 'because she wants to get her prince back'. Prince Ronald tells Elizabeth to clean herself up 'because he didn't like her being so messy'. He is a nice person and she should clean herself, just as Sebastian has to do when he is dirty, no matter how hard it is to get the dirt off. It is all right that they don't marry each other because 'he married someone else'. Just as Sebastian obeys his parents, so Elizabeth should obey Ronald. From Sebastian's point of

view she is simply a girl who got her gender relations wrong.

(Davies, 1989a, pp. 61–2)

In the follow-up interviews, Sebastian again constituted questionable secondary male figures as both central to the story and as heroic. This is one of the central mechanisms through which he maintains the gender order. One of the stories used in the follow-up interviews is *Princess Smartypants* (Cole, 1986). This is a story about a princess who loves to spend time with her grotesque animals and who does not want to get married. The king and queen insist and Smartypants sets impossible tasks for her suitors who give up and go away. Then along comes Prince Swashbuckle who, to her horror, can do everything that she sets him. She appears to capitulate, kissing him on the cheek, but he turns into a warty toad and flees in his red sports car, leaving Smartypants to lounge about by her swimming pool with all her animals.

Sebastian disapproved of Smartypants. When he was asked if he liked her he said:

S: Umm, no.
CB: What do you dislike about her?
S: Well I just don't think that she's very nice ... because you know
          um she knows that that guy could easily get killed by that, doesn't
          she, and she expects him to get in there (referring to prince
          Swimbladder retrieving the magic ring from the monster in the
          fish pond) and she turns this guy [Swashbuckle] to a toad.

From Sebastian's point of view Swashbuckle is not to be deprived—any more than Prince Ronald was four years ago—of his correct male positioning, that is, as one who has power. When asked 'Do you think it was fair that Smartypants turned him into a toad?' he said, 'Well in my opinion um, from the part we know, I reckon when she kissed him that if they kissed at the same time she would turn into a frog as well.' Thus Swashbuckle had power to equal Smartypants. He just didn't exercise it. When asked for an alternative ending, he had the king and queen throwing Smartypants out of the castle, and all she could do was go to Prince Swashbuckle and so they married and 'had nothing to do but live happily ever after'. When asked if they really would be happy he said 'no, because she would always have a frown on her face' and Swashbuckle would want her 'not to be smart'. Presumably this wish of Swashbuckle's, that Smartypants would not be smart, is to do with the maintenance of male dominance since, for Sebastian, smartness or reason is essential to maleness, and to the exercise of authority.

If Sebastian were Prince Swashbuckle he would first use the power of reason against Smartypants and rely on parental authority to ensure that he got what he wanted, namely, the line to the throne with all the power that entails. He says, when asked what he would do in Swashbuckle's place:

S: I would, I'd stay in the palace.

CB: Would you?

S: Yes because I've completed all the tasks that she wants and because of that, that means that he can marry exactly who she wants because he can, he can do all these tasks for her.

CB: Brilliant. So would she still have to marry him even though he was a toad?

S: Yes probably her mother or father would make her because she um he's tough and they all think that he's the exact kind of person that she wanted because if she didn't then she wouldn't have given him all the tasks, she would have given him different tasks. And I would just stay in the palace.

The rightful authority of the parents is used to back up Sebastian's use of reason, as it was four years earlier in justifying why Elizabeth should do what Prince Ronald told her to do. Sebastian thinks Smartypants is wrong to disobey her father, even though she doesn't want to get married, because parents make you do what is good for you. [...] From Sebastian's point of view, desire or want leads people to act in certain ways, but reasoned parental authority should override desire. Reason is generally a better basis for decision making than desire, and Smartypants is a good example of a powerful person following their desires to the detriment of less powerful others.

S: Well sometimes it, the people that, that think they are very powerful and, like princesses and princes, think they are very powerful and they can just do whatever they want, they think they can do that and they um they um ... they treat the other male or females ...

CB: mm

S: ... in not a very nice way.

CB: I see.

S: 'Cause they don't want to have anything to do with them.

However, when asked specifically about sex/gender difference, Sebastian asserted that males are more violent than females and, in response to the question, 'Do you think that boys are naturally more violent or do they learn to be more violent?' Sebastian relied heavily on desire as the defining feature of persons. Although desire needs to be tempered by parental authority it is none the less what gives rise to males and females learning different things. He had no idea, though, where desire might come from, except that one is not born with it:

S: They aren't, they aren't you know like born to be violent they just, they like things like wrestling, but I don't know why. And you know if you go to a karate thing, you you walk into a karate room grading, well, well I mean, the question is what would you be likely to see? And you would probably just see boys everywhere. You wouldn't see one female in there. And that's just because, females would think that it would be—you know, they don't like things like that, but um males do ... I don't know why. Boys could be, well, I don't know why.

In a later interview the issue of difference was raised again in relation to what he had done when he was at preschool, and Sebastian became quite irritated with the line of questioning.

CB: And why is it do you think that you didn't play with any of the girls?

S: They wanted to play different games than we did. They didn't like playing what we were playing.

CB: Uh um. Weren't there any times when the girls wanted to play with you or you wanted to play with the girls?

S: No, only when I didn't have anything to do

CB: And then what would you do?

S: I would no nothing. Just walk around bored stiff.

CB: You wouldn't play with the girls?

S: They just don't have the games that I want to play. They have (S bumps his head).

CB: Brain themselves?

S: Um. I don't want the kind of games they have, I didn't play with them.

CB: You really didn't, you just didn't want to play with them?

S: No. I didn't.

CB: What did you think of girls, honestly?

S: I thought just plain humans.

CB: Plain humans?

S: Because it's all boys, I thought that we were all plain.

CB: Yeah. Well, how come it is that you, if you were all plain humans, why is it that you only played with the boys? Why is it that you didn't play with the girls *and* the boys if you were all plain human?

S: I don't know, because they play different games to what we do. I told you that about two million times.

Despite his access to discourses of equity (we are all 'plain humans') masculinity for Sebastian is somehow intractable and the sexes just are different (cf. Seidler, 1989). The difference is related to personal desire and is not of a great deal of interest. Any reasonable person can observe it in the world around them. A thread running through much of his other talk was that masculinity is good and is worth pursuing. It is good to be competently male and that is clearly what one's parents want. Sebastian's preferred storyline, which he uses to make sense of both lived and told narratives, is one in which the male hero prevails despite the difficulties that competent females put in his path. The strategies the hero adopts are, first, the power of reason: his understanding of reason is closely linked to masculinity in that it is 'scientific', 'factual', 'objective' (cf. Seidler, 1989). Then adult and/or male authority, which is just and benevolent, is called on if reason fails. If both of these fail then force may be used.

The male/female dualism is thus a fundamental framework for his interpretation of text and of his lived experience. The male/female dualism is linked to the adult/child dualism, adults and males having authority, children and females having none. The maintenance of the gender order is important for his sense of himself as an accomplished male. In keeping with his reverence for reason the exceptions to the dualistic, hierarchical gender order must be explained. Scientist-like, Sebastian does not ignore what he sees, but looks to his storyline to find the ingredients with which to keep his storyline intact. His explanations are essentially that the males in question who are, by definition, agentic, choose not to exercise their power: Swashbuckle could have turned Smartypants into a toad; Prince Ronald didn't love Elizabeth anyway, so he was glad to see her go.

Position 2:
Difference between females and males is of some small interest but it is impossible to say whether there really is any observable difference. My own patterns of desire, however, are very much in line with my sex/gender.

Catherine:
In the original study, Catherine was generally to be found in the home corner. She dressed in a very feminine way and was clearly both competent and contented in the domestic setting of the home corner. On one remarkable occasion she donned male clothes to assert herself. A boy called George had come in and stolen her doll. She pursued him unsuccessfully. She came back to the home corner, very upset and refusing to be distracted by other offers of play:

> Catherine, ignoring John, goes decisively to the dress-up cupboard and puts on a man's waistcoat. She tucks the waistcoat into the dress-up skirt that she already has on, and marches out. This time she returns victorious with the dolly under her arm. She immediately takes off the waistcoat and drops it on the floor. She is now very busy and happy.
>
> (Davies, 1989a, pp. 16–17)

In this episode, Catherine revealed that she is perfectly capable of behaving in ways that are generally understood as male. She also revealed her understanding of such assertive behaviour as essentially male. She kept intact the male/female dualism through her very manner of choosing to transgress its bounds. She put on a male symbol in order to act assertively in a public place and thus regain her doll. Catherine was very much aware of the power that accrued to females in female places and also aware of the obligations her mother felt to be with her and to nurture her (Davies, 1989a, p. 80). But the episode with the waistcoat indicated that she did not define assertion or dominance in non-domestic settings, such as the preschool yard, as appropriate feminine behaviour.

In the follow-up interviews, Catherine revealed a continuing preference for a feminine style. She also talked about her fear of being hurt, indicating a sense of herself as fragile and vunerable. Her greatest wish was that people be kind to her and not hurt her. She did not talk at all about asserting herself.

Like Sebastian, she was very clear about the legitimacy of the authority of adults. In relation to sex/gender, although she displayed an intricate knowledge and competence in relation to femininity and was very interested in being good and kind and understanding, she was not particularly interested in masculinity and did not think that the differences between males and females were of significance. She mentions the difference in their voices (though what they talk about can be the same), or hair (though she acknowledges that men can have long hair), or makeup (some women wear makeup) and their genitals. Whatever the differences, though, she doesn't think that they affect what people can do. This significant difference between people is not so much their gender as whether they are mean or nice:

CB: Do you think having a girl's body ...
C: mm
CB: ... affects the things that you do? Can you do anything that you want to do because you have a girl's body, or ...?
C: No.
CB: Well, tell me about that Catherine.
C: Well all of the people are the same 'cept you've got different parts of your body different and that, some people are mean, some people are nice.
CB: Can you do anything with your body that a boy can do with his body? Is there something that you could do that a boy can't do?
C: Nup, I can't think of something.

Her stated acceptance of adult authority, like Sebastian, was unequivocal. Following a description of an incident where her father became angry with her and hurt her, she nevertheless argued for the legitimacy of adult authority in terms of adult rules saving children from being hurt:

CB: And how did that make you feel when your Dad did that?
C: Well it hurt.
CB: It hurt your feelings?
C: mm

CB:	Right. Do you think that it's fair that adults are always the boss? Do you think that kids should have more of a say about what goes on?
C:	Well I think the grownups are good to make rules beacause they are doing it for you so you don't get hurt.

Although she thought that exceptional or smart children might query adult authority, she was, she said, not one of those children. She said of Princess Smartypants:

C:	She looks happy. She doesn't, she can't marry the prince.
CB:	Can you understand, what do you think about the way Princess Smartypants behaved?
C:	Naughty.
CB:	You think she was naughty?
C:	Yeah, to make all the princes do those things.
CB:	Mm. What would she have done if she, if she'd been a good princess?
C:	She would have married a prince, and done the things that her mother and father did.
CB:	Right. So you think she should have obeyed what her mother and father told her to do?
C:	Yes 'cause most princes and princesses do what their Mum tells them to.
CB:	If you had've been Smartypants ...
C:	mm
CB:	... would you have behaved like that?
C:	Well if I was smart I would but if I was like me and I was Smartypants I would have obeyed my Mum and Dad.

Catherine's desire for her future is closely related to the kind of scenario that she played out day after day in the preschool home corner. Despite her strong belief in adult authority, she does have some conception of the rights of the individual not to have to get married and to make some choices of one's own based on personal desire. In response to the question 'Do you think it is important to get married?' she says:

C:	It's not if you're ... you don't want to, but like you can't get married if you are like my age (mm) and so you don't have to get married.
CB:	No, you don't have to.
C:	You can get married if you really want.
CB:	Right, do you think everyone should get married?
C:	Well ...
CB:	When they grow up?
C:	Well I don't know. They could make up their own minds.

CB: Do you want to get married when you grow up?

C: Yes.

CB: Do you?

C: 'Cause I want to have a few children.

CB: Do you?

C: 'Cause I think children are nice to have.

CB: What is it that is so nice about having children?

C: Well, in our house boys can be naughty sometimes.

CB: mm

C: Well I want to have a good boy and a good girl, like um me and Seth, my brother, I want to have, um, one girl and um, a boy and a girl—a boy and a girl.

CB: Do you?

C: Yes.

CB: Uh, huh. And who, do you have any idea who you would like to marry?

C: No. I don't have any boyfriends.

CB: No. Do you have any idea about the sort of boy you'd like to marry?

C: Well, a kind boy and loving, sorts of things like that.

Although Catherine talks of herself as not being smart, and therefore not being able to be like Smartypants, she also talks of loving school and of doing well at school and in particular in mathematics. She does not seem to have developed any patterns of desire around a future based on school work since the domestic fantasy (in which, for her, women are powerful) is the one that still seems to hold her. Doing well at school may well be, for her, another way of being virtuous, rather than something that opens up other possibilities. Her preferred storyline, then, is about vulnerability and the seeking out of kind people who will not hurt her. Agency comes not with opposing adult authority and gaining power in the short term, but with achieving adulthood and a place in her own domestic scene where as adult she will have legitimate authority. The male/female dualism has little salience in her storyline, in contrast to the adult/child dualism which is highly salient. But there is an interesting contradiction here, in her explicit theorizing about gender, for Catherine does not see the differences between male and female as being significant. But her practice is based on an implicit theory of difference. She has taken on as her own storylines and patterns of desire that are unequivocally feminine and which are embedded in the male/female dualism. These are evident in her constitution of herself as properly female, in her awareness of female power in the domestic realm and her conception of the future as one of domestic bliss. The contradiction is not evident to Catherine because she thinks of her position in terms of goodness and kindness (inside a kind/mean dualism) rather than in terms of femininity. One possible explanation for her ruling out the kind of 'masculine' competence that she displayed in the waistcoat episode is the humanist theory that her talk is couched in, in which the person is obliged to be unitary and non-contradictory rather than multiple and diverse. Thus, part of her goodness is precisely to rule out that which might be construed as inconsistent.

Position 3:

Difference between females and males is important because I value and want to do the things that are thought proper for the other sex. My strategy is to become exceptionally competent in the activities of the other sex rather than to philosophize about or to deny the differences.

Joanne:

At the age of four Joanne visibly struggled with the kinds of contradictions that were imposed on her by the attempt to render her appearance unequivocally female to any observer and at the same time to play the kind of 'male' games she liked to play that involved high levels of physical competence and daring that are more usually a feature of male play. Joanne tended to wear tracksuits all the time, at least during winter, these being much more suitable than dresses for the kind of outdoor activity she enjoyed. She had found that she was so often mistaken for a boy—presumably not just because of dress but the unusual physical presence that she had as she moved about the playground—that she decided to tie her hair up in a distinctly girlish top-knot in order to avoid being so mistaken. She did this because she found people's inability to see that she was female distressing, taking it as a signal of her failure to be correctly gendered.

Joanne liked to play with her best friend Tony and the dominant boys' group. But she was rarely accepted into the boys' group as one of them. Usually she was held outside their play, despite (or perhaps because of) her high levels of competence in all the things that they did—perhaps also because of her willingness to co-operate with female adults in their decision making. She said she used to play Voltron with the boys, a space heroes fantasy series then on television and based on transformer robot toys. Once they had allowed her to be the leader and she had loved that. But usually they insisted that she be the princess and she hated that.

Joanne's attitude to adult authority was complex in that she both accepted the legitimacy of their authority and yet was quite competent and decisive in her own decision making:

BD:	So you have to go to his place?
J:	If I want to.
BD:	And you don't want to?
J:	No, I don't know yet.
BD:	You don't know yet? How will you make up your mind?

J: When pre-school is finished, then I'll make up my mind.
                (Davies, 1989a, pp. 36–7)

Joanne sometimes revealed a struggle to be correctly gendered, that is, to desire the things that girls should desire and not desire the things that boys should desire. She had learned, for example, not to want to climb up on the fort with boys, but when new opportunities arose for acting powerfully she took them, though not without equivocation. [. . .]

   In the follow-up interview, Joanne presented quite clearly as a girl, but with all the same patterns of desire embedded in the same storylines as she had earlier. She brought Tony along to the interview, since they are still close friends though they now go to different schools. Both were very aware of the gender category maintenance work of others and, while they believed ideally it was a matter of persisting with deviant behaviour until others grew used to it, they also indicated a pragmatic retreat in the face of other's judgements. For example, since other children do not readily accept their friendship they sometimes choose to hide it. They display in their talk their knowledge of the generalizations that are made about gender; at the same time they reveal that they, as individuals, disrupt these generalizations. Their challenges to each other's generalizations are made with a pragmatic calm:

CB: Do you think that boys have the same sorts of feelings as girls Joanne?
J: No.
CB: You don't. Well how are they different?
J: They are tough, and they like playing with trucks and stuff and girls . . .
T: I don't like playing with trucks.
J: You play with other stuff and some boys like playing in the sand pit with trucks and stuff.
CB: Well don't some girls like playing with trucks too?
J: Yeah, I play with trucks now and then and boys don't like dollies.
T: Some boys do.
CB: Do you think that boys need the same sort of things that girls need?
J/T: No.
CB: Well what do boys need that girls don't need? And what would . . .
T: Football.
J: I've, I've got a soccer ball.

At the age of eight Joanne had noticeable competence in feminine style. However, she remains relatively scathing about 'girls' things' and indicates a continuing concern with developing male competencies.

J: Tony teaches me how to play soccer better ...

CB: mm

J: 'Cause we play soccer at school and I hardly ever get a go, 'cause the boys just take it.

CB: mm

J: My Dad, my Dad has been teaching me a few tricks too and now they don't think they have to pass it away from me, now I sort of get into the game more ... If you are friends with boys the boys can teach you to play with other boys and they'll not say 'Oh you're a little girl, you like dollies and stuff'.

One of the stories used in the follow-up interviews was *Crusher is Coming* (Graham, 1987). This is a story about a boy, Peter, who was having his friend 'Crusher' to visit and who hid all his soft toys because he assumed Crusher would think they were silly. As it turns out Crusher, though big and strong, loves stuffed toys and spends his time playing with Peter's little sister Claire, having a tea party and other such 'little girl' activities. Joanne's and Tony's comments reveal an intricate knowledge of the difficulties of stepping outside the gender boundaries. While they think that Peter should not have deceived his friend about what he liked, and that he should have insisted that Crusher get used to his difference, they do not think Crusher should risk showing his more 'feminine' side at school unless he was stronger than anyone else:

J: Well, um. I think the other kids thought he was mean and horrible because his name was Crusher and stuff. I thought he probably liked playing with babies, having tea parties and stuff, played football now and then. And loved playing ...

T: He [Peter] should have just kept how it was, and he [Crusher] would have had to get used to it. He, he liked playing with stuffed toys too ...

CB: Do you think that [Crusher would] show his caring side when he's at school?

T/J: Nah ah.

CB: You don't. Why not?

T: I don't know.

CB: Why don't you think he would show his caring side when he's at school? He's pretty big and tough.

T: Yeah. The other boys probably think he's stupid and he wouldn't.

J: Yeah he probably wouldn't, they'd probably think he plays with dollies and stuff. He's really stupid doing that.

T: Yeah then he could get up and bash them.

J: Yeah I know that.

CB: Then he could get up and bash them eh?

J: Depends—there might have been a bigger kid than him.

CB: Right.

T:	So then probably he'd probably hit them.
CB:	So if he was the biggest kid do you think that he'd show that he was also a caring boy?
T:	Yes.
CB:	You think that he would?
T:	Then he would get up 'em.

Thus boys are only able to behave in feminine ways inside a friendship in the domestic sphere or in public places if they are stronger than anyone else. Otherwise, others will give them a hard time. Joanne goes on to say that she would not let Crusher get away with feminine behaviour (which she thinks of as stupid behaviour). She would tell others and then it would be up to him to fend for himself. [...]

Crusher is Coming is not a story which reveals to Joanne and Tony that it is acceptable for boys to have 'feminine' qualities. It is about a boy who was running terrible risks. Competence in masculine terms does not include, from these children's points of view, any unnecessary displays of unmasculine behaviour in public places and requires a careful eye for the hierarchy, since it is in the terms of powerful others that one must achieve one's masculinity. Friends are vital, however, in so far as if they are the same as you they will accept you.

In their discussion of *Princess Smartypants* Joanne reveals much more sympathy for Smartypants than she did for Crusher. She fully supports her wish not to get married. Tony, in contrast, is more inclined to see things from Swashbuckle's point of view though they both imagine marriage as an extremely exploitative situation:

CB:	What sort of a wife do you think Swashbuckle would want Smartypants to be?
T:	Probably one that's like a slave sort of one.
CB:	Like a slave sort of one?
J:	Yeah, making dinner every time he comes home from work or whatever he does.
T:	He probably sits in a luxurious chair.
J:	Yeah.

When asked whether she thought Smartypants behaved correctly Joanne says:

| J: | I think that it was right because he thought aw he's just going to go in there and he's going to marry her and get rich and stuff and he's gotta, and she's going to have to sit down just being a queen when she wanted to go out doing stuff, and he just, aw he just going to go in and take over charge of everything. |

As to whether Smartypants should have to get married:

J:	I don't think that they should have to 'cause it's their decision.
T:	Not anybody else's?
CB:	Right. So you should be able to make up your own mind?
J:	Yep.
T:	Yep.

Joanne's preferred storyline is one in which the central heroic character follows her or his desire and follows on strongly, not being 'wimpish' and hurt at any difficulties that might get in the way. In pursuing that desire, heroes should develop special competencies that will enable them to withstand criticism, though part of that competence will be a detailed knowledge of where criticism is likely to come from and how best to deflect rather than confront it.

Joanne is aware of and accepts the requirement of the dominant discourses of gender that people appear to be clearly male or female, yet she appears as one who has transcended the confines/restrictions of the gender order because she displays the appearance and behaviour of both genders. There is a paradox here, however, because this semblance of liberation is located within a dualist conception of gender and as such helps keep the dualist gender order intact. Throughout, Joanne asserts the superiority of male pursuits and competences. She is unsupportive of males such as Crusher, who display feminine behaviour. Smartypants is seen as an acceptable female only because she refuses the gender discourse of femininity, displaying the male characteristics of determination and physical competence. Joanne continuously holds the male way of being as superior. Implicitly within her framework is the assumption that maleness is opposite and superior to femaleness. In such a model, male authority and power should always rightfully eclipse female authority and power.

Position 4:

Essentially there is (or should be) no difference between male and female, and I can be both. The social order is in error if it divides people according to the sex they happen to have been assigned. This is a much thought-through position.

Mark:

In the original study Mark was one of only two boys who were struggling to incorporate both masculine and feminine characteristics into their ways of being. In the preschool study his comments on the story *Oliver Button is a Sissy* were very telling. Oliver Button was a boy who wanted to do 'girls' things'. His Dad and the other boys gave him a hard time about this. His Dad eventually let him go to dancing class (for the exercise) and he became very good at dancing and won the friendship and support of his male peers. In a discussion of *Oliver Button is a Sissy* in *Frogs and Snails*, Mark was mentioned as an exception in his attitude to Oliver:

There were, however, two boys, Mark and Daniel ... (who) engaged in 'feminine' behaviours and claimed that they saw nothing wrong with this. They believed not only that Oliver Button should have been free to go to dancing school but that the older boys should have left him alone. Mark and Daniel both went to dancing lessons themselves, not like Oliver because they desperately wanted to, but because their parents were very keen that they not be caught up in masculine activities to the exclusion of feminine activities.

(Davies, 1989a, p. 52).

In the follow-up study it was possible to spend a lot of time with Mark and to discuss a wide range of stories. The following transcripts are based on readings of the stories in *The Wrestling Princess* (Corbalis, 1986) and *The Practical Princess and other Liberating Fairy Tales* (Williams, 1978). One of the predominant themes in these stories is the king wanting his daughter to marry and her finding a way not to, or at least to marry a man of her choice. Another major theme is that men do not have to be heroic to be likeable and worthwhile. We will not retell each of these stories as the discussions that follow do not rely on a knowledge of the details of the story to understand the various points that Mark makes. Mark felt that the old story of the male rescuing the female was out of date. Modern stories, he thought, would be about getting messed up with drug dealers and somehow gaining supernatural powers to defeat them, or saving the world from blowing up. Males and/or females would be heroic in such storylines. He referred back to the stories we had read and enjoyed years earlier. He said one of the stories, *The Paper Bag Princess*, reminded him of one of his current friends, Eloise, who is not well accepted in the class. When it was suggested that this was because she manifested both male and female behaviour which annoyed her classmates, Mark initially agreed, but in a later conversation he rejected this explanation largely because he did not accept the idea that there could be any rule that said boys had to be like boys and girls had to be like girls. The teasing or dislike of others did not for him establish a rule that said you had to do what the others thought was right (this point is elaborated later in this section).

On a reading of *The Wrestling Princess*, Mark talked about how he did not feel at all confronted by Ermyntrude, the tall, assertive and mechanically competent princess:

BD: What do you think of the story so far?
M: I think it has been quite funny.
BD: Mmm, in what way?
M: Um well it was actually better than the other three stories.
BD: Mmm
M: Because it actually had a different character. Like um all the others were um rather stupid males who didn't know much.

BD: Mm

M: And this was eh, um, a strong female um instead of the weak man.

BD: Ah hum ... So you like her better than you like those three blokes?

M: Yes.

BD: And what about her Dad?

M: I think that he was a pretty mean bloke.

In the following excerpt from that discussion Mark rejects several constitutive aspects of the male/female dualism such as size difference and age difference:

BD: Why do you suppose he did that, measuring the princes (who were suitors to his daughter)?

M: Um because he didn't want um, he didn't want there to be a quite large female and a tiny little male.

BD: Do you think that the woman always has to be shorter than the man?

M: No.

BD: So ...

M: It's the same thing with how old they are.

BD: mmm

M: They don't have to be older.

BD: Right. Does it seem strange to you if the man is shorter than the woman?

M: Um. No.

BD: It doesn't.

The idea of social pressure and of who Mark took himself to be was very interesting. Mark had no idea of being discursively constituted by others. He believed in an inner essential self who had to struggle with the personal tensions that others created for him. His struggle to establish an androgynous identity clearly creates great stress for him, but he does not imagine that he has any choice, since what he is springs from what he wants.

BD: Don't you think, don't you think that boys are under a lot of pressure to um prove that they are tough?

M: No. Some boys don't want to prove that they're tough.

BD: Mm

M: They just want ...

BD: Mmm?

M: Like me.

BD: Mm. So you don't feel that there's sort of a contradiction. Do you know what contradiction means?

M: Na.

BD: Means where ...

M: Absolutely have to?

BD: No, where um one thing's true, seems to be true, but the opposite seems to be true as well. Like you are supposed to be like a boy but you are also supposed not to be aggressive and um a bully and all those things.

M: Yeah. I'm not aggressive and I'm not a bully.

BD: But if you were too much like a girl the other kids would give you a hard time wouldn't they?

M: No, because I've got this rather large friend.

BD: Yeah?

M: And um he he just um says 'shut up' and that 'be quiet' and they do.

BD: Do they.

M: Yep.

BD: So you feel that you are really free to be anything that you want to be?

M: Yep.

BD: So what about, I mean you have to wear clothes like a boy don't you and you have to have your hair like a boy?

M: Na not necessarily. Everyone calls me a girl because I've got a rat's tail.

BD: Do they?

M: That doesn't mean I'm a girl.

BD: Oh no, it doesn't mean that.

M: And everyone calls me a girl because I wear a bit of pink socks or something. And I say to them my Dad's got a pink dressing gown and that makes them think twice.

BD: Mmm. So are you different from the other boys because your dad is different from other men?

M: No.

BD: No. Why do you suppose that you are different?

M: I don't know. I don't, I don't want to do the same things as other kids.

BD: Yeah?

M: I like to try a different approach to things. Try and do different things.

BD: But they do pressure you, don't they?

M: Yep.

BD: They say things like that. And you have just had to develop strategies to cope with that.

M: Yep.

BD: Does it, does it, is that part of what makes you feel tense?

M: Mmm

BD: It is yeah?

M:	Sometimes when I get, mostly when I get tense I feel like throwing up.
BD:	Yeah. Is that at school or at home or both?
M:	Both.
BD:	And, um, so that tension comes from that kind of um, conflict between what you want to be and what the world says you ought to be.
M:	Mmm
BD:	Um, so, now when you go off and play elastics with the girls is that one of the times that you get teased by some of the boys?
M:	Yep.
BD:	'Cause they think that you are doing it wrong. They don't see that you've got the right to be free like that and do what you want to do.
M:	Yep.
BD:	So, so how many boys would there be in your grade who you could say were feminist in that they think that you have the right to do anything that you want to do?
M:	Quite a few.
BD:	Quite a few?
M:	Um, aw then there's this other boy called Damien who is a complete nut.
BD:	Uh hm.
M:	He thinks, he thinks um the only way to be is um what he thinks is a boy.
BD:	Ah hmm.
M:	And if they're not ( ) he finds something that's funny about them and then just calls them by their name, whenever he sees them.
BD:	Oh really.
M:	Actually he calls me 'Ratty' because of the rat tail.
BD:	Right, right.
M:	It's really awful.
BD:	Uh hm. So how does that make you feel?
M:	Bad.
BD:	Why does it worry you, why does it worry you what kids like him think?
M:	Well I don't really like being treated like that.
BD:	Mmm. When you got your hair cut short and the ratty tail down the back what made you decide that?
M:	I um don't know, what I just thought was um, I just wanted to have a haircut like that. Now um there are four or five grade um four's that have had it shaved off, just got it spiky.
BD:	Uh mm, with a rat's tail or just shaved off?

M: They've just got it spiky here.
BD: Right, right so in a way short at the top like a traditional boy and
              long at the back like a traditional girl.
M: Yeah.
BD: Like a, an amazing combination.
M: I mi ... I might even try and get it long here.
BD: Yeah?
M: And then no one will be able to call me anything.
BD: Right, because you'll be both.
M: Yeah.
BD: Would you like that?
M: I'm trying to get this rat's tail to grow a bit longer.

Mark refuses to be positioned in terms of the dominant discourses on gender. He rejects the male/female dualism along with some of its constitutive dualisms. At the same time, and in contradiction with this position, he is reliant on aspects of the male/female dualism for the maintenance of his position: he needs a strong dominant male friend to defend his difference from the norm and he relies on his father's authority (as the wearer of the pink dressing gown) to legitimate his own deviation.

He believes he should remain true to his essential self and to the concomitant desires of having such a self. He believes his tension arises as a result of the confrontation between his essential self and the norms of the social world. The gender dualism merely reflects the views of some others and the categories male and female are impositions to be refused. His preferred storyline is one in which the heroic individual struggles in accord with their own deeply felt desires to be both masculine and feminine, against the pressures from others to conform to the gender order. He uses reason and relies on the force of his large friend to have the freedom to achieve this. Friends, male or female, who understand and accept and even support what you want to be are vital in this quest.

[...]

CONCLUSION

What we have shown in this detailed analysis of the children's talk when they were four and when they were eight is the extent to which their subjectivity and their interpretations of text are shaped by the discourses of gender to which they have access and which they have taken up as their own. We have also shown that desire is a central pivot in the process of interpellation and that this is closely linked to their imbrication in humanist discourses about the person. The particular patterns of desire that are made relevant in their preferred storylines are read by them as signalling 'who they really are', thus forming the basis of decisions about and interpretations of their actions and the actions of others in the everyday world. We have shown, as well, an interesting correlation between acceptance of the dominant discourses about gender and acceptance of the adult/parent authority as correct and benevolent.

One of the startling findings is the extent of the continuity in the storylines that the children apply to their experience and to texts to make sense of them. It would be easy to assume that this continuity demonstrates some liberal humanist version of the essential self and certainly that is the discourse that most children seem to have about the self. From our point of view, however, it would seem that the children use the same (known, familiar) storylines to pull out the same threads over time and thus to constitute themselves as persons with continuity. There is undoubtedly much more variety, discontinuity and fragmentation in their lived experience than comes over in their tellings of that experience. However, their preferred storylines and the cumulative experience of being positioned within those storylines in consistent ways enables them to tell stories that give the sense of a consistent and continuous person. That sense of continuity and stability in turn gives them a sense of control over their lives.

Having discovered feminist poststructuralist theory as a way of making sense of equity issues in classrooms in a way that moves us beyond many of the stalemates that sex role socialization theory had locked us into (Davies, 1989c, 1990c), we have increasingly become convinced that the children too need to be given access to some of the elements of poststructuralist theory if they are to be liberated from the burden of the unitary self and the limiting storylines that some of them are caught up in. Similarly, for those who are engaged in resisting the dominant discourses on gender, the reactions of others to that resistance could be far less painful if understood as category maintenance work which shores up their own storylines and the gender order in which they are embedded.

The second part of our primary school study is an exploration of this possibility. We are working with several groups of primary school children in school settings, introducing them to the concepts of discourse, dominant discourse, discourses of resistance, storyline, postitioning and desire. We are examining the ways in which they make sense of their lived experience and opening up the possibility of choice to them via an explicit introduction to feminist poststructuralist theory and the interpretative strategies which that opens up. We are convinced from our data collection and analysis to date that equity programmes which simply introduce the ideal of equity, and which rely on role models and access to non-sexist curricula, will not be enough to disrupt these strongly held theories of gender and patterns of desire (Davies, 1988, 1989c; Leach and Davies, 1990). This is so because those children who have been interpellated into the social world via the dominant discourses of gender, which serve to keep the male/female dualism intact, have taken those discourses on as their own. They have learned to interpret not just their own lives, but the lives of others, both in their everyday world and in the texts they encounter, within the terms of those dominant discourses. Their own deeply felt desires, imbricated in their preferred storylines and in the discourses through which they have taken up their personal being, cannot be undone by access to discourses which claim that girls and boys really are equal, or any exceptions such as occasional women with power, or a few texts in which females are the central protagonists. The children hear and see alternatives and even take them up as their own, believing them to be correct. Yet they are, in substantial ways, not able to translate those alternatives into their lived reality because their patterns of desire are imbricated in storylines which give substance to inequitable social structures. To deal with this contradiction we suggest they need to understand how they are interpellated, they need to understand how they have taken up various discourses as their own, and how desire is implicated in their preferred storylines. They need as well to grasp the contradictions that inevitably exist and which are not allowable in the humanist framework in terms of which most of them think. They need to understand how discourses of resistance work, if they are to begin to engage in any radical personal change which undoes fundamental elements of the male/female dualism.

References

Cole, B. (1986) *Princess Smartypants.* London: Hamish Hamilton.

Corbalis, J. (1986) *The Wrestling Princess and Other Stories.* London: Hodder and Stoughton.

Davies, B. (1988) *Gender, Equity and Early Childhood* (pp. 1–42). Canberra: Schools Commission.

—(1989a) *Frogs and Snails and Feminist Tales: Preschool Children and Gender.* Sydney: Allen and Unwin.

—(1989b) The discursive production of the male/female dualism in school settings. *Oxford Review of Education* 15 (3), 229–41.

—(1989c) Education for sexism: Moving beyond sex role socialization and reproduction theories. *Educational Philosophy and Theory* 21 (1), 1–19.

—(1990a) Agency as a form of discursive practice. A classroom scene observed. *British Journal of Sociology of Education* 11 (3), 341–6.

—(1990b) The problem of desire. *Social Problems* 37 (4), 801–816.

—(1990c) Lived and imaginary narratives and their place in taking oneself up as a gendered being. *Australian Psychologist* 25 (3), 76–90.

—(1992a) Women's subjectivity and feminist stories. In C. Ellis and M. Flaherty (eds) *Subjectivity: Investigating Research on Lived Experience.* Newbury Park, CA: Sage.

—(1992b) The concept of agency: a feminist poststructuralist analysis. *Social Analysis* 30, special edition A. Yeatman (ed.) *Postmodern Critical Theorising* pp. 42–53.

Davies, B. and Harre, R. (1989) Positioning: the discursive production of selves. *Journal for the Theory of Social Behaviour* 20 (1), 43–63.

De Paola, T. (1981) *Oliver Button is a Sissy.* London: Methuen.

Graham, B. (1987) *Crusher is Coming.* Melbourne: Lothian Publishing.

Henriques, J. Hollway, W. Urwin, C. and Walkerdine, V. (1984) *Changing the Subject: Psychology, Social Regulation and Subjectivity.* London: Methuen.

Leach, M. and Davies, B. (1990) Crossing the boundaries educational thought and gender equity. *Educational Theory* 40 (3) pp. 331–32.

Munsch, R. and Marchenko, M. (1980) *The Paper Bag Princess*. Toronto: Annick Press.

Seidler, V. (1989) *Rediscovering Masculinity: Reason Language and Sexuality*. London: Routledge and Kegan Paul.

Walkerdine, V. (1981) Sex, power and pedagogy. *Screen Education* 38 (Spring), pp. 14–24.

—(1984) Some day my prince will come. In A. McRobbie and M. Nava (eds) *Gender and Generation* (pp. 162–84). London: Macmillan.

Weedon, C. (1987) *Feminist Practice and Poststructuralist Theory*. Oxford: Blackwell.

Williams, J. (1978) *The Practical Princess and Other Liberating Fairytales*. London: The Bodley Head.

4 CONFLICTS AND TENSIONS IN THE FEMINIST STUDY OF GENDER AND SCIENCE

HELEN E. LONGINO AND EVELYNN HAMMONDS

Feminist thinking about the sciences in the last 15 years has produced an exciting proliferation of critical ideas and analytic approaches. The natural sciences have drawn our attention because of their multi-faceted participation in the subordination of women. In spite of gains in some areas, notably biology, they remain bastions of masculinity: the percentage of physicists who are women has hovered around 4%, of chemists 8%, of engineers 2%, of biologists 20%. The content of science is also hostile to women, from the biological research programs that suggest gender inequality is the ultimate outcome of genetic and physiological differences to the metaphorical identification of scientific inquiry with male sexual conquest. Finally, the procedures of science have been lauded as the very apex of human rationality—a height of human intellectual achievement of which women, stereotyped as incapable of detaching from our emotions, are believed incapable. Because the sciences are intimately embroiled with the structures of power in industrial (and post-industrial) societies, understanding their cognitive and social structure is high on the feminist scholarly agenda.

Accordingly, there are historical studies of the career patterns of women attempting to do science, studies of the history of exclusion of women, studies of the content of particular sciences both in their formative periods and in their contemporary manifestations. There is work appealing to science itself, rebutting the methods and conclusions of determinist research programs in biology. There are examinations of objectivity and rationality, of the affective dimensions of scientific practice. There are activist programs to increase the participation of women in the sciences. It should not be too surprising that this variety would generate conflicting analytical approaches. Science studies is in general host to wildly incompatible research programs. The conflicts that have developed among feminist scholars in this field, however, have a particular sharpness, sometimes evident in published work, but more often in interpersonal encounters harder to document. One scholar told one of us that she was leaving the field to get out of the crossfire.

In writing this article, we hoped to uncover the intellectual roots of

Source: Hirsch, M. and Fox Keller, E. (1990) *Conflicts in Feminism* (pp. 164–83). London: Routledge.

difference in this domain of feminist analysis and activism. Our different backgrounds suited us to different aspects of this task and so we have made separate contributions. Helen Longino, an academic philosopher, undertook to review the philosophical differences between a set of representative feminist theorists. Evelynn Hammonds, a physicist now studying the history of science, undertook to analyze the reception of feminist critiques of science by practicing women scientists. Our results were, to us, surprising and sobering. We offer them in the hope of furthering existing dialogues and sparking new ones.

POLITICAL DIMENSIONS OF EPISTEMOLOGICAL CRITIQUES — HELEN E. LONGINO

I approached the task of analyzing conflict from my location as a philosopher concerned with the implications of the current feminist critique of the sciences for the philosophy of science and as a participant in the development of that critique. I have been reading and listening to my colleagues in that endeavour as they write and speak about our common subject and about each other (in books and articles, public lectures and private conversation) for over ten years. I expected, on the basis of that experience, that a systematic comparison of central figures in our field would reveal three primary and related points of contention. From a metaphysical point of view, I expected no consensus on the nature of reality. Is reality one or many? Can we speak of a reality existing independently of our beliefs about it? Does it even make sense to speak of reality? Is reality knowable or will it constantly elude our attempts to find the appropriate description for what we can observe and the correct articulation of the orderly or lawful processes underlying the observable? From an epistemological point of view, I expected no consensus on the possibility and criteria of knowledge. Knowledge has traditionally been defined as justified true belief in philosophical circles. All of these defining terms are called into question in contemporary feminist thinking about the sciences. The desirability of justification is questioned by the claim that rationality is masculine or that rationality has been defined and appropriated in a way that privileges masculinity. The ideal of truth is undermined by perspectival accounts of knowledge and belief, which themselves draw some support from the whole tradition in contemporary philosophy of science. Finally, even belief is rejected by those who join Foucault in proclaiming the death of the subject and is replaced by authorless and subjectless discourse in which individuals may be positioned but for which they are not responsible. I hoped to locate our theorists in those various oppositions.

The third point of contention is rarely directly raised but gives the epistemological and metaphysical debates their urgency. Which philosophical position is most likely to promote social change? Clearly, answers to this question depend a great deal on the kind of change one wants. A list could include: expanding the community of scientists; increasing access for women; producing a biology whose contents do not diminish, neglect, or pathologize women; producing an alternative science; changing the priorities of science; releasing the grip of contemporary scientific theories on our imaginations. How one sets priorities among these desiderata depends in turn on a more comprehensive social and political analysis. Because of the connection between knowledge and politics, someone urging a view about scientific inquiry may be understood and read as supporting a political analysis, even when that is not her intent. We all care deeply about politics, hence there is more than enough room for misunderstanding and hurt.

I will outline the approaches of four principal writers in the feminist critique whose work illustrates the discrepancies and conflicts I have just mentioned.

Anne Fausto-Sterling

Anne Fausto-Sterling is a developmental biologist, still teaching and conducting research in biology. She is one of a number of biologists, including Ruth Bleier, Ruth Hubbard, Sue Rosser, Ruth Doell and Linda Birke (for an excellent bibliography, see Wylie *et al.*, 1989) who have drawn attention to the invidious treatment of women and the feminine in much biological research. Sociobiology, for example, claims in general that the social behavior of social species is biologically adaptive and genetically based—a favourite example being coyness in females, and sexual aggressiveness in males. Elaborate evolutionary arguments are developed and mechanisms invoked to support the claim that given behavior, or set of social relations, is an adaptation. Many other branches of contemporary life sciences harbour comparable sorts of views. For example, fetal testosterone is also invoked to explain the supposed greater aggressivity of males than of females, and the development of other elements of masculine temperament. Recently, premenstrual syndrome and menopause have been medicalized with, in some cases, bizarre outcomes for women. While those outside the sciences tend to view such ideas as quaint relics of a discredited nineteenth-century tradition, women inside know how seriously these approaches are taken and how well they are received in related fields. A network of purported results develops which seems to support the biological determination of a number of characteristics crucial to the perpetuation of a male dominant society.

Fausto-Sterling succeeds in showing that many of the contemporary genetic and biological determinist theories are untenable on 'internalist' scientific grounds. In her book, *Myths of Gender* (Fausto-Sterling, 1985), she reviews a number of research areas showing the deficiencies of particular studies and setting all the work in larger biological contexts, which suggest alternate ways of approaching the material. For example, in connection with research by John Money and Anke Ehrhardt on the fetal gonadal hormone influences on 'gender role behaviour,' Fausto-Sterling points to a number of problems. The controls used were inadequate: the patients with adrenogenital syndrome who were the focus of the study differed from their control populations in many ways besides hormonal exposures that could produce the behaviour studied. The observational data regarding the patients' behaviour was obtained from parents and others who knew of their condition and whose assessment may have been biased by that knowledge. And alternate explanations of the phenomena were not ruled out. So, by the rules of science itself, this research fails. It has succeeded in spite of this in attracting adherents, researchers, and supporters because it reinforces sexist attitudes in the culture.

Fausto-Sterling's vision of good science is work that is methodologically sound, but methodological soundness in a limiting or conventional framework is not enough. Her interest in criticizing the androcentric and sexist work is both to discredit it and to make room for more complex views of natural processes to emerge. Given our culture's longstanding misogyny, conventional science will inevitably derogate women and femininity. Good science about women, gender, and gender-linked processes can only begin to emerge in the context of a political women's movement which undercuts old stereotypes and provides a constituency for new research. In later work she is interested less in using science against itself than in showing the socio-political dimensions of a variety of biological research programs (Fausto-Sterling, 1989). For example, she analyzes the way conventional ideas about sex and gender limit and frame research on embryonic sex determination. She contrasts this work with results of research on embryonic development informed by more egalitarian views of sexual difference.

Many thinkers about the sciences, while not disputing Fausto-Sterling's particular arguments, are impatient with this method of demonstrating masculine bias in the sciences. They argue that there is something tainted about science itself which this approach does not reveal. In particular they claim that the approach of Fausto-Sterling and other scientists critiquing the androcentric biases in their fields leaves scientific method and the culture's glorification of rationality and objectivity untouched: Science is still master. As Audre Lorde has said, 'One cannot use the master's tools to tear down the master's house.'

Critics of the master's tools approach have gone outside of the natural sciences for a more adequate theoretical fulcrum—looking to psychology, sociology, history, literary theory, and even philosophy. Radical and feminist work in these disciplines offers ways to think about the sciences as a whole rather than engaging in the dismantling of one (or several) offending part(s).

Evelyn Fox Keller

Evelyn Fox Keller has straddled the boundaries between science and
metascience in both the research and teaching aspects of her professional
career. A mathematical biologist with an earlier training in physics, she
has become internationally known for her biography of geneticist Barbara
McClintock (Keller, 1983) and even more for her attempt to grapple with the
masculinity of science in her book *Reflections on Gender and Science* (Keller,
1985). This is not an idle academic problem for Keller. The kinds of analyses
developed in both these books help make sense of her own experience as a
scientist—the personal distancing by fellow (but male) graduate students and
the resistance to some of her ideas when a practicing theoretical biologist. Why
are the natural sciences a male and a masculine preserve? Why are the sciences
seemingly committed to linear casual analysis even when interactionist views
generate equal if not better analyses? Keller argues that these are two sides of the
same question. Her contributions to feminist science studies are multiple. She
draws attention to contemporary research programs that inscribe domination
in natural processes—searches for 'the master molecule' governing any given
biochemical process. She outlines alternative approaches actually pursued in
the sciences—McClintock's work on genetic transposition and on the interaction of chromosomes and the cellular environment, Keller's own work with
Lee Segel on slime mold aggregation. She offers an account, drawing on the
object relations school of psychoanalysis, of the interaction of cognitive and
affective processes. She argues, along with others like Carolyn Merchant and
Brian Easlea, that the sciences were appropriated (or re-appropriated) during
the seventeenth century as a masculine domain, in terms congenial not only
to the new experimental science but also to new ideals of gender.[1]

In all of this Keller is committed to the importance of science, and
seemingly to the power of scientific inquiry to reveal the character of
real processes in the real world. At least this is what one might conclude
on the basis of her very strong suggestion that a static objectivity (one
which emphasizes the differences between the inquiring self and the known
or knowable world) provides a familiar but distorted representation of
natural processes while an objectivity she characterizes as dynamic has the
capacity to provide a (different but) better or more reliable representation
of these processes. This latter representation reveals a world characterized
by interaction, interdependence, diversity, and self-organization. As Keller's
own work and her commentary on McClintock's work indicate, she is
herself more partial to models with these characteristics. To the extent
that certain methodologies of the modern and contemporary sciences are
incapable of revealing these aspects of nature, such methodologies, and the
presuppositions from which they arise, are inadequate to the task of science.
As Jane Martin (1988) and Ian Hacking (1989) have pointed out, one of
Keller's contributions here is to draw us (philosophers) away from our

obsession with propositional knowledge and the theoretical dimension of science to focus on the interactions of the scientist with her (material) subject matter. Keller engages in multiple analytic tasks—substantive, epistemological, moral—that are integrated through their ultimate grounding in psychoanalytic theory. But while the concepts of psychoanalysis act as a sort of discovery tool, readers can respond to (and have responded to) the ideas about the sciences—to ideas about causality, knowledge, discovery, and our relationship to nature—without adopting the psychoanalytic perspective.

In more recent work, Keller (1988) has approached these metascientific issues from a slightly different vantage point. In particular, her implicit judgments of the adequacy or inadequacy of a theory are (apart from issues of empirical adequacy) driven not by a commitment to a particular philosophy of nature but by views of human needs. Her view here is that the sciences provide models of nature with the aim of facilitating certain sorts of interventions, i.e. inducing changes in the real which affect our own relation to the real in certain desired ways. That we have any unmediated experience of the real, or that there could be a single correct model is not presupposed here. 'We have proven that we are smart enough to learn what we need to know to get much of what we want; perhaps it's time we thought more about what we want' (Keller, 1988, p. 28). Rather than the correct method, this work seems to set its audience the task of finding, choosing, or articulating the correct values from which will emerge a different science. As the paragraph ends, it becomes clear that Keller wants the sciences and those engaged in them to make a commitment to a particular value—survival. If we do think more about what we want, we will discover that this is the point 'where the convergence of our (diverse) interests might be said to be obligatory' (Keller, 1988, p. 28). Keller's essay is among other things a call to reorient scientific inquiry in the understanding that such reorientation cannot but change the character of scientific knowledge as well as the uses to which it can be put. Where in the earlier work she looked to the sources whence inquiry sprang, here she looks to the goals inquiry can help to fulfil.

While Keller's work has been taken up by feminist scholars and by historians and philosophers of science, her intended audience is scientists and her goal is the reform of the sciences. These intentions explain the rhetorical and argumentative strategies she has adopted throughout these discussions. Even as they have evolved they evince the desire for some invariant—whether it is a better developed cognitive attitude or a set of values—on which change can be grounded. These invariants are or could be characteristics of the practitioners of science. To the extent they recognize themselves in her portrayals they can find a rallying point and ground for effecting change in their specific fields of inquiry.

Donna Haraway

Donna Haraway, although herself trained as a biologist, seeks to distance herself from the sciences, at the very moment that she discusses them. She accomplishes this distancing through her choice of analytical tool—narrative theory. Rather than regard the sciences as a means of developing true representations or even instruments of prediction and thereby getting trapped by the epistemological quandaries this presents both for the scientist and for the critic of science, she treats scientific texts as stories, using the techniques of literary analysis to extract their meaning. The sciences she examines are the sciences of primatology—which tell stories of human origins and purportedly reveal what is natural about human nature. Haraway's (1989a) readings of these stories are complex, intertextual, and socially and politically situated. She examines the institutional contexts in which they were and are produced, the networks of instruction and affiliation in which their producers are enmeshed, and the multiple layers of meaning encoded and created in the texts. Such meanings come into being quite independently of the aims and intentions of individuals, and are a function both of the preoccupations of the social and institutional contexts in which the texts of primatology are produced and read and of the metaphors made current by such preoccupations. Haraway reads and encourages us to read primatological texts, therefore, not for what they tell us about human nature, or about the various primate species, but for what they tell us about their authors, not as individuals but as spokespersons for their cultures.

The stories told—of sexual relations, of social dominance, of stress, and of choice—are produced according to strict rules (scientific method). Primatology has always been ostensibly about the members of certain ape and monkey societies and as it has been professionalized it has developed explicit (if changing) rules about how to extract or elicit information from and about these societies. Nevertheless, primatology has also been about production, social management, communication, control, and investment strategies; about the conditions for managing social relations among inherently cooperative organisms and about the conditions for establishing order among inherently aggressive, mutually antagonistic organisms. By showing the mutability of primatological visions in response to different human social and economic preoccupations, Haraway invites us to cast away our own preoccupation with objectivity, truth, and getting it right.

Her joyfully deconstructive approach to traditional boundaries between nature and culture, human and animal, organism and machine, and her dismissive attitude towards traditional epistemological concerns may lead readers to ascribe to Haraway an anti-realism that licenses any claim so long as it is in opposition to accepted mainstream discourses. Such a reading is itself too mired in the epistemological. Haraway is not telling us how to do science or how to create new knowledge. She is telling us how to read science—'primatology is politics' proclaims one of her titles—and telling us, if anything, how *not* to create knowledge of human society and human justice. The primatological texts she analyzes are produced from social positions reflecting certain interests. Many are produced as the basis for manuals of social manipulation and control, while others are produced with one hand extended to contemporary liberation movements. One of primatology's self-appointed explanatory goals is to develop some account of a transition from nature to culture. To speak of a transition must assume some distinction between the two, at a juncture inevitably constructed by the very socio-political preoccupations which the texts are meant to inform. Haraway's aims and audience are thus quite different from those of the authors previously considered. She is not contesting (though she does expose) androcentric or masculinist representations in science nor is she trying to recruit scientists to an alternative or oppositional scientific practice. While hoping to be read by her subjects she writes primarily for a lay-reader—a left-wing intellectual at least sympathetic to feminism and concerned with contesting the hegemony of scientism. Surely one hoped-for outcome would be the ejection of science, not from its role as representer of natural processes, but from its role as arbiter of politics. The sciences can tell us about the chemistry of immunity, even in highly politicized metaphors. They cannot tell us about justice; that is for us to define and realize.

Haraway's claims that a new social order will evoke a new biology may be read as a suggestion that science is just ideology. Haraway is not a simple relativist, nor can she be read as anti-realist in any metaphysical sense. In an essay that explores the metaphors of militarism, difference, and integrity constructing the meaning of selfhood in contemporary immunology, Haraway (1989b) stops briefly to answer an imagined question about the facticity of biological entities as opposed to the ficticity of science fiction's fantasies. Bodies, by which I understand 'entities,' are 'material semiotic actors.' They are not simply ideological constructions, but actively participate (as do the chimps of *Primate Visions*, Haraway, 1989a) in the construction of knowledge about them. What Haraway denies is only that bodies (from amino acids to you and me) uniquely and solely determine what counts as knowledge about them. Bodies certainly impose constraints on what can be said about them. These are just not the constraints Haraway is interested in exposing. The constraints which interest her are those imposed by politics, by the play of power among those who seek knowledge.

Sandra Harding

Unlike the previous three thinkers, Sandra Harding is an academic philosopher—explicitly concerned with epistemological questions and their convergence with issues in social and political theory. Empiricism, which she identifies with positivism, has failed, in Harding's view, as an account of human knowledge—scientific or otherwise. Harding endorses and extends the arguments of philosophers such as Quine against positivism by foregrounding aspects of positivism that work against an understanding of the operation of gender in science. Much of her book, *The Science Question in Feminism* (Harding, 1986) can be read as a canvas of feminist theory for an adequate replacement to positivism.

The rejection of positivism is for Harding not just the rejection of a normative view about the forms of justification appropriate to the sciences. Harding implicitly treats positivism as correctly reflecting the methodology of mainstream science. The rejection of positivism is, thus, simultaneously a rejection of mainstream science. Harding concludes *The Science Question in Feminism* with a new vision of the unity of science, a vision in which reflexive and self-critical social sciences occupy the foundational place occupied by physics in the positivists' vision. She offers the promise of a science transformed in her reversal of the traditional unity of science, but it is also a science made unrecognizable. Part of the problem is the identification of scientific inquiry with the logical positivists' image of science. This is a misreading of the endorsement of logical positivism by some scientists. Such endorsement was really directed at positivism's privileging of scientific over other forms of knowledge rather than at its account of scientific practice. It is the positivists' image of scientific inquiry that must be rejected.

Harding locates her work within the feminist project to remake knowledge. It seems to be Harding's view that an adequate epistemology is a prerequisite for an adequate science. Her strategy in developing such an epistemology has been to look to the argumentative and rhetorical practices of self-identified feminists working in sociology and in biology. It is here that she has found the theories she identifies as feminist empiricism and feminist standpoint theory. She draws out the philosophical commitments and implications of these views partly by tracing the connections among their various feminist exponents and partly by reviewing their philosophical ancestry—classical empiricism, logical positivism, and Marxism. And surely there are elements of empiricism in the biologists' critique of sexist science, as well as elements of standpoint theory in Keller's account of objectivity. The women primatologists studied by Haraway include exponents of empiricism as well as claimants to a special access to the lives of other female primates or to the workings of primate societies. What has most occupied Harding are the conflicts between 'empiricism' and 'standpoint theory,' which she is never able to resolve in favour of one or the other (Harding, 1986, 1989a). Even during her flirtation with a version of postmodernist anti-epistemology, she claimed that it could not displace empiricism and standpoint theory, both of which were still necessary. Given her explications of empiricism and standpoint theory, this has left her seemingly in the grip of a contradiction. In *The Science Question in Feminism*, Harding constructs an epistemological dialectic in which the internal contradictions of feminist empiricism give way, in turn, to feminist postmodernism. Nevertheless, the projects of feminist empiricism and of feminist standpoint theory must be carried on.

This position seems paradoxical, at best. Here, too, considerations of audience are useful. Harding writes for several audiences. One is the ever increasing multidisciplinary group of Women's Studies teachers and scholars. For these, she provides a guide to the literature about science, a way to see its various aspects in relation to each other. Both scholars identified as feminist empiricists and those identified as feminist standpoint theorists have made distinctive and crucial contributions to feminist scholarship. She may think, therefore, that it would be perverse to claim that either approach was based on so fatally flawed a philosophical view that it ought not be pursued. Harding identifies another audience in a recent exchange with Dorothy Smith: administrators of universities and foundations, the people who sit on grant committees, tenure committees, and thesis committees (Harding, 1989b). Here she is a feminist activist, striving to make the value of feminist work evident to those with the power to choke it off or let it grow. Here again she would undermine her aims by judging between the positions she describes. But a segment of Harding's audience, certainly her internal audience, consists of philosophers and this audience requires attention to philosophical topics, hence she must acknowledge, even while she does not resolve, the conflict between positivist and Marxist theories of knowledge. She is respectful of the situated character of the feminist research programs whose tensions she explores. The philosopher's impulse to universality sits uneasily with that respect.

REFLECTIONS

Each of these thinkers, and we with her, confronts a scientific world shaped by the concerns and interests of Euro-American middle-class males. Each stands in a different relation to that world and to the political movements that challenge Euro-American middle-class male supremacy, and each engages in a different mediation between these two worlds. Neither the scientific world nor these political movements constitute exclusive monoliths. They are each composed of a complex of partially overlapping communities, some of which participate in both worlds.

Each of the positions in which our actors find themselves is a node in a force field that defines a different set of possibilities and political tasks. The developmental biologist practicing in the laboratory who is a woman and feminist challenges the representations of women and the use of gender stereotypes in contemporary biology. Is it possible to do better? She answers by citing an example of a scientist who works in a manner accountable to women. The theoretical biologist, edged out of physics because of her sex, advocate of non-standard models, speaks to and for other such advocates, speaking at times out of a shared form of non-standard, because non-masculinist, relationship to nature and at times out of hope of a shared value around which deviant scientists can rally to produce an alternative representation of natural processes. Another biologist leaves the discipline altogether, finding a new home in history and cultural studies. The analytical tools of these disciplines and her insider's knowledge of the world of biology are resources which she makes available to the political movement outside biology. Haraway's rhetoric presupposes a commitment to anti-colonialism, anti-capitalism, anti-sexism on the part of her readers. Her analysis seeks to demystify science for such readers. By contrast, Keller seems to seek a more common denominator—perhaps a wise decision given the already small size of the pool from which she can expect recruits/allies. And Fausto-Sterling, while empowering women outside of science, does so by enabling them to talk back to their definers in a language they understand. That is, she shows the inadequacies of the biological representations of the female by reference to the very standards the promoters of those representations endorse. Finally, Harding claims to make the activities of feminists in science intelligible and legitimate to the administrators who have power over their projects. If in the process she succeeds in nudging the scientists themselves into even more self-reflection on their practice and the philosophical reconstruction of their practice, so much the better.

As a philosopher, however, I want to ask what the real philosophical differences are here. On first reading, and, as I said, hearing the reflection of their views in the feminist debates about the sciences, we might anticipate deep and interesting metaphysical and epistemological differences. When we look for explicit arguments, however, and discount for rhetoric aimed at certain audiences, these anticipations turn to dust.

For example, we find statements in Fausto-Sterling's book to the effect that the biological determinist view does not do justice to the facts of biology. 'Facts,' we might say, 'this shows Fausto-Sterling thinks that there are facts—she's a realist—and that biology can find them. She believes scientific method can reveal the real as it is in itself.' But this rhetoric can also be read more modestly. Set in the context of Fausto-Sterling's other statements, it can mean merely that among the methodologies and theories in contemporary biology there are resources to draw on in countering the ideas of the determinists. We can read her strategy as bringing out the diversity and richness of biological thinking rather than claiming any privileged access to truth when the scientific method is properly applied.

Similarly, as we follow Haraway treating the texts of primatology as stories, we may be tempted (as some of her readers have been) to read her as saying they are 'just stories' or 'just fictions.' Hence, anything goes. This is to ignore her assertions elsewhere that the production of these accounts is rule-governed and that representations produced according to rules of inquiry in given fields have made it possible to interact with our material surroundings in reliable ways. This, too, is not to say that the rules provide a privileged access to the real, but it should warn us against interpreting Haraway as licensing any claims whatever in science since they are all fiction anyway. (And the novelists among us might remind us that if there is a fiction in the discourses of truth, so there is a truth in the discourses of fiction.)

While I read, therefore, no firm commitment to scientific realism in these authors, neither do I find a commitment to any of the current alternatives to scientific realism in post-positivist philosophy of science. (This is not to say that when pressed they might not make such a commitment.) An interesting philosophical project would involve determining which of the various alternatives is most compatible with the ontological commitments in the work of any of the feminist scientists I've discussed. But this is a job for philosophers. The scientists themselves aren't interested unless we can persuade them that it matters.

It is equally hard to find commitments to particular epistemological theories, where by an epistemological theory we mean a justificatory theory. Instead, we find recipes for inquiry, suggested procedures for deciphering nature, none of which amount to criteria of justification. One point of difference here does lie in attitudes toward the pursuit of alternative accounts within the sciences. Both Fausto-Sterling and Keller seem to urge this project, whereas the historian explores tensions and conflicts among the various alternatives pursued by women in primatology, and the philosopher explores tensions and conflicts between metascientific views. Here again, I think it a mistake to read these differences as metaphysical or epistemological. It might be possible to read commitments to partial, local knowledge on one side as against the hope for a new but comprehensive framework on the other. But, for reasons already explored, it would be difficult to construct stable alignments along these axes and, secondly, the grounds for the attitudes towards alternative scientific practices and research programs are not primarily metaphysical or epistemological, but political.

Each of these theorists would claim that the sciences are a central conceptual (as well as material) support of the structures of power feminists wish to change. Where they disagree is on how best to weaken this particular foundation—from within or from without. Fausto-Sterling and Keller believe that the supportive role of science is acquired at the cost of constricting the variety possible within science and falsifying its epistemic character. Their work is directed at loosening in different ways the external constraints imposed upon scientific activity and thereby cracking its positivist image. Scientific research deviating from the mainstream may be of use to those seeking political change. More immediately it weakens the support the sciences can give to established power, by challenging the hegemony of a privileged world picture. Keller also sometimes seems to suggest that the sciences can contribute to changing the world. Rather than trying to produce the diversity of which scientific activity is capable, Haraway reveals that diversity—by documenting the mutability of mainstream primatology which is capable of including Carpenter, Yerkes, and Washburn as well as feminist (or female-centered) accounts of primate behavior. While her coolly ironic presentation may seem an attack from outside the walls of science, it depends crucially on the diversity within science. She contests not Science, but certain claims on behalf of Science. Harding does locate the origin of her critique firmly outside the sciences. By identifying the sciences with their positivist image, she treats arguments against positivism as effective against the claims of science. From this perspective, attempts to do science differently than prescribed by the established modes are doomed reformism. The only value of such attempts is that they will result in alienation of those scientists from the sciences, i.e. in a withdrawal of allegiance that will destabilize the claim of the sciences upon our belief. Science entire, not just particular claims and theories, must be created anew in a new social order.

If I am correct in seeing these conflicts as differences in political analysis and strategy, why do they get read and expressed as epistemological and metaphysical? Part of the problem lies in the language available to analyze the sciences. Here, feminists are badly served by traditional philosophy of science. As feminists, we are concerned with the sciences as a set of institutions. The critical language provided by philosophy to analyze the sciences is an epistemological one. But the transition between a critique of epistemological presuppositions and a critique of institutions is very treacherous, not least because traditional epistemology is framed in individualist terms, while institutions must be analyzed with social categories.[2] Traditional philosophy of science and its categories are ill suited to the critical analysis that our own kind of critique of the sciences demands. Feminist work in and about the sciences raises *new* questions not confinable to traditional issues about rationality and objectivity. Such questions include, among others: Just what *is* the relation between social change and scientific change? Is it possible to engage in theorizing that does not intimately articulate with existing social distributions of power? What are the consequences of directing our philosophical attention away from propositional knowledge to the relationship between scientist and phenomena?

Why do we persist in framing our arguments within the traditional categories, thus magnifying our differences? Here are some suggestions. First, one unspoken tension in this field lies between psychoanalytically based theorists and theorists based in Marxism. Are epistemological questions carrying the weight of conflict over these analytic approaches? If so, we need more direct and comparative discussion of what can be accomplished within these intellectual frameworks. Second, unlike some other areas of feminist scholarship, there are relatively few central participants in the debates over gender and science, and the field of feminist science studies is, compared with areas such as women's history or feminist literary criticism, still very small. Does this lead us to see our potential audience as a scarce resource? or to think that there is room for only one correct line? Third, could it be that our construction of these differences is itself refracted through the father's eye, through *his* language, *his* questions, for *his* attention? If we could free ourselves from this internal bondage, our disagreements surely would not disappear, but they might generate more creative and productive difference. Such disagreements would expand our intellectual horizons, as well as the domain of science studies, rather than fostering competition over limited concepts.[3]

THE MATTER OF WOMEN IN SCIENCE— EVELYNN HAMMONDS

Feminist studies of science face many other, considerably more vexing areas of conflicts, that arise between working women scientists and feminists critical of contemporary science. In fact, the reception of the feminist critique of science by practicing women scientists has not been an altogether positive one. Some of the reasons lie with the perceived political project of the feminist critique (and in this post-Reagan era much of the public perception of feminism is negative) and others lie with the failure of this critique to offer examples of the gendered structure of the physical sciences and mathematics. The central conflict, however, is over the interpretation of 'science,' 'gender,' and 'feminism.' This conflict can be expressed in two questions: working women scientists persist in asking 'What is it about women and women's lives that have kept them from doing science?' whereas feminist critics of science ask 'What is it about science that has limited the participation of women and, by extension, other marginalized groups?'

Many women scientists continue to perceive the feminist critique as putting forth a simple characterization of science that reinforces traditional stereotypes both of women and of science. While many of us engaged in feminist studies of science see this work as ultimately helpful to women scientists, far too many of these women (perhaps especially those who have made it into the enclaves of the 'hard' sciences) do not see it that way. In their view, the feminist critiques of science hurt, rather than advance their cause.

Professional organizations of women scientists and engineers were established to 'promote equal opportunities for women to enter the professions and to achieve their career goals.'[4] They believe that the problems women face in science and engineering can be traced first and foremost to environmental issues—how women are treated in schools and in the workplace; if they just work harder, show that they are team players, don't drop out when they have children, develop more confidence in themselves, put aside their desire for emotional connectedness in their work, dismiss stereotypes that science and engineering are 'thing-oriented' professions, increase the numbers of women in science, the environment will change and the problems will be solved. As one scientist reassuringly insists, 'The reality about women is that there need be no conflict between being fully-fledged scientists and being fully female: we get to be both' (Mierson, 1989).

In her Presidential Lecture to the AAAS, Sheila Widnall (1988), MIT Aeronautical & Astronautical engineer, notes that women and minorities are needed to fill the anticipated gaps in scientific personnel in the future. She discusses recent studies which show that graduate school environments have had an effect on the completion rates of women and minorities in the natural sciences and engineering. She asserts that the issue is not that women are not capable of doing science but that the environment they encounter in their education fails to enhance their self-esteem and provide positive professional experiences. Her charge to her colleagues is: treat women better, we need them, we will all benefit by the improvement in the educational environment. More importantly this can be accomplished ' ... while being no less insightful and scientifically critical ...' (Widnall, 1988, p. 1745). Widnall, like many other women scientists and engineers, makes no connection between the problems women encounter and the structure of scientific knowledge and scientific education. They persist in arguing against the perception that women can't do science while never attempting to address the source of such perceptions.

Widnall does however see a potential problem in the future funding of science if it continues to be perceived as an activity solely for white males. 'The years ahead may be troublesome for the support of science, and the image of science as a community accessible to all will be important to maintain public support,' she concedes (1988, p. 1741). It is clearly not Widnall's intent to portray the exclusion of women and minorities from science as merely an image problem, but her comments do suggest that the perception of exclusion lies with the excluded and not within the scientific professions.

To confront culturally defined stereotypes about women's nature and about what scientists do, women scientists tend to offer two strategies. The first is to expose the 'private world' of scientific work. As one woman mathematician notes:

> It would appear that there is a private and public world of mathematics. The private world is where struggle, failure, incomprehension, intuition, and creativity dominate ... The public world is where the results of the private struggle make their appearance in a formal, conventional abstract formulation from which all evidence of false trails, inadequate reasoning or misunderstandings have been eliminated. Unfortunately for our pupils, the majority are given access to only the public world.
>
> (Leone Burton, quoted in Jackson, 1989, p. 672)

By exposing this private world where values more often associated with women are displayed, these women scientists hope to show how women can fit into science without changing themselves. The second strategy suggests that women do have to change their view of their own abilities in order to be successful in science. Admitting the truth of some culturally familiar notions about women's problems with science and technology, articles about women's relationships to physical objects encourage them to overcome their fears of alienation from technology by developing more aggressive behaviours and more confidence in themselves. Such articles reinforce the belief that there are behaviours and attitudes peculiar to women that hamper their progress within science. This is the very idea women scientists want to dispel.

Many of these women scientists focus on 'fitting' women to science, while denouncing the idea that science is a necessarily male activity as merely a stereotype. They do not believe that gender has any bearing on scientific work. Gender is not itself a scientific issue, it is a purely social one. Science, they argue, as understood by those who really do it, is an activity devoid of any connections to social behaviours. It follows then that science cannot be implicated in the 'legitimation of society's gendered beliefs and norms' (Bleier, 1988).

As Widnall's remarks suggest, many of the professional women scientists neither hear nor understand the feminist critique. Their deep belief in the meritocratic ideology of science is unexamined and unshaken. For the most part, they are unfamiliar even with the history of women in science, except for the uncritical portraits of great women of the past, so often published in the professional journals. What tends to go especially unnoted is the important critical analyses of many of these women's careers. For example, a review of Anne Sayre's (1975) book on Rosalind Franklin (in *U.S. Woman Engineer)* reads: 'today we can look at Franklin's story as a lesson to keep an open mind, to listen to others, to avoid being overly dogmatic; and most importantly; to speak out when one is sure of the facts—not an easy balancing act!' (Murray, 1988). The complicated circumstances which led to the suppression of Franklin's contribution to the discovery of the structure of DNA is clearly not known to this reviewer. Instead, Franklin's story is reduced to a lesson in assertiveness training for women who want to be successful scientists. Unmarked by the alternate narratives of feminists, the professional journals of women scientists and engineers continue to reinforce the notion that women can do science and do it well, even while doing all the other things that women do. They portray the many successful women in the field who juggle home life and work, and insist that being a successful woman scientist is not different than being a successful woman in any other profession. The 'science' that they want to do is the 'science' that men do. Even if they acknowledge that women might want to engage in scientific work more directly connected to human concerns, they suggest that this can be done within the wide range of scientific work available. It is not necessary to go outside of science to accommodate such goals. The literature argues, in fact, that the prevailing image of scientists as dispassionate human beings with no need for close human contact or nurturance are nothing but stereotypes, stereotypes most detrimental to women. 'Then women scientists are told that we are not good at and do not need what is almost considered a defining characteristic of our sex. We get appreciated for being different from other women rather than recognized for the characteristics we have in common' (Mierson, 1989, p. 13).

Unlike those who would merely encourage more women to enter science, or those who envision some uniquely 'feminine' way of doing science, some working women scientists have attempted to understand and sympathize with the feminist critique of science, though they often find it unfamiliar and disturbing. For example, a recent article in the *Notices of the American Mathematical Society*, raises a number of by now familiar points against the feminist critique of science. The main objection is that it might work to discourage women from entering mathematics and science ' . . . because this literature perpetuates stereotypes and misconceptions about mathematics and science . . .' (Jackson, 1989, p. 669). The author argues that feminist critics present the nature of science in such a way that it alienates women and perpetuates a strong anti-science bias. Few, if any, distinctions are made between feminist critics of science; the critique is represented as a static unified body of work. More significantly, there seems to be no understanding of the questions that feminist critics of science have attempted to address. Women mathematicians cited see the feminist critics as *accepting* stereotypical notions about women rather than *questioning* them. This is a very curious reading of the feminist literature. Ideas about how gender is constructed within scientific discourses are constantly read as statements *about* women scientists. One mathematician writes: 'They reiterate rather than question our society's belief that women are closer to nature, that they are more instinctive, intuitive' (Jackson, 1989, p. 671). Another claims, 'One of the main objections to the critiques is their view of science and mathematics as inherently masculine. This view is based on stereotypes of science and mathematics: the problem is that some of these scholars have taken the stereotypes literally' (Jackson, 1989, p. 672).

A more problematic point of contention between feminist critics and these women mathematicians is the inference or claim that mathematics and other mathematized sciences are also gendered. In fact, feminist critics have made little headway in specifically articulating how gender is inscribed in these sciences. Many, if not most, of the examples used in feminist critiques have come from the biological sciences where gender bias in language and practice seem more easily described. Women in the mathematical sciences object to the practice of extending generalizations based on biology to their own disciplines. They argue that strict adherence to scientific method makes mathematical science gender-free.

For these women scientists, science simply works; the laws of physics are what they are, proven by their consistency with experiment, and by the great technological advances they have spurred. To them, science is *defined* as the product of scientific method—a method that self-corrects for all human biases—including any that could arise from biases of gender. As one mathematician put it: 'One still wants to know whether feminists' airplanes would stay airborne for feminist engineers' (Levin, 1988, p. 105). Discussions of science in any other terms is incomprehensible to these women scientists. To them, the only possible connection that feminism could have to science would be to make it possible for more women to do science under the most equitable circumstances.

CONCLUSION

Women scientists are educated, as men scientists are, with no self-critical perspective about their own disciplines. Reflexivity and self-criticism are neither valued nor encouraged. It is therefore not surprising that they find little commonality with a feminist critique premised on just such a perspective. What is more troubling, however, is that women scientists have so little sense of history. The strategies proposed by feminists and non-feminists to help women achieve their career goals and to bring more women into the scientific professions are virtually identical to those of women scientists before World War II. As Margaret Rossiter (1982, p. 316) notes, the separate organizations of women scientists found that efforts to provide psychological self-help to their members or lobbying professional organizations for more recognition of women failed. These groups ' ... were not designed or able to change the established structure of scientific employment in a sexist society.' The feminist critique of science begins, in part, with the acknowledgment that these strategies have failed.

That science is in fact neither fully objective nor value-free, that it serves particular social, economic, and political interests, is in some cases not too difficult for many women scientists to accept—the 'private world' of science has always revealed to them such flaws. Yet, the absence of a clearly articulated alternative to conventional practices remains a critical stumbling block to a rapprochement between even these women scientists and feminist critics. What options do practicing women scientists have, other than to apply the existing method more faithfully? Feminist critics have articulated a sophisticated argument about the inscription of gender in the language and norms of scientific practice, but they have been less successful in demonstrating, at least to the satisfaction of practicing scientists, how the scientific method, especially in the 'exact' sciences, is itself inscribed by gender. Above all, we have yet to demonstrate how the scientific method can provide successful representations of the physical world while at the same time inscribing social structures of domination and control in its institutional, conceptual, and methodological core.

Notes

1. Several writers have described a masculine appropriation of knowledge and science in the sixteenth and seventeenth centuries. Carolyn Merchant in *The Death of Nature: Women, Ecology and the Scientific Revolution* (1980); Brian Easlea in *Witch Hunting, Magic and the New Philosophy* (1980); and Keller in *Reflections on Gender and Science* (1985) all describe a struggle between the hermetic/magical tradition in natural philosophy and the newer mechanical philosophy. This struggle is expressed in a rhetoric of gender and sexuality that eventually makes of nature a female to be conquered and the scientist her male conqueror (by charm, wile or force). The triumph of the mechanical corpuscularist philosophy of matter deanimates nature and by extension woman—matter and the female become a metaphor each for the other. The legacy of this ancient struggle is a natural science preoccupied with power and domination, expressed vividly in this century in the quests for the secrets of the atom and later the secret of life—the gene.
2. Harding's restrictive account of the sciences locates the exclusionary power of the sciences in epistemology, rather than in the social and political interactions of scientists and scientific institutions. While it seems to be a more radical critique of the sciences it achieves its radicality at the price of denying evident features of scientific thought and practice even when we remove our positive spectacles.
3. I am indebted for this vision to Valerie Miner's image of expanding the bookshelf rather than fighting for a designated space in it in her essay 'Rumors from the cauldron: Competition among feminist writers,' in Miner and Longino (1987).
4. Motto of the Association for Women in Science.

References

Easlea, B. (1980) *Witch Hunting, Magic and the New Philosophy.* Brighton: Harvester Press.

Fausto-Sterling, A. (1985) *Myths of Gender.* New York: Basic Books

—(1989) Life in the XY corral. *Women's Studies International Forum* 12 (3), 319–32.

Hacking, I. (1989) Philosophers of experiment. In A. Fine and J. Leplin (eds) *PSA 1988* (pp. 147–56). East Lansing, MI: Philosophy of Science Association.

Haraway, D. (1989a) *Primate Visions: Gender, Race and Nature in the World of Modern Science.* New York: Routledge.

—(1989b) The biopolitics of postmodern bodies: Determinations of self in immune system discourse. *Differences* 1 (1), (Winter), 3–44.

Harding, S. (1986) *The Science Question in Feminism.* Ithaca, NY: Cornell University Press.

—(1989a) How the women's movement benefits science: Two views. *Women's Studies International Forum* 12 (3), 271–84.

—(1989b) Response. *Newsletter on Feminism and Philosophy* 88 (3), (June), 46–9.

Jackson, A. (1989) Feminist critiques of science. *Notices of the American Mathematical Society* 36 (6) (July/August), 672.

Keller, E. F. (1983) *A Feeling for the Organism: The Life and Work of Barbara McClintock.* San Francisco, CA: W. H. Freeman.

—(1985) *Reflections on Gender and Science.* New Haven, CT: Yale University Press.

—(1988) Critical silences in scientific discourse: Problems of form and reform. Paper presented at the Institute for Advanced Study, Princeton, NJ, 4 February. This material is incorporated into Keller's chapter: Gender and science. *The Great Ideas Today.* Chicago, IL: Encyclopaedia Britannica 1990.

Leavitt, J. W. and Gordon, L. (1988) A decade of feminist critiques in the natural sciences: An address by Ruth Bleier. *Signs* 14 (1), 182–195.

Levin, M. (1988) Caring new world: Feminism and science. *The American Scholar* Winter, 105.

Martin, J. (1988) Science in a different style. *American Philosophical Quarterly* 25, 129–40.

Merchant, C. (1980) *The Death of Nature: Women, Ecology and the Scientific Revolution.* San Francisco, CA: Harper and Row.

Mierson, S. (1989) We're OK; Internalized sexism: Issues for women scientists. *AWIS Newsletter* 18 (3), (May/June).

Miner, V. and Longino, H. (eds) (1987) *Competition: A Feminist Taboo?* New York: The Feminist Press.

Murray, E. M. E. (1988) Review of A. Sayre (1975) *Rosalind Franklin and DNA. U.S. Woman Engineer* May/June, 33.

Rossiter, M. (1982) *Women Scientists in America: Struggles and Strategies to 1940.* Baltimore, MD: Johns Hopkins University Press.

Sayre, A. (1975) *Rosalind Franklin and DNA.* New York: Norton and Co.

Widnall, S. (1988) AAAS Presidential Lecture: Voices from the pipeline. *Science* 241 (30) (September).

Wylie, A. Okruhlik, K., Thielen-Wilson, L. and Morton, S. (1989) Feminist critiques of science: The epistemological and methodological literature. *Women's Studies International Forum* 12 (3), 379–88.

5 GENDER AND GIRLS' PHYSICAL EDUCATION: FUTURE POLICY, FUTURE DIRECTIONS

SHEILA SCRATON

The relationship between gender and girls' physical education is of particular importance given that physical education is the only separate and distinct curriculum area in secondary schooling which remains predominantly single-sex taught by women to groups of girls and young women. It has inherited particular historical traditions which inform this unique separation. [...] There is parallel work to be developed on boys and young men and on the relationship between gender, sexuality and masculinity in the context of physical education.

Four significant dimensions of inquiry and analysis have developed out of my research project: (1) teachers' perceptions, attitudes and ideas, (2) institutional analysis, (3) the historical context of contemporary debate, (4) cultural responses and resistances. All four dimensions have proved crucial to the development both of a theoretical understanding of gender *and* an informed, critical analysis of the teaching of girls' physical education. Gender and girls' physical education are in a dialectical relationship in which gender is identified as a central construct of girls' physical education, the analysis of which provides an essential contribution to the theoretical debates concerning gender. The project emphasizes the importance of the connection between theory, practice and politics. For example, the research identifies the need to recognize and assess the importance of physical power relations as part of the social relations of gender. This has been considered both at a theoretical level and at the level of everyday practice in girls' physical education teaching. Arising from this consideration is the question of whether and/or how the social relations of gender could be challenged or modified through the transformation of girls' physical education. In other words, whether the politics of girls' physical education can include strategies and policies which not only will change girls' physical education but also will contribute to changes in the social relations of gender.

Source: Abridged from Scraton, S. (1992) in S. Scraton (ed.) *Shaping up to Womanhood: Gender and Girls' Physical Education.* Buckingham: Open University Press.

THEORY, PRACTICE AND POLITICS

Teachers' perceptions, attitudes and ideas

The interviews identified the presence of powerful assumptions about femininity in relation to girls' and young women's physical ability/capacity, sexuality, motherhood and domesticity. These gender stereotypes were accepted and explained by most heads of department interviewed as being 'natural'. This 'naturalism' was defined as either a biological or a cultural inevitability. The interpretation of gender differences as 'natural' is surprising particularly with regard to physical ability/capacity, because the reality is so obviously different. The stereotype of girls as weaker, less powerful, neater and more precise in their movements is factually inaccurate. The research observations confirmed that the physical differences within one sex are far greater and more obvious than those between the sexes. Furthermore, the appearance of many of the teachers themselves was in direct contradiction to their own stereotyped views, as many were strong, powerful, muscularly developed women. Bob Connell (1987) argues that in understanding gender, 'nature' is often used as a justification rather than as an explanation. This suggests that the teachers felt the need to justify their practice of stereotyping and used biology as an explanation even though their own reality and experiences were at variance with their views. What this suggests is the existence of a powerful ideology of biology which will be considered in more detail later in this article.

A major explanation put forward for gender stereotyping is sex-role theory, which concentrates on the importance of socialization and sex-role learning. This is a central consideration within liberal feminist analysis. There are many critiques of this perspective emphasizing the lack of an adequate theorizing of power relations within liberal feminism; the neglect of an historical analysis; the over-reliance on individualism and voluntarism; the tendency to reduce gender to the biological dichotomy of male and female (Connell, 1983, 1987). [...]

In considering attitudes and ideas the research confirms that women teachers have clear expectations about girls and young women which are constructed around a notion of 'femininity'. This 'femininity' encompasses ideas about physical ability/capacity, sexuality, domesticity and motherhood. Crucially the research demonstrates that it is a construction which does not remain simply in the minds of individual teachers but one which is generalized, both informing and influencing physical education practice. This is reflected in the choice of 'suitable' activities for girls, class organization and teacher–pupil interaction. Clearly, then, in their professional practice, women physical education teachers are agents of socialization, transmitting gendered messages to pupils through their interaction, language and teaching. It is a process derived from expectations around femininity.

It is necessary, however, to return to the criticism of this analysis. While research into attitudes and ideas contributes significantly to an understanding of the importance of gender in girls' physical education, at the level of description, it fails to give an adequate account of the *relationship* involved. In focusing on attitudes and ideas there is a tendency to concentrate on *differences* between the sexes. The teachers interviewed emphasized differences between girls and boys (both physical and social) and the importance of these differences in practice. Given their training this position is understandable, but if the analysis remains limited to this level, there is a danger of considering femininity and masculinity as polar opposites, thus assigning girls to ascribed roles and behaviour by using the dichotomy of sex as its organizing principle. The 'problem' of gender then becomes reduced to biological sex differences. What is missing here is the vital element of *structure* and, implicit with this, an understanding of power relations. Girls' physical education cannot be studied divorced from its historical and structural context. It does not exist in a vacuum influenced only by individuals with 'free-floating' ideas that can be changed simply by raising awareness and challenging attitudes. Such initiatives are significant but they need to be located and analysed within the broader relations of ideology and situated within contemporary structural and institutional contexts. The 'tip of the iceberg' has been illuminated by researching attitudes of teachers but the broader underlying structural complexities require further investigation and analysis.

Institutional analysis

The case study material, obtained from periods of observation in the selected schools, concentrated on the daily reality of teaching physical education in its institutional setting. From the evidence it is clear that gender is a significant factor in the structuring of girls' physical education, which can be identified through its organization, staffing, facilities, aims and objectives and curricular content.

However, the research also contributes to an understanding of the structures of gender as power relations. Three significant areas emerged from the research. [...]

1 Patriarchal power: the importance of the 'physical' Two important issues emerged which warrant consideration. First, it is necessary to question the use of 'male' power as a definition of structural power relations. There is a tendency, not surprisingly, to associate power with all *men*. While acknowledging that this is an accurate application in many, or indeed most situations, the power of men over women cannot be viewed as a universal and inevitable theory of domination. Hester Eisenstein (1984) introduces the concept of 'false universalism' to describe literature and analysis which talks of the experiences and subordination of all women regardless of other structural relations such as race, ethnicity, class and age. Similarly, 'false universalism' can be applied to the notion of 'male power'. Yet there remains a need for a concept that adequately describes the relevance and importance of patriarchal power relations without resorting to simple biological reductionism. The significance of this research project is that it identifies the presence of gender power relations in an area which usually is exclusive to women. In fact everyone concerned with the research—advisers, teachers and pupils—were women. Therefore it is not direct, overt 'male power' which is identified in the teaching of girls' physical education but, as Bob Connell (1987, p. 43) observes, the power of 'hegemonic masculinity' or 'the maintenance of practices that institutionalize men's dominance over women'.

[...] Gender needs to be theorized as being structured by a dominant hegemonic masculinity which not only forms the basis of male–female relationships but also is conveyed and internalized through institutions and social practice. Girls' physical education does not exist in isolation outside the hegemonic order. Despite being a female institution, it remains an institutional form which internalizes, supports, maintains and reinforces hegemonic masculinity.

The second area identified by the research is the centrality of physical power relations as a construct of hegemonic masculinity. There is a clear relationship between men's physical activity, prowess, strength and contemporary Western definitions of masculinity. This relationship finds particular expression in the competitive sporting world. Within feminist literature the importance of men's power has been defined primarily in terms of economic, social and political power. However, the research highlights the need to define a politics of *physical* power with the physical as a central construct.

The recognition that ideologies of the physical contribute to the definition of woman-as-object and reinforce women's physical subordination both at the overt level of physical violence and confrontation and at the more subtle level of self-confidence, bodily awareness and the stereotyping of women as weak and passive, should underpin all analyses of gender power relations. [...] By focusing on an aspect of social practice which is concerned with the body and physical activity, biological explanations for the totality of gender differences can be challenged effectively. As noted in the research, one of the reasons sport and physical education have been neglected by feminist analyses is that research that focuses on the body and physical action is assumed to be rather too close to biology for comfort! [...] The research, clearly related to 'women's bodies' and women's physicality, stresses the need to move away from analysis which focuses on assumed 'differences' and to recognize how social practice can easily be reduced to biology by emphasizing and naturalizing difference. The interviews demonstrate the strength of ideologies of biology which find expression in and are conveyed via the teaching of girls' physical education.

2 Sexuality   An analysis of gender must include sexuality as a central concern. What is apparent is that the construction of an 'ideal' heterosexuality is a crucial aspect of the structuring of gender relations. Physical education is a major influence in the process of sexualizing young women as heterosexual 'objects'. This finds expression in the persistent concentration on appearance, clothing, specific behaviour and desirable body shape which, taken together, contribute to the reinforcement of 'feminine' heterosexual appeal. 'Sexuality' for girls and young women does not develop in isolation; it is a social construction with male heterosexuality of central significance in its formation. As Bob Connell (1987) argues, 'emphasized femininity' is the response to the dominance of 'hegemonic masculinity'. Girls' physical education is shown to be part of the social process whereby girls and young women, during the period of adolescence, are encouraged to develop an 'acceptable' feminine sexuality organized around heterosexual appeal, desire, objectivity and subordination. This is not a simplistic, over-determined process readily received and incorporated into the lives, experiences and behaviours of all young women. These structures and relations of gender power are by no means totally determining but are complex and also produce strategies of resistance and negotiation in girls and young women. It remains important, however, to identify the structural relations of gender within social institutions and practice. Girls' physical education contributes significantly to the maintenance and reinforcement of a subordinate 'feminine' sexuality and as a consequence feminist analyses of schooling should recognize girls' physical education as potentially a most significant site for the building and maintenance of gender and sexuality.

The body and sexuality are not related simply through biology but through the social construction and use of the female body as a sexual object, be it an object of 'desire' or an object of reproduction (O'Brien, 1981). Adolescence is a vital period in the lives of young women. Physical and biological changes have a profound and social significance. At this stage of physical development and sexual maturation women's bodies become public property, developed for and controlled by others. In many spheres women's bodies are on show, open to comment and abuse. The body moves to public ownership and control which for many young women creates private anguish. The conflict for young women at this stage is immense. Unless they conform to 'ideal' femininity in relation to appearance and presentation of self, they are open to verbal abuse and their sexuality becomes questioned and scrutinized. Physical education provides a situation where 'the body' is on show and therefore at its most vulnerable. This is evident in the recognition by women teachers that many young women have to face comment and abuse in mixed settings such as swimming galas and athletic meetings. However, this 'public possession' of, or public control over, women's bodies is not a 'natural' development—a biological inevitability. It is part of hegemonic masculinity whereby men can gain and maintain control over women, not only in relation to their sexuality, but also in relation to the use of social space. Physical education in secondary schools must be made conscious of this conflict for young women and recognize how it contributes to the maintenance of hegemonic masculinity. It is not necessarily a conscious reinforcement but through the language used by teachers and the organization of physical education (content, kit, changing rooms, etc.) the conflict betwen body image and ideal femininity is emphasized.

3 Division of labour An analysis of gender and girls' physical education should also consider the relationship between schooling and other social institutions. It is clear from the research that female teachers and female pupils are influenced considerably by family relations. The sexual division of labour within families whereby women, as wives, mothers and daughters, bear the major responsibility for both domestic work and child-care, was identified as having major implications for teachers and pupils in physical education (e.g. opportunities to participate, extra-curricular programme, teacher career structures, and so on). [. . .] In girls' physical education, despite being a subject exclusively female in its teaching and practice, the relative financing of male and female departments is also significant. The research shows that where the female and male departments coexist in a mixed school, there is often gender differentiation both in terms of salary scales and status. Even though girls' physical education has its own history and cultural context, it is usually the male department which retains and wields the economic power. Where there are two distinct departments in a school, the holding of economic status and power by the male departments often has implications for the future development of the female department. The research highlights the need to consider carefully the staffing implications of initiatives such as mixed physical education where economic power and status are likely to move increasingly into the male physical education world.

[. . .] There is also a need to understand the *sexual division of leisure*, particularly in the transition from school to leisure where future oppor-tunities and leisure experiences are concerned. The research shows girls' physical education contributes to a gendered leisure and sports experience for women. Clearly gender divisions in leisure are not solely dependent on girls' experiences at school but their physical education experiences are a significant part of their reproduction. It is interesting to note that for girls this is often a negative experience, whereas it tends to be positive for boys. In constituting a critical analysis of leisure, other institutional contexts are significant (i.e. family, sport, etc.) but it is clear that girls' physical education is central to the development of these complex and interrelated determinants.

Consideration of the 'division of labour' and the 'division of leisure' emphasizes the need to theorize the complex relationship between gender and class. Although the research is concerned primarily with gender and girls' physical education the class location of schools, teachers and pupils emerges as significant. Throughout the research the impact of class on the experiences of both women teachers and female pupils was evident. The inadequacy of analyses which concentrate solely on class, incorporating gender as a secondary determining structure, or which point to the universality of patriarchy and relegate class to the periphery, is confirmed in this research. Certainly hegemonic masculinity and sexuality have been discussed and shown to be important, regardless of class location. It is important to stress, however, that gender, through ideologies of femininity and the materiality of masculine power, is not static, pre-given and experienced as a common, universal form. While gender both constructs and is reinforced by girls' physical education it is constantly cross-cut by class location and it is dependent on specific contexts for its expression and influence. This con-clusion is closest to feminist analyses which identify capitalism and patriarchy as comprehensive social systems which interact, and are most usefully defined as constituting a capitalist patriarchy (Eisenstein, 1984). While this brings the theoretical understanding of the complex interaction of class and gender no nearer, it contributes research evidence to the proposition that an analysis focusing on an understanding of capitalist patriarchy provides the potential for a more adequate, coherent and comprehensive theory of social rela-tions. [...]

While the research illuminates the need for an integrated analysis of gender and class, the neglect of race throughout the research has become apparent. Again, the research shows that the analysis of gender, within a schooling system which is a predominantly white, middle-class, male institution, must attempt to theorize the inter-connections between gender, race and class. Black feminists (hooks, 1980; Carby, 1982; Amos and Parmar, 1984) have correctly identified the ethnocentrism of much feminist analysis and research. The research project began with a concern to explore the relationship of gender and girls' physical education but it concludes that race and institutionalized racism needs to be incorporated into future work in this area. Certainly the research shows how aspects of gender cut across race divisions and are experienced by all girls and young women. [...] One outcome of this research is the recommendation that there needs to be future work which considers the experiences of black young women particularly in relation to the teaching of girls' physical education.

The historical context of contemporary debate

In discussing sport in North America, Helen Lenskyj (1986) comments:

> Medical professionals played a major role in determining those sports and levels of participation that were safe for female anatomy and physiology. Not coincidentally, these activities were seen to enhance femininity, a socially constructed and historically specific concept encompassing personality, appearance and comportment. Acceptable

activities promoted the physical and the psychological characteristics that males, as the appropriate dominant sex, pronounced appropriate and appealing for females: general and productive health, heterosexual attractiveness, passivity and conformity. *On all these issues, physical educators*, sports administrators, journalists and the general public *treated medical opinion as the voice of reason and authority.*

(Lenskyj, 1986, p. 139, emphases added)

Similar influences can be identified in the development of girls' physical education in nineteenth-century Britain. The roots and underpinnings of this female subject, as noted, are centred on male medical opinion which was conveyed and institutionalized as ideologies concerned with girls' physical ability/capacity, motherhood/domesticity and sexuality. It is important to situate contemporary analysis within its historical contexts in order to recognize that 'structure is not pre-given but historically composed' (Connell, 1987, p. 63). An historical analysis contributes to a fuller understanding of gender and girls' physical education, because it demonstrates that 'femininity', while continually present and central, is not a fixed or an immutable category. The identification of gender in girls' physical education in the 1980s and 1990s cannot be interpreted as identical to that which emerges from historical accounts. Femininity is not to be equated with some transcendent biological category of being a woman but is both socially constructed and historically specific.

However, by identifying the influence of male professionals and the strengths of ideologies of gender on the development of girls' physical education, it becomes possible to understand the part played by this subject in the institutionalization of gender rather than understanding gender as simply the manifestation of attitudes and ideas held by unenlightened individuals. Thus historical evidence gives weight to the argument that a structural analysis of gender and girls' physical education is crucial while identifying where change and negotiation can and does take place.

Cultural responses and resistances

[. . .] Although gender can be shown to be reproduced through the institution of girls' physical education, structured by a hegemonic masculinity, this is not the whole story. The research also highlights aspects of girls' physical education which involve resistance and negotiation to the structures of gender. All girls do not accept passively the definitions of femininity which place them in a weaker and physically subordinate position. Teachers are not all passive agents within a process of cultural reproduction. In their responses and practices some women staff negotiate gender stereotypes and encourage girls to develop and challenge 'femininity'. Girls resist some of the institutionalized definitions and practices of girls' physical education which relate to femininity (appearance, suitable 'ladylike' behaviour, and so on). [. . .] While the research identifies the power and influence of hegemonic masculinity over girls' physical education which maintains, reinforces and reproduces femininity, it also demonstrates the potential of resistance and challenge. It is with this potential that the foundation of transforming girls' physical education and the social relations of gender can be laid.

FUTURE POLICY, FUTURE DIRECTIONS

Many strategies for increased participation and interest adopted in girls' physical education are based on their potential appeal to young women (e.g. health and beauty, keep fit). Inevitably such strategies reinforce the culture of femininity, locking girls' physical education within an 'emphasized femininity'. However, the research also shows that girls' physical education has the potential to develop policies and directions which could transform physical education and provide a platform for building resistance to the culture of femininity. The case studies highlighted the autonomy of physical education within the overall school system. Physical education departments are usually situated away from the rest of the school, the heads of department have authority over the curriculum and, in most instances, the teaching is carried out in a private sphere unfettered by the restrictions of examinations or the critical eyes of school hierarchies. Thus girls' physical education has the potential for change even within a schooling system which is becoming more rigidly defined by central government interventions and the National Curriculum. [. . .]

Two main approaches have emerged as challenges to sexism and gender differentiation in schools: an equal opportunities approach, concentrating on equality of access to all educational benefits (girl-friendly); and an anti-sexist approach concentrating on girl-centred education with its main objective being the relationship between patriarchy, power and women's subordination (Weiner, 1985). The 'equal opportunities' approach encompasses initiatives in girls' physical education which emphasize equal access to facilities, activities and curricular/extra-curricular time. Co-educational grouping is one organizational change which is increasingly being developed in order to ensure equality of access. As pointed out in the discussion of mixed physical education initiatives, there are problems with strategies based on equal access which fail to question the structures and power relations of the institution to which equal access is sought. 'Equal opportunities' initiatives stem from a liberal feminist perspective on gender and schooling. Gaby Weiner (1985) articulates the main criticism of this approach:

> Expanding equal opportunities is not just a question of juggling resources or rearranging option choices . . . To liberalize access to an inadequate system may be acceptable in the short term but for more permanent change a major restructuring of all social institutions, including schools is needed.   (Weiner, 1985, p. 10)

However, it is important to acknowledge that some 'equal opportunities' initiatives, introduced by teachers committed to reform, represent an important political response to generations of limitations imposed on young women in all aspects of school and related activities.

Pessimism in the face of structural and institutional inequalities provides no route towards change. Although this research firmly establishes that a feminist analysis of gender and girls' physical education must be situated within a structural analysis of capitalist patriarchy it acknowledges the usefulness of some short-term strategic reforms. Indeed, unlike Gaby Weiner (1985), who draws clear-cut boundaries between the inadequate equal opportunities approach and the more long-term radical anti-sexist strategies, this research recommends that strategic gains can be made in both areas. The important issue is that policy does not remain locked into an equal opportunities approach but must work towards a more radical restructuring of girls' physical education in order to attempt to transform the power bases of gender identified throughout the research. This challenge is not a straightforward task. The powerless can attempt to appropriate their rightful situation but for the powerful to relinquish their position demands considerable material change. As Bob Connell (1987) recognizes:

> In a gender order where men are advantaged and women are disadvantaged, major structural reform is, on the face of it, against men's interests.
> (Connell, 1987, p. 285)

Further, although this research and its recommendations are concerned with gender and girls' physical education, a more integrated strategy for change must also be recognized. [...] The complexities of the interrelationship between gender, class and race are essential to the analysis, and changes in the structure of gender relations should be concerned with structural inequalities of race and class. Consequently the connections between and across institutions and strategies for institutional change should be analysed and developed.

Progressive initiatives in girls' physical education must be made with the awareness of the need for long-term fundamental changes in the structures of the family, the labour process, sport, leisure, and so on. At first sight this appears to be a substantial and unattainable objective. The importance of inter-institutional links, however, points towards more positive directions. There is considerable evidence to demonstrate that young and adult women's experience are not totally determined by structural inequalities. Since the early 1970s there has been a substantial shift, through the development of new directions, in the reconstruction of women's sexuality and consciousness. These include the development of self-help groups in medical care and mental health; the emergence of well-woman clinics and other all-women projects geared to giving women more control over their own health and bodies. Women's groups have developed, resisting male violence through rape crisis centres, women's refuges and counselling. Within education new initiatives, such as 'new opportunity for women' courses, 'outreach' projects and women's writing groups, have emerged and have encouraged women to gain confidence and assertiveness in intellectual situations. The availability of self-defence and assertiveness training and women's fitness programmes, geared to developing health, strength and physical well-being, rather than the stereotypical construction of 'femininity' around appearance and body physique, gives women greater control over their physicality. These latter developments indicate a qualitative shift in definitions of the 'physical'. Women in these programmes are reclaiming the right to physical development and appearance on their own terms rather than on the terms laid down in the traditions of 'feminine culture', learned and reinforced in youth and, as this research shows, in their physical education experiences at school. [. . .]

The historical analysis shows that girls' physical education and women's sport in the nineteenth century contributed positively to a redefinition of women's femininity and, in particular, women's physical potential. While this remained within the clear boundaries of 'acceptable' behaviour, women's struggles in the twentieth century have shown that women can challenge inequalities at all levels. Girls' physical education has the real potential to challenge contemporary patriarchal definitions of women's submissiveness, passivity and dependence. While this is not straightforward the following recommendations provide a foundation for future policy directions. These recommendations are not ranked but should be interpreted as the basis for constructive moves to a more critical and radical feminist form of physical education teaching:

- girl-centred organization
- female-only space
- collectivity and confidence
- physicality: muscles, strength and physical power
- consciousness-raising
- future research.

Girl-centred organization

The earlier discussion of co-educational grouping indicates that girl-centred organization should be retained. This raises the problem of retaining boy-centred organization in male physical education and its attendant implications. In the short term, however, girls require both the space and the time to develop their potential. In some instances this could involve the retention of a single-sex programme as the norm throughout the secondary school with selective periods of mixed teaching, if appropriate, for specific activities. It is crucial that the politics of gender and sexuality are understood by the staff involved in mixed activity sessions. With sensitive, understanding teaching, which may require positive intervention and leadership, mixed grouping can provide the forum for increased pupil awareness of gender issues and also can challenge existing gender expectations and inequalities.

If single-sex grouping remains the long-term goal, then the future is bleak for a comprehensive overthrow of gender inequalities. Yet there needs to be a short-term strategy to ensure girls receive opportunities, time, space and understanding to redress the traditional base of gender imbalance.

Female-only space

This is linked directly to the arguments made for girl-centred organization. For it is not only the formal organization of single-sex grouping which must be retained but also the provision of informal female-only space. Girls and young women need space to develop their confidence and realize their interests and to be in control of that social space. In co-educational schools the evidence shows that boys and men dominate space, physically and verbally, in all social situations (Young, 1980; Spender, 1982). In both co-educational and single-sex schools the main female-only space is in the toilets, the cloakrooms and the changing rooms. These are the areas where young women 'hang out', where they spend time together away from 'the lads' and/or the teachers. It would be a positive move for women physical education teachers to recognize the need for young women to have their own space for conversation, making plans or simply 'having a laugh'. Clearly this poses problems for school organization and the enforcement of school rules and regulations. However, it can be a positive move to open up changing rooms and facilities during breaks, lunch-time and after school, to provide open access to extra-curricular time and to encourage girls and young women to use the space available for their 'leisure' whether it be 'formally' for netball and table tennis or 'informally' for chatting with a friend. Too often young women's access to the physical education wing is restricted solely to participation in organized, formal activities. It would be a significant development to enable young women to develop greater control over their extra-curricular activities and therefore provide the space for meeting and socializing without interference from boys or teachers. A further symbolic—and practical—policy change would be to allow girls effective choice concerning clothes worn for physical education. The research shows that formal kit or uniform remains the norm. While there are arguments for and against school uniform it is clear that, within specific safety guidelines, adolescent girls should be able to determine appropriate clothes for physical activity. The earlier discusssion argued that from puberty girls come to experience their bodies as 'public property'—defined, compared, criticized and often degraded. Within physical education especially, given the contexts of movement, girls need to have effective control over the 'presentation' of their physicality in dress and style. Consequently, teachers need to develop a greater sensitivity to and awareness of the pressures on young women regarding body shape and appearance. Young women's bodies are on display during physical activity and physical education teachers must realize the ease with which they can contribute to the alienation of young women with regard to their bodies.

Collectivity and confidence

Physical education is in an ideal situation to offer young women opportunities for collective support through co-operative and enjoyable physical activity. While the relationship between teacher and student inevitably will reflect an institutionalized power relationship based on age and status, young women can be encouraged to work closely together, and with their teachers, through activities such as dance, outdoor pursuits and self-defence. Many boys and young men thrive on their collective 'rugby club' experiences. Indeed hegemonic masculinity is sustained and reinforced by male collective experiences. Young women also need the space for collective physical experience while rejecting and challenging the competitive 'macho' values of the male sporting ethos. [...] Physical education can contribute to developing a sense of solidarity between young women, thus defining a female-based construct of confidence and motivation. In many ways the 'movement' approach of girls' physical education prevalent in the 1960s and 1970s, and to some extent perpetuated in schools today, has emphasized these qualities. Where it has failed, however, is in its tendency to reinforce gender stereotypes and to emphasize gender divisions while encouraging a level of co-operation and a sense of community.

What is clear is that equal access to the contemporary sporting world would involve access to male-defined dominant, aggressive institutions. [...] Sport in British society is dominated by competition, commercialism, sponsorship and professionalism. Revolutionary change would be required even to begin to challenge a sporting world predominantly controlled and defined by men and situated within a capitalist economic structure. Yet change within sports institutions has to be a long-term objective for feminist struggle, given that sport directly reinforces and reproduces hegemonic masculinity. Part of this long-term struggle must come from physical education within the schools, at both primary and secondary levels. Changes in sport institutions will not come from policy introduced from the 'top' or dominant hierarchies involved in sport. As Celia Brackenridge and Anita White (1985) have shown, sport is owned, controlled and organized by white middle-class men. Sport can be redefined only if those involved in sport at this level begin this process of redefinition. Paul Willis (1982) reflects this position:

> A sport could be presented as a form of activity which emphasizes human similarity and not dissimilarity, a form of activity which expresses values which are indeed immeasurable, a form of activity which is concerned with individual well-being and satisfaction rather than with comparison.
> (Willis, 1982, p. 14)

Within physical education it should be a priority to consider alternative forms of sport which, in the long term, will not only encourage different values but also encourage girls and boys, and eventually women and men, to enjoy sport on equal terms. This may mean that educators and those involved in sport need to develop new games and activities and take seriously sports such as handball and korfball (a cross between netball and basketball developed in Holland, with eight a side—four men and four women) as activities appropriate to both girls and boys. Although physical education is not synonymous with sport, sport remains the emphasis within the curriculum. This emphasis will remain, particularly if physical education continues to be identified as preparation for future leisure activities. If girls' physical education is not going to simply reinforce the gender divisions of leisure and sport in society then it must begin to question what it is preparing for and how it can begin the process of challenge and redefinition.

Physicality: muscles, strength and physical power

The research highlights the need to locate physicality and physical power relations as central to the analysis of gender relations. Therefore the development of individual potential in physical strength and power for girls must be a primary objective of girls' physical education. This requires effective challenges to the ideology of the physical, so that girls can develop confidence and assertiveness and, ultimately, greater control over their bodies. The most obvious recommendation is the inclusion of self-defence as an essential core element of teaching. Just as adult women are claiming the right to control and develop their own bodies for intrinsic satisfaction rather than sexual exploitation, so physical education must emphasize these values for young women. They must be encouraged to enjoy physical movement, to develop strength and muscular potential; to work together to discover body awareness and confidence. As Helen Lenskyj (1982) states, women tend to be alienated from their bodies and unaware of their physical potential. Girls' physical education should move away from stereotypical expectations of girls' physical potential and look to new directions which can motivate young women to be active, fit and physically developed. This might mean the development and introduction of 'new' sports and/or the development of new teaching approaches to the traditional games. The practical implications are difficult to determine and will require considerable action research in the schools.

[...] Girls and young women need to be encouraged to see the positive arguments concerning the development of physical strength and to challenge their construction as the passive recipients of male aggression and strength. 'Women fighting back' is an important slogan in the struggle to gain equality between the sexes. Part of this 'fight back' must be the realization that women too can be 'strong and resilient, capable of hard work and hard play' (Lenskyj, 1982). As Helen Lenskyj argues, in a development of her work:

> Women's increasing participation in fitness-related activities, from dance exercise to body building, is potentially liberating. To feel at ease with one's body and to be aware of its strengths and weaknesses is to know oneself better. Moreover, the sense of achievement derived from physical

fitness gains encourages women to tackle either physical or mental
challenges.   (Lenskyj, 1986, p. 137)

[...]

Consciousness-raising

In order to achieve the first four recommendations of this research, teachers,
advisers and pupils need to develop an awareness of the significance of these
issues. [...] But Rosemary Deem (1986) emphasizes, in relation to policy
implementation, teachers must admit first that there is a problem before
they can or will question their practice. Pratt (1985) found that in general
physical education teachers remain unsympathetic to the notion of equal
opportunities between girls and boys in school. Yet teacher commitment
is necessary for change to be implemented. It is vital, therefore, that gender
is discussed and action initiated at advisory level, in teacher education and in
in-service training. Initially the setting up of teacher support groups for those
teachers with a personal commitment to anti-sexist strategies within physical
education would be a positive move for those isolated at work in sceptical, and
even hostile, environments. Within schools, physical education can contribute
to the creation of a positive 'female' atmosphere by the use of photographs
and displays in the teaching areas. The research found in many schools either a
lack of display material or the inappropriate use of posters exhibiting typically
male sporting 'heroes'. There should be positive images of women which challenge the stereotyped ideas of women in relation to appearance, body image,
shape and dress and which encourage young women's participation in, and
enjoyment of, physical activity.

Related to this is the need to promote active teacher—pupil discussion about
the main issues of 'physicality' and 'sexuality'. Adolescent young women
require encouragement in addressing these issues within a broader political
framework. If physical 'education' is to move beyond its rigid traditions then
it must tackle directly issues contextualized within the politics of sexuality
and the structure of gender divisions. This confirms the priority of situating
physical education within broader structural relations not only theoretically
but also at a practical level with the pupils. There must be an awareness that
social relations outside the school (e.g. in the family) directly influence gender
in the school. Pupils need to be aware and question who it is who supports
their physical education by providing them with clean kit and, indeed, what
the reality is and where the responsibility lies, for out-of-school and post-
school sport and leisure opportunities for young women. These issues need to
be addressed not only formally in physical education time but also constantly
in the informal contacts between staff and pupils.

Future research

Boys, masculinity and physical education   If gender divisions are to be challenged then there must be concern for the physical education of both girls and boys. There is a need for research which looks at the relationship between boys' physical education and the reinforcement, production and reproduction of hegemonic masculinity. If girls' physical education reproduces an ideology of the physical which constructs young women as physically subordinate to men then there is a need to consider the proposition that male physical education reproduces an ideology of the physical which underpins a culture of masculinity emphasizing strength, toughness, competitiveness and physical domination. Without identifying and challenging the dynamics of gender in the schooling of boys, male–female power relations cannot change.

Towards an analysis of race, class and gender   There is a need for future research to concentrate on the relationship between race, class and gender within physical education. There is a lack of research into race and sport or leisure although race and schooling is a developing area. Future research into physical education should centre its analysis on an understanding of race, racism and physical education teaching.

Pupils' perceptions and expectations   There is a need for more in-depth cultural research which would provide analyses of pupils' perceptions and expectations about gender and physical education. At present the emphasis has been on teachers and it needs to shift to consider pupils' attitudes and ideas.

Initial training and in-service training   This area is recognized as of crucial importance for future policy initiatives. Future research needs to assess the impact of current debates about gender on both physical education initial and in-service courses. This research is necessary in order to identify the gaps and weaknesses in these areas, assess current projects, courses and intiatives relating to gender and point towards future directions.

Sport, leisure, family and the division of labour   More research concerned with the relationships between institutions needs to develop in order to provide a fuller analysis of gender, race and class. Research, for example, which looks at the connections between the family and physical education experiences and teachings, the relationship between physical education and future leisure and sport activities.

Primary school physical education and gender   Throughout the research it became clear that the teaching of secondary school physical education is heavily dependent on the primary school curriculum. There needs to be in-depth qualitative research which questions both girls' and boys' experiences of physical education at primary school level, and a structural analysis of primary school physical education looking at the primary school curriculum and teaching in relation to gender, class and race.

The National Curriculum, gender and physical education   The 1990s is a time of considerable change in the structure of secondary schooling and research is necessary to consider the implications of the National Curriculum for the future physical education of both girls and boys. In particular, it will be important to monitor the impact of the National Curriculum on equal opportunity policies and initiatives (Flintoff, 1990).

[...] Gender relations cannot be altered fundamentally by women alone. It is for men also to take up the challenge, both in physical education and in wider society, for any future radical restructuring of gender relations to take place. However, this research demonstrates that feminist analyses of schooling must always include a full consideration of the complex relations between gender and physical education. Physical education *is* in a position to initiate change which could influence not only those teachers and pupils directly involved in feminist innovations but also, in the long term, to a redefinition of gender. There is a need for feminist analyses and approaches to physical education in order to inform policy and contribute to a fuller understanding of gender relations in society. M. Ann Hall (1985) points out that:

> nowhere is there a recognition among feminist theorists/scholars as to the fact that sport plays a considerable role in the reproduction of a specifically patriarchal social order and could, therefore, be significant in the transformation of that order. At the very least it can provide a site of resistance. Let us get on with the analysis and historical work necessary. By doing so we will be making an important contribution to some essential thinking about the sociology of sport—as well as to feminist theory.
>
> (Hall, 1985, p. 40)

M. Ann Hall's concern for the sociology of sport needs to be extended to a critical analysis of physical education. For the future it is important that critical work in physical education is maintained and extended to ensure that not only girls and young women but also boys and young men receive a *physical* education that is sensitive to, aware of and prepared to challenge gender inequalities.

References

Amos, V. and Parmar, P. (1984) Challenging imperial feminism. *Feminist Review* 17, 3–20.

Brackenridge, C. and White, A. (1985) Who rules sport? *International Review of the Sociology of Sport* 20 (1/2), 95–107.

Carby, H.V. (1982) White women listen! Black feminism and the boundaries of sisterhood. In Centre for Contemporary Cultural Studies (ed.) *The Empire Strikes Back*. London: Hutchinson.

Connell, R.W. (1983) *Which Way is Up? Essays on Class, Sex and Culture.* Sydney: Allen and Unwin.

— (1987) *Gender and Power.* Cambridge: Polity.

Deem, R. (1986). Bringing gender equality into schools. In S. Walker and J. Barton (eds) *Changing Policies, Changing Teachers.* Milton Keynes: Open University Press.

Eisenstein, H. (1984) *Contemporary Feminist Thought.* London: Counterpoint.

Flintoff, A. (1990) Physical education, equal opportunities and the National Curriculum: Crisis or challenge. *PE Review* 13 (2), 85–100.

Hall, M.A. (1985) How should we theorize sport in a capitalist patriarchy? *International Review of Sociology of Sport* 20, 109–15.

hooks, b. (1982) *Ain't I a Woman? Black Women and Feminism.* London: Pluto Press.

Lenskyj, H. (1982) I am strong. *University of Toronto, Women's News Magazine* March–April, 13.

— (1986) *Out of Bounds: Women, Sport and Sexuality.* Toronto: Women's Press.

O'Brien, M. (1981) *The Politics of Reproduction.* London: Routledge and Kegan Paul.

Pratt, J. (1985) The attitudes of teachers. In J. Whyte, R. Deem, L. Kant and M. Cruikshank (eds) *Girl-Friendly Schooling.* London: Methuen.

Spender, D. (1982) *Invisible Women.* London: Writers and Readers Co-operative.

Weiner, G. (ed.) (1985) *Just a Bunch of Girls: Feminist Approaches to Schooling.* Milton Keynes: Open University Press.

Willis, P. (1982) Women in sport in ideology. In J.A. Hargreaves (ed.) *Sport, Culture and Ideology.* London: Routledge and Kegan Paul.

Young, I. (1980) Throwing like a girl. *Human Studies* 3, 7–13.

Part 2: Curriculum and Classroom Practice

6 LIFE IN THE CLASSROOM

HEIDI SAFIA MIRZA

Of the many theoretical perspectives that have contributed to the debate on the nature of the educational experience, two ideological camps are distinguishable. On the one hand there are those that emphasise the institutional level, the structure, operation and functions of schooling: on the other, there are those that find analysis at the personal interactive level more important. These theorists, who emphasize the inner workings of the classroom, focus in particular on the relationships between teacher and pupil.

Attempts to describe the black educational experience have been characterized, in the main, by research designs ideologically disposed towards the latter perspective, with early studies investigating the causes and effects of negative black self-esteem (Milner, 1975, 1983; Coard, 1971). Employing the notion of the self-fulfilling prophecy and the mechanism of labelling, these studies focused on the effect a teacher might have on a pupil's self-image.

A central proposition of such research is that pupils tend to perform as well or as badly as their teachers expect. The teacher's prediction of a pupil's behaviour, it is suggested, is communicated to them, frequently in unintended ways, influencing the actual behaviour that follows. Thus it is only logical to assume that if teachers hold stereotyped opinions and expectations of black children, this may lead to different teaching techniques and classroom treatment which works to the detriment of these children's education. (See Stone, 1985).

[. . .] However, while the evidence presented in this article does suggest that teachers do have interpretative schemes upon which they make predictions concerning pupil ability, the findings of the following study do not uphold the notion of the self-fulfilling prophecy as a central explanation for black underachievement.

THE STUDY

[. . .]

The 62 young black women in the study, aged between 15 and 19 years, attended two comprehensive schools in south London. The girls and their black and white male and female peers, 198 in all, could objectively be identified as coming from working-class homes. They answered questionnaires, and were interviewed and observed in their homes and classrooms over a

Source: Abridged from Mirza, H. S. (1992) *Young, Female and Black* (chapter 4, pp. 1–3; 54–83). London: Routledge.

period of 18 months.

In each school a random sample was drawn from the fifth- and the sixth-form pupils. From St Hilda's, a co-educational Catholic school, 128 (65%) black and white male and female pupils were taken whereas 70 (35%) were taken from St Theresa's, a single-sex Church of England school. Of these 62 (31%) were African Caribbean young women; 13 (7%) were African Caribbean young men; 77 (39%) were 'other' young women; and 46 (23%) were 'other' young men.

The two schools were studied simultaneously; that is, I spent one day in one school and then the next day in the other. Depending on the time-table, some days I would spend half a day in one and the other half in the other. On other occasions I might spend several days at one school only.

General observations were made about the school, the daily regime, the headteacher's role, and so on. General staffroom observation was also undertaken, and school meetings were attended. Classroom observation constituted a major part of my time spent in the field. I attended many classes and lessons, in which my interest was not only to observe teacher–pupil interaction but other classroom situations. In particular, I was interested in curriculum content and teaching effectiveness.

[...]

THE PUPIL PERSPECTIVE: A CHALLENGE TO THE SELF-FULFILLING PROPHECY

There appeared to be two major reasons why the self-fulfilling prophecy failed to provide an adequate understanding of the observed classroom process. Firstly, there was nothing in the evidence to suggest that teachers were successful in eroding black female self-esteem. Secondly, the findings do not show that teachers transmitted their apparent negative expectations to the black pupils they teach. According to the logic of the self-fulfilling prophecy, these two aspects of the labelling process are fundamental to its successful operation.

There was no indication that young black women had negative feelings about being black or female. The girls greatly valued their cultural and racial identity. Of young black women, in answer to the question 'Who is the person you most admire?' 48% indicated that this person was herself.[1] Furthermore, when the qualities of the person each pupil indicated as the person they most admired were analyzed it was found that 55% of the black women had chosen a person who was black, as did 50% of the young black men. The young black women also frequently chose a female person as 'the person they most admired' (11% chose their mother, 5% a female relative, 9% a female historical figure).

There was also little evidence of young black females suffering psychological damage from being 'put down' as a consequence of their teachers' negative evaluations of them. Clearly the girls did not accept the negative evaluations of themselves and their academic abilities, as the following example shows. Ms Wallace, when describing a predominantly black fifth-year class designated as of 'low ability', said: 'These girls have absolutely no motivation. They feel you are here to think for them.' Yet these same girls said of their teachers: 'They hold you back. Teachers always put you down, then they say, "You can't manage." . . .' (Dianne: aged 16); 'When you come you sit a test and then after that they never give you a chance to prove yourself' (Tony: aged 16).

The young black women, when interviewed, were aware of their teachers' negative feelings towards them:

> You feel the discrimination, they try to hide it but you can see through it. They try to say, 'We're all equal', but you can tell: they talk to you more simply. (Maureen: aged 16)

Although the girls were resentful of these attitudes, there was little evidence that they were psychologically undermined by this differential treatment. On the contrary, the girls often challenged these assumptions about their ability and confronted the situation openly. [. . .] An outcome of this pupil awareness of negative teacher evaluations of them was that black children refuse to present their real selves in school. It was apparent that the black girls would avoid asking for help. The girls would only approach certain members of staff known to be compliant, or only participate keenly in certain lessons taught by such sympathetic teachers. They would also avoid choosing certain subjects if the teacher was recognized as being difficult. [. . .]

It was a fact that in many cases the girls' academic energies were often diverted to strategies aimed at avoiding unpleasant scenarios within the school environment, rather than in the activity of learning.

If the explanation for the way in which teachers affect pupil performance does not lie within an understanding of the notion of the self-fulfilling prophecy, the question remains as to how exactly does teacher–pupil interaction function to disadvantage the black child? The evidence seemed to suggest that the process of discrimination operated by means of the teachers' access to physical and material resources, restrictions to which would result in the curtailment of opportunities. Clearly teachers do have the power to effect changes and limit or enhance pupil opportunity. As an outcome of their power within the institutional infrastructure teachers are in a position to enforce their prejudices by restricting access to information and educational resources. The positive pupil perspective, which has been persistently overlooked in the trend to highlight black negative self-esteem, brings to the fore the importance of power and control in the classroom.

RACISM AND REACTION: A TEACHER TYPOLOGY

The findings of this study revealed many shades of teacher reaction to the race, gender and social class of their pupils (see also Mac an Ghaill, 1988). In the following pages I attempt to analyse some of the attitudinal charateristics I found among staff in the schools, and assess the outcome of their specific beliefs and values on the black female pupils in their classrooms. Five general teacher responses were identified. These were grouped as follows: (1) the 'Overt Racists', (2) the 'Christians', (3) the 'Crusaders', (4) the 'Liberal Chauvinists' and (5) the 'Black Teacher'.

(1) The 'Overt Racists'

As high a proportion as 33% of teachers interviewed in the study held what can only be described as overtly racist opinions. [...]

Examples of overt racist sentiment and practice were not always confined to isolated incidents or statements, but were often the consequence of long-standing, bitter feuds between certain members of staff and pupils, situations fuelled by racist action and pupil reaction.

Mr Davidson was a young history teacher who derived a definite pleasure from taunting the black pupils, particularly the boys. One black male pupil reported the following incident, apparently one of many, in confidence:

> Mr Davidson called me a wog. Me and my friend we turned round and saw Davidson looking at us and then he said get inside. He also said, 'Don't drop peanuts or coconuts on the floor', the peanuts belonged to a white boy behind him. But Davidson said nothing to him. After school he kept me and some other black kids. *(sic)*
>
> (Davis: aged 16: aspiration, armed forces)

[...] He also claimed, in his capacity as history teacher, that:

> African history is so boring ... I had to do it at college, it was part of the course. Old civilizations are boring and the discussion of slavery is monotonous in school teaching ... it has no bearing on anything.

[...] While Davidson's racist behaviour was more overt than that displayed by others, incidents of overt racism were by no means an exceptional occurrence. Many members of staff deeply resented the presence of black pupils in their school and often articulated this point of view.

Ms Bland, an Art teacher for many years, explained how she felt about her black pupils:

> I'm fed up with them. Everyone is fed up ... only they won't say it. They are so loud and inconsiderate. ... They are always talking about being black, chip on the shoulder, haven't met one who hasn't. ... Why can't people be people. Everyone's so over-sensitive nowadays!

[...]

Sister Margarita, a nun and first-year head at St Hilda's, had a reputation both in the school and in the wider community (young mothers at the local youth centre made a reference to her attitude), for not only being a difficult and often unpleasant, humourless, person (she was *very* strict), but also, as one colleague called her, 'a bit of a bigot'. Her particular attitude was one that was characterized by ignorance and intolerance, as the following incidents illustrate.

Sister Margarita was called to interview some prospective parents to the school. However, the school secretary delivering the message that they were on their way up, also whispered to her that they were 'black'. Sister Margarita immediately became agitated and said to the secretary. 'I'm busy, tell them to wait'. Eventually, after some time, she did go. However, when she returned she exclaimed suprised, to several colleagues, 'Do you know he was a doctor ... a black doctor!' Sister Margarita's limited racist perceptions had, in this instance, received a jolt.

[...]

The existence of several studies that have also found overt forms of racism prevalent among teachers in schools suggest that the presence of this form of racism is more widespread than is often recognized (DES, 1985: Wright, 1986, 1987; Mac an Ghaill, 1988; Gillborn, 1990). Apart from the situations mentioned so far, the passing of references to assumed inherent characteristics of black students was often to be heard in the staffroom and openly stated to me. For example, one pleasant and helpful young male teacher (he was doing an MA in Education) warned, 'You have to watch them (that is, black girls), they can be sly.' Another explained, 'They are angry and frustrated with their lot, and can get very hostile when they get into a group.'

[...] People do make, and find it necessary to make, generalizations about people from limited information in everyday life. However, the type of assumptions being made by certain members of staff about black pupils were clearly negative and thus had consequences for the black student.

(2) 'The Christians'

The 'Christians' were a distinct group who lived up to their name. These teachers were identifiable by their capacity for compassion towards and conviction about the equality of their black brothers and sisters.[2] The particular concept of equality employed by the 'Christians' led to a consensus that, in general, characterized this attitude: that is, the 'colour-blind' approach to the education of the black child. What guided this approach was the philosophy that 'We are all the same ... there are no differences, *and there are no problems':* a celebration of 'sameness'. As one teacher pointed out, 'We see them as pupils first, not if they are black or white.'

The following extract from St Hilda's school newsletter, written by the headmaster, Mr Madden, exemplifies this 'Christian' orientation to the black presence in British schools.[3] He writes:

Headmaster's letter to Parents: Spring Mid-Term 1984
    Dear parents,
    Multi-Ethnic Education
    I am convinced that you, like me, wonder what this is all about? What are these words, ethnic, racialism, discrimination, minorities, equal opportunities, the British Movement and the National Front, etc. etc. and etc.? White parents and black parents pride themselves on treating all children, whatever the colour, in the fairest way possible. After all we are all Catholic men and women and we all know the story of the Good Samaritan in the Gospels where the foreign visitor took great care of his enemy, the badly injured Jewish traveller ... I could go on extolling our virtues but it would be incorrect.
    Today in our schools, in our neighbourhood, in the place where we work, in the pubs, discotheques and everywhere we go, we will have children and adults who are not white and who may have different ideas about many different aspects of life, etc. to which they are fully entitled.
    I think the general attitude from white people at best is to tolerate them and their differences although we really like charming French accents or chic Italian-style shoes. To be honest with ourselves we haven't really tried to come to terms with these black children and adults and all you have to do is to look around the school or perhaps look at the number of black teenagers who are unemployed ...

This extract illustrates not only the 'well-intentioned' nature of this ideological perspective, but it also highlights the gulf of experience that exists between the white staff and the black pupil: a 'them-and-us' situation mediated by the belief in tolerance and understanding as a solution to the endemic problem of racial discrimination.

What gave this particular 'Christian' orientation its negative impact was the reaction it engendered from the teachers to any form of positive action that aimed to redress racial discrimination. At St Hilda's, for example, the setting-up of a Multi-Racial Working Party[4] was objected to on the grounds of a general consensus that all pupils were treated equally in the school and that therefore there was no racial discrimination, in spite of evidence to the contrary.

    [...]

There was a strong belief that racism was not present in the school nor was cultural diversity an issue they needed to address, as several of the staff explained:

I really don't think we are affected as other schools. We are all Christians here. That is our culture, and our way of life, black and white, I really can't see that there has been a spread of any other different culture.

(Ms Cole: Religious and General Studies teacher)

[...]

There was also a strong feeling among the staff that they did not need to be told how to conduct their internal affairs, not only because that was tantamount to interference, but also, as one teacher explained, because it could lead to problems when, as they agreed, there were none:

By talking about racism, making it an issue, coloured pupils can get aggressive. I've seen it at St Joan's ... the atmosphere is so tense. You feel threatened just going in there. Teachers have been attacked there, terrorized, I've heard. I don't want that here, not here. We have a happy and healthy atmosphere here.

(Ms Cole: Religious and General Studies teacher)

[...]

Furthermore, the unwillingness to take a strong stand on educational issues concerning the black child for fear of 'rocking the boat', a basic characteristic of the 'Christian' attitude, had the effect of both misleading and misinfoming black parents about the progress of their children, as the following example illustrates, Marion's mother had been under the impression that her daughter's progress at school was satisfactory. Marion's reports all indicated that she was working well—'Progress good' was what was written in the annual reports. Ms Dale, Marion's mother, was therefore very surprised when she was called to the school for a formal meeting to discuss Marion's poor levels of attainment.

I thought she doing OK. They said she doing good, and doing good is doing good, not so? But now the teacher say I must understand that doing good is a relative thing. Marion was doing good for Marion, not just doing good.

Ms Dale felt that she had been misled about her daughter's progress, because, as it transpired, the teacher concerned did not want to disappoint her black pupil. The effect of this teacher's 'kindness' was not only upsetting for both Marion and her parents, it was also detrimental to her long-term progress. Marion was unprepared for her exams and eventually had to give up two subjects in order that she might be able to cope with the rest of her work.

[...]

The evidence was clear, the 'Christian' approach, despite its benevolent and passive characteristics, can have negative consequences for black pupils. By adopting a 'colour-blind' perspective, the staff and the schools concerned created an atmosphere where ignorance and fear remained unchallenged. Any reference to colour was, among the 'Christians', an accepted taboo, as its very mention implied that there existed racial differences.

(3) The 'Crusaders'

In contrast to the 'Christians', the 'Crusaders' were prepared to acknowledge that racism was present within educational establishments. This group of teachers held strong beliefs that this racism among their colleagues and the pupils they taught should be challenged. [...]

The distinctive characteristics of the 'Crusaders' were their colour (white), their youth and their commitment to their cause. This latter aspect that in particular identified this group, the commitment to their cause, was characterized by a strategy that sought to 'educate' colleagues into the wrongs of the past and the injustices of the present. [...]

The experiences of Rachel Spencer, a young Drama teacher at St Hilda's, illustrates the frustration and futility of the often over-zealous and misguided anti-racist campaign that was the hallmark of the 'Crusaders'.

In accordance with the guidelines of the ILEA's directives on anti-racism (ILEA, 1983), Ms Spencer had been engaged for several months in the difficult (but voluntary) task of setting up a Multi-Racial Working Party in her school, St Hilda's. One day, totally exasperated with her struggle, she explained: We are *breaking* ILEA policy, actually going against it by not doing anything positive. We *must* do something.' She had come up against several obstacles in her attempts to establish the Working Party, not least because of the headmaster's own objections. His dissent was grounded in his feeling that the Working Party was an intrusion and a violation of the school's private affairs by an outside body, the ILEA, mediated by Ms Spencer. Mr Madden also felt, like many others, that racism was not an issue. As Spencer explained, her campaign was frustrated at every turn:

> Madden has no interest in working parties ... so he does not attend, not even to give any moral support. So you can imagine this lazy do not bother to attend, maybe one or two out of how many of us? Thirty or so? Well, I suppose there are no promotional prospects in attending ... so why bother? No one's going to stay on till 5.30 when they can go home at 4.00 if they don't have to, are they? Even at lunch-time there is a problem. I'm really fed up, dealing with people that just don't care. Yesterday I wanted to call a meeting at lunch but because some of them wanted to play football they said I can't have it at lunch. Everyone moans, they can't come at that time or at this time. They don't seem to understand that it is school policy I am talking about. No one has shown any interest in that plan of mine to speak to the fifth and fourth years ... You won't believe this, Madden actually said that I cannot go to the meeting that I arranged with Mr Bacchus (Borough MRE inspector). Guess his excuse? There is no one to cover for my lesson ... A bit weak, I think.

[...] While Rachel Spencer saw her colleagues as suspicious, backward and inherently prejudiced, they on the other hand regarded her and the other committed anti-racist campaigners in a not too serious light, as somewhat eccentric and going through a 'phase', a bit of a nuisance. [...]

There was little doubt that the 'Crusaders' were dedicated to the cause of anti-racism: however, their actions were not always in the best interests of the black pupils in their care. Often, because of the futility and frustrations of their actions, a great deal of the 'Crusaders' teaching energies were concentrated on their staffroom campaign. It was also clear that the well-meaning but self-conscious treatment of black pupils in their classroom did not satisfy the immediate needs of the black students. The multi-racial input of the 'Crusaders' into classroom work did not appear to have much effect on the black pupils in the lesson, though, it must be said, it did make these lessons and teachers more popular and liked. These teachers were regarded as more caring, less strict and more approachable.[5] For example, though one young black woman described Rachel as 'sweet', this did not mean that these teachers had the trust or confidence of the young black women in their classes. The young black women explained that they often felt patronized and were aware of these teachers' efforts to be 'nice'. 'You think he is nice and all. He'll come up and speak to you nice, but you can't trust him, he'll stab you in the back' (Verne: black girl, fifth year, St Hilda's, talking about Mr Sutton, the fifth year head).

[...]

Some pupils found their teachers' efforts to include in the lesson what they considered to be socially relevant 'black' experiences amusing, as Brenda explained: 'Miss, it was a laugh, Miss Spencer made Verne be a social worker, right, and then I was sent to her as I was caught missing school, right ... It was funny, miss' (Anita, talking about her fifth-year drama lesson). Not only did the girls in this group have no experience of truanting, they had never been near a social worker. Ms Spencer had assumed that such experiences were a reality for the pupils in her class, an unwarranted assumption.

Ms Spencer's perspective on the lesson was markedly different from that articulated by the black girls in the class, as she explained: 'It was a very good session, the black kids got into it. It's important that the material is socially relevant for them. I think they could really understand what it was all about, it was good.'

In conclusion, the evidence suggests that the outcome of the 'Crusader' anti-racist campaign was less productive than they themselves believed. The efforts of these well-intentioned teachers were lost on both their colleagues and their pupils: the former alienated, and the latter they neglected, if not misunderstood. This failure of the anti-racist campaign was not only attributable to the way they went about things and the attitude of their colleagues, but was also the inevitable outcome of the fundamental flaws in their philosophy. Gilroy (1990) suggests the reductive concept of culture and 'race' embodied in antiracist ideology trivializes black life as nothing more than a response to racism. This had the effect of not only alienating the majority of black people (from whose experience the antiracists derive their authority to speak), but it also pushes racism to the margins of the mainstream political agenda.

(4) The 'Liberal Chauvinists'

Unlike the 'Crusaders' the 'Liberal Chauvinists' were not campaigners for social justice. These teachers did, however, attempt to 'understand' (albeit only within the context of their own perspective), the cultural, class and gender characteristics of the various minorities they came into contact with. Armed with information, mostly gleaned from secondary sources such as television, books, travels, friends, rather than personal experience, these liberally inclined teachers were often convinced, with a curious arrogance that characterized the 'Liberal Chauvinists', that when it came to their students, they knew best. There were many examples of such liberally orientated staff in the schools in the study. Approximately 25% of the teachers held beliefs that would classify them in this category.

There were many differet types of 'Liberal Chauvinism' to be found among the staff in both the schools, each form having its own unique characteristics and therefore specific outcome for the young black women who found themselves on the receiving end of this type of 'unintentional' racism. Turning to an examination of one of these forms of 'Liberal Chauvinism', I cite first the case of Mr Sutton.

Sutton, the fifth year head at St Hilda's, believed that he, better than any other member of staff, 'understood' *his* black female students. In his efforts to 'understand' the young black women in his classrooms, Mr Sutton had become preoccupied with the issue of the sexuality of the black female pupils in the fifth year, as indeed were many other members of staff. It seemed that for Mr Sutton the answer to everything, when it came to young black women—success, failure; good or bad behaviour, happiness or sadness—lay in an explanation that had as its central causal concern the dynamic of black female sexuality. In the fifth year at St Hilda's there were several Band 1 black girls who were not achieving as expected, he explained:

> I do feel ethnic monitoring or at least keeping a record of black pupils could help us understand what's going on better. It has occurred to me, just by looking at the reports, that something is very wrong, very wrong indeed: how much is actually concerned with behaviour and not achievement? In a few weeks these girls suddenly do badly ... so much going on inside them. What I mean is that they are maturing, becoming young ladies. It seems at this point their performance slips ... as if school is, well beneath them. Yes, I do think many of them begin to feel that school is beneath them.

The fifth-year reports of the black female pupils, written by Sutton and other members of staff, reaffirmed the popular notion linking sexual maturity to levels of achievement. In these reports, which make often overtly sexist comments regarding particular feminine characteristics, behaviour is employed as the medium through which achievement and maturity are assessed. The following extracts from the school reports of young black women in the fifth year illustrate my point:

> Sandra must learn to behave like a woman if she is to be treated like one ... (Mr Farr: fifth-year class tutor commenting on Sandra, aged 16)

> Charm and good manners are as commendable in a young woman as work and punctuality!   (Mr Sutton: commenting on Donna, aged 16)

> It is clear from this report that the staff and I feel that Frances is maturing gradually. I hope the sensible approach has not come too late.
> (Mr Sutton: commenting on Frances, aged 16)

However, when discussing black girls the teachers would also complain more specifically about boyfriends, aggressive and unruly behaviour, and in general, assertiveness, which was often interpreted as being 'cocky'. It appeared that the girls' status as young women had contradictory outcomes in the way they were regarded. Being mature, on the one hand, was seen as the explanation for responsibility and taking schoolwork seriously. On the other hand, a 'developed' sense of maturity was regarded as a reason for lack of concentration and dissatisfaction with schooling. In this regard the black girls could not win. Their sexuality was perceived to be continually at odds with their educational achievement. Whether 'developed' or not, it was clear that their sexuality had to be contained.

[...]

However, the theory pertaining to black female sexuality was only one of a number of 'informed' beliefs held by the 'Liberal Chauvinists' to explain the educational performance of the black girls in their classrooms. Ideas about the nature of the cultural and family background of West Indian female pupils were also culturally 'distanced' and as such often misunderstood. For example, it was not uncommon to find that many teachers felt that their black pupils possessed a cultural handicap that inhibited their successful educational participation. This belief, it must be stressed, emanated from a so-called 'informed' perspective that these teachers thought they had about West Indian life, and was therefore different in kind from the attitude displayed by the 'Overt Racists', who held a similar but more genetically orientated view.

In staffroom discussions teachers, who regarded themselves as informed, often showed a complete lack of understanding when it came to the cultural values or social lives of young black people. There was often surprise (and horror) at the extent to which young black girls helped and were expected to help with household chores. Some 'progressive' members of staff, most of whom were women themselves, felt it was a handicap to the girls' educational advancement. In one instance a mother, who was herself an educational welfare officer, was summoned to the school to be told to stop 'putting upon her daughter'. Ms Parker, believing in her estimation and using the yardstick of her own experience, that this was indeed not only an endemic but also detrimental aspect of West Indian culture, decided that this was an explanation for Sherry's recent deterioration in her (high-ability) work. She took matters into her own hands, saying:

> She (Sherry's mother) is one of those who believes you must work hard to get anywhere, you know, to work and work to better one's self. I think she's too hard on Sherry. She drives herself so hard, she's now started fainting during school time. It is emotional stress, if you ask me. I understand the father left home, then came back and he treats them very badly, they have no beds at the moment, and if Sherry does not help at home she gets no food. A bit of a problem, don't you think? It is difficult to know what to do. We are considering sending her to the school psychologist.

Whatever the cause of Sherry's distress over her schoolwork, the pathological sensationalism of Ms Parker's explanation displayed in this extract had clearly been fed by the impoverished images she had of cruel black men and over-ambitious black women. Yet Ms Parker had derived her explanation from her own evaluation of West Indian culture.

It was apparent that pictures of black pupils coming from, on the whole, socially deprived backgrounds, and thus in need of care and assistance, were being pieced together from information teachers read or saw and understood within their own cultural framework. These assessments of their pupils had important consequences for the black girls in their care. Their ideas impinged on the expectations and attitudes they had toward certain girls, who became labelled as problem children or not from the impressions that they derived, from often very limited contact with the parents of the girls.

[...]

Unrealistic expectations and over-ambition was another aspect of West Indian 'culture' with which the 'Liberal Chauvinists' preoccupied themselves. It was felt among the staff that these demands were imposed on the children of West Indian households as a matter of course. The staff tended to regard the hopes of parents for their children not as considered aspirations, but as symptomatic of what they 'knew' to be the unrealistic cultural orientation of black families (an over-ambition that also determined what they considered to be the unacceptable levels of discipline in West Indian households). Thus the common complaint of 'too high aspirations' among West Indian parents was met with a general concern among the 'Liberal Chauvinists' that the daughters of such unreasonable parents should be preserved from such demands, as the following example shows:

Linda's mother is very strict, one of those religious West Indian families, you know. She even says 'God bless you' when you ring. Now, she wants Linda to do 'A' Level RE, but she hasn't got a clue about her daughter. She's not even up to grade 3 CSE. She lives in another world, both of them.

(Ms Parker: fifth-year head at St Theresa's, discussing Linda, aged 16)

Ms Wallace, careers mistress, counsellor and English teacher at St Theresa's, felt deeply committed to 'her girls'. She was indeed a dedicated teacher with a long-standing reputation for 'caring and helping', yet she too harboured her convictions about the 'hopeless' position concerning the future of most of the black girls with whose charge she was entrusted.[6] She was prepared to discuss her concerns about individual fifth-year girls:

Miriam is being unrealistic ... She is not equipped academically or as a person to do probation work or any sort of social work, she will only be disappointed, yet another case of one who wants to be but won't be. But how do you deal with these situations, you tell me, it is very touchy. (Four years later, in a follow-up study, Miriam had completed the social studies course she had wanted to do at the local FE college in Brixton.)

Laurie I would call a fairly competent sort of girl, but she needs to focus more clearly on what she really will be able to do. (Laurie was an outstanding tennis player with high hopes of becoming professional, but this was considered unrealistic by the school. She also had excellent academic credentials.)

Of Rubina, who wanted to study law and showed every indication that she was capable academically of pursuing such a career (she already had several CSE and 'O' level passes from her previous year in the fifth form), Ms Wallace was not prepared to offer any undue encouragement. She said: 'She may go on to do A Levels, but she is so ambitious, may be a bit too anxious.'

Ms Wallace's pessimistic assessment of these high ability and achievement-orientated young black women was not shared by the black careers officer, Ms Forte, who visited St Theresa's on a regular basis to interview girls and counsel them on their future choices. Ms Forte had views of her own, contrary to Ms Wallace, concerning the girls' capabilities: 'I think Miriam is fully capable of undertaking a social work course ... Ms Wallace presumes sometimes that these girls have less of a mind than they really do.'

[...]

Ms Andrews, a third-year mistress, explained that one of her third-year students, a black girl, was insistent on taking history as an examination subject for the future. However, she felt:

Andrea is just not capable and she has been strongly advised not to. She is disorganized and a lazy girl, and slow. Even if she were able to do the CSE she could not complete the course work. She

wants to do it so badly but we know she'll fail. I cannot allow
it.

Such concern could easily be regarded as an honest assessment, advice that, in order to avoid disappointment, sensibly takes into account the limitations of a pupil's ability. However, when another teacher's evaluation of Andrea is taken into consideration, this assessment begins to seem unfair. Another teacher revealed: 'It is not that she (Andrea) is lazy or not able to manage, it is just that she tries too hard. For instance she'll rewrite four lines in one lesson just to get it right and looking good.'

Tomlinson (1981, p. 59) has found that many teachers do operate within a framework of stereotypes which are more often reinforced than negated by pupil response. She argues that it was not uncommon to find that teachers regarded their West Indian pupils as generally slow, docile and underachievers on the one hand, and hyperactive and anti-authoritarian on the other. In the case of Andrea the primary response of the teacher was to categorize her as slow and lazy. This meant that the teacher overlooked and failed to encourage the qualities of perseverance and commitment that Andrea obviously had. Thus, rather than attemping to develop her potential, Ms Andrews labelled Andrea as lazy and slow, relegating her to the category of 'difficult and problematic'.

[...]

In conclusion, there were numerous examples of teacher's negative assessments, most of which were based on what they believed to be 'informed judgement'. These negative assessments often led to the curtailment of opportunities that should have been available to the black girls in the study in view of their ability and attainment.

(5) The 'Black Teacher'

There is an expectation that, with a positive policy of recruitment towards black teachers, not only will it present a more representative picture of the population of the inner city, but that they will also be placed in the forefront of the demand for a more progressive and egalitarian educational system. However, in the schools studied the black members of staff, who numbered only four, did not participate in the obvious arena that had been constructed to encourage such change. The anti-racist campaign, which on the whole was monopolized by the 'Crusaders', did not attract black support, as Mr Green, a young black male teacher at St Hilda's, explained: 'I just let them get on with their business. I don't bother with them. They feel they know what it is all about so who am I to say. I find it just gets on my nerves, I keep well out of it.' *(sic)*

This negative feeling about the 'liberal white tokenism' that dominated the race issue in schools was articulated by the other black teachers:

The ILEA has set about 'investigating' the 'problem of race'. Everyone is rushing around 'investigating race', talking about 'running out of time', having to do it now. A curious way to go about things. (Ms Lewis: head of Biology department, St Theresa's)

It was not that these black members of staff did not sympathize with the need to reassess the issue of race in the schools, but that they shared[7] a definite and alternative perspective on the nature of the black educational dilemma and the solution to that problem. This orientation was clear from the statements these teachers made about the role and development of multi-racial education. For example, when Ms Lewis was asked what she felt about multi-racial education and equal opportunities policies, she said: 'So what about them? What needs to change, if you ask me, is ourselves and our attitudes as teachers, rather than the girls.'

[...]

As the issue of role models is often discussed in relation to the recruitment of black teachers, an aspect that is worth investigating is pupil response to their presence. It was apparent in the schools that the race of the teacher was not as significant as the quality of their teaching and their ability to communicate with the girls. Of course the race of the teacher did automatically increase their ability to empathize with the girls and so increased their popularity, as the girls explained:

> Ms Lewis, she's a good teacher. She makes you work, but she's always fair.
> (Fifth-year black girl)

> She never picks on anyone, not like Ms Webster ... best of all she never shouts at you.
> (Fifth-year black girl commenting on Ms Lewis)

The feeling was mutual: the exchange between black teacher and black pupil showed no elements of favouritism or special recognition; they were regarded simply as pupils by the teachers and teachers by the pupils.[8] Mr Green demonstrated this when he warned me about several black male students in the school: 'Those boys, they are trouble makers. They try to disrupt everything for you. Just ignore them and keep out of their way, that is what we all do.'

Similarly, Ms Lewis explained that she did not give any particular preference to the young black women she taught just because she herself was a black woman. She explained her philosophy on the matter, a philosophy that was in marked contrast to that expressed by many of her white colleagues and documented earlier in this article.

> No matter who we are we can only do what we can ... there is no point in trying to be or do what you can't. No matter if you are black or white we all have limitations. The important thing is to recognize what those limitations are in terms of your academic ability and work on your strong points.

Being a black woman and having a black perspective on issues concerning the pupils was, as in the case of Ms Forte, the careers liaison officer at St Theresa's, of immense value when it came to advising and understanding the girls' needs. In her realistic appraisal of the career situation for young black women she was able to relate the desire for certain jobs to family background, the migrant experience and social class influences among West Indians. As a black female careers officer, Ms Forte felt she was in a difficult postition, but she did not give the girls false hope or misleading information just because she felt that black women should aspire as high as they could, she explained:

> As a careers officer my role is to prepare them for a job. To broaden their interests and to provide information, but also to be aware of how we as careers officers can affect their opportunities ... It is difficult to assess what job they would like and how to give advice. You can't say 'no, you can't be such and such'. You have to be realistic, it just may not be possible. Ultimately, it's your job to help them stop wasting time wanting to be a doctor by giving them realistic advice. Some girls, for example, are late developers. You have to then just give them the facts and help them make their mind up. If they want to work hard give them the time and don't say you can't. They may feel you are discouraging them if you don't give them alternative advice, but then as a black officer, and this goes for black teachers, we are perceived as part of the system, the authority. It is very frustrating.

[...]

On the whole, everyday working relationships between the black members of staff and their white colleagues were amiable. However, in one instance racial strife in the classroom caused one black teacher to complain about the lack of support and understanding among white colleagues. Dr Ashraf, a chemistry teacher at St Hilda's, had been having a great deal of trouble with one particular fifth-year chemistry group. The racism of the pupils was evident as he became the object of their abuse. The class constantly made fun of him, mimicking his 'Indianness' and calling him derogatory Indian names. The pupils even began to boycott his lessons and taunt him that they were not going to attend the final exam. These events caused Dr Ashraf much distress. He had appealed to the headmaster, Mr Madden, and the staff, but found not only disbelief but little sympathy and support. They, he felt, regarded him as an incompetent teacher and he was aware that the non-entry of substantial numbers of fifth-formers for the chemistry examination would fuel that belief. However, though Dr Ashraf had outstanding credentials[9] and was a dedicated teacher, he was aware of the lack of recognition and racism he had suffered not only in the job market, but also from his colleagues, who judged him primarily on his accent and ability to speak English. The lack of support over the fifth-form incident, he felt, was a further insult to his integrity. He was aware that in the staffroom he was regarded as very much an outsider:

I feel very alone. I can't tell anyone anything. I am aware that a lot of what is going on is because I'm Indian and everyone else here is Catholic. Parents, teachers, together they will say I'm not able to manage the class. Parents, they especially have a lot to do with it. They influence their children at home and that is why they feel they can come here and say and do these things like this.

The irony of this incident was that it took place in a school, St Hilda's in which the staff were most vociferous that racism was not present among them.

In conclusion, the experiences and values of the black teachers in the study differed radically from those of the white teachers. On the whole, black teachers were more in tune with the needs of their black female pupils, often offering a more positive solution to the education of the black child.

CONCLUSION: THE STRATEGIC AVOIDANCE OF RACISM

The evidence of this study shows that while young black women (who clearly displayed their positive self-esteem), challenged their teachers' expectations of them (expectations that were often characterized by overt racism on the one hand or unintentional racism on the other), they were in no position in the 'power hierarchy' to counteract any negative outcomes of these interpretations.

All too often the recognition of these negative assessments led the girls to look for alternative strategies with which to 'get by'. These strategies, such as not taking up a specific subject or not asking for help, were employed by the girls as the only means of challenging their teachers' expectations of them, and as such were ultimately detrimental to the education of the pupils concerned.

However, the attitudes and orientations of black teachers presented a positive example of how some of the processes of disadvantage could be avoided. These teachers neither patronized nor misinterpreted their black students' reactions and were insistent on the maintenance of high standards of teaching and learning.

Notes

1. This response of 48% was in marked contrast to their white peers who, in answer to the same question, were far less likely to indicate themselves (e.g. only 25% of white females and 16% of white males indicated that they would like to be like nobody but themselves). Black males, like their female counterparts, were more likely to indicate themselves; i.e. 50%.
2. It must be noted that this orientation was by no means only found among practising Christians; it was an attitude that extended to non-religious teaching staff and was identified by the philosophy of colour-blindness, not Christian belief.
3. This newsletter caused outrage among black parents and pupils in the school, who felt it was offensive. One parent, for example, found being likened to French accents and Italian clothes particularly offensive, while others felt it stupid and shallow. Teachers, however, although they too felt it was a rather

awkward statement, put it down to the 'hamfisted' eccentricity of Mr Madden and were therefore prepared to overlook it.

4. The MRE Working Party at St Hilda's constantly met with opposition. The Working Party's status was under threat, not least by the head, who felt it was an unnecessary committee. In several instances he went out of his way to obstruct the holding of meetings, giving no time allowances to the staff involved. He himself only attended one meeting when the Multi-Racial Inspector of the borough came to review the school's progress on the matter.

5. Green (DES, 1985, p. 52) found that with tolerant teachers who used the indirect teaching method, black girls received more than their fair share of attention and also received less criticism about their work.

6. It should also be noted that Ms Wallace was engaged on a part-time MA in Education, and was particularly interested in the issue of gender in schools.

7. The black teachers appeared to 'share' this common orientation even though they were not all from the same school and thus did not know one another.

8. Ray Rist (1970) comments on the fact that black teachers responded in the class in such a way as to show no difference between black and white pupils.

9. Dr Ashraf had a PhD from India, had completed two years' post-doctoral research at a college of the University of London and had a PGCE.

References

Coard, B. (1971) *How the West Indian Child is Made ESN in the British School System.* London: New Beacon Books.

DES (Department of Education and Science) (1985) *Education for All: The Report of the Committee of Inquiry into the Education of Children from Ethnic Minority Groups* (The Swann Report). London: HMSO Cmnd. 9453.

Eggleston, J., Dunn, D., Anjali, M. and Wright, C. (1986) *Education for Some. The Educational and Vocational Experiences of 15–18 Year Old Members of Minority Ethnic Groups.* Stoke on Trent: Trentham.

Gillborn, D. (1990) *'Race', Ethnicity and Education: Teaching and Learning in Multiethnic Schools.* London: Unwin Hyman.

Gilroy, P. (1990) 'The end of anti-racism'. *New Community* 17 (1) (October).

Green, P. (1985) Multi-ethnic teaching and the pupils' self-concepts'. In DES 1985, *Education for All* (The Swann Report). London: HMSO Cmnd 9453.

ILEA (Inner London Education Authority) (1983) *Race, Sex and Class* (Nos 1–6). London: Inner London Education Authority.

Mac an Ghaill, M. (1988) *Young, Gifted and Black: Student Teacher Relations in the Schooling of Black Youth.* Milton Keynes: Open University Press.

Milner, D. (1975) *Children and Race: Ten Years On.* London: Ward Lock Educational.

—(1983) *Children and Race: Ten Years On.* London: Ward Lock Educational.

Rist, R. (1970) Student social class and teacher expectations: the self-fulfilling prophecy in ghetto education. *Harvard Educational Review*, 40 (August), 411–50.

Stone, M. (1985: 1st edition 1981) *The Education of the Black Child: The Myth of Multi-cultural Education.* London: Fontana.

Tomlinson, S. (1981) *Educational Subnormality: A Study in Decision Making.* London: Routledge and Kegan Paul.

Wright, C. (1986) School processes—an ethnographic study. In J. Eggleston, D. Dunn and M. Anjali (eds) *Education for Some: The Educational and Vocational Experiments of 15–18 Year Old Members of Minority Ethnic Groups.* Stoke-on-Trent: Trentham.

—(1987) The relations between teachers and Afro-Caribbean pupils: Observing multi-racial classrooms. In G. Weiner and M. Arnot (eds) *Gender Under Scrutiny.* London: Hutchinson in association with the Open University.

7 BOYS: FROM SEA-COOKS TO CATERING MANAGERS

DENA ATTAR

A boy sings on one of my tape-recordings of a home economics lesson. In the transcript I have noted fourteen bursts of song and thirteen outbreaks of whistling, as well as boys talking in funny voices, jokes, laughter and somewhere a rhythm being played on a saucepan or lid. I have no other tape like this one. It records a fourth-year practical CGSE 'Home Economics: Food' lesson in a boys' school, and confirms evidence from other sources about the important difference between boys' and girls' experiences. Boys have fun in home economics.

Frankie, the boy who sang the most, was in danger of having too much fun. At one point in the lesson the teacher rebuked him, although not in a very serious way:

Teacher: Frankie, when you come to do a practical exam how are you going to learn to keep quiet? I think you should start practising ... You can smile, we like you looking happy, but try, try to control ...
Frankie: I'm only happy when I'm singing.
Teacher: Then I'm afraid we're going to have to make sure you're sad.

The outstanding feature of this encounter is its rarity. Nothing remotely like this happened in any of the lessons I observed—the majority—where girls were present. Frankie's whole class appeared to share his mood. Girls sometimes told me they liked home economics, but no girl provided such evidence of enjoyment. The mood in other classes, as far as I could detect it, was usually serious and sometimes discontented, but never lighthearted. No girls sang.

In recent years feminists have begun to write about the differences between raising sons and raising daughters. The pain, the conflicts and the rewards are not and cannot be the same. Sons grow up to acquire the privileges of maleness in a society dominated by men, while daughters have to learn what it is to be oppressed as girls and women. We need to talk more too about the differences, for women, between teaching boys and teaching girls. Much of the discussion so far has taken as its focus boys' harassment of women teachers, or boys' sexism, and how to deal with them. That is only part of the story. The other part, often acknowledged by staff in mixed schools, is

Source: Abridged from Attar, D. (1992) *Wasting Girls' Time. The History and Politics of Home Economics* (pp. 114–35). London: Virago.

that teaching boys is generally easier. Boys are more likely to reward teachers by showing that they are enjoying themselves. Even their deviancy is more likely to be passed off as a joke.

[...] Frankie could enjoy the lesson but at the same time make clear that its content didn't much matter. A girl of fourteen or fifteen who was dismissive of criticism or cared little for detail would be making a different kind of statement. As I argue later, whether they are conforming or resisting, home economics has to matter more to girls. Boys have less at stake.

[...]

The scramble to transform home economics from a girls' to a gender-free subject may obscure the fact that boys have already been studying it for a long while, sometimes even taking separate specialised boys' courses. In general they have concentrated on cookery, which is still the overwhelming case now. It is comparatively rare for boys to opt for child development courses, and almost unheard of in many areas for them to opt voluntarily for needlework, dress or textiles courses—a teacher in one school told me that she had 'never known a boy to take textiles'. This pattern of choice, which appears so strongly throughout British schools, is not universal. Its cultural specificity is shown up by the example of another school I visited where many of the pupils or their families had come originally from Bangladesh. Because of the high level of demand from boys and their parents, the school had arranged extra classes in tailoring. No girls opted for it, but as a vocational course relevant to their immediate employment prospects it was extremely popular with the boys.

Cookery, as a professional activity, has traditionally been dominated by men in terms of the most prestigious jobs and the best pay. There have been many instances of men oraganizing to keep women out of the male profession of cookery (for examples see Mennell, 1985; Attar, 1986). Only the domestic, unpaid version has been universally allotted to women. In training and education this has led to a predictable split, with boys going off to colleges to take vocational courses in catering, often leading to the City and Guilds of London Institute qualifications which are required for many jobs, while girls take courses at school which concentrate on cookery for home and family and gain them professionally useless qualifications, if any.

College catering courses have had a distinctly masculine image. It used to be difficult for girls to gain entry to them, and girls were often steered towards the least skilled and least well-paid fields. This was logical since it was consistent with discriminatory employment practices. Courses were linked to apprenticeship schemes which excluded girls, and orientated towards the requirements of large hotels and restaurants which would employ only men as chefs. [...]

The division between professional training together with formal apprenticeships for boys, and school lessons serving as informal domestic apprenticeships for girls, led to another split in the content of food and cookery teaching. For boys, the emphasis was placed on the craft skills they needed to compete in the labour market, not on the themes of sound nutrition and thrift which were constantly emphasized to girls. In the annual catering competitions which gave young trainees—almost always male—a chance to show off their skills, the great set pieces were traditionally required to be impressive displays of technical proficiency; they did not have to be particularly edible.

[...]

Within schools, too, home economics for boys has had its own separate history. In the early years of domestic economy teaching, boys living in seaport towns were given a special dispensation by the Board of Education to attend cookery classes in the elementary schools (Yoxall, 1913, p. 49). It was otherwise almost unheard of for boys to take domestic subjects, and in the period of payments by results they could not be counted towards the grant if by some chance they were entered for examination along with the girls.

When any consideration was given to cookery lessons for boys it was always within a specific, limited and well-defined context. If they were not prospective sea-cooks, boys wanting to take cookery lessons were probably Boy Scouts. Yoxall, who in 1913 mistakenly thought that 'the question of cookery instruction for boys in general will soon receive careful consideration', wrote that Boy Scouts often asked if they could join classes as they needed to learn to make porridge and soup in order to become Scouts of the first class.

[...]

From teachers' accounts of their work it emerged that courses for boys could be of three types: vocational in the serious sense of equipping them for paid employment once they left school; purely recreational; or basic, in the form of short 'survival' courses preparing them for looking after themselves in circumstances which were seen as exceptional rather than normal.

[...]

Several of the boys I spoke to in mixed schools in 1988 who had chosen home economics—but none of the girls—mentioned wanting to be a chef as their reason for taking it. Some may really have had serious ambitions to become chefs, but their answers also reflected the pressure they were under from teachers, parents and other pupils to provide an acceptable motive, compared with girls who did not have to explain themselves and need give no reason at all.

[...]

Attitudes towards cooking as a recreational subject for boys have varied according to pupils' ages and abilities. For boys in a school for slow learners, pastry-making could be seen as a therapeutic extension of sand and water play, according to one teacher (Hinsley, 1971). For sixth-formers who could afford to choose additional courses for no very serious reason, cooking could be enjoyed as a hobby.

Two pupils who provided personal accounts of their experience of recreational home economics in the *Housecraft* special issue on boys and home economics made the point that boys had to face taunts of homosexuality from their peers if they did choose it:

> ... you will probably have to withstand being called a sissy, bent, queer, etc. but don't give it up ...   (Jaques, 1971)

> ... many people consider boys who enjoy cooking rather 'effeminate' and this is such a pity ... it dissuades many from taking it up as a hobby.
> (Dick, 1971)

The opportunity to cross sex-role boundaries could none the less be attractive and could offer boys easy access to high achievement, or at least a sense of it, since they were only comparing themselves with girls. One pupil described how he chose home economics because he wanted to do something different, and thought it would be a challenge to himself and to the girls in his class. He eventually formed an ambition to become a lecturer in food and nutrition at a home economics college. The conspicuous position this pupil was in seems to have worked to enhance his self-esteem and confidence. As Jenny Shaw (1984) has pointed out, boys in mixed classes tend to see girls as a 'negative reference group' and assume either that girls are performing worse than themselves or that girls' superior performance can be discounted. When girls form the only reference group and a boy taking home economics can consider his mere presence on a course as outstanding, it is understandable that he could easily perceive himself as doing extremely well and ready to aim for the furthest point ahead that he can see.

Most courses designed specifically for boys were of the 'bachelor living' type, aiming to teach them a handful of essential facts and skills for looking after themselves. In the *Housecraft* articles, teachers referred specifically and repeatedly to a need for boys to learn how to look after *themselves*, with no suggestion that they might also have to look after others.

Nutrition education for boys also tended to place them as consumers rather than providers. One teacher even argued that disharmony in the home was created by men's faulty eating habits, because they rejected their wives' attempts to offer them a more varied diet. The answer to this was to teach boys nutrition so that they would be more appreciative of their future wives' efforts. The traditional rationale, given or accepted by boys, for learning to cook the few quick, convenience meals these courses featured was that in a crisis they might need to fend for themselves—when a girlfriend walked out, or a wife was in hospital.

[...]

One London teacher argued that teaching about hygiene and grooming could enable boys to take advantage of the home-like ambience of the home economics department, a privilege usually enjoyed exclusively by girls:

> Boys ... should be equally welcome to join in the lunch-time freedoms which girls have always had—to pop in to remove a stain, sew a button, wash and iron a muddied shirt to prevent a 'telling-off' from an over-worked mum, or just to offer help in getting something repaired or ready for the next lesson. We know that for the most part they are all excuses to come for a chat. The housecraft room really is the home within the school and girls have tended to regard this as their own—a jealously guarded sanctum. (Myers, 1971)

There have been few signs at any period that girls were going to lose their sanctum to boys, as the numbers on these courses were always small. The ATDS survey of 425 mixed schools in 1967 found that in nearly half no boys at all were participating in domestic science lessons. The number of boys taking domestic science in the remaining schools was tiny. Sixty of the schools offered single-sex classes for boys, although it was never a compulsory subject for them, as it frequently was for girls. [...]

The era of supposed equal opportunities put an end to the provision of separate courses for boys in mixed schools, although it did not bring about equality between schools. In the late 1980s home economics departments in boys' schools were still unusual. A Kent teacher wrote in 1987 of the hard work needed 'to establish a Home Economics department in a secondary boys school' (*Modus,* 1987) and several London boys' schools were still at the stage of hoping to start their own departments. They faced the problem of a scarcity of resources, shared also by schools which had set up home economics departments. One teacher I spoke to in a boys' school calculated that craft, design and technology had six times the resources of her own department and said it gave the impression of occupying a vast proportion of the school's space, whilst she had one room and was the sole teacher in her subject area.

Boys who do choose home economics seem in general to come from a narrower range of ability groups, and probably also a more unified social class background, than the girls. Examination statistics show not only that relatively few boys choose home economics compared with girls but also that their examination results are considerably worse. [...]

The examples in Tables 7.1 and 7.2 reveal a wide gap between boys' and girls' achievements, which needs to be explained. Boys taking these examinations were at least twice as likely to fail—and in one case about five times as likely—as girls. Girls' greater familiarity with the content of the course—and even boys' over-confidence, as discussed above—are possible factors, but the most plausible explanation lies in the screening process which lets some pupils into home economics, and keeps others out.

The minority of boys who opt for home economics are likely to be perceived as less academically able ('opting' can of course be a misleading word;

TABLE 7.1 Comparison of boys' and girls' results in JMB Home Economics (Food) GCE ordinary level examinations*

	1984–5 (%)			1985–6 (%)			1986–7 (%)		
	No.	C+	E+	No.	C+	E+	No.	C+	E+
Girls	23,682	39.2	69.6	24,579	66.7	73.0	26,489	40.5	75.8
Boys	2,762	13.6	39.2	3,379	16.3	46.2	4,556	16.6	51.1

Source: Adapted from Joint Matriculation Board Statistics of Examinations, Manchester, 1986, 1987, 1988.
* Including Joint O level/CSE and Alternative Ordinary examinations.

TABLE 7.2 Grades achieved by percentages of girls and boys in a sample of O level home economics examinations, June 1983

	A	B	C	D	E	U	Total number
Girls							
AEB	5.0	21.9	37.0	16.6	16.9	2.6	13,812
London	6.7	26.1	34.4	11.0	8.7	13.1	6,661
Boys							
AEB	2.4	9.2	29.0	15.6	31.6	12.1	620
London	1.2	15.1	30.6	14.3	9.7	29.1	258

Source: Adapted from University of London and Associated Examining Board GCE Examination Statistics 1984.

the boys from a lower-stream class who were timetabled to do home economics 'as a joke' in an incident described in one of the study schools presumably were not given much option at all). [. . .] Clever boys don't choose, or are not allowed to choose, home economics; clever girls are discouraged too, as the ATDS often used to complain, but not nearly to the same extent. Boys' career prospects matter more than girls' do—to parents, schools, and not least to pupils themselves. The low-status subject of home economics is regarded as good enough for a few boys without much expectation of academic achievement, but not for the rest. It is good enough for girls, though, even if they are academically able.

[. . .]

In the mixed lessons I observed, teachers were generally on the lookout for boys trying to pass their share of tidying or washing up on to the girls in the class, although it still sometimes happened. The greatest difference I noticed between girls and boys was in calling-out behaviour—boys were much more likely to call out to the teacher, and often seemed to think a whistle would fetch her over to them. They were usually seeking the answer to a question the girls did not need to ask, such as what to do with an empty tin, or where to look for ingredients or equipment.

The most marked example of this type of behaviour occurred not in a mixed class, but in a boys' school. [. . .] In the third-year practical which I observed, I recorded a total of 92 requests for the teacher's attention in the space of 46 minutes, in addition to another 23 shouts of 'Miss!' and occasional whistles directed at her. From where I sat I could not observe the whole room, so my total was certainly an underestimate, besides leaving out of the count the first few minutes of the lesson. Boys seeking the teacher's attention often went up to her, physically surrounding her or following her around the room. As there were occasional periods of comparative calm, there were also periods of frantic persistence on the part of pupils, with as many as five boys trying to get her attention at once. There were 15 boys in the class, and their task was to prepare and eat a snack—sandwiches, or baked beans on toast, with a drink.

A number of studies have shown that boys demand more teacher time and attention than girls (for example Spender, 1982; Stanworth, 1983). In the example above, where there was no question of competition between boys and girls, the physical situation—a class of boys with one woman teacher, in a room which was effectively a kitchen—seemed to intensify this pattern of behaviour. Boys' tendency to monopolize equipment in mixed classes has also been recorded (see, for example, Kelly, 1985). While I noted no particular instances of this in the lessons I saw (and I had not set out to record any), something else struck me: boys were more likely to use machinery unnecessarily. One boy used a food processor to slice a single tomato. Girls were not denied access to machines, but did not use them without good reason.

In the past teachers have seized on machines as a way of drawing boys into home economics, along with the opportunity to fix things and fiddle with hardware in general.

> . . . Boys have a natural curiosity that stimulates the development of every lesson. Water and waste pipes are trailed to their destinations and they want to know how all the equipment works. There is never any shortage of willing hands to mend a sink plug and check loose screws on grill pans or ideas to reorganize work space and assist with furnishing the housecraft flat. (Myers, 1971)

> . . . The popularity of needlework for the boys was less predictable (than for cookery), there is no doubt that the electric sewing machines were an attraction . . . (Ellwood, 1971)

More recently computers and industrial machinery have been brought into home economics, to help establish its new identity as a branch of design and technology while also, deliberately or coincidentally, making it more masculine. The greatest change has probably happened within textiles as a school subject. Needlework was once the most feminine subject of all, and as such repelled boys almost without exception. Now that some courses have been redefined and turned into textiles technology, with computer-programmable knitting machines and industrial overlockers taking the place of familiar domestic equipment, they aim to attract the interest of many more boys (though as yet there is little evidence of their success). In a sense the new curricular environment of technology represents a return to craft skills as the essential basis of home economics, with industrial and commercial settings replacing the traditional domestic context.

Courses which focus on the industrial uses of food and textiles technology, rather than seeing food and textiles as linked elements of one overarching subject concerned with home and family life, are more compatible with the aims of the national curriculum than with the criteria for GCSE examinations. Design and technology in the national curriculum will change the whole framework for teaching home economics, and in one very specific sense will make textiles and food courses more masculine. Although pupils' design briefs are supposed to relate to home life and leisure activities as well as to manufacturing and retailing, when the underlying model for their activities has been derived from commerce and industry rather than from the home the stress falls very differently.

Shedding the 'soft' image of home economics so that it can compete with the 'harder' areas of design and technology also conflicts with the use of home economics as an anti-sexism training ground. Teachers who ran 'skills for living' and anti-sexism courses in a small number of boys' schools (described in, for example, Askew and Ross, 1988), far from trying to make home economics masculine, were asking boys to look at and challenge their own assumptions about male and female roles. It was essential to these courses to preserve and use home economics' emphasis on home and family, both as a way of socializing boys into more caring and co-operative forms of behaviour and to make the point that the home was not only, or necessarily, a woman's place.

[...]

Compared with the efforts which have been made since around 1980 (Kelly, 1985) to encourage more girls into science and technology, the efforts of the small number of teachers and advisers concerned with the role of home economics in boys' education have been almost insignificant. Girls' lack of participation in scientific and technological education at 16 and beyond was seen to have serious consequences for themselves and for the whole of society, and as a problem demanding a number of approaches. Researchers examined classroom behaviour, teacher attitudes, course materials and careers advice and generally concluded that everything needed to change. There was no parallel development for home economics, in spite of evidence that it was the worst case of gender differentiation in the curriculum.

Boys' lack of participation in home economics was simply not seen as the

same order of problem; the textbook and syllabus changes prompted by equal-
opportunities legislation and regulations were not supported by a thorough
appraisal of classroom practice, and certainly not by high-level expressions of
concern. [. . .]

The first feminist scrutiny of home economics to result from the new
wave of feminism dating from the 1970s set out to detect forms of blatant
stereotyping and pressures towards domesticity aimed at girls. The question
of boys' participation was raised only briefly as an issue of equal opportunities. Wynn (1983), for example, argued that home economics teaching ought
to reflect and encourage equal roles in the home for men and women.

Equal opportunities were still the theme of the *Genderwatch!* (Myers, 1987)
self assessment notes for teachers, but the approach Nicky Wadsworth (1987)
advocated went beyond making home economics gender-free or offering it on
an equal basis to boys and girls. She raised the issue of the nature of boys' participation, asking whether they were taking the same type of course as girls
or experiencing the same type of involvement. She suggested, too, that home
economics teaching could in some way compensate boys for deficiencies in
their education or upbringing. The basis for her approach was nevertheless
still equal opportunities. In presenting sex differentiation in home economics
as simply a reversal of the situation of male domination in science and technology, Wadsworth produced a strangely unreal account of the 'problem' of
female domination.

Using a model of male domination in mixed classes as described by a
number of researchers, Wadsworth asked teachers to consider whether the
group leaders in mixed classes were always female, and whether compensatory support was offered to male pupils (1987, p. 181). [. . .]

Another question indicated how male support could be engaged: 'Do you
encourage male colleagues to come to your lessons and share their culinary
expertise?' (p. 184). The list of 'strategies for change' again stressed male
teachers as a resource, recommending: 'Male teachers in schools should be
encouraged to participate in teaching every aspect of the subject, working
alongside qualified female staff' (p. 185).

On the question of adapting courses to encourage boys into home economics, the recommendations were much less clear. Teachers were asked
whether they had considered 'introducing any changes to encourage more
male pupils to opt for home economics' (p. 186), but as they were also advised
not to let boys concentrate on catering or emphasize the narrowly vocational
aspects of the subject, the potential nature of such change was unexplained.
[. . .]

Maleness alone, in the *Genderwatch!* proposals, provides enough of a qualifi-
cation for male colleagues to help teach 'every aspect of the subject', alongside
'qualified' female staff. Yet pupils are not supposed to draw the obvious lesson
from this—that men have more authority and expertise than women, as television commercials, cookery programmes and countless other sources have

already told them. Instead it is envisaged that they will only receive the
message (assumed to be something of a new idea to them) that men, too,
can cook, care for children and take an interest in home and family life.
   [...]
The view of female dominance as a problem, which I think is miscon-
ceived, arises from an attempt to see home economics as a subject exactly
like any other except with the power relations changed around. Boys' reluctance to choose it can then be seen as a consequence of stereotyping which
can be dealt with by a shift of emphasis towards boys and men. An alternative feminist view in the 1980s took a harder look at boys' conditioning,
and offered courses in home economics as a means almost of civilizing pupils
who were pictured as unable to work co-operatively or express their gender
emotions without what amounted to remedial help.
One aim of the small number of anti-sexism courses introduced into a few
London boys' schools in the 1980s, according to Sue Askew and Carol
Ross, was to

> ... provide equal curriculum opportunities (including childcare studies
> and domestic crafts) to help boys to learn to take domestic responsi-
> bility and not to regard this as a woman's realm.
>   (Askew and Ross, 1988, p. 75)

The authors were aware that providing a basic level of information and skill
would not be enough to guarantee future domestic equality:

> Learning to cook, or learning about children, does not necessarily change
> boys' stereotyped notions about roles in the home. We have often heard
> comments such as: 'It's useful for when my wife goes into hospital' or
> 'It's a good idea because I might be on my own for a while before I get
> married'.   (Askew and Ross, 1988, p. 75)

They advocated challenging boys directly or indirectly about their attitudes,
looking at stereotyping itself and at boys' concepts of masculinity. Rather
than simply teaching skills and imparting knowledge, home economics lessons
in some schools were used to develop the social skills which boys were seen
to lack:

> For example, boys worked together in a small group making a meal and
> then eating if (often with a guest), as an opportunity to develop their
> ability to work collaboratively as well as develop a sense of respon-
> sibility for another person's well-being. The assessment built into the
> work allowed the boys to reflect, not on how good their finished
> food was but on how well they have worked together.
>   (Askew and Ross, 1988)

The courses described by Askew and Ross were mainly compulsory courses for boys in the early years of secondary education at single-sex schools. It was the aggressive and often misogynist ethos of boys' schools, as much as anything, which set the scene for the type of compensatory education they offered. In common with the *Genderwatch!* recommendations, they stressed the necessity for boys to learn about parental responsibilities and the needs of young children, but as a way of understanding themselves too. The authors acknowledged that there were limits to what could be achieved by such courses on their own, when boys' schools were socializing pupils in a different direction in so many other ways.

The concept of boys' inadequacy as a problem for home economics to solve is as unconvincing to me as the problem of female dominance. There is enough available evidence that boys, and men, are able to work co-operatively when they wish to (leaving aside some more dubious theories about male bonding). Learning how to behave as a member of a football team arguably involves at least as much skill in co-operation as learning to make tea and toast.

[. . .]

Strategies for dealing with female dominance or with boys' inadequacy start from the same assumption: that boys have a problem with home economics, which it could be restructured to solve. My observation of boys' lessons led me to the opposite conclusion. Boys do not appear to have problems with home economics (other than the one they share with girls of trying to understand what the subject is now supposed to be about). They have more freedom to enjoy it than girls do, and are more likely to reap praise from their teachers. If they do not choose home economics options (and few academically able boys do), their decisions are not the unthinking result of stereotyping but have an entirely rational basis. They judge home economics as not particularly valuable for them in the future, compared with other subjects—and in general they judge correctly.

Accounts of home economics lessons as a form of anti-sexist evangelism and accounts of traditional lessons a generation earlier are united by one theme: it is wonderfully rewarding to teach boys. I heard boys praised for taking an interest in the facts of childbirth, for owning their own pairs of rubber gloves, for saying that they wash up at home. Most of all, it seems that boys endear themselves to their teachers because they are having so much fun.

Reading the past thoughts of home economics teachers on teaching boys, easily the most striking feature, absent from descriptions of teaching home economics to girls, is the enjoyment which both teachers and pupils express. In all the literature I have surveyed, girls may be represented as 'bustling', 'pottering', 'competent', 'interested', 'enthusiastic', 'responsible' and so on, but there is never much doubt that they are rehearsing for the serious business of adult life. [. . .]

Boys came in for gushing praise and were clearly expected to know and care a lot less than they actually did, so that their achievements were disproportionately admired:

> They buy their own fabric and since they do not have much experience, very often the fabric is difficult to handle, uneven stripes and checks, slippery satin, fine lawns, but they have a definite sense of colour and seldom do their ties clash with their shirts ... With painful persistence they match almost all the checks and produce fine French or run and fell seams ...   (Myers, 1971)

A teacher in a further-education college, writing that the sheer pleasure boys got from making meat patties, apple pies and doughnuts had to be seen to be believed, found that ... 'the nicest thing about teaching boys is their sense of humour, they never burst into tears when things go wrong or get in a flap' (Gillett, 1971). She asked rhetorically: 'Who but a boy would decorate a pie not with pastry leaves but 'Chelsea for the Cup' and plan real turtle soup and stuffed grouse for his next lesson ...'

Who indeed. It is more pertinent to ask when girls were ever praised for their curiosity or wild and clumsy enthusiasm. Yet the paeons of praise for the keenness of boys still rang late into the 1980s. One article about setting up a home economics course in a boys' school described the need to bring all the enthusiasm into order (Bell, 1987): it is still boys' unthinking enjoyment, rather than their lack of interest, which created problems for teachers.

The question is not whether boys really are so wonderful; as I argued before, in some ways teaching boys may offer greater rewards. A more important question is whether the praise they collect is at the expense of girls, whose achievements in home economics (let alone their possession of aprons and rubber gloves, endearing persistence at hemming or failures to match every last check) are not so unequivocally admired.

Teachers undoubtedly have lower expectations of boys in home economics, as expressed in the *Genderwatch!* suggestion that they be offered compensatory teaching. There is also evidence that in other subjects boys and girls are praised for different achievements and behaviour, with boys assumed to have more natural curiosity and enthusiasm (see, for example, Walkerdine *et al.*, 1989). Yet the observable difference between boys and girls in home economics needs more of an explanation. Boys' enthusiasm, despite the attention it gets, does not really need to be explained, but there are many reasons why girls should have to stifle theirs.

The effect of gender on home economics is an infinitely more subtle matter than the questions of gender-stereotyped roles—who is shown doing what, or which pronouns or nouns are used. It lies at the heart of home economics; it relates to concepts of domestic labour as a service which a subordinate group provides.

As most references to boys' participation make clear, whatever boys have learned to do they almost always learned for themselves. They knew they were not learning how to service others, except sometimes in the context of paid employment. The 'servicing' aspect of home economics, recently re-emphasized by the GCSE National Criteria, was absent from courses geared for boys, but it runs throughout the new home economics syllabuses and textbooks, just as it did in the earliest versions. There never was much mention of fun.

As home economics is already as thoroughly male-defined as anything else in the curriculum, there can be no route to radical social transformation through making it more friendly to boys. The problem of home economics is still primarily a girls' problem: how they can secure access to an education which is *not* geared towards their subordination. It is a problem of who has the power, not who has the craft skills. Unless we seriously believe that men have left the burden of most domestic chores to women simply because they do not know how to do them, there is little point in concentrating educational resources on boys instead of girls when girls already receive less than their fair share.

It has always been open to men to step into the supposedly female-dominated domains of home economics: they have simply shown less interest in fields which are unpaid or exceptionally low-paid, and lacking in status. There has been little to stop them becoming paediatricians, gynaecologists, chefs, clothing designers or even lecturers and researchers in home economics if they wished. Yet paediatricians have sometimes made bad fathers, and men who know how to cook for themselves have declined to do so. It is too wildly hopeful to assume that explaining to men the necessity for sharing and caring, which they have not realized until now, will cause them to abandon their abuses of power. In the last resort equality is not real if it can be chosen by some and not others. Educating boys to equal roles they can still refuse is a less urgent task than empowering girls, who still have far less choice.

References

Askew, S. and Ross, C. (1988) *Boys Don't Cry: Boys and Sexism in Education.* Open University Press.

ATDS (1967) *A Survey of the Teaching of Domestic Science in Secondary Schools in England and Wales.*

Attar, D. (1986) A dabble in the mystery of cookery. *Petits Propos Culinaires* 24 (November).

Bell, J. (1987) In a class of its own. *Modus* 5 (7).

Dick, P. (1971) What do the boys think about it? *Housecraft* (June).

Ellwood, G. (1971) Middle school common course. *Housecraft* (June).

Gillett, C. (1971) Teaching young men in FE. *Housecraft* (June).

Hinsley, A. B. (1971) Teaching boys in a school for slow learners. *Housecraft* (June).

Jaques, J. (1971) What do the boys think about it?. *Housecraft* (June).

Kelly, A. (1985) The construction of masculine science. *British Journal of Sciology of Education* (2).

Mennell, S. (1985) *All Manners of Food.* Basil Blackwell.

Modus (1987) Wanted: a fuller perspective. *Modus* 5 (4) (May).

Myers, J. (1971) Real enthusiasm. *Housecraft* (June).

Myers, K. (1987) *Genderwatch!* EOC/SCDC.

Shaw, J. (1984) The politics of single-sex schools. In Rosemary Deem (ed.) *Co-education Reconsidered*. Open University Press.

Spender, D. (1982) *Invisible Women: The Schooling Scandal*. Writers and Readers.

Stanworth, M. (1983) *Gender and Schooling: A Study of Sexual Divisions in the Classroom*. Hutchinson.

Wadsworth, N. (1987) Home economics and child development. In K. Myers (ed.) *Genderwatch!* EOC/SCDC.

Walkerdine, V. and The Girls and Mathematics Unit, Institute of Education (1989) *Counting Girls Out*. Virago.

Wynn, B. (1983) Home economics. In J. Whyld (ed.) *Sexism in the Secondary Curriculum*. Harper and Row.

Yoxall, A. (1965, first published 1913) *A History of the Teaching of Domestic Economy*. Cedric Chivers.

8 'GIRLS' STUFF, BOYS' STUFF': YOUNG CHILDREN TALKING AND PLAYING

NAIMA BROWNE AND CAROL ROSS

This article is based on conversations with, and observations of, a large number of very young children in nursery and infant classes. It explores how young girls operate within nursery and infant schools and the degree to which gender influences children's involvement in science-orientated activities. Many of the observations relate to constructional play, as this is an area with a high science, maths and technology content. Furthermore, it is an area of concern for many teachers as they believe that the activity is dominated by boys.

The nursery and infant classes differed in terms of their cultural, linguistic and ethnic composition. Most classes had approximately equal numbers of girls and boys, but in a few classes either girls or boys predominated. The adults in the classes varied in respect of their awareness of, and commitment to, the various issues connected with equal opportunities in education. The observations took place over a period of four years and a number of issues emerged which are particularly pertinent to those concerned about the science education of girls in the early years of schooling.

FROM A VERY YOUNG AGE CHILDREN SEEM TO HAVE CLEAR IDEAS ABOUT WHAT GIRLS DO AND WHAT BOYS DO

In our observations of the play preferences of nursery and infant children there were clear demarcations along gender lines. Figures 8.1 and 8.2 provide an indication of how marked this demarcation was in the case of two activities: creative activities (e.g. painting, collage, printing, etc.) and constructional play. The various patterns of children's play preferences have been discussed elsewhere (Clarricoates, 1980; Walkerdine, 1989; Whyte, 1983; Thomas, 1986) and need not be discussed here.

Our conversations with children in nursery classes suggested that children as young as three were very conscious of what they played with and appeared to have mapped out in their mind which toys and activities were 'for girls', which 'for boys' and which were gender-neutral.

Source: Browne, N. (ed.) (1991) *Science and Technology in the Early Years: An Equal Opportunities Approach* (pp. 37–51). Buckingham: Open University Press.

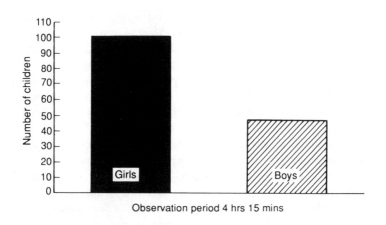

FIGURE 8.1 Involvement of girls and boys in creative activities

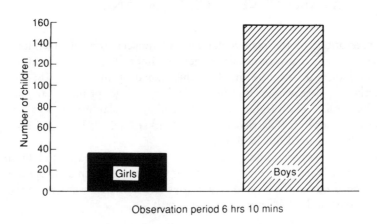

FIGURE 8.2 Involvement of girls and boys in construction play

Many of the infant children also held very strong views. The following exchange was typical of many conversations with six-year-olds:

Boy 1: I don't play with dolls—they're girls' stuff.
Adult: What do you mean 'girls' stuff'?
Boy 2: It's girls' toys.
Adult: Do you think there is anything else that's 'girls' stuff'?
Boy 2: Barbies and Sindies and painting is girls' toys.
Girl 1: Some boys can do painting.
Adult: What's 'boys' stuff'?
Girl 2: Action Force.
Boy 1: Yeah, and transformers.
Girl 2: Ludo's for girls and boys.

Some of the infant and nursery children were shown a selection of photos of different toys and asked to choose two toys with which they would most like to play. In an effort to avoid influencing the children, the toys had been photographed against a plain background without packaging and no child was shown in the picture. Despite these efforts the resultant choices were frighteningly predictable. Every girl chose a doll and then one of following: felt pens and paper, a doll's house, jigsaw puzzles, books or sand. One six-year-old girl's immediate response on seeing the photo of the Lego was to say, 'I *hate* it'. No other toy elicited such a negative response from the girls. Every boy chose Lego and one of the following: Mobilo (a construction toy), wooden bricks, woodwork, puzzles, books or sand. When the children were asked to sort the toys out into those that girls would like to play with and those that boys would like to play with they sorted them as follows

For girls	*For boys*	*For girls and boys*
doll	Lego	books
doll's house	Mobilo	puzzles
felt pens and paper	wooden bricks	sand
	woodwork	

When talking about different activities the children frequently made spontaneous comments in which they linked activities with gender. This would seem to indicate that very young children understand that gender is used as a means of organizing people and society.

IDENTIFICATION OF ACTIVITIES IN GENDER-RELATED WAYS AFFECTS HOW CHILDREN USE MATERIALS

On observing girls engaged in constructional play we began to suspect that girls' and boys' learning experiences may be quite different even when they are using the same materials. It was apparent throughout our observations that not only did young children have clear ideas about what girls and boys play with, but they also had firm ideas about how resources were to be used by each other.

In one infant class we observed a group of girls and boys as they settled down to play with Lego. There was a total assumption on the boys' part that the girls would make houses and the boys would make vehicles or guns. This was clearly demonstrated by the way in which the boys immediately, and without discussion, sorted out the Lego, giving the windows, doors, base boards and larger bricks to the girls and the wheels and rotatable connectors, etc. to the boys. The girls did not protest, although one girl who had planned to make something other than a house changed her mind saying, 'Oh, all right, I'll make a house'.

When children in another infant class were shown a photo of Lego the comments they made revealed that they were also very conscious of the different ways girls and boys used it.

Girl 1:   I make houses out of Lego ...
Boy 1:   We always make cars.
Boy 2:   I make guns too. We make guns and have fights.
Girl 1:   The boys in our school always make cars.

Nursery-aged girls and boys also frequently used the same material in quite different ways. The differences in use were related to the children's sense of what was appropriate for each gender. For example, five nursery children were working at a table set up for cutting, sticking and stapling paper. The boys were making loops out of paper which they slipped on to their arms. The girls were cutting out oval-shaped pieces of paper which they stuck on to sheets of paper.

Adult: (To boys) Are you making arm-bands?
Boy 1:   No, they're muscles.
Girl 1:   We're making flowers.
Boy 2:   We're making muscles to play He-Man
Girl 1:   They always make muscles.
Girl 2:   Sometimes they make He-Man belts.
Adult: (To girls) Do you sometimes make muscles and He-Man belts too?
Girl 3:   (laughing) That's silly!

The children's view of how certain resources should be used in gender-related ways often effectively excluded girls from particular construction materials which were not seen as having the potential for 'girls' play'. The materials which children identified as being used to make cars, aeroplanes and guns were almost constantly boy-dominated. In the classes we observed, boys tended to use constructional materials in more sophisticated ways, making more use of them as a medium and exploiting their three-dimensional properties (e.g. capacity for movement, balance, potential for complexity of configuration). The boys also tended to approach constructional play as an individualized activity. Girls, on the other hand, frequently made very simple structures and, moreover, they often used them as a foil for social play. In one class the girls worked co-operatively to construct a simple house and a few basic tables and chairs from Lego. They then fetched some 'Play People' and used their Lego house to engage in play centred around families at home. In contrast, the boys worked on their own and constructed cars, aeroplanes and guns. These Lego constructions were quite complex and many incorporated movable parts. They played briefly with these models using appropriate sound effects and then changed their construction into something else. The boys were engaged in a constant process of making and remaking Lego constructions.

Similar patterns were observed in many early-years classes. This would suggest that girls and boys may focus on two very different processes when playing with construction toys. Girls appear to be more concerned with the process of social interaction and boys with the process of making things. These observations would strongly suggest that ensuring girls and boys engage in the whole spectrum of activities on offer in nursery and infant classes is not in itself necessarily going to ensure that girls' and boys' learning experiences in school are not qualitatively different from each other.

THE VICIOUS CIRCLE

Children's choices of activity were not solely influenced by judgments about whether or not it was 'appropriate' in gender terms. This may have been an initial determining factor on first encountering the activity but the girls' comments suggested that lack of confidence and feelings of inadequacy about their ability to handle specific activities rapidly became an additional factor which inhibited their involvement.

Adult:	Do you play with the Lego?
Girl:	(aged 6) Sometimes ... I make cars—I can't do it. I make grass, flowers ... I can make a house. Sometimes I can't do it.
Adult:	What do you do then, who helps you?
Girl:	When I can't do it I just go away and do a drawing.
Adult:	(To boys) What about you, who helps you when you can't do something with the Lego?
Boy 1:	I can do it.
Boy 2:	I can always do it.
Adult:	But there must be times when you find it difficult—you can't make what you want to. What do you do then?
Boy 1:	I just do it.

Many of the girls described constructional activities as 'boring' but this may have been their way of opting out as the same girls became quite enthusiastic when given time, space and encouragement.

An analysis of nursery children's first choice of activity was revealing. On entering the classroom at the beginning of the day, many nursery children tend to choose to become involved in those activities they feel most confident about. Many girls chose to play in the 'home-corner', do a drawing, become involved in a creative activity (especially if an adult was present), read a book or talk to an adult. It was extremely rare to observe a girl choose to play with a construction as soon as she entered the class whereas it was very common to observe boys doing so.

CONFIDENCE AND POWER IN RELATION TO GENDER DOMAINS

The notion of territories or domains was highlighted by the way in which the children's confidence and assertiveness varied depending upon whether they were in or out of 'their' territory (see also Walden and Walderdine, 1982). The degree of confidence was reflected in the way that children approached activities.

Boy: I've made a dragon (shows model made from Mobilo).
Girl: Can you make me one?
Boy: (Incredulously) Can't you do it?
Girl: Do I need this?
Boy: No, you don't need that. You need a yellow one, one of these.
Girl: (Collects pieces to make model) That goes there. Did you put one of these in?

This constant questioning and checking continued until the girl had completed her dragon.

The children wielded power over the other sex when in their 'own' territory. Sometimes this power was apparent in the way the children dictated the terms or the rules of the game. Sometimes it was used to exclude would-be interlopers. Variations on the following exchange were frequently heard in nursery classes.

Girl 1:   (To two boys playing with large bricks) Can I play?
Boy: No ... Well, don't put your hands on the bricks 'cos I've wiped them.
Girl 2:   Can I play?
Boy: No, not *another* girl.

A third boy joined the group and was immediately included in the building activity. When the girl made a suggestion about the structure being built, one of the boys pushed her away and shouted, 'No! I told you not to touch the bricks'.

In those schools where the adults expressed disapproval about exclusion on the grounds of gender, children would offer an alternative justification for the exclusion. In one such nursery school ten boys were playing with large bricks when a girl attempted to join them.

Boy: This is a rocket, not she stand on it!
Adult: She can stand on it.
Boy: Who said you could play? Who said you could play?
Adult: She can play.
Boy: No she can't.
Adult: Why?
Boy: 'Cos she's got a horrible nose.

When in 'their' domain the girls were equally assertive. Three girls were playing in the home corner and a boy appeared at the door of the home corner.

Girl: (Before the boy had said anything) No!
Boy: I want my baby.
Girl: No! Go away.
Boy: (Pleading) I want it.
Girl: Here it is. Now run away.
              (In very adult tones)

In some classes the adults provided support and encouragement to children who wanted to move into previously unexplored 'territories'. It was interesting to note how children playing in areas they did not feel entitled to, frequently showed anxiety when children who normally dominated the activity began to join in. This anxiety led children to turn to an adult and make requests such as 'Don't let him play', or, in relation to her own model or the construction pieces, 'Don't let him take it'. When children were operating beyond their perceived gender domain their confidence was very easily undermined. For example, a four-year-old girl was in the process of grappling with a problem with a construction toy when a boy approached. He watched her for a moment and then said, 'That's not how you make a car. I know how'. He then began to tell her what to do. The girl responded by adopting a helpless demeanour and made no comment. Following the boy's intervention the adult tried to encourage her to continue but she refused saying 'I can't do it'.

GIRLS' STRATEGIES FOR GAINING ACCESS TO 'BOYS' DOMAIN

It was encouraging to notice that many girls did not passively accept the gender-based boundaries and developed their own strategies to gain access to 'boys' activities.

Boys who wanted to play in areas usually dominated by girls often ensured that they were able to do so by employing tactics which included disruption and fighting. Girls rarely employed such overt or violent means of gaining access. Many girls would try and gain access by attempting to show the boys that she was 'one of them' or by making it explicit at the outset that she was not going to attempt to dominate the activity and that she was willing to become involved on the boys' terms. In the following example a girl used both of these strategies, with varying degrees of success.

Three boys were playing with bricks. A girl had tried, unsuccessfully, to verbally negotiate an entrance to the activity. She then went away, built a machine-gun out of Duplo and returned to show it to the boys and said, 'I made a gun ... Look! I've got a gun'. The boys, who frequently engaged in gun play, could not resist a quick glance but they made no further response and continued to play with the bricks. The girl returned the Duplo to its tray and came back.

Girl: Can I be the baby girl? (repeated three times)
Boy: No, you can't be anything.

A few minutes passed and the girl remained where she was.

Boy: Oh, all right then.
Girl: Baby girl?

The boy nodded and the girl joined the group.

Gaining access to an activity was often not the end of the battle as those who regarded the activity as 'theirs' often insisted on taking the lead and dictating the terms of play. Sometimes girls were determined not only to play with toys normally dominated by boys but also to play with the toys on their terms. A three-year-old in a nursery decided that she wanted to play with the trains which, in this particular class, the boys had claimed as 'theirs'. As soon as she started playing she came into conflict with the boys who tried to insist that her train move in the opposite direction. One boy verbally threatened her, glared at her and repeatedly said 'No!'. When this failed to deter the girl he resorted to appealing to a nearby adult for help by crying. 'She's breaking up my train'.

The two examples show the degree of confidence, resolve and tenacity required on the part of girls who want to engage in activities normally dominated by boys.

GENDER OR CULTURE AS THE BASIS FOR PLAY CHOICES?

In the schools observed, there was no evidence of girls or boys choosing activities on the basis of their cultural, linguistic or religious background. Rather it was the case that children who were presented with a range of new activities tended to be drawn to those they were familiar with until they had developed the confidence to try something new. The pattern of girls playing with dolls and boys with cars and Lego was consistent across cultural and social groups. Gender appeared to be the major factor influencing children's play preferences. Children were also influenced by the degree of language that was an intrinsic part of the activity. If the activity required that the children talk to each other (e.g. solving a problem in pairs) there was a tendency for children from the same linguistic group to play together.

SABOTAGING OF TEACHERS' ATTEMPTS TO INVOLVE GIRLS IN CONSTRUCTIONAL PLAY

We found that the girls were very adept at sabotaging teachers' efforts to ensure that they engaged in an activity they would not normally choose. One of the strategies girls employed was to move to a completely different area of the classroom or nursery where the teacher could not see them in the hope, often fulfilled, that the teacher would forget about what she had asked the child to do. Another involved merely sitting near the activity for a short while and keeping a low profile until they judged it was safe to move away. If the task involved constructing something, a third strategy was to ask another child to make the model which they then showed to the teacher. This strategy was not used very often as it required the co-operation of other children. The fourth strategy, which was often used by girls when asked to make something using a construction toy, was for the girl to produce a model of minimal complexity which involved very little effort, problem-solving or thought. Girls were observed to connect a few bricks together and on showing it to an adult often received a great deal of praise. This last strategy was employed frequently and would suggest that at a very young age the girls concerned had worked out that not much was expected from them in the field of constructional activities and that a minimal effort would result in praise. Ironically the teachers who were most liable to be overgenerous with their praise were those who were keen to develop girls' constructional skills.

THE 'MAGNETIC' ADULT

Most cross-domain play occurred when an adult was involved in the activity. Figures 8.3 and 8.4 show the effect of an adult presence on the involvement of girls and boys in creative activities and constructional play. This pattern has also been observed by others (e.g. Whyte, 1983). The degree to which

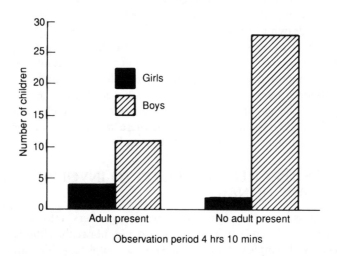

FIGURE 8.3 Effect of adult presence on involvement of girls and boys in creative activities

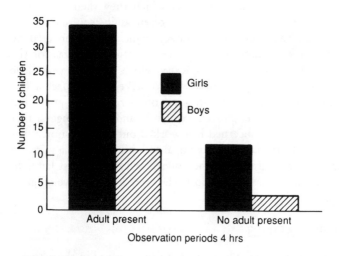

FIGURE 8.4 Effect of adult presence on involvement of girls and boys in construction play

the adult was a 'magnetic' influence depended upon the extent and nature of the adult's involvement. Adults who were enthusiastic and actively involved attracted more children than did those adults who 'serviced' activities.

In multilingual classes, bilingual children were attracted by adults who spoke their home languages. The children may have been attracted because they welcomed the opportunity to engage in stimulating discussion or because the adult was able to make the activity appear interesting. In nursery classes where there were women and men on the staff, girls were more likely to become involved in a 'boys' activity if a female rather than a male member of staff was present. Similarly, boys were likely to engage in 'girls' activities if a male member of staff was present. In one class when the male teacher was working with children in the creative area there was a predominance of boys. On other days, when the female teacher was working in the creative area girls predominated. When no adult was present the area was dominated by girls.

PERCEPTIONS OF SCIENTISTS AND TECHNOLOGY

It has been argued that girls 'switch off' from science and technology because both are associated with men and 'maleness'. Whilst none of the nursery children we talked to had formed ideas about what scientists are and what they do, comments made by under-fives suggested that many very young children have begun to develop clear ideas about the scientific and technological abilities of women.

Girl	
(aged 4):	My sister got a typewriter.
Adult:	Do you play with it?
Girl:	Mmmm. . . . It's broken.
Adult:	Oh dear, how did it break? Can you fix it?
Girl:	(Laughs) No!
Adult:	Why not?
Girl:	'Cos I can't.
Adult:	What about your Mummy, could she fix it?
Girl:	No! My Daddy does.
Adult:	Why not your Mummy?
Girl:	'Cos she's no good.

Not many of the infant children had clear ideas about what scientists do. The following is a record of a fairly typical conversation with a group of 6- and 7-year-olds.

Adult:	What is a scientist?
Boy 1:	A scientist? I dunno.
Boy 2:	It's a man . . .

Boy 3:   It's a man, it's a doctor and he helps women and helps children, he gets his case and helps them.

Girl 1:   It's a doctor, a woman (whispered), no, a man (said loudly).

Girl 2:   It's somebody who finds out what makes people sick. Testing things like yoghurt because hazelnut yoghurt got a poison in it and makes people sick. (This was a reference to a recent outbreak of botulism which was traced to hazelnut yoghurt.) He tests water. It's a man. It's a man who tests medicines and make-up. He works in a school laboratory.

Girl 3:   You need science for doctors and nurses.

Girl 4:   It's like Doctor Who. They go in space.

Most young children assumed that scientists were male and explained this by saying, 'Because they are'. It seems clear that for many children, science and science-related activities are perceived as a male domain. However, this perception is influenced by the types of activities which are identified as being 'scientific'.

CONCEPT DEVELOPMENT AND GENDER DOMAINS

The fact that science is perceived by many children to be about men in white coats doing experiments and going into space may result in girls feeling unable to engage in overtly scientific pursuits. However, activities defined as being 'for girls' also involve a range of scientific concepts. Our observations indicate that girls and boys often apply similar conceptual understandings in different situations. Many apparent gender differences in scientific understanding may have more to do with the context of conceptual application than with differences in conceptual development. This consideration assumes a new importance with the introduction of the National Curriculum and the 'testing' of very young children in order to ascertain their levels of attainment.

Girls engaged in a range of activities associated with girls and women (e.g. cooking, sewing, some forms of craftwork) are introduced to a wide range of scientific concepts. It is clear from talking to young children who have had experience of cooking that they are developing scientific understandings related to the properties of materials (e.g. their appearance, the effect on them of different temperatures, how they combine with other substances). Similarly, it was apparent from watching a girl making a dragon from junk materials that she had learnt a great deal about the characteristics of card, plastic, wood, paper and polystyrene, knew what would happen to these materials if they were squashed, had some idea about their relative strengths and had begun to explore how to make strong, stable structures.

One step towards enabling girls to view themselves as scientists may be to find ways of validating their understanding of scientific concepts by helping them, and boys too, to recognize that scientific concepts are applied in a range of contexts. Helping girls recognize their scientific understanding within applications where they have confidence, gives these activities status and also provides a basis for enabling them to transfer their knowledge to other contexts which may lie within 'male' domains.

It is widely recognized that children may have an understanding of a concept within one context but this understanding will not be apparent if the child is asked to apply this concept in another context (Donaldson, 1978; Hughes, 1986). We suggest that the existence of gender-related domains can be a major factor in influencing how well children can apply their understandings and capabilities. Although it is well documented that girls do not use constructional and mechanical toys as often as boys, they certainly have the necessary understanding to perform competently in spatial and mechanical activities and have developed a range of skills associated with CDT. Many 'female' activities (e.g. making dolls' clothes, dolls' houses, paper baskets) involve the process of conceptualizing a finished product, considering how to construct it from a range of non-specific components, executing a plan and modifying it as necessary. The same process is involved in building something from a construction toy. It seems reasonable to assume that the use of construction toys is influenced by sense of entitlement and confidence, rather than simply about possessing a particular type of knowledge and aptitude.

One approach to helping girls gain access to scientific application within male domains which we have found to be relatively successful is to begin with activities with which girls are familiar and feel confident about and move gradually into situations where they can apply their abilities to less familiar contexts. For example, an exploration of movement with five infant girls began with drawing animals, making movable paper puppets of the animal and finally making a model out of the construction toy Mobilo, a resource which offers scope for the exploration of forces and movement but one which these children had refused to use up to this point. Helping these girls transfer their understanding and interests into realms they defined as 'male' (e.g. construction toys) enabled them to extend their use of materials and begin to question the 'ownership' of materials and resources.

There is no simple way of promoting equal opportunities in science, maths and CDT. The observations outlined in this chapter highlight the complexity of the issue. Children's attitudes towards science and technology reflect deep-seated social patterns and therefore cannot be modified by a single, simple strategy. Real progress is dependent upon changes occurring in society as a whole. However, teachers cannot wait for such changes to occur and, within the classroom, teachers can have some impact on children's developing attitudes, confidence and choices. In order to do so we need to adopt a range of approaches which aim to promote equal opportunities. For example, ensuring girls spend more time with construction toys should be seen as only one way of dealing with a multifaceted issue. Approaches must also address other aspects such as attitudes towards various activities, the way activities are defined and identified, the degree and nature of adult involvement and methods of assessment.

Note

We would like to thank the children and staff of the 29 schools in which we observed and worked.

References

Clarricoates, K. (1980) The importance of being Ernest, Emma, Tom and Jane: the perception of categorisation of gender conformity and gender deviation in primary schools. In R. Deem (ed.) *Schooling for Women's Work*. London: Routledge and Kegan Paul.

Donaldson, M. (1978) *Children's Minds*. London: Fontana.

Hughes, M. (1986) *Children and Number*. Oxford: Basil Blackwell.

Thomas, G. (1986) Hallo Miss Scatterbrain. Hallo Mr Strong: Assessing nursery attitudes and behaviour. In N. Browne and P. France (eds) *Untying the Apron Strings: Anti-sexist Provision for the Underfives*. Milton Keynes: Open University Press.

Walden, R. and Walkerdine, V. (1982) *Girls and Mathematics: The Early Years*. Bedford Way Papers 8, University of London Institute of Education.

Walkerdine, V. (1989) *Counting Girls Out*. London: Virago Education Series.

Whyte, J. (1983) *Beyond the Wendy House: Sex Stereotyping in Primary Schools*. York: Longman for Schools Council.

9 REWRITING READING

GEMMA MOSS

The relationship between English teaching and feminism is not always an easy one to tease out. Feminism, has traditionally operated in non-hierarchical ways. English teaching takes place within stratified institutions where structural distinctions are always drawn between teachers and the taught. Feminism depends upon identifying oppression through the sharing of women's experience and so turns the personal into the political. English teachers may encourage personal expression, but how and where that translates into political action is a moot point. Different things happen to the category 'personal' in these two different contexts. Given these kinds of contradictions it is perhaps not surprising that English classes have seldom looked like consciousness-raising groups, even when gender issues are being most strenuously addressed. Most of the attention on sexism in English has focused on what teachers can do with books, a comparatively clear-cut issue, which seems relatively straightforward to address. Yet there has to be more to the relationship between the two areas than the kind of uneasy compromise I have sketched out above. Indeed, as I hope to explore below, it is high time for a radical reappraisal of the contribution feminism can make to English teaching.

Of course, English teaching itself is not homogenous. There are at least four major strands. One prioritizes the teaching of literature, another the teaching of basic skills. One sees the prime aim of English teaching as being the encouragement of personal growth, another as helping pupils develop the ability to question the social world. At the level of rhetoric these remain distinct positions; in practice, most English teachers use all of these approaches some of the time. Despite the fierceness of the debate, there are hidden continuities and overlaps. Those seeking to improve language skills are unlikely to rely solely on the use of decontextualized drills, no matter how hard the Secretary of State for Education may seem to be pushing teachers in that direction. (The compromise effected by Baroness Cox has been to itemize some skills but to insist on placing them in a context where meaning is stressed.) Those who emphasize the place of literature in the classroom often see reading as a morally uplifting activity, not just the means to knowledge of a cultural heritage.

Source: Kimberly, K., Meek, M. and Miller, J. (eds) (1992) *New Readings: Contributions to an Understanding of Literacy* (pp. 183–93). London: A. and C. Black.

Those committed to either child-centred or radical pedagogies seek to build from what children already know and so privilege autobiography, though for very different reasons; yet neither tradition excludes reference to other forms of literature, nor seeks to dispense with basic skills. If disputes between such diverse traditions can be so easily reconciled in practice, does feminism have anything to offer in the way of a radical critique of English teaching? Or can it, too, be appropriated readily, becoming just another strategy alongside the rest?

Of course, in one sense feminism may already be said to be represented in the English classroom, in the form of anti-sexist strategies. But anti-sexism is not synonymous with feminism. At best it remains one particular strand in feminist thinking, one which in the context of English teaching, I would want to argue, has been appropriated to fit existing approaches rather than constituting a challenge to them. This is not to say that the appropriation is altogether a bad thing. It has led to some very real achievements. Many English Departments have reviewed the kinds of literature they offer in the main school. There has been a sustained effort to include more books with female central characters and to exclude some of the existing stock. Anti-sexism can be a powerful weapon in the hands of female teachers wanting a better deal for their pupils in this respect, one which has been very effectively used against colleagues.

Other gains are less clear-cut. I have said that anti-sexism has been appropriated within existing approaches in English teaching. What I am getting at here is that it leaves intact many of the existing assumptions that English teachers already make, most notably about the relationships between texts and pupils. Anti-sexism joins in a rather odd alliance with Leavisism and the kind of vanguardist Left perspective associated with media studies in treating particular kinds of texts as potentially powerful in their effect. Linked to the notion of powerful texts is a notion of vulnerable readers. As a consequence of these views the teachers' role becomes one of regulatory control: without teacherly intervention, the assumption is, pupils may go astray. This kind of argument is most strongly played out around the sorts of text which are represented as being of dubious quality. Whilst opinions differ on which are the preferred texts, there is a fairly broad consensus in terms of what constitutes trash, and formulaic writing of the kind epitomized by the romance genre is pretty high on the list of dislikes. The effect of such a broad consensus is to close down debate about the model of reading which is involved here. Yet it is precisely this model of reading which I want to go on to examine, not least because it poses some problems for feminists when it comes to considering the girls in our classrooms. After all, many of the latter are avid consumers of precisely those kinds of texts which this argument views with suspicion: romances and photo-love stories. Accept this model of reading, and what do we make of the girl readers of such texts? That they are passive victims of a set of values which work against their own best interests? That they are learning a set of behaviours they would be better off without?

The view that texts are powerful and can fundamentally influence their readers, whether for good or bad, works from the assumption that particular textual features have particular fixed meanings, and that consequently the message any one text holds is quite easy to determine: by exercizing skill and judgement teachers can identify what kind of text they have in front of them, and whether its effects will be good or bad, an image positive or negative. But there are difficulties here. For instance, a recent issue of *My Guy* included a photo-love story whose central character was an unmarried mother/ teenage single parent. She meets the potential new man in her life when she's out with her child. Is this a positive image or not? How do we judge? Do we assume that any story in which girl meets boy is negative, reinforcing heterosexual desire (in which case do we pass the same judgement on a text such as *Pride and Prejudice*)? Or does the inclusion of the child in the story disrupt the romanticized representation of girls' sexuality more ordinarily associated with girls' teen magazines? Should the fact that the young mother appears neither upset, ashamed nor embarrassed about her lot be welcomed as a change from the stereotype, or is the association of women with children reinforcing women's reproductive role? In which case should we reject all stories which include women as mothers as being dangerous texts? Of course, without the original in front of you it is hard to judge. But even if it were reproduced here I'm not sure on what grounds we would settle the argument. The image is contradictory, capable of being read in several ways.

Even seemingly more straightforward positive images are not without their difficulties. *The Turbulent Term of Tyke Tyler* is a case in point. If we imagine that all stories about girls show them as passive and resourceless individuals, involved in soppy plot-lines revolving round flowers and cuddly toys, then *Tyke Tyler* provides a useful corrective. But in turning Tyke into an active and resourceful individual with a strong role to play, the book also effectively transforms her into a boy. Indeed, this is part of the point the book has been designed to make. By disguising Tyke's identity until the final chapter the idea is that expectations about gender role can be challenged—the message can be put across that girls can behave like boys. But is this the only way that girls' behaviour can be valued, if they can pass as male? Interestingly enough, Tyke's elder sister, clearly identified as female throughout the story, gets the same kind of disparaging treatment normally reserved for girls in more obviously conventional texts. So just what has been changed? At least some of the subtext still seems to be that girls being girls in some way don't count, their interests and concerns only matter when they look like boys. Specific textual features *are* contradictory. Yet within the current terms of debate, it is not always easy to see how to respond. On the one hand, it is tempting to persist in denying that there is any difficulty. Some teachers, faced with a difference of view, insist that their interpretation is right and just try harder to persuade their pupils to subscribe to the teacher's tastes. In this way, battle lines get drawn and opinion is sharply polarized. Either pupils concur with the teacher's view or they don't. If children get the point the teacher is driving at and come into line by dropping their reading of second-rate teencomics, for instance, all well and good. They win the teacher's approval. If they don't it is hard to know what to do next. It is the classic vanguardist dilemma. What do you do when the followers refuse to be led? The alternative is to accept that the meaning of any text is ambiguous, and open to more than one interpretation, but then to make the adoption of one interpretation rather than another a matter of purely individual choice. Consequently, the teacher ends up advocating an entirely hands-off approach, in which anybody is entitled to think anything they like: the classic *laissez-faire* liberal tactic, which obscures any political dimension to debate.

I have suggested some difficulties in holding to a view of powerful texts. If texts contain contradictory images, it is hard to see how we could imagine that they exert a simple effect. On the other hand, admitting some of the difficulties involved in getting pupils to agree with teachers about the meaning of what gets read doesn't in itself provide much of an alternative. Within the existing consensus in English teaching, the choice of response seems to come down to old-fashioned liberalism or the kind of policing of children's reading which smacks of hard-Left vanguardism. Meanwhile, a specifically feminist contribution to this debate is missing.

What way out of this impasse does feminism suggest? The single most important point which has got lost in feminism's appropriation as anti-sexism is the pro-woman line, by which I mean the assumption on feminists' part that women are not to blame for the inequalities of patriarchy, and that on the contrary, what they do is a legitimate response to the realities of male power. An example of what this means in practice can be provided by looking at the debate about promotion prospects for women teachers. One explanation of why so few women hold senior posts goes something like this: women themselves are under-confident. They have been handicapped by not being brought up to behave like men. What they need is assertiveness training. Once they have gained their confidence, then they will be able to compete equally with male colleagues and take their rightful place in the hierarchy. The pro-woman perspective would start from the assumption that it is not women's confidence or lack of it which is at fault. The fact that women don't apply for senior posts is due to a realistic assessment on their part of what would be involved in climbing the career ladder. They are not prepared single-mindedly to pursue promotion in a system which makes unacceptable demands on those who compete within it. In contrast, the men who are prepared to make that sacrifice can do so only because much of the work has been taken out of their personal lives by the women they live with. In this analysis it is accepted that women don't fit the system, but the conclusion is that it is the system which needs changing, not the women themselves. The point of a pro-woman line is not to show that women are always right but, by starting from the premise that women's behaviour makes sense, to challenge what men are up to. If we accept the analysis that the current set-up works in the interests of men not women, that is surely what we need to do.

In the classroom, taking a pro-woman line would get us out of the vanguardist perspective so often associated with anti-sexism, whereby teachers assume all the responsibility for telling students what they need to know. Such an approach consistently underestimates girls' experience. They do not arrive in our classrooms as blank slates, waiting for teachers to tell them the score. Of course, girls know that they get a rough deal. How could they avoid being aware of what is only too clearly spelt out to them by boys' behaviour every day of their lives? The confusion arises simply because they are not taking stridently militant action. Well, is that the only legitimate way of dealing with male power? Hanging around a neglected area of the playground with your friends to chat about the kinds of things that boys aren't interested in may be just as profitable as having the hassle of competing with them for space to play football. Why does the latter seem to win all the approbation? What is actually being decided in this way?

Taking a pro-woman line would also get us away from the kind of contempt that often trails in the wake of anti-sexism. In attempting to resolve the differences between girls' and boys' behaviour anti-sexism puts a high priority on getting them both to behave in the same way. But often in practice this means encouraging girls to behave like boys, in which case no radical re-evaluation of girls' activities takes place, and no real challenge is made to boys' behaviour. Instead, girls become the problem. 'Since girls in general are so severely conditioned and repressed and so turned in upon themselves, they fall victim to fantasies in consequence,' Bob Dixon (1977) has written. Girls are assumed to be lacking in a way in which boys are not. Where there is an attempt to encourage boys to behave like girls the assumption is that the former are oppressed by gender stereotyping in exactly the same way as the latter. But how can this be the case? Asking girls to take on boys' behaviour means asking the powerless to appropriate the strategies of the powerful; asking boys to take on girls' behaviour means expecting the powerful to appropriate the strategies of the powerless. The invitations are not equivalent.

Unless we revalue what girls are up to in the way that a pro-woman line suggests, it remains possible to use the discourse of anti-sexism to put women in their place. Judith Williamson (1981) in a piece entitled 'How does girl number twenty understand ideology?' writes about an incident where exactly this happens. A boy making a presentation in a media studies class on Images of Women has chosen girls' comics as his topic.

I can see why Mark has chosen this topic: it's easy work, in a way, we can all see how stupidly girls are shown and that's what this course is all about, isn't it? He thinks I'm going to approve. But as we go through his careful presentation—packed with gems of teaching material—my flesh creeps at the note of scorn in his voice. After all, girls read this rubbish, don't they? It just goes to show how stupid they are. The problem arises openly in class. *Why* do girls read these? *We* can see at a glance how unrealistic the stories are, how trashy the images. So why do girls read them? It just confirms, for the boys at least, that girls *are* somehow silly or dumb.

                                                            (Williamson, 1981)

Taking a pro-woman line and starting from the assumption that girls' behaviour makes sense, mean re-evaluating male behaviour. It can no longer be treated as neutral, the norm against which other ways of operating can be judged. Instead it becomes visible as a strategy for taking and holding on to power.

Positively valuing girls' activity and raising questions about boys' provides new and much more useful approaches to questions about reading (and writing). For it also suggests a different way of thinking about the relationship between pupils and texts, both the texts they read and the texts they produce. Rather than trying to establish once and for all what a text means and then trying to police children's reading of that text, or alternatively endorsing any and every response, the pro-woman line shifts attention to the context in which any one reading takes place. In this way there is no difficulty in understanding how a boy can use teenage girls' comics to denigrate female pupils. It is precisely the kind of power play one might expect. For what matters about texts is not the content alone, but the way that content can be mobilized and used by readers. And feminists would expect differences here to be governed, not by randomly individual choice, but by social and collective histories. In other words, we would expect there to be conflicting readings, which could not be settled by reference to the text alone. Rather than attempting to close things down by fixing once and for all what the text means, feminism would fore-ground the social strategies readers bring to the text.

This means putting to one side the kind of rudimentary content analysis which has been used to establish whether a book contains positive or negative gender representations. Such analysis will not tell us very much about the reading strategies pupils use, nor, consequently, what the books 'mean'. Anybody in any doubt about this should try applying this sort of checklist analysis to texts which aren't reading schemes or school textbooks. The results look decidedly odd. Jane Austen would appear to be unacceptable because her female characters occupy an unhealthy limited range of social roles. Shakespeare would have to be rejected on the grounds that he dangerously under-represents women. *Hamlet* would have to be considered a deeply unsatisfactory text because women readers can only identify with either Gertrude or Ophelia, neither of them positive role models. As Jane Miller (1986) has already pointed out, this would hardly sum up the possibilities for women readers. If we allow that women readers may have other options when reading these texts, why shouldn't the same be true when they pick up a magazine? The categorization of content should not lead to assumptions about how a text gets read. Instead of extrapolating back from content to reading strategies, we should start the other way round, with the readers themselves and the social contexts within which texts are produced and circulated.

Adopting this perspective means reconsidering some of the other assumptions on which current practice is based. It would certainly raise doubts about the value of stressing a personal response to text. If we accept that response to texts is socially constructed then the search for the individual and unique experience is rendered illusory. Perhaps we should replace the personal response principle with an ethnography of reading? An ethnography of reading would stress the role which diverse social and cultural practices play in shaping how texts get read. This would enable contrasts to be made between different forms of reading, association with different kinds of texts and different groups of readers. Such an approach suggests a new study of comics, magazines and generic fiction. The latter are hard to accommodate whilst the stress is on the uniqueness of the reading experience, for such texts are deliberately constructed to make the most of familiarity with the conventions of the form. They play on repetition (Neale, 1983). An ethnography of reading would expect such literature to be read differently from, rather than in the same manner as, other kinds of texts. At the same time, because they are aimed at gender-differentiated markets, they provide a focus for exploring the different ways in which boys and girls read. We could begin by asking some of the following kinds of questions. What is the significance of the fact that the magazines teenage boys purchase appear to be aimed at an adult readership, when girls seem to choose magazines explicitly targeted at a teenage audience? What is the appeal of the stress on technical language, or the apparent need for expertise on the part of male readers, which boys' magazines cultivate? What range of images of masculinity are to be found in girls magazines? What is the function of the 'pretty boy' version of masculinity associated with many of the pin-ups? What effect does the selection of this image (rather than any other) have? What makes it so difficult to persuade boy readers to cope with genres which they consider to be primarily aimed at girls? What is at stake here? This kind of approach, expecting difference and asking questions about it, could usefully be extended and applied to children's writing too. Do the genres of romance and science fiction have a different function in children's writing? What are the implications of the virtual absence of female characters in the genres boys use in their writing? What function does the double perspective of the romance (the boy's view of the girl's view of the boy) have in girls' writing? In asking these kinds of question we would be re-casting writing as primarily a social, not a private and personal, activity.

So far I have been indicating the role a feminist perspective could have in re-shaping the ways in which English teachers think about reading and writing. Turning our attention to the function texts have for their readers or writers means concentrating first of all on differences and beginning to account for the patterns which emerge (Moss, 1989). At the same time this has implications for the way in which gender is addressed in the classroom as an explicit topic, not least because it emphasizes finding ways of exploiting potentially conflicting points of view. Making the most of such conflicts depends on taking a pro-woman line. In what follows I want to give a clearer indication of how this perspective might work out in practice, by looking in detail at a particular lesson I had with a fourth-year English group.

I had set the class a writing task which was gender-specific by asking them to write as realistic an account as they could manage of the sort of talk that went on in small groups during registration, with this proviso: they were to restrict themselves to the sort of talk that went on in single-sex groups and were to begin with their own sex. Once they had done this they were to go on and write down what they imagined the conversation would be like between members of the opposite sex in the same circumstances. So each individual wrote two pieces, one entitled 'Girls' Talk', one entitled 'Boys' Talk': one piece drawing on what they knew from first hand, the other speculative. When the tasks had been completed, I divided the blackboard into four columns, two headed girls' talk, two headed boys' talk. We began to write down all the subjects that had been mentioned by the class in their writing. In this way we established an impression both of what the girls and the boys had actually been talking about and what they thought the other sex would have been talking about. What emerged was as follows: the girls thought the boys would have been talking about sex and violence. The boys described themselves as talking about sex and violence, although they had also talked about hobbies (something the girls hadn't thought of).

> 'Geoff,' Neil and I shouted in unison as Geoff walked through the door.
> 'Ah,' as Geoff heaved his bag off his back,
> ' . . . caught three chub yesterday, down Keynsham.'
> 'Oh yea,' said Neil.
> 'Yea,' said Geoff, 'I've frozen them. You can see 'em tonight if you want.'
> 'You're on. Coming tonight, Rich?'
> 'Might as well. Nothing else to do.'
> 'Call about 5,' said Geoff. 'After, I'll get my radio-controlled car out.'

The boys thought the girls would have been talking about boyfriends, pop groups and records.

'Hello Sarah,' said Catherine as she walked in.
'Right. Hey I got my Wham fan club letter back today,' said Debby.
'Hey, what did it say?'
'Well it said all about their coming tour and . . .'
'Hey, guess what,' said Louise running in, 'Jeremy is going out with that new girl. You know, the one with spots all over her neck and the fat legs.'
'How could he stand it?' said Sarah.
'How could she stand it?' said Debby. 'How could they stand it?' said Louise.

None of the girls had described herself as talking about pop groups. They had described themselves as talking about boyfriends, but they had also covered a much wider array of topics: clothes, friends, teachers, homework, parents, watching television, buying presents. The list went on. But at the same time there was a common thread running through much of what they wrote about. Almost regardless of the subject matter, the conversation would be used to define relationships.

'Me and Christine went up Kingswood on Saturday right?' Sharon said to me. 'I bought a chip-fryer for my Mum and a big doll for my sister and I made Christine carry it all the way home.'
'Yeh, they were really heavy and I couldn't see where I was going and I hit my head,' said Christine. 'And Sharon just stood there laughing.'
Alison then came into the room and told a dirty joke.
'My Mum nearly hit me when I told her it,' she said after.
'I should think she did,' Christine replied.

It was once we'd established these broader headings that the conversation became interesting. At first the boys were quite happy to have the subjects of their discussion listed as sex, violence and hobbies. The mention of sex and violence produced loud laughter and a variety of other noises from the boys in the class. But as the conversation developed around the differences between the boys' treatment of these subjects and the complexity of the girls' writing, other things began to happen. The girls became increasingly restless, both impatient with the way the boys had underestimated what they were up to and critical of the topics the boys had chosen. This culminated in Angelique turning round to the boys and saying: 'The trouble with you lot is you just haven't got any feelings.' In the rather stunned silence that followed I picked on the one boy in the class who I thought would be prepared to give me a straight answer and said: 'That's a very serious charge. What have you got to say about it?' Suddenly the whole tenor of the conversation changed. The boy began to talk about how difficult it was to express your feelings as a boy talking to other boys, how the pressure was on to disguise the feelings you have, or if you couldn't do that, show them through violence. The whole basis for the boys' pride in their ability to talk about sex and violence had been undercut.

That is the brief outline of the lesson. Now let me consider in more detail just what was going on here. When the boys wrote about what they imagined the girls' talk to be, they wrote about it with contempt. Richard, whose piece of girls' talk I quoted from above, had this comment to make when, following the lesson, I asked the class to summarize the discussion that had gone on under the heading 'The differences between boys' and girls' talk':

> Girls talk about boyfriends and how well they get on with them. Also they talk about more trivial things than boys and things which are less important. Girls always seem to talk about clothes right down to the last detail. Boys like being fashionable but girls are more fussy.

The topics that the boys chose for the girls were ones they considered trivial and not serious. At the same time they also misrepresented how the girls actually talked about boyfriends. They imagined that such talk was either about status (so Jeremy can be mocked for going out with an unglamorous girl) or revealed the girls as being fixated on the boys (given over to their power?) or showed them to be soppy (given over to feelings) unlike the 'hard' boys. Here is Richard again:

> The main difference in boys' and girls' talk is that boys think about the rougher side of life and girls think about appearance and relationships more.

So in other words, in their account of girls' talk the boys were attempting to 'do power' over the girls. When it came to discussing what they had written in the lesson, the boys' initial concern was both to show that they were different from the girls and to show that the girls' concerns weren't up to much. However, in the process of discussion the girls became increasingly vociferous in refusing the boys' evaluation of them. They were trying to get out of the position in which the boys were trying to place them and to defend their own interests against the boys. I went along with what was going on and supported the girls by encouraging them to look at what they themselves had written, and to find ways of validating it. I did this both by asking them to reflect directly on their own work—'How is what you've written about different?'—and by giving them the space in the discussion to do so—in other words, shutting up the boys.

The key to the radical shift in the conversation came when Angelique directly challenged the boys about what they were up to by applying the criteria the girls had established in their own work to the boys. By saying that this was a very serious charge and insisting that a particular individual answered it rather than dismissing it, I changed the whole grounds of the discussion. Now the boys had to reconsider what they had been talking about from another perspective, one which had been identified as the girls'. The outcome was that the girls got their own power back and refused the boys' definition of them, whilst the boys had the opportunity to rethink their own position in different terms.

What was the gap in the discourse which allowed this to happen? In the version of their own talk that they had given in their writing the boys had been pushing away feelings so that they could rehearse a strong objective masculinity, dealing in the impersonal. In so doing they were claiming adult male status. Their version of boys talking about girls was to talk about girls as sex objects, rather than who they were interested in going out with and how they might manage that: 'Angela's a bit of all right. Cor, what a pair of knockers.' In writing about violence they were most interested in establishing the status of the participants according to who was most prepared to throw punches:

> 'Did you see that scrap last week? Terry really gave it to him. You should have seen the blood. Paul got it right on the nose.'

But in saying this they were not giving the complete truth about themselves. They were covering over certain areas of their lives in an attempt to give a strong public performance which could establish their status in relation to the other boys. At times their writing showed another side to the way things were even if only by implication. Richard's piece of conversation, which had been summed up under the heading 'Hobbies', is also in an oblique way about friendship. Even if the tone is casual—'Coming tonight, Rich?' 'Might as well. Nothing else to do.'—it's also about being friends and the relationships between boys. In a way the boys' biggest mistake, which was ultimately to lead to them failing to 'do power' over the girls, was in accepting the summary of their agenda as sex, violence and hobbies. They accepted it because it looked impersonal and also made them look big. In their own terms handling these subjects in rather racy conversation was proof of the masculinity to which they aspired. It was what made them different from the girls:

> If someone notices boys have feelings and consideration for girls they will call them soppy and other stuff. So just to prove to their mates, when the girl isn't around he will talk about her with his mates saying 'Oh, she's all right, but a bit of a cow at times' ... Boys don't involve girls in their conversations because they think she wouldn't know what she was talking about. If it was a girls' conversation he wouldn't be interested because if he was his mates would call him sissy.
>
> Boys think about the rougher side of life and girls think about appearance and relationships more. The rougher side of life is horror films, rough sports and fighting, etc. Also things like cars and bikes, etc., are often talked about.

But it was also their undoing, because this impersonal agenda is not a complete representation of who the boys are, and once questions had been raised by the girls about feelings, the boys' bluff had been called. So the terms of the conversation were switched by directing attention back to what the boys were trying to exclude. Instead of trying to argue with what was there in the boys' talk—this sex and violence is repulsive—the girls won back the agenda by pointing to what was absent in the boys' talk: feelings. They identified the absence by establishing the difference between what was present in their own work and what was present in the boys', but also by taking their own work as the norm against which the boys' could be judged. It was this sort of positive comparison between the two that pushed the discourse over into something new.

Of course, that doesn't mean to say that the particular strategy the girls used here will always work, nor that it is the only one. But it does indicate that a useful starting-point can be made by exploiting the differences between perspectives in the classroom. If we are serious about our politics, it is not so much a matter of coming to the classroom with a fixed position, a set of ready-made answers, as setting the agenda for the discussion and, through our support of the girls, setting out how that discussion will take place.

Feminism has much to offer English teaching. The kind of pro-woman perspective I have been outlining suggests new ways of taking up gender issues in the classroom. At the same time it raises questions about many of the kinds of practices which English teachers take for granted in their classrooms by stressing the place of social and cultural histories rather than privileging personal and individual expression.

References

Dixon, B. (1977) *Catching Them Young, I: Sex, Race and Class in Children's Fiction.* Pluto Press.

Miller, J. (1986) *Women Writing About Men.* Virago.

Moss, G. (1989) *Un/Popular Fiction.* Virago.

Neale, S. (1983) *Genre.* BFI.

Williamson, J. (1981) How does girl number twenty understand ideology? *Screen Education* 40 (2).

10 BOYS WILL BE BOYS? RACISM, SEXUALITY, AND THE CONSTRUCTION OF MASCULINE IDENTITIES AMONGST INFANT BOYS

PAUL CONNOLLY

> I think it is very important to describe the values of masculinity in the working class. It's a social fact like any other, but one that's badly understood by intellectuals [...] It goes without saying that I don't present the lifestyle of the working class and its system of values as a model, an ideal [...] I try to explain the attachment to the values of masculinity, physical strength, by pointing out for example that it's characteristic of people who have little to fall back on except their labour power, and sometimes their fighting strength [...] the idea of masculinity is one of the last refuges of the identity of the dominated classes.
>
> (Pierre Bourdieu, 1993, p. 4)

There is no uniformity in the particular aspects of masculinity and physicality that are valued amongst working-class boys (Dollimore, 1986; Brod, 1987; Hearn and Morgan, 1990; Segal, 1990). Specific values will differ not just for White, Irish and Black[1] boys but also in terms of how the discourses on 'race', gender, class and sexuality articulate for these boys in specific contexts. This article is concerned with the construction of masculine identities amongst a friendship group of four-, five- and six-year-old boys, collectively named the 'Bad Boys'[2] (one African/Caribbean, two mixed-parentage[3] and one White). It aims primarily to address the way in which, as Bourdieu commented, masculinity is 'badly understood' by intellectuals. It is an attempt to shift the focus away from innate cultural and familial-based explanations of masculinity towards an explanation of masculinity as a response to broader social processes—a shift from 'blaming the victim' to problematizing 'society'. The article draws upon data from a much broader ethnographic study of a multi-ethnic, inner-city primary school—a study concerned with examining the ways in which racialized and gendered cultural identities are formed amongst infant children.[4]

The African/Caribbean[5] boys considered in this paper see themselves not just as working class but also as Black. So these boys have more than their labour power to fall back on. Their masculine identities are also formed within the context of, and resistance to, racism. However, racism and class

Source: This article has been specially commissioned for this Reader.

relations are neither expressed nor experienced uniformly (Cohen, 1987; Donald and Rattansi, 1992). In general, the African/Caribbean children in the school studied have very diverse biographies: they bring differing experiences to the school and respond to situations with differing knowledge bases and, accordingly, in differing ways (Fuller, 1980; Gillborn, 1990; Mac an Ghaill, 1988; Mirza, 1992). Moreover, the nature of relations within the school will largely depend on how various discourses articulate and manifest themselves in specific contexts. Nothing is predetermined. The boys discussed here are in no way representative of other African/Caribbean boys in the school. The aspects of masculinity that they valued, especially in relation to sexuality, differ markedly from the other Black boys. The main concern of this article is to examine the specific nature of their masculine identities and identify the way in which particular social processes have contributed to their construction. Rather than making any claims to be representative, the article therefore starts from the premise of diversity. It attempts to understand how discourses on racism, gender, sexuality and class articulate within specific contexts to inform the formation of masculine identities among the Bad Boys. Their focus on physical competence (at sports and fighting) and sexuality is not because they are Black[6] *per se* but because of the specific contexts and set of social relations in which they are located.

In focusing upon the complex nature of masculine identities and the variety of social processes that articulate in their construction for the Bad Boys, the article will also illustrate the active role that infant children themselves play in negotiating and forming social relationships. It will show the cognitive ability of children as young as five and six to make sense of and actively construct their own identities around a number of discourses on childhood, masculinity, racism and sexuality (James and Prout, 1990; Chisholm *et al.*, 1990: Wagg, 1988).

In doing this, the article will draw out the contradictory nature of children's experiences of schooling and their responses to it. It will be shown how gendered and racialized identities are relatively fluid and contingent and, as a consequence, how the construction of identities are only ever contradictory in their outcomes. In this sense, the Bad Boys are not only *Black* but they are also *boys*. Their construction of specific masculine identities in response to schooling and racism are, especially in their reliance upon particular discourses on gender and heterosexuality, never simply 'progressive' in their own right. As Walkerdine has argued:

> The contradictions, the struggles for power, the shifting relations of power, all testify the necessity for an understanding of subjectivities not a unique subjectivity. These contradictions also point to the necessity to re-think our strategies for action within education. It shows too how resistance on the part of children is not necessarily progressive in and of itself, and that the consequences of resistance are, to say the least, contradictory.   (Walkerdine, 1981, p. 24)

MANOR PARK ESTATE AND ANNE DEVLIN COUNTY PRIMARY SCHOOL

The 'Bad Boys' all live on the Manor Park estate which provides the main catchment area for Anne Devlin County Primary School.[7] It is a distinctly working class, inner-city council estate located in the heart of an English city with high levels of unemployment and a high population of young children and single-parent families. Manor Park is composed of maisonettes and high-rise tower blocks, separated from its immediate surroundings by four main dual-carriageways and with its own shopping precinct, neighbourhood and health centres and tenants' association. Whilst there are high proportions of Black (mainly South Asian) people to be found in the immediate neighbourhoods, the estate itself is predominantly White with only 14% South Asian and 8% African Caribbean.

Within this overall context Manor Park has gained a notoriety with the police and other professional agencies serving the area for being 'rough'. Whilst such a reputation has, as with many others, been the product of various moral panics (Cohen, 1972; Hall *et al.*, 1978) and is not one particularly shared by the residents themselves, the estate does experience higher rates of crime (particularly burglary, theft and robbery) and higher levels of domestic violence compared with the county as a whole. The incidence of racist attacks is also relatively high and many of the (particularly Asian) parents are unable to use the local playgrounds and other facilities without fear of verbal abuse or attack—often by children from Anne Devlin primary school. Such attacks could partly be related to contestations over territory amongst the White working-class youth on the estate (see Cohen, 1987) and their perceptions of being one of the 'last posts' or White areas within a city 'dominated' by Black communities. This was certainly one of the underlying themes that emerged in discussions with the children and parents on the estate.

Five years old at the start of the school year, the Bad Boys had come to construct and negotiate their identities largely in the domestic environment of parent(s), older peers and friends living on the estate. The emphasis on Manor Park was one of survival and this provided the context for the creation of specific forms of working-class masculinity which emphasized its 'street-wise' nature and drew heavily upon various expressions of popular culture. Such cultural forms and identity played a large role in the Bad Boys' attempts to re-construct and re-negotiate their masculine identities within the more public arena of the school. It is here that the Boys, in being confronted with social relations on a much larger scale and more ethnically diverse than before, whilst also being the object of various discourses on racism and childhood, drew upon and introduced these wider working-class cultural forms in their responses.

The Anne Devlin is a relatively large school with 407 children on roll at the start of the 1992/93 academic year. It is more ethnically diverse than its catchment area with roughly half its children being White, a quarter South Asian and the other quarter African/Caribbean and mixed-parentage children in equal numbers. Each child on the estate is entitled to spend at least one term full-time in one of the school's three nursery classes before moving up to the Reception/Year 1 classes. There are four Reception/Year 1 classes (three of which formed the basis of my study). Children move up to these classes at the start of the term following their fifth birthday. At the start of the 1992/93 academic year each of the Reception/Year 1 classes began with a total of 18 or 19 children rising, by the summer term, to between 24 and 27.

RACISM, SCHOOLING AND THE BAD BOYS

The Bad Boys—Stephen (African/Caribbean), Jordan (mixed-parentage), Paul (mixed-parentage) and Daniel (White)—who provide the focus of this paper were all in the same Reception/Year 1 class—Mrs Scott's class. They had all been there for two terms prior to the start of the academic year 1992/93 and were all five years old at the start of that academic year. For much of the time these four (or at least a combination of three of them) could be seen together, either sitting at the same table in the classroom (unless purposively split up by Mrs Scott) or outside in the playground playing football or other group games such as tick or wrestling.

The Bad Boys' experiences of schooling need to be located within the broader schooling experiences of African/Caribbean boys. In essence, it was one of greater surveillance, chastisement and disciplining from teaching and non-teaching staff compared to any other group within the school (Wright, 1986, 1992a, b; Mac an Ghaill, 1988; Gillborn, 1990). Such control was heavily dependent upon the specific contexts. Teachers were more likely to make important distinctions between African/Caribbean boys in terms of beliefs and actions in more relaxed, less stressful situations. This was also true in more one-to-one, private contexts (Connolly, 1993). It was, in the more public, and often highly stressed context of classroom management, however, that these boys were more likely to share a relatively common experience of surveillance and control.

It was common practice in the school for staff in public situations such as in assemblies, the playground, dinner hall or classroom to 'single out' certain children quite publicly when order was being challenged. By directing their wrath at one or two individuals rather than the group as a whole and quite publicly chastising them, order was soon regained. It was in this context that the Bad Boys' more adverse experiences of schooling needs to be located. For it was their 'visibility' as *African/Caribbean* children which meant that they were by far the most likely to be called to the front of assembly, excluded from the classroom and made to stand in the corridor, or ordered to stand by the wall in the playground.

The Bad Boys' increased 'visibility' to school staff, at times when staff are struggling to maintain order, is in part underwritten by the broader racialized view of African/Caribbean boys being stubborn, aggressive and moody. The fact that they had formed a friendship group and were therefore more 'visible' as a *group* of African/Caribbean boys, increased their likelihood of being singled out by school staff relative to other African/Caribbean boys. This was certainly the case for Mrs Scott whose end of year school report[8] for Jordan commented on how:

> He persists in kicking and thumping other children despite the fact that he has been kept in at playtime frequently. He takes no notice at all [. . .] colouring seems to have a calming effect on him [. . .] I must add that Jordan's stubbornness prevents him from doing as well as he could; today he refused to look at the alphabet on the wall when trying to write about his new baby. He can be *extremely* difficult to deal with. [original emphasis]

Similarly, during a brief talk I had with Mrs Scott in the playground one morning she also had this to say about Paul's father who was in prison:

> I shall imagine Paul's father is a big West Indian man, because Paul is quite big and the mother's blonde, and I can imagine, you know, perhaps have to be in maximum security if he's got a temper or some other thing.'

These broader views of the Bad Boys were often reinforced in public situations. A typical example of this was in the following incident in the classroom where Mrs Scott, sitting at a table with Stephen, Daniel and two other children, was asking Stephen about his planned visit that evening to his father in prison. Interesting here is not only the public vilification of Jordan but Stephen's contradictory identity as created by Mrs Scott; 'good' at one level but always within the shadow of being Black (with the potential this creates for a 'deviant' way of life'):

Mrs Scott: So you might be visiting him tonight?
Stephen: [*nods*]
Mrs Scott: You're good. I don't think you'll be going to prison [*louder, some children in the class look up*]. You'll have to remember when you're a man not to fight, steal, throw bricks. [*pause*] In fact even when you're ten.
Daniel: Can you go to prison when you're ten?
Mrs Scott: Well not prison but you can certainly be taken away.
Daniel: Go to a naughty children's home eh?
Mrs Scott: Something like that—a young offenders' centre they call it,

that's right; a young offenders' centre. [*She then looks over to Jordan on another table on the far side of the room who is busy with his head down, colouring in his picture and shouts over*] You'll have to remember that over there! [*Most of children in class stop what they are doing and look over to Jordan's table*] If you kick and fight when you are over ten you'll have to go to a special school—a young offenders' centre.

(For an explanation of typographical conventions used in transcribed dialogue see end of article.)

PEER GROUP RELATIONS

It is this frequent public reinforcement of African/Caribbean boys as 'bad' that provides the specific context for the playground interaction with their peers and thus the basis within which their masculine identities are then constructed. These continuous public vilifications of African/Caribbean boys generally helped to create and reinforce a distinct reputation they had for being 'troublesome' within the school. For the Bad Boys, being seen as a *group* of African/Caribbean boys, this was a reputation much more marked. It was a reputation that created, for some of the White boys in the school, a number of responses. On the one hand, whilst the Bad Boys have obviously been set-apart and racialized by such processes, the White boys, in comparison to their almost universally derogatory views of the Asian boys, held a kind of grudging 'respect' for the Bad Boys. They were in their eyes, after all, obviously strong and defiant—why else were they attracting the wrath of the teachers so much? Moreover, they were also regarded as 'good at sport' and especially football—something that the school encouraged the boys to be involved in (Connolly, 1994; see also Carrington, 1983). The centre-stage, both visually and spatially, that the older African/Caribbean boys took in the playground at dinner time with their highly organized games of football, provided both distinct role-models for the younger boys and consolidating evidence, for the White boys, in their views.

On the other hand, such competent displays of masculinity were also the main source of feelings of insecurity and of threat for the White boys (Hewitt, 1986; Back, 1991). It was a 'threat' experienced more acutely in public situations and when African/Caribbean boys played together and were thus more 'visible'. The consequent need, amongst the White boys, to 'prove themselves' and re-assert their own 'macho' credentials provided the context for regular public contestations. Such contestations were at times particularly violent and would be set off for no particular reason. Not surprisingly, the Bad Boys were more likely than other African/Caribbean boys to be singled out and challenged by the White boys. These resultant contestations were witnessed periodically throughout the year, arising at certain conjunctures and within specific contexts and occurring often enough to become a significant experience in the lives of the Bad Boys (Daniel, by association, being implicated in this as much as the others).

On most occasions, however, these attacks and confrontations were sparked off by a complex mixture of factors. One main factor was group loyalty. Groups were constantly formed and reformed in various contexts and, for the boys, most commonly around the factors of age, which classes they were in, and 'race'. Membership of a group demanded loyalty to other members and the ability to help and/or defend them at times of either verbal or physical conflict (Hewitt, 1986). This construction of the group or 'gang' had important implications for a second main factor which influenced confrontations between boys and that was gender. Girls were treated as property that boys could lay claim over either by defining them as girlfriends or, more generally, by virtue of the girls being in their class. The fact that the Bad Boys could be seen playing kiss-chase and other games with girls from another class was interpreted by one particular gang of White boys, who were a year older and predominantly from that class, as a challenge to their status. Moreover, the fact that the Bad Boys were Black and the girls were all White appeared to exacerbate the situation and render conflict inevitable. This is illustrated in the following interview with Jason and Craig, two of the leading members of the White gang, who were telling me why they had attacked Daniel and Paul:

PC:	[. . .] but tell me about before, you know Daniel and Paul
Jason:	Ah yeah!
PC:	From Mrs Scott's—what was all that about?
Jason:	Erm, er, were you [*to Craig*] playing with us? [*Craig nods*] That means Mark, Nicky, me, Craig started it [. . .] we started it but/
Craig:	/and, and, and we made a plan didn't we
[. . .]	
PC:	You started it—you started it with Daniel and Paul? Why?
Craig:	It, it started when/
Jason:	/Ah-a-a, I'm saying it, because erm, you know John, John was catching Christine
PC:	Yeah
Jason:	That's why we just done it
PC:	John from Mrs Scott's class?
Jason:	Yeah—they got Christine in *our* class
PC:	Right, and you didn't like that?
Jason:	No!
Craig:	No!
PC:	Why not?
Jason:	[*to Craig*] You saying it not me now—I've said something
Craig:	No, you, I didn't even do anything/
Jason:	/Yes you did you said your gang had a plan did they?

Craig:	The plan was to, erm, get John out of the way [. . .] with er just me right who made the plan up
[. . .]	
PC;	I don't understand if you were trying to get John then why were you fighting with Paul and Daniel?
Jason:	But Paul and Daniel are on their side!
PC:	Oh, right! So what were Paul and Daniel doing then?
Jason:	Er, erm/
Craig:	/Chasing after Jason's girlfriend!
Jason:	Oye! Shush!
PC:	Jason's girlfriend? Who's that?
Craig:	Emma!
[. . .]	
PC:	Do you not like them chasing after Emma then?
Jason &	
Craig:	No!
[. . .]	
PC:	So do you think Emma likes to be chased by the boys?
[. . .]	
Jason:	I don't know!
PC:	You don't know? So why did you try and stop John then if you don't know whether she liked/
Craig:	/I, I was trying to stop him!

The sense of ownership of girls provided one key context for conflict between boys and for affirming classroom loyalties. But the fluid nature of such groupings became apparent as the confrontations which developed over the following few weeks became less class-based and distinctly racialized, drawing in other boys from different classes and differing ages into the conflict. At its peak there were between 10 and 15 boys involved split quite visually into two groups—one all-White and one predominantly African/Caribbean. The highly physical and vicious nature of the fights ensured that a certain level of tension and resentment between the two groups remained and would flare up, on occasion, throughout the year.

Such attacks, both physical and verbal, against the Bad Boys were not only found to emanate from these specific groups of White boys but from other infant children—both boys and girls—in their and the other Reception/Year 1 classes. John, for instance, was heard later on that year telling some of the girls in his class not to play with Stephen and Jordan because they're 'bad boys'.[9] Indeed this label of 'bad boys' that having been created by a combination of the teachers' tendency to publicly chastise the Bad Boys and other African/Caribbean boys more generally together with the presence, moreover, of racist discourses within and beyond the school, was now being taken up by significant numbers of the infant children to varying degrees in the classroom and playground. It created the classic self-fulfilling prophecy where the Bad Boys were forced into more fights and were then identified and publicly vilified by the teacher for being more aggressive (note Jordan's school report above). The boys were then set up with an even stronger 'masculine' identity which other boys within the school felt it necessary to challenge.

A similar process was also observed to be the case in the classroom where children would jump, without hesitation, to blame misdemeanours on the Bad Boys when they had not been involved. During story time one afternoon at the end of the day, for instance, when all the children were sitting on the carpet, one of the children near the back belched; Mrs Scott stopped reading, closed her book and asked in a stern voice who it was. Without hesitation, two girls sitting at the front offered Jordan's name as the culprit even though he was not at school that day.

RACISM, MASCULINITY AND RESISTANCE

It is within this overarching context of racism, manifest both in pupil–teacher and pupil–pupil interaction, that the construction and negotiation of the Bad Boys' masculine identities takes place. From the foregoing discussion it is not surprising to find that the first, and central, tenet of such an identity is associated with the ability to defend yourself and to fight back. This was particularly true for the Bad Boys who, more than other African/Caribbean boys in the school, were more frequently singled out and attacked. This tenet of their identity can be seen in the following discussion between Paul and Daniel following the first physical encounters with Jason and his gang over Christine and Emma. Whilst there was obviously some exaggeration and bravado in the account, it does reflect quite accurately the physical nature of the confrontations described earlier and the way in which physical strength and the ability to 'look after yourself' are negotiated, constructed and re-constructed in the act of story-telling and recounting of incidents:

PC:	You said when they came up to you to start with you were playing with some girls?
Paul:	Yeah, I had some fighting but he [*Daniel*] didn't!
Daniel:	Yes I did!
Paul:	No you didn't!
Daniel:	Jason pushed me in a puddle!
Paul:	Yeah, what did you do?—nothing!
Daniel:	No
Paul:	So you didn't fight did you?—I did! Cos I got, erm, one of them over
Daniel:	Yes I did fight! when I was running, I was going to kick them
Paul:	But missed them didn't you!
Daniel:	What?

Paul:	Missed them!
Daniel:	No I never!
Paul:	Well I got, I got, I had two people over from me
PC:	You had two what Paul? What did you say—you had two people what?
Paul:	Down!
PC:	Down?
Paul:	Three!—Sean, Craig and Jason
Daniel:	Yeah, I, I, you got Sean down by kicking him didn't ya?
Paul:	No! He ran and I got my foot out so he tripped over
Daniel:	Yeah and then he was going to kick you weren't he?
Paul:	Yeah but he couldn't—he was running and trying to get me but [*gets up to rehearse the actions—Daniel also gets up*]/
Daniel:	/But he missed didn't he?/
Paul:	/I put my foot out and he went over!
[. . .]	
Paul:	Then I tripped Karl over, and I punched Jason down so he was, so he was down

Much obviously depends upon how such episodes are remembered and recounted. The contestation between Daniel and Paul both over the nature of the events and the status that rides with it was as much for my benefit as their own. Indeed, my role, as an adult providing an audience for such arguments, is a significant one. It is in these interviews, through the introduction of 'adult' ways of knowing, talking and acting that the Bad Boys could subvert their position as objects within specific discourses on childhood and gain a certain level of power. As will be seen, it is through the introduction of certain 'adult' themes that the boys know are 'taboo' for children of their age, such as those associated with violence, sexuality and 'cusses' (curses or swear words and/or phrases) that my authority, as an adult within the school, was challenged (Walkerdine, 1981).

Interviews were therefore very popular with the children as an arena where past events could be re-constructed and re-told and 'adult' knowledge could be paraded and exchanged. The central role played by the acquisition of 'adult' knowledge for the construction of masculine identities generally is illustrated in the following transcript where, with myself temporarily absent from the room, a whole range of violent and sexualized cusses are exchanged and learnt. There was no animosity between the children but rather the context was one of a contest or verbal sparring match. Note the active role played by the peer group itself where such cusses are not simply handed down from older peers but are taken up, customized and re-used in an almost rhythmic manner, by the boys themselves in interaction with each other.

| Stephen: | Come on then you fuck-in bitch! |
| Jordan: | Come on then! |

Stephen:	Come on sit down!
Jordan:	Eh! Miss Williams! [*pointing to photo on wall*]
Stephen:	You fucking Sappa!
Paul:	Zappa!
Stephen:	Sit in your seat! Quick!
Jordan:	Oye! There he is!
Paul:	Who?
Stephen:	You're a fucking bastard!
Jordan:	You fuckin' dick-head!
Stephen:	You fuckin' dick! Bitch!
Jordan:	Bitch! Ass-hole!
Paul:	Arse-hole!
Jordan:	Ass-hole! Bitch! Dick-head! Fuck off dick-head! Fuck off fucker!
Paul:	Fucker! Fuckin' bastard bum-bum!
Stephen:	Come on then you fucking bastard! Calling me fucking names!
Jordan:	Yeah like/
Paul:	/you bastard!
Jordan:	Fucker! Dick-head!
Stephen:	Lickin' your arse off, pussy-sucker! You White pussy-sucker!
Jordan:	You Black/
Paul:	/You're blind you Black/
Jordan:	/You Black bastard!
Stephen:	you White/
Jordan:	Pussy! you smell pussy!
	[*inaudible—Creole accent. Boys seem to be standing and play fighting*]
Jordan:	Booofff! [*play-hits Stephen*]
Stephen:	No don't—don't fight me! Paul sit down quick! Quick Paul!
Stephen:	[*banging out beat on table making bass noise through lips*]

The general use and appropriation of cusses—especially the more complex ones—was heavily guarded. In this, Stephen appeared to be the expert. In one interview he recounted the following rhyme at a speed which was intentionally hardly audible to the other boys: 'Hey Pakistani, Let me see your fanny, Let me smell [*sniff sniff*], fuckin' Hell!' The distinctly gendered and racialized nature of this is a theme that will be covered shortly; for now, the significance lies in the way that Stephen spent much of the session listening to the other infant boys trying to guess the rhyme and telling them that they were wrong, whilst refusing to repeat it.

More generally, this drawing upon, experimentation with and adaptation of various discourses on adulthood emphasizes the importance of popular culture. It is the representations of women and sex in the tradition of American films such as *Police Academy*, and its language which has permeated through to popular youth cultures more generally (ie 'pussy', 'bitch', 'ass-hole', 'pussy-sucker'), that provide specific cultural building blocks from which identities, through interaction, can be constructed. The Bad Boys however, are also able to draw upon, and interweave within this, a whole host of Black cultural themes such as the use of creole, particular styles of dress and music. They are themes that often draw upon African and Caribbean heritage, focus on racism and, as such, are heavily guarded more generally amongst African/Caribbean youth. The appropriation of these Black cultural forms is therefore more problematic for White and South Asian boys who, as a consequence, find such themes less accessible (see Hewitt, 1986; Jones, 1988).[10]

The use of these Black cultural themes was noticeable with Stephen for instance who, at the end of the above transcription, was beating out the rhythm to 'Jump! Jump!' on the table—a rap-song by Kriss Kross, a popular teenage duo of American Black boys. In other interviews, where just Stephen and Jordan were present, they sang this song right through together with the dance actions. Stephen also tried to teach Jordan a song from the movie *Boyz 'n' the Hood*. These cultural forms, in drawing from Black cultural themes to varying degrees, do offer the potential for resistance; one which is treated with a grudging respect by many of the other (White) peers (Hewitt, 1986; Back, 1991). The increased victimization of the Bad Boys relative to other African/Caribbean boys, and the particular sub-cultural responses generated between them, provided a fertile context within which such cultural forms were appropriated.

The ability to take up and use such Black cultural forms was, however, often contradictory and conditional. Daniel, the only White boy of the four, faced the most difficulty. Whilst being keen to learn and use various cusses he rarely entered into verbal competition with the other boys. His almost passive acceptance of their 'prior claim' to use such Black cultural capital was quite observable through interaction (Hewitt, 1986). For Jordan and Paul, being mixed-parentage meant that their access to and use of these Black cultural forms were no less precarious; their identity had to be worked on. In the context of (often racial) verbal sparring and insult-trading their light skin colour led to their identity as African/Caribbean being questioned and contested, as the following transcript illustrates:

PC:	What about the girls in your classroom do you play with any of them?
All:	No-oo! No!
Daniel:	Some are Indians!
PC:	Are they? What, do you play with Indian girls then?
Stephen:	NO-WAY!
Daniel:	Jordan kisses um!
Jordan:	NO! I'm West Indian!

Daniel:	Eh?
Jordan:	I'm West Indian—I'm English and I'm half-White ain't I?
Paul:	Yeah but then if you say that—d'you know what?—you're an *Indian*!
Jordan:	No! ... Are you still my friend then?
Paul:	Not if you talk like India! No—talking like an Indian!
Jordan:	I bet I am!
Paul:	If you do I'm not, we're not playin' with ya!
PC:	Why's that Paul? Don't you like/
Paul:	/We don't like Indians!
PC:	Why?
Paul:	We don't like Indian talkers!
PC:	Why?
Jordan:	[*indignantly*] Well I ain't a Indian!

What the above transcript illustrates is the way in which such racist taunts are often highly gendered and also the contradictory and fluid nature of racial identities (Cohen, 1987, 1992). This 'carving out' of a distinct identity by the five- and six-year-old-boys, partly in terms of what they are not provides a significant context for the reproduction of various racist discourses. These are aimed almost exclusively at South Asian children in the school and are overwhelmingly clustered around notions of inferiority and disdain unlike the discourse within which African/Caribbean children are located. Such discourses are most likely to be found within distinctly public spaces within the school where identity and status are much more keenly displayed and guarded. Football, because of its high status amongst boys and its inevitably public nature, provided one of the key sites at Anne Devlin where racist discourses flourished and Asian children were systematically excluded (see Connolly, 1994). For the present paper, however, we will focus on the discourse on sexuality and how it came to inform the Bad Boys' views of girls whilst also mediating relations between the sexes. What will be shown is not only the largely symbolic and public nature of boyfriend/girlfriend relationships but also the ways in which they form a central component of these five- and six-year-old boys' masculine identities and are, as a consequence, highly racialized.

KISS-CHASE, GIRLFRIENDS AND SEXUALIZED IDENTITIES

Certain derogatory and sexualized images of girls and women central to masculine discourses have already emerged above. The main arena through which sexuality most overtly manifests itself, however, is through the rituals of kiss-chase and the identification of boyfriends and girlfriends. Kiss-chase was a game consistently present in the playground throughout the year of the study. It involved both girls and boys encouraging and initiating the chases. A range of actions were observed to take place when a child had been caught. They might be let go, kissed or, on occasions, a group of boys would hold girls down on the floor, or pin them against the school gates and sexually abuse them. This might involve groping them or simulating sex on top, or against them. These games were played equally by Black and White children. South Asian children were never observed being encouraged to play kiss-chase by other children—either boys or girls—in the playground during the whole year of observations.

Discourses on Black, particularly African/Caribbean, male sexuality have a long history in popular culture. They are discourses which are equally likely to circulate amongst infant children and inform peer group relations. The Bad Boys' reputation for being 'hard', and the way in which they were constituted as highly 'visible' subjects within such discourses, provided the context within which these discourses on Black male sexuality were more likely to become prominent. They were discourses manifest, most directly, in the greater attention that some of the infant girls paid to the Bad Boys compared to other boys. It was interesting to note that the (mainly White) girls in Mrs Scott's class together with Emma and Nicky (the two girls at the heart of the fighting during the Autumn term) were more frequently observed encouraging and initiating kiss-chase games with the Bad Boys than with any others. Of course, the more the Boys were encouraged to play kiss-chase the more they gained a reputation in this area. This was a process quite specific to the Bad Boys compared to other African/Caribbean boys who were only ever tangentially involved, if at all, in such games.

These processes can be seen as providing one key aspect of a complex self-fulfilling prophecy within which the Bad Boys, specifically, constructed identities around notions of heterosexuality. The more they responded to the girls and engaged in games of kiss-chase and boyfriend/girlfriend relationships, the more they developed a reputation in this area. Moreover, notions of sexuality and the construction of sexualized identities amongst infant children was regarded as one of the most 'taboo' subjects for children as young as these. The appropriation of such discourses can be seen as constituting a powerful means to resist such dominant discourses on childhood on the one hand, and reinforcing a distinctly male and adult identity on the other. Thus the more the Bad Boys were encouraged into games of kiss-chase, the more cultural building blocks they had with which to construct a specific identity along these lines.

It was within this context that the Bad Boys constructed masculine identities which drew upon a range of discourses on heterosexuality as in 'kiss-chase' and the identification of 'girlfriends'. Whilst boys and girls would often be seen playing together in the more personal and private spaces of the playground (by the walls, in the bushes, behind the benches), kiss-chase involved the use of large areas of playground space and was therefore, by definition, an essentially public activity. In this sense kiss-chase was another public parading and exhibition of status but it was also the only 'legitimate' arena within which the Bad Boys could play with girls so openly. As the following quote illustrates, a distinction was made between girlfriends and girls-as-friends for, whilst girls provided one crucial way in which masculinities can be forged, the girls themselves, outside of their roles as girlfriends, were treated with distaste and belittled. To have a girl as a friend would bring the Boys' masculine identities—so heavily guarded and carefully constructed—crumbling down. The following argument, between Stephen and Daniel concerning the ownership and control of girlfriends, illustrates the way in which, within such arguments, Daniel's attempts to associate Stephen with girls-as-friends can be seen as an insult:

PC:	So Stephen, before, remember before break time when Nazia [*South Asian girl in his class*] wanted to look at your work and you wouldn't let her? Why didn't you let her have a look?
Stephen:	I hate girls!
PC:	You hate girls?
Stephen:	Yeah!
[. . .]	
Daniel:	Why, well why do you chase girls then like ours?
Stephen:	No I don't chase you lots of girlfriends!
Daniel:	Yes you did!
Stephen:	No I didn't!
Daniel:	Yes you did!
Stephen:	No I don't, no I never this morning!
Paul:	No, last morning didn't you?
Stephen:	Last morning? What last morning? What last morning? Yesterday—that was yesterday though—that was yesterday!
Paul:	After dinner that thingy! Yes you do get a lot of girls!
Stephen:	No I not, no I don't Paul!
Daniel:	You do!
Paul:	Why do you get Nicky and Emma then?
Stephen:	No I don't—I only got 'em yesterday!
Paul:	So why did, so why sometimes you chase your girlfriends so why, so you must like girls!
Stephen:	[*angry*] So what if I've got a girlfriend! It doesn't mean I like girls does it?
Daniel:	Yes it does!
Stephen:	[*to PC*] Does it?
PC:	Doesn't it?
Stephen:	[*more subdued*] No it don't!

Within the context of these interviews where the arena is set for the re-interpreting, verbal jousting and construction of fantasy, discussions of girlfriends, sex and sexuality take on a specific form; especially with myself as a spectator to such contestations and an adult in a position of power over the children (Wolpe, 1988; Walkerdine, 1981). Sexuality, especially its emphasis on violence and power, manifested itself most frequently in the boys' conversations in terms of verbal abuse and insults (see also Willis, 1977). Such themes of power and violence are also significantly evident in specific conversations about girlfriends. The following transcription illustrates both the knowledge that these five- and six-year-old boys have about sex as well as the symbolic power that kiss-chase has come to hold for them:

PC:	I was just wondering what you've been playing in the playground recently?
Jordan:	We're playing races, kiss-chase
PC:	Kiss-chase? Who with?
Stephen:	Kissy-cat!
PC:	Kissy-cat?
Jordan:	Yeah, when you catch somebody then you kiss them on the lips!
PC:	Who've you played that with?
Stephen:	Our girlfriends!
PC:	Your girlfriends Stephen? Who's that?
Stephen:	[*laughs*] I said it last time!
Jordan:	Marcia!
Stephen:	And Samantha!
[. . .]	
PC:	So what do you play with them?
Stephen:	Kiss
PC:	Kiss?
Stephen:	-Chase!
PC:	Do you?
Stephen:	And you have to kiss 'em and sex 'em!
Jordan:	Ahhh! No!
PC:	And sex them? What does that mean?
Stephen:	Arhh—I'm not saying that!
PC:	You can tell me if you want to
Stephen:	No way!
Jordan:	Do you want me to tell him?
PC:	Yeah you tell me what it means Jordan!
Stephen:	I know—up and down!
PC:	It means shagging? What do you mean by 'up and down' Stephen?
Jordan & Stephen:	[*loud laughter*]
Jordan:	Stick in your fanny!
Stephen:	Snogging!
PC:	Stick in your fanny you said?

Stephen:	Yeah he just said!
Jordan:	He's well dirty!
Stephen:	Not like you are!

The specific issue of power and the objectification of girls can be seen in the following conversation where the context provided by the interview setting of competitive and verbal sparring adds significantly to this process. Girls are situated within such a discourse as being emotionally dependent and possessive upon one boyfriend whilst the boys come to treat girls as little more than inanimate objects to 'sex' in a kind of production-line fashion:

PC:	Which girls do you like to play with the best?
Paul:	Nicky and Emma!
Daniel:	And Emma!
Stephen:	I like Natasha [*mixed-parentage*] and Marcia and Samantha. I like, I've got fourteen girlfriends!
Paul:	Woo-woo!
Stephen:	I've got a hundred girlfriends!
Daniel:	If you've got one you can't have no more!
Stephen:	Yeah!
Daniel:	Your girlfriend will tell you off!
Stephen:	No!
Daniel:	Yeah!
Stephen:	No!
Paul:	How you going to sex 'em then?
Stephen:	I'll put all of them on top of each other and when I've done one—put her over there, then when done another one put her over there, then another one put her over there, then over there, and over there and over there
Paul:	I've got, I've got a million!
Stephen:	I've got four hundred and eighty-two!
[…]	
PC:	Stephen, when you say you've done one what do you mean when you say you've done one?
Paul:	Sexy baby!
Daniel:	He throws it over and then he puts, then he has another one then he picks her up throws her over and has another one

Contradictions emerged later in this conversation, where all the boys accept that girls can also have a hundred boyfriends. Whilst wider discourses on power are deeply engrained, it would seem that, in the realms of fantasy and the telling of stories, there is a certain inherent logic which opens up a significant array of contradictions and spaces for the introduction of alternative stories and understandings (Billig *et al.*, 1988). The overwhelming message from these discussions, however, is one of power, violence and domination (see also Mahoney, 1989). This can be seen in the following extract where I asked the other three boys where Jordan was that day:

PC: Where's Jordan today?
Stephen: He's at home boiling his head off!
Paul: No! Kissing his girlfriend!
PC: Kissing his girlfriend? Who's his girlfriend?
Stephen: He's waiting at his girlfriend's house
PC: Is he? Who's?
Paul: Yeah, waiting for her
Stephen: And when she comes in, he's hiding right, and when she comes in he's going to grab her and take her upstairs and then she's going to start screaming and he's going to kiss her ... and sex her!
PC: And sex her? And why's she going to be screaming?
Stephen: Because she hates it!
PC: Because she hates it?
Stephen: Yeah!
PC: So if she hates it why does he do it?
Stephen: I don't know!
Paul: Because he loves her!
Stephen: He'll sing 'I want to sex you up!'

This creation of a distinctly uneven and disturbing power-relationship with girlfriends seems, to a certain extent, to be symbolic of the actual relationships that the boys had with their 'girlfriends'. Paul and Daniel, especially, could be observed fairly frequently in the playground physically abusing Emma and Nicky; pushing them over, swinging them round and kicking them.

GIRLFRIENDS, RACISM AND SEXUALITY

Discourses on girls, girlfriends and sexuality are highly racialized, as illustrated in some of the transcripts reproduced earlier. Having a girlfriend is a particularly public affair and thus to be associated with an Asian girlfriend is definitely a term of abuse. This is illustrated in the extract below where the conversation is preceded by a general argument about whose girlfriend is whose. Annette (mixed-parentage) occupies a contradictory position; on the one hand, she is the only girl in the class who is treated by the Bad Boys as a member of their group and whose physical and sporting prowess is acknowledged. On the other, this distinctly masculine identity renders her less attractive and desirable as a girlfriend:

Paul: Annette does love you! Annette does go out with you!
Stephen: I bet! Is that why ... Alright then, if Annette goes out with me then Nazia goes out with Daniel!

Paul:	You have two girlfriends—Nazia, Kelly [*mixed-parentage*] and her, Annette.
Stephen:	And I know, and I know you go out with Rupal, Rakhee and [*saying last name slowly and pulling face*] Neelam!
[. . .]	
Daniel:	You've got a Paki girlfriend!
Stephen:	Who?
Daniel:	That one there with that dot! [*on another poster*]
Paul:	[*laughs*]
[. . .]	
Stephen:	You go out with Neelam!
Daniel:	And so do you!
Stephen:	You go out with all the girls in our class!
Daniel:	You go out with all the Pakis! [*laughs*]
Stephen:	I said you go out with everyone in the whole world mate!
Daniel:	So do you [*laughs*]!
Stephen:	How can you say I do when I've already said you do!
Daniel:	You do!
Stephen:	You do!
Daniel:	You go out with all of the Pakis, I go out with all the Whites [*laughs*]
Stephen:	You go out with all of the Pakis! Because I, do I look like a Paki though—you do! You go the Mosque mate where all the Pakis go! [*general laughs*]

When pressed to justify their derogatory views of Asian girls, the boys not only illustrate their cognitive ability to reason at a relatively sophisticated level but, as a consequence, raise a whole host of contradictions:

Daniel:	[*laughs*] and do you know what? He's [*Paul*] got a girlfriend in that class! [. . .]—Nadia! [*laughs*]
Paul:	No I haven't—he's lying! I ain't got a girlfriend anyway!
PC:	Who's Nadia?
Daniel:	A PAKI!
[. . .]	
PC:	Do you, do you like/
Paul:	/Indians!
PC:	Indians?
Daniel:	No!
PC:	Why?
Paul:	[*to Daniel*] Why you say it then?
Daniel:	Because they're brown!
PC:	They're brown? You don't like them because they're brown?
Daniel:	Yes

[...]

PC: What are you Paul?
Paul: Brown
PC: So you like Paul don't you Daniel?
Daniel: Yeah 'cause he's in our class!
PC: He's brown!
Daniel: Only people in our class!
PC: So Prajay is in your class—do you like Prajay?
Daniel: Yeah!
Stephen: He's an Indian! And you like him?
PC: And you like Neelam and Rakhee?
Daniel: Yeah

The contradictions inherent within the above as lines of friendship are drawn and re-drawn around differing boundaries—gender, 'race', their own class-loyalty—can be seen as can the spaces created for work to be done in challenging and offering alternative perspectives with which the children can make sense of their world. This contradiction is apparent within the Bad Boys racial discourses on Asian girls where, in opposition to the distinctly non-sexual and derisive view of Asian girls outlined above, there exists a parallel discourse which raises the supposed exotic, unknown and threatening sexuality of Asian girls. The following extract, from an interview with three White boys, illustrates both of these themes:

Dean: He don't know what I mean, he don't know what I mean, he talks English
Jason: English, I'm talking English now!
Dean: Yeah like Paki [*laughs*]
Jason: You talk French!
Dean: You talk like Paki language [*laughs*] you talk ...
PC: What's that language?
Jason: You talk French
Dean: When you got a girlfriend, no way you want to play with them [*Asian*] girls, right, they might, you might, you might, you might [*in soft voice*] 'come on baby want to suck you off'
PC: You want to what?
Dean: Nnaaahhhh not ...
PC: What girls are those? What do you mean by them girls?
Jason: Downstairs
Dean: In our class/
Jason: Like Reema
              [*laughs*]
PC: You don't want to play with those then?
Dean: No
PC: Why?

Dean: She's a Paki!

This is a contradiction, to a more coded, and less frequent extent, reproduced by the Bad Boys in this study. In the following extract, Asian girls are characterized as tigers who are unpredictable and dangerous as girlfriends:

Daniel:	I don't like 'um [*Asian girls*]
PC:	Why don't you like 'em?
Daniel:	Because they're Tigers! [*laughs*]
PC:	They're Tigers?
Daniel:	Yeah! They've got a mask on their face like a Tiger!
Paul:	Daniel, if there, if you go with one of them—you know what will happen, you know what, what they'll do?
Daniel:	What?
Paul:	Bite ya!
Stephen:	Eat you!
Daniel:	Bite your bum off!

African/Caribbean girls are also subjects of such discourses on sexuality and desirability but in a more 'positive' and sexual manner:

Stephen:	I'd just go to my Black girlfriends!
PC:	Your Black girlfriends?
Stephen:	Yeah [. . .] And do you know why I like 'em?
PC:	Why?
Stephen:	Because they're sexy!
PC:	Because they're sexy?
Jordan:	No dirty words today!
PC:	Well you can if you want! Who's, who's sexy then?
Stephen:	My girlfriend
PC:	Your girlfriend?
Jordan:	Yeah and my girlfriend!
PC:	Why are they sexy?
Jordan:	'Cos, erm, 'cos they're shiny!
[. . .]	
PC:	So who's, who's shiny then? Jordan?
Jordan:	Erm Marcia
Stephen:	My girlfriend—especially my girlfriend!
PC:	Why especially your girlfriend?
Stephen:	Cos my girlfriend puts too much cream on her
Jordan:	Mine, er, mine just puts some cocoa-butter on and she puts some cocoa-butter on
PC:	What Samantha [*who's White*] put some cocoa butter on?
Jordan:	Yeah
Stephen:	Yeah but she don't even know what cocoa-butter is—she asks her mum what cocoa-butter is

PC:	What Samantha does?
Stephen:	Yeah she goes: 'mum, what's cocoa butter?'
PC:	What else makes them sexy then?
Jordan:	[*inaudible first two words*] skirts
Stephen:	Skirts—we have to pull down their knickers!
PC:	You pull down their knickers?
Stephen:	Yeah to see them sexy! Init Jordan?
Jordan:	[*giggles*] No! I don't!
[. . .]	
Stephen:	[*singing*/chanting] And I wanna kiss my girlfriend, and I wanna love my girlfriend, and I wanna sex my girlfriend, and I wanna snog my girlfriend!
Jordan:	Don't Stephen!

IDENTITIES OF RESISTANCE: SOME CONCLUDING REMARKS

This article makes no claims to be representative. Indeed, the Bad Boys were unique amongst other African/Caribbean infant boys in the school in relation to their appropriation and combination of physical and sexual themes in the construction of their identities. The main concern of this article has been to examine how and why various discourses on 'race', sexuality, childhood and gender articulated in the specific ways that they did for the Bad Boys. It was their presence in the school as a *group* of African/Caribbean boys that was central in increasing their 'visibility' and subjecting them to a number of racist discourses. These discourses operated in a complex manner and, through their articulation with other discourses, helped to create a complex set of social processes whereby the Bad Boys were constituted as aggressive, hard and sexual.

The Bad Boys were far from passive subjects within such discourses, however. This paper has highlighted, more generally, the active role that children as young as five play in the construction and negotiation of their identities. It has illustrated the relative sophistication of the children's understandings of issues of racism, gender and sexuality at that age and, moreover, the cognitive ability they have in terms of being able to draw upon and re-frame such discourses in the course of trying to make sense of their own experiences. However, as also highlighted, such views are riven with contradictions and are inherently fluid. In this sense the paper has highlighted not only the need to do anti-racist and anti-sexist work with young children but has also pointed towards some of the spaces—within the contradictions of the children's own perceptions and narratives—where such work could be done (see also Carrington and Short, 1989, 1992; Troyna and Hatcher, 1992; Thorne, 1993).

Furthermore, the paper has, within this, drawn attention to the complex nature of masculine identities and the variety of processes that articulate in their construction and negotiation. Above all it has argued for the need to locate the forging of Black masculinities within the specific contexts provided by racism (see also Westwood, 1990). It is here where the ongoing debates surrounding African/Caribbean boys and their 'underachievement' [*sic*] should be located. What the paper has shown is not only the central role of the school and its teaching staff in the labelling of African/Caribbean boys as 'bad' and the consequent self-fulfilling prophecy that results (see, for instance, Wright, 1986, 1992a, b; Mac an Ghaill, 1988; Gillborn, 1990) but also the importance, within this, of peer-relations and their role in the creation of specific masculine identities amongst some African/Caribbean boys as young as five. Significantly one of the teachers in this study had complained despairingly to me that she had read all the research regarding African/Caribbean boys and the self-fulfilling prophecy and was ever-mindful of that in her own work and yet, unfortunately, found that all the African/Caribbean boys in her (Reception/Year 1) class were already 'aggressive' and/or exhibiting 'behavioural problems'. This, more than anything, emphasizes the need to develop a more comprehensive understanding of the schooling experiences of Black children, one which incorporates the active role of peer group relations with that of student–teacher interaction (see Connolly, 1993).[11]

Finally, this article has drawn out the contradictory nature of children's responses to schooling. In this sense the Bad Boys' forging of masculine identities of resistance, whilst needing to be located quite specifically within the context of racism and the school, also needs to be understood in terms of its highly gendered and sexualized nature. The Bad Boys are not only *Black* but are also *boys* and *children*. They therefore occupy a number of subject positions. Their use and adaptation of Black cultural forms and a 'hard', street-wise image in response to racism forms only one facet of their identity. It is also their use of and experimentation with adult ways of knowing, in response to the discourses on childhood manifest within the school, that plays a significant part in the formation of their masculine identities. Whilst the adoption of Black cultural forms and a street-wise image represent attempts at 'being an adult', it is apparent from the above that it is not so much that the Bad Boys are experimenting with being 'adults' generally but with being 'men' more specifically. Their introduction of adult themes are therefore highly gendered and draw upon an array of representations and meanings that tend to provide the backdrop to boy–girl relationships.

The status of the data reproduced above obviously needs to be borne in mind. The transcripts are not simply a clear representation of 'reality' but of boys, in a specific context, taking up, experimenting with, and adapting a variety of discourses on adulthood. The use and adoption of such identities varied from one context to the next. Consequently, their masculine identities emphasized above were specific to the interview context. They structured interaction in the classroom and playground only ever partially and complexly and represented more of an ideal-typical fantasy picture of masculinity for the boys rather than what was conveyed day-to-day through interaction with others. Nevertheless, such discourses are powerful and emphasize the contradictory nature of children's responses to schooling and the need to be more critical in understanding resistance on the part of children rather than simply assigning it as 'progressive' and celebrating it in its own right (Walkerdine, 1981).

Key to transcriptions

/ indicates interruption in speech
[...] indicates extracts edited out of transcript
[*text*] indicates descriptive text added by myself to clarify/highlight the nature of the discussion.
 ... indicates a pause

Acknowledgements

The above data is drawn from my broader doctoral research funded by an ESRC Postgraduate Training Award. I would like to thank my supervisor, Sallie Westwood, and Janet Holland, Maud Blair, Karen Winter, Cecile Wright and Steve Wagg for their insightful comments and guidance on earlier drafts of this article.

Notes

1. 'Black' here is used as a political term to denote those of African/Caribbean and South Asian heritage. Whilst I am mindful of the fact that such a term is essentially socially constructed and is inclusive of a range of people whose identities appear to be becoming increasingly fractured and diverse (see Rattansi, 1992; Cohen, 1987, 1992) there is a space where a qualified use of the term 'Black' is still appropriate in relation to the general marginalization, alienation and conditional citizenship that South Asian and African/Caribbean people experience.
2. This was a name used by the boys themselves during one interview where, in complaining about the way in which the teachers and their peers label them as poorly behaved and 'bad' (see also note 8), they significantly reverse the meaning of the term ('bad' now meaning 'good'), as in broader Black cultural forms (Hewitt, 1986), and reclaim it for themselves.
3. Unless stated otherwise, mixed-parentage refers to those children who have a White mother and African/Caribbean father.
4. The data reproduced below forms part of a much broader ethnographic study of a multi-ethnic, inner-city primary school where I spent a full academic year focusing on the school's three parallel, vertically grouped Reception/Year 1 classes (Connolly, forthcoming). Methods included participant observation, semi-structured interviews with all teaching and non-teaching staff and a series of group interviews with the children. The data drawn on for this study derives from ten interviews held with two or more of the 'Bad Boys'—in various combinations—over the whole of the academic year. Three other interviews with differing groups of White boys from two Year Two infant classes are also drawn upon.

These interviews varied from 10 to 50 minutes in duration and were held in a separate room within the school away from other children and teachers and were distinctly non-directive; with the children being given the space and opportunity to discuss whatever they felt to be relevant and/or significant with the assurance of total confidentiality.

5. In this article 'African/Caribbean' includes those children of mixed-parentage (see note 3 above) unless stated differently. Whilst their specific racial identity is significant in certain contexts, in many respects mixed-parentage children do occupy similar subject positions to African/Caribbeans within the school with regards to the prevalent racist discourses which emphasize the aggressive, sporting and sexual nature [*sic*] of such boys.

6. See Willis (1977), for instance, and the way in which the 'Lads' in his study—a group of White, working class adolescents—greatly valued notions of aggression and sexuality.

7. All names of places and people in this study have been altered to maintain confidentiality.

8. I have drawn upon both reports written for, and sent home to, the parents for each child and also their 'internal' reports, which are kept in the child's individual file at the school and are mainly for internal consumption. As such, many of the teachers admitted that they felt they could be more truthful in these than in the ones written for parents.

9. Indeed it was when this was discussed with the Bad Boys during one interview that they adopted and inverted the term 'bad' to describe themselves.

10. Again it needs to be stressed that these boys have agency and that nothing is predetermined. Indeed the appearance of *Apache Indian*, a South Asian male rap artist is a case in point. The issue is, however, that for such a man the ability and effort it takes to construct and maintain such an identity will be much greater than for an African/Caribbean.

11. Maybe this is where Foster's (1990) work could have been more fruitfully focused. His research claimed that there were no instances of racism in the sample school he studied, whilst also explaining away the differing social and educational experiences of African/Caribbean boys in his study in terms of their possibly higher levels of aggressiveness and/or lower educational ability within that year (see also Connolly, 1992). His measure of 'racism' was, not surprisingly, focused almost entirely upon the role of teachers and their detrimental treatment of Black students.

References

Back, L. (1991) Social context and racist name calling: An ethnographic perspective on racist talk within a south London adolescent community. *The European Journal of Intercultural Studies* 1 (3), 19–38.

Billig, M., Condor, S., Edwards, D., Gane, M., Middleton, D. and Radley, A. (1988) *Ideological Dilemmas: A Social Psychology of Everyday Thinking*. London: Sage Publications.

Bourdieu, P. (1993) *Sociology in Question*. London: Sage Publications.

Brod, H. (ed.) (1987) *The Making of Masculinities: The New Men's Studies*. London: Allen and Unwin.

Carrington, B. (1983) Sport as a side-track: An analysis of West Indian involvement in extra-curricula sport. In L. Barton and S. Walker (eds) *Race, Class and Education*. London: Croom Helm.

Carrington, B. and Short, G. (1989) *'Race' and the Primary School: Theory into Practice*. Windsor: NFER-Nelson.

—(1992) Researching 'race' in the 'all-White' primary school: The ethics of curriculum development. In M. Leicester and M. Taylor (eds) *Ethics, Ethnicity and Education*. London: Kogan Page.

Chisholm, L., Buchner, P., Kruger, H. and Brown, P. (eds) (1990) *Childhood, Youth and Social Change: A Comparative Perspective*. London: The Falmer Press.

Cohen, P. (1987) The perversions of inheritance: Studies in the making of multi-racist Britain. In P. Cohen and H.S. Bains (eds) *Multi-Racist Britain*. London: Macmillan Education Ltd.

—(1992) 'It's racism what dunnit': Hidden narratives in theories of racism. In J. Donald and A. Rattansi (eds) *'Race', Culture and Difference*. London: Sage Publications Ltd.

Cohen, S. (1972) *Folk Devils and Moral Panics: The Creation of the Mods and Rockers*. Oxford: Martin Robertson.

Connolly, P. (1992) 'Playing it by the rules': The politics of research in 'race' and education. *British Educational Research Journal* 18 (2), 133–48.

—(1993) Racism, schooling and resistance: The construction of masculine identities amongst African/Caribbean boys. Paper presented to postgraduate conference 'Representation, Identity and Agency', University of Manchester, December.

—(1994) Racism, anti-racism and masculinity: Contextualising racist incidents in the primary school. Paper presented to International Sociology of Education Conference, University of Sheffield, January.

—(forthcoming) The formation of racialised and gendered cultural identities amongst working class infant children: an ethnographic study of a multi-ethnic, inner-city primary school. Unpublished PhD thesis, University of Leicester (in process).

Dollimore, J. (1986) Homophobia and sexual difference. *Oxford Literary Review* 8, 5–12.

Donald, J, and Rattansi, A. (eds) (1992) *'Race', Culture and Difference*. London: Sage Publications Ltd.

Foster, M. (1980) *Policy and Practice in Multicultural and Anti-Racist Education: A Case Study of a Multi-Ethnic Comprehensive School*. London: Routledge.

Fuller, M. (1990) Black girls in a London comprehensive school. In R. Deem (ed.) *Schooling for Women's Work*. London: Routledge and Kegan Paul.

Gillborn, D. (1990) *'Race', Ethnicity and Education*. London: Unwin Hyman.

Hall, S., Critcher, C., Jefferson, T. Clarke, J. and Roberts, B. (1978) *Policing The Crisis: Mugging, the State, and Law and Order*. London: Macmillan.

Hearn, J. and Morgan, D. (1990) *Men, Masculinities and Social Theory*. London: Unwin Hyman.

Hewitt, R. (1986) *White Talk, Black Talk: Inter-Racial Friendship and Communication Amongst Adolescents*. Cambridge: Cambridge University Press.

James, A. and Prout, A. (eds) (1990) *Constructing and Reconstructing Childhood: Contemporary Issues in the Sociological Study of Childhood*. London: Falmer Press.

Jones, S. (1988) *Black Culture, White Youth: The Reggae Tradition from JA to UK*. London: Macmillan.

Mac an Ghaill, M. (1988) *Young, Gifted and Black: Student–Teacher Relations in the Schooling of Black Youth*. Milton Keynes: Open University Press.

Mahoney, P. (1989) Sexual violence and mixed schools. In C. Jones and P. Mahoney (eds) *Learning Our Lines: Sexuality and Social Control in Education*. London: The Women's Press Ltd.

Mirza, H.S. (1992) *Young, Female and Black*. London: Routledge.

Rattansi, A. (1992) Changing the subject? Racism, culture and education. In J. Donald and A. Rattansi (eds) *'Race', Culture and Difference*. London: Sage Publications Ltd.

Segal, L. (1990) *Slow Motion: Changing Masculinities, Changing Men.* London: Virago Press.

Thorne, B. (1993) *Gender Play: Girls and Boys in School.* Buckingham: Open University Press.

Troyna, B and Hatcher, R. (1992) *Racism in Children's Lives: A Study of Mainly-White Primary Schools.* London: Routledge.

Wagg, S. (1988) Perishing kids? The sociology of childhood. *Social Studies Review* 3 (4), 126–31.

Walkerdine, V. (1981) Sex, power and pedagogy. *Screen Education* 38, 14–24.

Westwood, S. (1990) Racism, black masculinity and the politics of space. In J. Hearn and D. Morgan (eds) *Men, Masculinities and Social Theory.* London: Unwin Hyman.

Willis, P. (1977) *Learning to Labour: How Working Class Kids Get Working Class Jobs.* Hants: Saxon House.

Wolpe, A. M. (1988) *Within School Walls: The Role of Discipline, Sexuality and the Curriculum.* London: Routledge.

Wright, C. (1986) School processes: An ethnographic study. In J. Eggleston, J. Dunn and A. Madju (eds) *Education For Some.* London: Trentham Books.

—(1992a) Early education: Multiracial primary school classrooms. In D. Gill, B. Mayor and M. Blair (eds) *Racism and Education: Structures and Strategies.* London: Sage Publications Ltd.

—(1992b) *Race Relations in the Primary School.* London: David Fulton Publishers.

11 'WITH GENDER ON MY MIND': MENSTRUATION AND EMBODIMENT AT ADOLESCENCE

SHIRLEY PRENDERGAST

> Biological, anatomical, physiological and neuro-physiological processes cannot be automatically attributed a natural status. It is not clear that what is biological is necessarily natural. Biological and organic functions are the raw materials of any processes of production of indeterminate forms of subjectivity and material, including corporeal existence. If this is the case, universal givens, such as menstrual, anatomical and hormonal factors, need to be carefully considered as irreducible features of the writing surface, distinct from the script inscribed: a 'texture' more than a designated content for the 'text' or the 'intextuated' body produced.
>
> (Grosz, 1990, p. 72)

This article explores young women's accounts of menarche and early menstruation. It suggests that their experiences are fundamentally shaped not by some universal attributes of menstruation *per se*, but also by the social and material conditions in which they, and women more generally, must learn to manage and cope. There is no essential biology, only the socially constructed intermediary of the body which is in a constant dialectical process of being shaped by and shaping the everyday social world. In this particular example, schools play a significant role in mediating the meaning given to the 'biological' and how the biological is constructed as 'feminine', and the process whereby individual women might come to live and feel authentically gendered in their everyday lives.

Most research has a personal history behind it. That history has been an important part of my own work, relevant both to my initial interest in embodiment and gender and to the unfolding of ideas and the exploration of new knowledge that has resulted. A few years ago, as part of an ethnographic study of sex education and school learning, I and a colleague watched a film about birth, alongside groups of pupils in at least a dozen classrooms. Each time the mother in the film was about to give birth some of the boys (sitting on one side of the classroom) began to laugh, while most of the girls (sitting on the other side) hugged their shoulders, twisted themselves round, crossed their legs, averted their gaze, and generally made themselves as small as possible on their chairs (see Figure 11.1).

Source: This article has been specially commissioned for this Reader.

FIGURE 11.1 Postures of schoolgirls while watching a film about birth.

In a paper written at the time we discussed the ways in which children were inducted into a medicalized view of parenting and childbirth, one which muted the mother's experience, rendering her subservient to the gaze and control of medicine (Prendergast and Prout, 1990). I put to one side the image of the girls twisted on their chairs, but like all powerful images it did not go away. It remained troubling, with a significance that I could not grasp. It wasn't until I came across an extraordinary book of photographs by the anthropologists Gregory Bateson and Margaret Mead (1942) that what we had seen began to make sense.

In *Balinese Character*, written in 1942 within the context of pre-war debates about culture and personality, Bateson and Mead attempted to show the ways in which, from earliest babyhood, the physical body shapes and is shaped by, and comes to express key aesthetic and cultural values of Balinese society. They argued that the Balinese world-view is dominated by conflicting opposites of balance and extension, teasing and denial, learned and expressed through, for example, bodily care, control, movements and gesture. They noted how mothers feed their babies from above, not below the breast as in Western culture (see Figure 11.2). Consequently, if the child loses concentration, or drops asleep, the breast falls from the child's reach, and the child may be removed. In addition, crying babies may be suckled by women who have no breast milk, momentarily quietened only to become more frustrated and upset. As Bateson says in the introduction, the book is not about Balinese kinship, law, religion or custom as such, but is about the Balinese as living persons. How everyday acts such as feeding babies, instructing them how to sit or stand, teaching them to point, to dance etc, actually *embody* that abstraction that we call culture.

The photographs of Bateson and Mead helped me to 'make strange' what was happening in the classroom. The boys joked; girls, observing birth, represented in the film as woman's quintessential experience, reflected pain, bodily shame and disgust. So used to listening, to interviewing I had failed to *see*—to see something about the process of *embodied, gendered* learning, from the pupils' perspective which may quite literally be beyond words at that moment.

The failure to see the body, to account for embodiment, let alone the *gendered body* is not mine alone. As Russell Keat (1986) has noted it springs in part from a general reluctance within the social sciences to address the relationship between the biological and the social. Until recently, mainstream sociology and social psychology have made little contribution to the debates that have been taking place in this area. He points out that the significance and role of the body as a defining feature of similarity or difference between human and other life forms is a recurrent issue in philosophy and the human sciences. Is the body central to that which can be marked as distinctively human, or are its qualities something that we share in common with other living beings? Are language, purposive action, conscious experience, sociality, historicity, cultural diversity the essential and unique defining aspects of

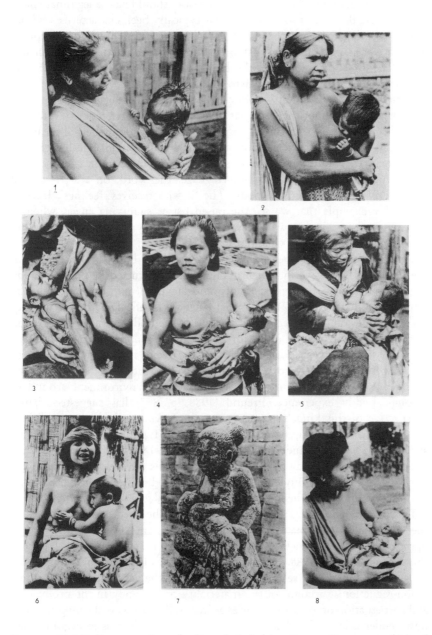

FIGURE 11.2 Balinese mothers feeding their babies. *Source:* Bateson and Mead (1942)

being human? If so, what of the capacities and qualities of the human body as the *source* from which these spring?

The question of whether *bodily* characteristics should have a legitimate place in the object-domain of social theory has typically been characterized within the social sciences as whether *biological* characteristics should have a place. The answer is generally 'no'. At best, perhaps in our attempts to answer and silence the sociobiologists, the body is identified as the *social construct* 'biology', and again therefore put to one side.

A further area of difficulty, as Michael Jackson (1983) suggests is that most current thinking about the body has been vitiated by a tendency to interpret embodied experience in terms of cognitive and linguistic models of meaning. Although bodily experiences, both ontogenically and phylogenically, precede and remain beyond semantic analysis and description, in this logo-centric world meaning is reduced to *sign*, language, the word, on a separate and superior plane to the *act*, the body. The 'I' who receives 'feelings'. Jackson argues for example that we see the raised fist as signifying anger, when in fact it is anger itself that we see. We 'read' the body through the conscious knowing subject, still the same old Cartesian split.

This priority of mind before/over body disallows both the materiality of the body and the ways in which it might be constructed or produced, and the ways in which bodily experience and language may fundamentally be intertwined. Johnson (1987) argues that language is reflexively bound up with and elaborates on fundamental orientations of the body-in-the-world through metaphoric constructions. Thus for example our sense of being 'grounded' or 'rooted', or conversely 'having the ground swept from beneath our feet', are powerfully evocative of emotional as well as literal aspects of human experience. We live within and interact with the environment around us through bodily experience. Freund (1988, p. 857) has suggested that a perspective of this kind 'that recognizes the ways in which the conditions of gender socialization, work environment and public social spaces can shape our *soma* and understand how members of a society view such a socially constructed body as "natural"' is the basis for a radical sociology of knowledge. Frederick Buytendijk (1974) has called this relationship between mind, body and place the 'constellation of *psyche, soma and social existence*'.

This phenomenological approach, which sees 'the lived body as integral to the continual transformation of self in situated contexts where self reflects upon self' (Olesen, 1992, p. 205) exemplified in the work of Johnson, Buytendijk, Freund (1988, 1990) and others such as Iris Marion Young (1989) is particularly useful in relation to discussion of the gendered body. It offers a non-reductionist account of the materiality of the body in the production and perpetuation of gender categories as 'natural' and a way of thinking about how gender is learned and enacted. In so doing it enables us to begin to map the transformations that take place between the social, as ideological context, and the individual, the body as lived experience.

Using a phenomenological framework, and drawing upon the accounts given by girls of between 13 and 16 years of their experience of menarche and early menstruation this paper asks some questions about how embodiment takes place within our own culture and what it might signify. Following Bateson and Mead, it attempts to make a link between the everyday experiences of the body *as lived* with the body *as theory*. It suggests that in young women's narratives about the difficulties of caring for the body in school we find one example of the way in which 'biological' aspects of the body are constructed as 'feminine', and how material aspects of the everyday world can shape the ways in which the biological is given social value. In this fashion the inscription of meaning on the body at adolescence might be seen to stand for more general aspects of 'gender' and how women individually and authentically might come to live and feel gendered in their everyday lives. Lastly, it suggests that this embodied 'cultural materiality' is not only essential in the symbolic production of gender, but, in the conditions and definitions we place upon it, fundamentally shapes the experience of menstruation itself.

GIRLS' EXPERIENCE OF MENSTRUATION IN SCHOOL: SOME FINDINGS FROM THE RESEARCH

> 'I'd say periods are totally a disadvantage. It's all the trauma of getting used to it at first, the pain and embarrassment and everybody finding out. It's worse at first, but it does stay with you. It changes everything, you are limited in what you can do, you limit your actions, stops you doing things.'   (5th-year student)

School offers an interesting way of exploring the role of social context in shaping the experience of puberty. It is a place where young people must spend their 15,000 hours, where, quite unlike the privacy and individuality of home, there are standardized formal rules, obligations and lessons concerning the body. Unlike home, too, where one lives with people at different stages of development, school provides a consistent public location where changes to the body are learned about, experienced and managed in the company of others of the same age. For many, school provides the only formal learning about bodily events and sexuality that they will ever have (Allen, 1987).

Over the course of a recent study about 70 girls between the ages of 13 and 15 spoke in great detail about their experiences of menarche and early menstruation, and about how they learned about it and 'managed' in the context of school (Prendergast, 1987, 1994). A number of key narratives, or story themes, were particularly marked within these interviews. They can be summarized as follows:

(1)   Stories about own private, personal experiences, mostly about physiological effects, emotions and feelings.

(2)   Revelation stories about accidents, mistakes—things that went publicly wrong.
(3)   Stories about male gaze, about teasing and harassment.
(4)   Stories about coping in school—practical facilities and school rules etc.
(5)   Stories about lessons and classroom teaching.

(1) Stories about own private, personal experiences, mostly about physiological effects, emotions and feelings

> 'I had pains from my stomach downwards, really sharp pains, and I couldn't walk, and the only thing that stopped it was bending over. Then I got a headache and had to lie down. I couldn't get dressed because there was so much heavy bleeding and that.'   (5th-year student)

The first set of stories accentuated both the private and the personal nature of menarche and menstruation, and a kind of fatalism, the key articulation of which was the sense of being 'taken over' by the experience. All the girls could remember exact details of the onset of their first period: where it first happened, who they were with, who they went to for help, and their feelings about it. Their accounts were dominated by a terminology of shock and accident: of being 'taken over', 'knocked out', 'a blow', being 'thrown off balance', 'clobbered', lucky or unlucky in their experience.

   Later experiences of menstruation also took girls over but compared to the early experiences later ones were related to physical and emotional effects of the cycle. They spoke of being 'crippled' or 'dragged down' by pain, 'flaring up', 'lashing out' with irritability, uncontrollably weeping or depressed. Irregular periods and heavy bleeding were allied to images of the body as 'flooding', 'leaking', 'staining', threatening to breach some unspecified but significant boundary of self. Girls seemed to feel that there was little that they or anybody else can do to alleviate these effects, and rarely discussed them with other girls.

(2) Revelation stories about accidents, mistakes—things that went publicly wrong

> 'Oh God, I'm always thinking what if it happens to me now. And then I'm worried when I'm on, and if it's leaked. That's always a worry for me ... and if I feel I am sweating, I think, oh no, I've leaked and better go to the loo.' (3rd-year student)

In contrast the second set of stories were often embarrassing and sometimes funny. They were about the consequences when what girls dreaded—the breaching bodily boundaries—actually happened, when private knowledge and experience was made public. They were expressed as a series of anxieties:

- about staining clothes
- having to ask for emergency help in school
- about feeling ill in class, missing an event
- about boys discovering their 'stuff' (towels and tampons)
- about carrying supplies around in school
- doing games, taking notes, having showers, feeling ill.

Thus girls worried that if they did not carry 'stuff' (spare towels and tampons) around with them all the time, they may begin their period unexpectedly and have no way of coping. They worried that the male games teacher would disbelieve a letter from home and ask personal questions. They worried that boys would turn out their school bags, looking for stuff, and throw them around the classroom. They worried that unless they constantly changed towels or tampons they would stain their clothes.

These were not unreasonable things to worry about, indeed they happened all the time. However, unlike the first set of stories, where the body took over and there was little that girls could do to mediate or relieve the effects, these were incidents which might, with extreme watchfulness, monitoring and advance planning, be avoided. They relate to the practical day-to-day management of menstruation, particularly in keeping knowledge of it away from boys. Constant surveillance on many fronts was necessary to manage menstruation with proper discreetness—in essence total invisibility—in school, and girls blamed themselves if they failed.

(3) Stories about male gaze, about teasing and harassment

'At my last school there was a girl, and the boys found things and tampax in her bag, and they were chucking it round the classroom and kicking it down the corridor. And she was just crying and really they didn't care, they don't really feel or anything.' (3rd-year student).

The third set of stories concerned boys, and reached a peak in the second and third years of secondary school. Certain groups of boys appeared to delight in using their often new-found knowledge of menstruation to tease and torment girls. In all the mixed schools this had been the case. They watched to see if a girl took her bag to the toilet or missed games. They went into girls' toilets and wrote things on the walls, called girls names, pretended that they had stained their skirts in lessons. Boys turned out girls' school bags, hung towels and tampons around the playground, and threw them in the classroom.

There was a great deal of group hostility from boys, often combined with physical harassment, in which girls were touched, pushed and squeezed. Girls were furious about such things, but rarely if ever spoke to a teacher. They responded with as much dignity as they could muster. In practice this often meant avoiding boys, never letting go of their school bags, wearing special clothes on certain days.

(4) Stories about coping in school—practical facilities and school rules etc.

> 'Oh God, the toilets! They are awful! Sometimes when I am dying to go, I would sooner wait until I can go home because they are so disgusting, they really are. There's no machines to get towels out of, the toilet paper is really hard. Nobody pulls the chain and there are towels on the floor.'
> (5th-year student)

The fourth set of stories concerned the ways in which school facilities, school rules and procedures influenced the ways in which girls were enabled to practically cope and adequately care for themselves in school. One true story: Amy described how the teacher would not let her leave the classroom to use the toilets. Amy bled heavily each period. By the end of the lesson the blood had soaked through her skirt on to the chair, and she was terrified of getting up to leave. She burst into tears and inevitably other pupils noticed. The boys called her Bloody Mary, a name that had stuck for the 18 months that had elapsed before she was interviewed in school.

In these stories girls described the sometimes almost total lack of practical provision in schools necessary to deal with menstruation in a civilized and dignified fashion. For example, whole toilet blocks were often locked during lesson time. It could be hard to get permission to go to the toilet, often involving a lengthy and humiliating search for a teacher with a key. Even the most basic facilities such as soap and toilet paper were not reliably available, disposal bins, paper towels or hand dryers and locks on doors were variable, while vending machines for emergency supplies totally unavailable. Girls described waiting to use lavatories out of school at dinner time, having to change while they blocked the lavatory door closed with one foot, taking away used towels wrapped in paper to dispose of elsewhere, and the disgust they felt at not being able to keep clean or wash their hands.

(5) Stories about lessons and classroom teaching

> 'And all the boys and girls were together in the first year, and the boys just started laughing whenever we said something [about menstruation] so we laughed back. We didn't really learn anything. We had heard something at primary school, but the boys didn't know anything.' (5th-year student)

The final set of stories concerned teaching in the formal curriculum. Girls described the ways in which sex education lessons were dominated by boys' behaviour and responses. For example, very like the birth film incident described above, they spoke of boys' laughter and crude comments about women's bodies as they watched many of the videos and films. This was exacerbated because much of the official content of sex education focuses on reproduction rather than sexuality, and therefore is dominated by references to and images of women's reproductive cycle. While the biology of reproduction must refer to the erect penis, and therefore to some notion of male desire and pleasure, there may be little to suggest an active, positive female sexuality. The onset of maturity for boys is marked, it seems, with wet dreams; for girls it is menstruation.

In summary we can say that the average girl who wishes successfully to manage menstruation in school must keep a number of issues in mind when she has her period:

- She must know in advance that her period is likely to start that day and be prepared with appropriate supplies (towels, tampons, tissue, painkillers, etc.).
- She must keep these in a safe place so that they are both readily accessible but not likely to be found deliberately or accidentally by boys.
- She must judge the appropriate time to change in order that blood does not leak on to her clothes, and co-ordinate this with lesson breaks, and find a toilet that has the facilities (disposal bin, lock, lavatory paper, soap, hand towels etc.) that she needs.
- She must assess how she is likely to feel in the day, and be appropriately prepared for headache or period pain, for example. She must try to stay alert in lessons, and manage feeling sleepy, irritable or unwell so that other people do not notice.
- She must have considered the day's lessons, and brought a note from home if she wishes to be excused from any of them.

It is against this framework that schools promote the idea of menstruation as a perfectly 'normal and natural thing'.

GIRLS' ACCOUNTS: SOME DOMINANT THEMES

These fragments of data, girls' stories, are about the ways in which menstrual experience, what Grosz (1990) has called one of the 'universal givens', is shaped by the social and material processes of school. Taken as a whole, they reflect a negativity and disgust that go beyond individual experience: no girl, however positive her beliefs, could escape completely unaffected by the conditions in most schools in the study. Among the consequences of this are:

- the adolescent body's response to the scrutiny of the (predominantly) male gaze
- the sense that girls have of their bodies becoming disorganized and out of control
- the regulation of the self as a model for future gender roles.

These consequences are discussed further below.

The scrutiny of the (predominantly) male gaze

Barrie Thorne (1993) has noted the ways in which pre-pubertal children often describe girls' bodies as sexual, and the prevalence of games such as 'cootie touch' and 'girl stain' as negative elements in both boys' and girls' play. Although Thorne felt this was not an explicit reference to menstruation, it was clear from girls in the study that, by early puberty, menstruation did provide young teenage boys with powerful ammunition: judgement of the female sexual body as polluted. While we are familiar with the ways in which women must *produce* their bodies (via make-up, hair and clothes) for the judgement of men, these stories were also about the ways in which the body must be repressed, guarded and contained so that its secrets could not be known. As girls enter puberty they must take on these new tasks in close proximity to boys, an audience who are watchful, often antagonistic and looking for trouble. Pressured and teased by boys, few girls in the study had managed to break the spell and speak their anger. Those who had were legendary—jokers, heroines, powerful girls who had risked boundaries.

This repression of the menstruating body is physically expressed. During the interviews, I saw girls recreate a morphology of shame. As they told their stories they tightly closed themselves in. This itself mimicked the postures I had seen earlier but not understood as girls watched a woman give birth (Figure 11.1). The significance of a woman's open legs, of her exposure or imagined exposure to male gaze, even in birth, must be set against 'page three' of the *Sun* and the 'open crotch' shots in top-shelf magazines. This is not an unrealistic fear among girls. Holland, Ramazanoglu and Sharpe (1993) describe how many young men in their study reported pornographic magazines as an important source of learning about sex. Such magazines are commonly shared between boys in and out of school. The body's performance of that which is female, but which cannot be fully subsumed into predominant definitions of the sexual, must be shielded from the gaze that would judge it lacking, vulnerable or, even, disgusting.

Embodied knowledge of this kind builds upon a history of the gendered body from early childhood. These gendered expressions of movement in space, and gendered differences in posture have been more generally described by Iris Marion Young (1989) and captured in photographs by Marianne Wex (1979). Wex photographed what happened when she asked young women and young men to sit 'like a girl' and then to 'sit like a boy' (see Figure 11.3) Both the women and the men could instinctively and accurately take up the other's archetypal pose. Wex captured something of the modern Western notion of an ideal female body as it has been dominantly portrayed for women: childlike, thin, small-breasted, fine-boned. Compared with a man, a woman should take up little space, be light and graceful, keep her legs together. Young suggests that in this way a young woman learns to regard her body as an object, as other, as the intention of another subject, rather than as a 'living manifestation of action and intention' of her own (p. 155).

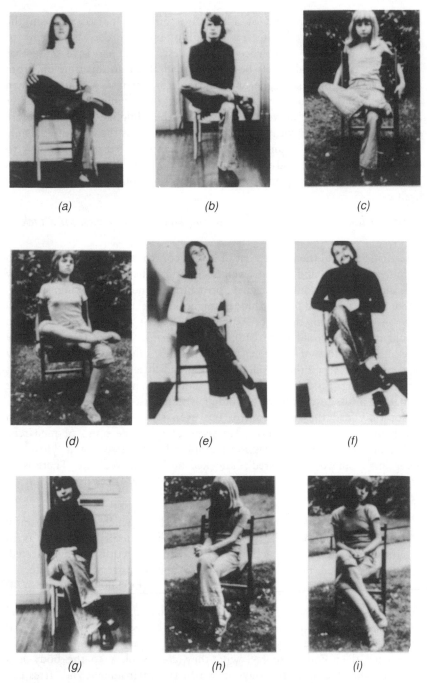

FIGURE 11.3 Women and men adopting archetypal 'feminine' (a–d) and 'masculine' (e–i) poses. *Source:* Wex (1979)

One might speculate that at adolescence girls are poised between the experience of bodily shock, fragmentation and disorder that seems to accompany menstrual experience in the West, and a pervasive sense that in fact this is their body at its best, its most ideal. From this time on, from the immanence of this fragile and contradictory arrival, a young woman has much to lose: to grow up, to mature, to become adult and enter childbearing can only move her away from this childlike body. There are clear connections here with what has been described as the current epidemic of eating disorders in young women: the attempt to freeze adolescence, to hold on to a childlike body, and to control it rigidly through diet. Perhaps significantly, one consequence of anorexia and bulimia is that menstruation itself ceases.

Menstruation as loss of control: Crossing bodily boundaries, an attack on self

A second powerful theme was that of loss of control at the most intimate and seemingly personal and unique level. Each month the body appeared to draw girls into a time of doubtful agency, breaching boundaries. Leaking, staining, flooding, what should be kept hidden might become exposed, inside–outside, private–public. This might be expressed as loss of *temporal* control (when would it come, would it be late), loss of *practical* control (can't stop the bleeding), and loss of *emotional* control (can't stop crying, feeling angry or depressed). At another level, girls often had little understanding of what was happening 'inside', or what to do about it. What was normal? Wasn't it making a fuss to complain? Shouldn't women just grin and bear it?

Not only had they lost control but even stronger was the idea of an attack or assault on their everyday sense of self. The onset of menarche and menstrual experience was most graphically expressed, as a 'blow'—as being 'hit', 'landed', 'clobbered', 'knocked out', 'shattered', etc. There is an extraordinary parallel here with what Buytendijk (1974) has described in his *Prolegomena to an Anthropological Physiology*:

> There is no mode of being in man [*sic*] in which the polar unity of bodily and personal subjectivity manifests itself so clearly as in those situations in which he refers with the words: being affected, upset, touched, moved, struck, shocked, alarmed, overwhelmed, etc.
>
> (Buytendijk, 1974, p. 174)

Buytendijk sets out what he calls the constellation of 'psyche, soma and social existence' a continuous stream of affect between the everyday social environment and the ways in which people might come to subjectively experience their bodies, to feel who they are. A blow to the body is a blow to 'self'. He notes the ways in which the environment and stress can affect bodily posture, blood pressure, blood sugar, hormone levels, immunity, respiration, etc., and names some of the consequences as: fatigue, aches and pains, headaches, dizziness, anxiety, palpitations, depression, 'nerves;. The general overlap of this list with women's everyday experience of menstruation is striking. Clearly defensive body postures, watchfulness, secrecy, anxiety, stress, all the things that girls describe in school, are not natural correlates of menstrual experience, but might come to shape, quite literally our sense of self.

Regulation of the self

As we have seen above, girls in school must keep a mental list of practical tasks, be constantly watchful and on their guard in order to keep menstruation hidden. This included not only watchfulness of the body, constant monitoring to forestall accidents such as staining their clothes, but also watchfulness of bags and possessions and of their own and others' actions. For example, even if they would prefer not to, girls must remain aware of what groups of boys might be up to and take adequate precautions. The combined effect of these kinds of watchfulnesses, both in producing and repressing the body, might be summarized more abstractly as 'regulation of the self':

- to regulate emotions including depression, anger and anxiety
- to regulate responses like embarrassment, shame
- to regulate the expression of physical discomfort, including sometimes severe pain
- to regulate body movement, posture and clothes so as to maintain secrecy
- to make clean, comfortable and invisible those body processes seen as publicly unacceptable
- to plan ahead and be prepared for both cyclical and daily events and bodily changes
- to manage all these things in adverse conditions, against the odds.

We can sum this up by saying: for young women (perhaps all women) menstrual experience must be constantly present in their thoughts in order that it remains invisible to the outside world. As Buytendijk notes, these are the ways in which 'the body is in the mind'. This is essentially exhausting and negative energy, keeping things hidden, because the consequences of them becoming public can be dire.

There is a close analogy here with the tasks that make up the proper role of adult women in managing the bodies of babies, children, the elderly and the sick, as well as those of families and husbands, as carers both in work and at home. Again, as in the presentation of her own body as object of the gaze, it gives to women the task of both producing the social and collective body, the growth and health of children particularly, and repressing it, removing the detritus of growth, the unwanted products of living. This is what Emily Martin (1989) has called quite literally 'housekeeping the body'. While these tasks must be done, it is essential that they are done discreetly, invisibly, and without intruding.

This list also looks very like a preparation for the workplace, teaching girls the rules of presenting and containing femininity in public, in reminding women that its structures, values and organization are basically masculine—ones that women must adjust to and co-operate with if they are to succeed there.

DISCUSSION

> There are no 'facts', biological or material, that have social consequences and cultural meanings in and of themselves. Sexual intercourse, pregnancy and parturition are cultural facts, whose forms, consequences and meanings are socially constructed in any society, as are mothering, fathering, judging, ruling and talking with the gods.
>
> (Yanagisako and Collier, quoted in Thorne, 1993, p. 204)

This article has laid out one very specific example of how the spaces of school, pedagogical, social and material, may critically shape bodily experience and wider sense of self for young women at this time. Learning takes place at many levels, most particularly in the unconscious taking up of an authentic, seemingly natural, gendered embodiment which lies at the heart of what is considered properly feminine. At the same time this notion of the 'natural, properly feminine' body, and the processes which contribute to shaping it in school reflect a crucial paradox in Western societies about the wider value given to the reality of adult womanhood. Not only is the 'properly feminine' body one which does not live out its full potential in terms of strength, extension and space in the world, but girls also learn that their bodies are not good enough as they are.

At adolescence girls discover that in order to be acceptable, women's bodies must be 'enscribed' (Grosz, 1990), embellished, shaped and styled as surface and as three-dimensional text: that which is central, definitional of womanhood, bleeding, must be suppressed. This suppression can never be complete or entire. As Mary Douglas (1966, p. 8) says of the failure to contain bodily boundaries, 'the polluter is always in the wrong'. Although puberty is a time when the young girl is said to 'grow up' we do not match this with even the most practical recognition of her most basic material needs. More than this, young women must keep silent about what has happened.

The valuing of menstruation must be set beside what is openly acknowledged in young men: height and strength (Simmons, Blyth and McKinney, 1983). When at menarche a young woman makes a dramatic shift towards her adult female self, we do not speak about it publicly, we do not generally celebrate it and many young women are not properly taught about menstruation in advance of it happening. McKeever has noted:

> Female children approach puberty in a disadvantaged position. They
> have little or no knowledge of menstruation, and are poorly equipped
> conceptually and perceptually about their genital structures. In addition
> they have lived a decade or so in a society where they have learned
> that their genitals must be hidden from language, sight and thought.'
>
> (McKeever, 1984, p. 40)

In the early production of menstrual experience in school we see one marker
in what Connell (1987) has called the 'ongoing making of gender', constantly
being remade, subject to both continuity and to change throughout the life
course. The remaking of gender takes place within material environments
which continue to shape body/mind. Not only does early menstrual experience
rehearse adult roles, but the theme of the embodiment of gender continues to
be affirmed and reconstituted by the unpaid and paid work that women do.
Hochschild's (1983) study of the gendered 'emotion work' of air hostesses
and debt collectors, Lawlor (1991), on nursing, or Game and Pringle (1986)
on relations between secretaries and bosses lay out most clearly the ways in
which the requirements of some work roles carry gendered implications in
terms of the mind/body/environment.

This article does not claim that girls' experiences of school are always
everywhere the same. Neither does it suggest that women's experience of
menstruation is universal, or that we can make universal judgements about the
nature of menstruation *per se*. Clearly, if we claim that there is no fixed and
rigid biology, it is likely that different cultures will construct meaning around
events of the body in different ways (Johnson, 1987; Gottlieb and Buckley,
1988). Within a broad definition of Western culture, however, it has been
suggested that at puberty something happens to girls which does not happen
to boys: the body becomes the dominant agency whereby they are 'brought
into line'. Sophie Laws (1991) has described how menstrual etiquette, the
generally unvoiced cultural assumption that women may not refer to periods
in any public situation, is internalized and enacted by women: the policing
of menstruation is done in relation to the definitions and desires of men.
Judith Butler (1993, p. 16) has asked how might one begin to 'think through
the matter of bodies as a kind of materialization governed by regulatory
norms in order to ascertain the workings of heterosexual hegemony in the
formation of what qualifies as a viable body?' At no time is the hold of
heterosexual values more powerfully pursued and enforced than during
adolescence.

What is central to this social mapping of gender and difference around
menstruation and the body in school is the naming and disguising of
what are in fact social processes, material circumstances, ideological forms
as 'biological', and therefore natural, legitimate and inevitable. When girls
speak so eloquently of the onset of puberty as a 'blow', about being 'hit',

'clobbered', I suspect that this is partly what they comprehend, a metaphor for what is to come, the unfairness of being a girl, inexorably bound to a body that is treated as, and feels unequal, about which they can do very little.

Acknowledgement

The research upon which this article is based was funded by the Health Promotion Trust, Cambridge. I gratefully acknowledge the Trust's support of this study, but take full responsibility for the content.

References

Allen, I (1987) *Education in Sex and Personal Relationships*. Policy Studies Institute Research Report No. 655. Dorset: Blackmore Press.

Bateson, G. and Mead, M. (1942) *Balinese Character*. New York: New York Academy of Sciences.

Butler, J. (1993) *Bodies that Matter. On the Discursive Limits of 'Sex'*. London: Routledge.

Buytendijk, F. J. (1974) *Prolegomena to an Anthropological Physiology*. Pittsburgh: Duquesne University Press.

Connell, R.W. (1987) *Gender and Power*. Oxford: Polity Press.

Douglas, M. (1966) *Purity and Danger*. New York: Praeger.

Freund, P. (1988) Bringing society into the body: Understanding socialised human nature. *Theory and Society* 17, 839–64.

—(1990) The expressive body: A common ground for the sociology of emotions and health and illness. *Sociology of Health and Illness* 12 (4), 452–77.

Game, A. and Pringle, R. (1983) *Gender at Work*. Sydney/London/Boston: Allen and Unwin.

—(1986) Beyond gender at work: secretaries. In N. Grieve and A. Burns (eds) *Australian Women: New Feminist Perspectives*. Melbourne: Oxford University Press.

Gottlieb, A. and Buckley, T. (1988) *Blood Magic: New Anthropological Approach to Menstruation*. Cambridge: Cambridge University Press.

Grosz, E (1990) Inscriptions and body maps. Representations and the corporeal. In T. Threadgold and A. Cranny-Francis (eds) *Feminine, Masculine and Representation*. Sydney: Allen and Unwin.

Hochschild, A. (1983) *The Managed Heart: The Commercialisation of Human Feeling*. University of California Press.

Holland, J., Ramazanoglu, C. and Sharpe, S. (1993) *Wimp or Gladiator: Contradictions in Acquiring Masculine Sexuality*. London: Tufnell Press.

Jackson, M. (1983) Knowledge of the body. *Man* (NS), 327–45.

Johnson, M. (1987) Premenstrual syndrome as a Western culture-specific disorder. *Culture, Medicine and Psychiatry* 11, 337–56.

Keat, R. (1986) The human body in social theory: Reich, Foucault and the repressive hypothesis. *Radical Philosophy* 11, 24–32.

Lawlor, J. (1991) *Behind the Screens: Nursing, Somology and the Problems of the Body*. Churchill Livingstone.

Laws, S. (1991) *Issues of Blood. The Politics of Menstruation*. London: Macmillan Press.

McKeever, P. (1984) The perpetuation of menstrual shame: Implications and directions. *Women and Health* 9, 33–47.

Martin, E. (1989) *The Women in the Body*. Milton Keynes: Open University Press.

Okely, J. (1987) Privileged, schooled and finished education for girls. In G. Weiner and M. Arnot (eds) *Gender under Scrutiny*. Hutchinson.

Olesen, V. L. (1992) Extraordinary events and mundane ailments. In C. Ellis and M. Flaherty (eds) *Investigating Subjectivity. Research on Lived Experience*. London: Sage.

Prendergast, S. (1987) Girls' experience of menstruation in school. In L. Holly (ed.) *Girls and Sexuality, Teaching and Learning*. Milton Keynes: Open University Press.

—(1994) *This is the Time to Grow Up. Girls' Experience of Menstruation in School*. London: FPA.

Prendergast, S. and Prout, A. (1990) Learning about birth: parenthood and sex education in English secondary schools. In J. Garcia, R. Kilpatrick and M. Richards (eds) *The Politics of Maternity Care: Services for Childbearing Women in Twentieth-century Britain*. Oxford: Clarendon Press.

Simmons, R. G., Blyth, D. S. and McKinney, K. L. (1983) The social and psychological effects of puberty on white females. In J. Brooks-Gunn and A.C. Petersen (eds) *Girls at Puberty: Biological and Psychosocial Perspective*. New York: Plenum Books.

Thorne, B. (1993) *Gender Play: Girls and Boys in School*. Buckingham: Open University Press.

Young, I. M. (1989) *Throwing Like a Girl and Other Essays in Feminist Philosophy and Theory*. Bloomington: Indiana University Press.

Wex, M. (1979) *'Let's Take Back Our Space': Female and Male Body Language as a Result of Patriarchal Structures*. Berlin: Movimento Druck.

Part 3: Research

12 QUANTITATIVE AND QUALITATIVE METHODS IN THE SOCIAL SCIENCES: FEMINIST ISSUES AND PRACTICAL STRATEGIES

TOBY EPSTEIN JAYARATNE AND ABIGAIL J. STEWART

Within the last decade, the feminist research community has engaged in a dialogue concerning the use of quantitative versus qualitative methods in social research. Much of this debate has concerned the claim that quantitative research techniques—involving the translation of individuals' experience into categories predefined by researchers—distort women's experience and result in a silencing of women's own voices. Advocates of qualitative methods have argued that individual women's understandings, emotions, and actions in the world must be explored in those women's own terms. Defenders of quantitative methods in turn have worried that qualitative methods often include few safeguards against the operation of researcher biases and that abandonment of all aspects of traditional methodology may carry political and scholarly costs. In addition, some have pointed out that although quantitative methods can be and have been used to distort women's experience, they need not be. Although feminist advocates in this debate have generally embraced qualitative methods, they have expressed a range of views on the use of quantative research, from condemning quantitative methods wholesale to promoting research which incorporates aspects of both qualitative and quantitative methods (Birke, 1986, Healy and Stewart, 1991; Jayaratne, 1983).

The purpose of this article is to review the evolution of this dialogue, to evaluate several issues which continue to be problematic in this literature, and to propose productive and practical strategies for feminist researchers concerned with these issues. In particular, this essay will emphasize the value of quantitative methods as effective tools to support feminist goals and feminist ideologies, while rejecting those traditional research procedures which are antithetical to feminist values.

We believe that much of the feminist debate about qualitative and quantitative research has been sterile and based on a false polarization. Moreover, as we will show below, solutions offered for methodological problems have frequently been either too general or too constraining to be realistically incorporated into research activity. Finally, much of the discussion

Source: Abridged from Fonow, M.M. and Cook, J.A. (1991) *Beyond Methodology: Feminist Scholarship as Lived Research.* Bloomington and Indianapolis: Indiana University Press.

of feminist methodology is really a discussion of basic epistemological issues (for example, the validity of various forms of knowledge); the dialogue is, therefore, fundamental but relatively esoteric and inaccessible. The nonempirical basis for discussion makes translation of the feminist philosophical perspective into testable research questions or acceptance by many researchers impractical. Given this state of affairs, we think a more practical, less abstract analysis of this topic is overdue. We hope the formulation of some pragmatic and useful recommendations for conducting feminist research will allow a variety of options and strategies to those who wish their empirical research to be consistent with feminist values.

THE FEMINIST METHODOLOGY DIALOGUE

Feminist criticism

The initial dialogue on feminist methodology originated from feminist criticism of traditional quantitative research. [. . .]
   Specific criticisms of this research have included:

1. The selection of sexist and elitist research topics (Cook and Fonow, 1984; Grady, 1981; Jayaratne, 1983; Scheuneman, 1986) and the absence of research on questions of central importance to women (see Parlee, 1975; Roberts, 1981).
2. Biased research designs, including selection of only male subjects (Grady, 1981; Lykes and Stewart, 1986).
3. An exploitative relationship between the researcher and the subject (Mies, 1983; Oakley, 1981) and within research teams (Birke, 1986; Harding, 1987).
4. The illusion of objectivity, especially associated with the positivist approach (Bleier, 1984; Stanley and Wise, 1983).
5. The simplistic and superficial nature of quantitative data (Jayaratne, 1983).
6. Improper interpretation and overgeneralization of findings (Jayaratne and Kaczala, 1983; Westkott, 1979), including the use of person-blame explanations and application to women of theory tested on exclusively male subjects.
7. Inadequate data dissemination and utilization (Tangri and Strasburg, 1979). Mies (1983) nicely sums up these criticisms by noting a fundamental contradiction between methodological theories which are currently accepted in the social sciences and the goals of the feminist community.

Many classic studies in social science may be analyzed now in terms of these criticisms. For example, Milgram's (1974) famous studies of 'obedience,' in which participants were led to believe they were administering painful shocks to another person (actually a 'stooge' of the experimenter) in the name of 'teaching,' may be considered in light of these issues.

First, Milgram's definition of 'obedience' (following the experimenter's instructions) relied on the rather abstract authority of the 'scientist' and ignored both economic and personal safety factors which may in fact motivate 'obedience' among those without power. [. . .] Second, *all* of Milgram's studies involved a male victim or 'learner' and a male experimenter. In addition, most of his studies included only white, male, well-educated subjects in New Haven, Connecticut. [. . .]

Third, the entire research design depended on maximizing the hierarchical distance between experimenter and research participants; in addition, the experimenter actually deceived the participants throughout the experiment. [. . .]

Fourth, the 'indicators' selected for analysis were thoroughly 'objective,' for example, the actual voltage of the current, apparently administered to the stooge 'learner' by the research participant. Similarly, fifth, analysis of the data was conducted in the most quantitative terms; thus, the participants' beliefs about their actions, and their feelings in the situation, were often not assessed at all. [. . .]

Sixth, despite the rather narrow definition of 'obedience' and the limited range of people included as research participants, Milgram believed that

> the essence of obedience consists in the fact that a person comes to view himself [*sic*] as the instrument for carrying out another person's wishes, and he therefore no longer regards himself as responsible for his actions. . . . The question of generality, therefore, is not resolved by enumerating all the manifest differences between the psychological laboratory and other situations but by carefully constructing a situation that *captures the essence of obedience* . . . [italics added] (Milgram, 1974, p. xii)

The critical question, of course, is how we know that the 'essence of obedience' has indeed been captured. Although Milgram invokes an internal, self-definitional process as accounting for 'obedience,' he does not in fact assess directly any aspect of that process. Moreover, although he explores a number of contextual factors affecting rates of obedience, he concludes—without proof—that the 'essence' of it is captured in all variants of the experimental paradigm. [. . .]

Feminist criticisms of traditional research practice are relevant not only to some social science research, but to many of the most respected and significant 'landmark' studies.

Sources of feminist criticism

The specific feminist criticisms of traditional methodology derive from at least three sources. First, criticism has resulted from negative personal experiences with traditional research (for example, see Weisstein, 1977). Thus, Reinharz (1979), in describing the disillusionment she felt when participating in a research study at Columbia University, states that there were enormous discrepancies between her idealized version of research and her actual day-to-day experiences on and observations of this research project. [. . .]

A second source of criticism is political, stemming from a concern that existing methodologies support sexist, racist, and elitist attitudes and practices and therefore negatively affect peoples' lives. [. . .] Research which only documents differences between the sexes offers no understanding of why those differences exist or how such differences may be attenuated and therefore may reinforce (or create) the public's preconceived and sexist attitudes.

Thus, for example, Eccles and Jacobs (1986) report that media coverage of social scientists' research on sex differences in math ability results in differential parental encouragement of boys and girls equally gifted in math. The importance of this fact is underlined by Eccles and Jacobs's documentation of the power of parental encouragement of children's math efforts as a key predictor of children's performance over time.

[. . .]

A third source of feminist criticism is philosophical and is based on a general rejection of positivism, its claim that science is value neutral, and that the scientific method protects against contamination of findings by 'subjectivity' (see Wittig, 1985). Thus, for example, Unger (1983) argues that

> the ideological framework of positivist empiricism defines the relationship between researcher and subject as an impersonal one. The logic of these methods (and even their language) prescribes prediction and control. It is difficult for one who is trained in such a conceptual framework to step beyond it and ask what kind of person such a methodology presupposes.
> (Unger, 1983, p. 11)

Many feminist critics have argued that the person 'presupposed' is a male scientist trained to ignore or mistrust feelings and subjectivity (see, for example, Keller, 1985).

Partly because the accepted methods of research in the social sciences have been quantitative, the focus of all three kinds of feminist criticism has been on quantitative research.[1] [. . .]

Feminist support for qualitative methods

In response to these criticisms, some feminist researchers recognized the need to discover or develop research methodologies consistent with feminist values that could be advocated for general use in the social sciences (Mies, 1983). The methodology which they embraced was primarily qualitative. It was promoted for numerous reasons, often parallelling the reasons for rejection of quantitative methods. Running through much of this enthusiasm for qualitative methods has been an understanding that many aspects of women's experience have not yet been articulated or conceptualized within social science. A deep suspicion of quantitative methods as having concealed women's real experience has motivated much preoccupation with, and advocacy of, qualitative methods as methods which permit women to express their experience fully and in their own terms. Thus, for example, Smith (1987) argues that social scientists' methods must permit respondents to describe the world as they experience it.

> There are and must be different experiences of the world and different bases of experience. We must not do away with them by taking advantage of our privileged speaking to construct a sociological version which we then impose upon them as their reality. [...] Their reality, their varieties of experience must be an unconditional datum.   (Smith, 1987, p. 93)

One frequent source of enthusiasm for qualitative methods stems from their potential to offer a more human, less mechanical relationship between the researcher and 'the researched.' For example, Oakley (1981) suggests that 'the goal of finding out about people through interviewing is best achieved when the relationship of interviewer and interviewee is nonhierarchical and when the interviewer is prepared to invest his or her own personal identity in the relationship' (p. 41). [...]

Feminists', as well as others', advocacy and use of qualitative methods has not generally been welcomed in the social sciences. Despite the argument that qualitative methods provide more accurate and valid information about respondents' experience, use of qualitative methods, and especially qualitative feminist research, often produces strong negative reactions in the mainstream academic community (Cook and Fonow, 1984; Du Bois, 1983, Healy and Stewart, 1991; Reinharz, 1979), primarily because it is thought to be 'unscientific' or politically motivated, and therefore overtly biased. [...]

An inclusive feminist perspective

Over time, feminist theorists and researchers have increasingly distinguished between qualitative methods and a feminist approach to social science research, thus deemphasizing the critical focus on quantification. For example, Stanley and Wise (1983) have argued that 'methods in themselves aren't innately anything' (p. 159). They point out that although 'positivist methods and world views are objectionable, sexist even, ... what should be objected to about them isn't quantification or their use of statistical techniques' (p. 159). Instead, the ways in which research participants are treated and the care with which researchers attempt to represent the lived experience of research participants are of more central concern. In fact, in reviewing recent discussions of feminist methods, Harding (1987) argues that

> feminist researchers use just about any and all of the methods, in this concrete sense of the term, that traditional androcentric researchers have used. Of course, precisely how they carry out these methods of evidence gathering is often strikingly different.   (Harding, 1987, p. 2)

She concludes, 'it is not by looking at research methods that one will be able to identify the distinctive features of the best of feminist research' (p.3).

An inclusive viewpoint on methods, which appears to be increasingly accepted in feminist research circles, takes the form of promoting the value and appropriate use of both qualitative and quantitative methods as feminist research tools. The emphasis here is on using methods which can best answer particular research questions, but always using them in ways which are consistent with broad feminist goals and ideology. Thus Jayaratne (1983) and Wittig (1985) have argued that both types of methods can be effectively utilized by feminists and can be implemented in ways which are consistent with feminist values. Procedures commonly used in quantitative research which are inconsistent with feminist values can be altered without abandoning the quantitative strategies which can be beneficial to feminists. Moreover, combining methods, sometimes termed 'triangulation' (see Denzin, 1978; Jick, 1979) permits researchers to 'capture a more complete, holistic, and contextual portrayal . . .' (Jick, 1979, p. 603). As Jick points out, 'the effectiveness of triangulation rests on the premise that the weaknesses in each single method will be compensated by the counter-balancing strengths of another' (p. 604).

Yllo (1988) is most persuasive in making this case with respect to research on marital rape. As she points out, the true nature of marital rape cannot be captured in statistics; the experience of violent victimization at the hands of a loved one in an act grotesquely similar to and totally different from an act of love cannot be conveyed in traditional questionnaire or survey format. Yllo conducted extensive qualitative interviews with a sample of women who volunteered to be in a study of marital rape. She points out that this analysis yielded a new typology of marital rape (Finkelhor and Yllo, 1985, p. 32). 'I learned a greal deal about wife abuse from those 50 women that the quantitative data on over 2,000 couples could not begin to reveal'.

Yllo also points out that associations which are powerfully significant to an individual woman cannot be understood in terms of their generality without careful survey research.

> For example, we found that a large portion of the marital rape victims had also been sexually abused as children. We cannot discover the extent of the relationship between child sexual abuse and marital rape unless we construct a controlled study using a representative sample. It may be that child sexual abuse is no more common among marital rape victims than among other women. But, only by comparing marital rape victims with nonvictims could we come to any adequate conclusions.
>
> (Finkelhor and Yllo, 1985, p. 35)

CURRENT ISSUES IN THE FEMINIST METHODOLOGY LITERATURE

Although there seems to be increasing consensus in the feminist community that quantitative methods are legitimate research tools and that methods should be chosen based on an appropriate fit with the research question, there remain at least three conceptual areas in discussions of feminist methodology where the dialogue remains problematic. First are definitional difficulties with the terms 'quantitative,' 'qualitative,' 'method' and 'methodology.' Second is the tendency of many authors to take an essentialist position, which assumes that female researchers feel comfortable, and are competent using only certain 'female' methods. The third problem concerns the epistemological issue of objectivity/subjectivity, a continuing central focus for debate.

Definitional issues

A number of terms used in the feminist methodology dialogue have different implicit or explicit definitions, resulting in some confusion. This difficulty is particularly apparent with regard to the distinction between 'methods' and 'methodology' and between 'quantitative' and 'qualitative' processes. [...] Harding (1987) has suggested one set of distinctions among terms. She identifies 'methods' as particular procedures used in the course of research (e.g. interviews), 'methodology' as a theory of how research is carried out or the broad principles about how to conduct research and how theory is applied (e.g. survey research methodology or experimental methodology), and 'epistemology' as a theory of knowledge (e.g. the 'scientific method' which aims to establish the truth-value of various propositions). It follows from these definitions that first, quantitative and qualitative 'methods' are simply specific research procedures; second, 'feminist methodology' or a 'feminist perspective on methodology' must be taken to refer to a much broader theory of how to do feminist research. There may, then, be a 'feminist methodology' without any particular feminist 'methods.' [...]

Besides distinguishing methods and methodology, we also distinguish historical from logical associations between specific procedures and specific ideologies. For example, quantitative methods have been associated historically with sexist and antifeminist attitudes. We propose that although quantitative research may have been used in the past to obscure the experience of women, it need not always be used in that way. That is, the association is an historical one but not a logical one. [...]

However, despite the prevalence of these historical associations, there may be some absolute constraints or limitations associated with each type of method. Thus, for example, quantitative methods may never provide the kind of richly textured 'feeling for the data' that qualitative methods can permit. [...] It can also be argued that multivariate statistical analyses of large data sets may provide the most truly 'contextual' analyses of people's experience. This is because certain multivariate statistical procedures allow the incorporation of a large number of contextual variables, permitting the simultaneous testing of elaborate and complex theoretical models. It has been argued that such analysis is more 'ecologically valid' (Bronfenbrenner, 1977).

One common stereotype of qualitative methods is that they are unsystematic and thus unscientific. Clearly such methods can be unsystematic, but they need not be. Hornstein (1991) is able to spell out detailed procedures for a 'phenomenological approach to the study of lives.' She describes three stages in the researchers' analysis of a phenomenological account. In the first stage the researcher is 'attempting to uncover the structure of an experience,' and therefore 'takes each bit of the subject's report and scrutinizes it to uncover its meaning.' She points out that 'crucial to this process is a way of thinking termed *imaginal variation*, in which a given feeling, thought, or outcome is compared with other possibilities' (pp. 6–7). The second stage of analysis involves construction of 'analytic categories' that emerge from the themes identified in the first stage. 'To the greatest extent possible, one strives to allow the categories to emerge from the data themselves, rather than from a preconceived theoretical or empirical framework' (p. 7). Finally, the researcher attempts to describe the relationships among the various categories in order to identify the 'pattern' or 'structure' of the experience—the ways in which the elements combine to create a unified whole (p. 8). This approach is wholly qualitative and rigorously systematic. [. . .]

Thus, we would distinguish between methods which are systematic and methods which are quantitative. Quantification, in a strict sense, only refers to the transformation of observations (by a researcher or participant) into numbers. It can occur in the context of unsystematically collected data, and it need not occur in the context of systematically collected data. It may permit one form of systematic analysis, but it also permits unsystematic, ad hoc analyses. Thus, while historical associations between quantitative and systematic methods can be documented, logical associations between them are debatable, suggesting that a feminist methodology cannot ultimately be tied to either qualitative or quantitative methods.

An additional difficulty with the terms 'quantitative' and 'qualitative' is that they have frequently been used to refer to an absolute methodological dichotomy, so that the entire research process or methodology is characterized as discretely quantitative or qualitative. However, if we think of a research project as involving a group of separate procedures or methods, it is useful to reconceptualize each procedure as located on a qualitative to quantitative continuum (Healy and Stewart, 1991). [. . .]

'Essentializing' the issue: What is 'women's research?'

Although it is our view that many feminist critiques of traditional quantitative methods have considerable merit and that qualitative research is often more consistent with feminist values, we also believe that many authors incorrectly base their criticisms on what we term 'the different voice' perspective. This perspective, represented in Gilligan's (1982) *In A Different Voice* emphasizes the difference between the male voice, which defines the self in terms of distinctness and separation from others, and the female voice, which defines the self in terms of connections and relationships. Numerous discussions of feminist methodology have applied this essentialist view to the quantitative and qualitative dialogue concluding that the female voice is, in fact, qualitative. [. . .]

In general, those who take an essentialist position believe that women are more able than men to study issues of importance to women. According to Mies (1983), because of women's personal experience with oppression they 'are better equipped than their male counterparts to make a comprehensive study of the exploited groups' (p. 121). While we generally agree that women, on the average, *should* have a better understanding of issues important to feminists, it is unclear whether this *is*, in fact the case, and, if it is true in general, under what circumstances it is true. Overall, evidence in support of the essentialist position is lacking, and thus a more cautious approach to evaluating this belief is appropriate. Moreover, differences among women are ignored and rendered invisible by this exclusive focus on inter-sex differences.

[. . .]

We suggest several problems with the essentialist position, in addition to the lack of empirical support. First, it amounts to wishful thinking by confusing an ideal with reality. In other words, although essentialist beliefs appear consistent with feminist values, they may have no basis in fact. The underlying values expressed in this literature could, however, function more usefully as ideals. For example Du Bois' (1983) call for a wholistic (contextual and non-linear) approach, is clearly stated as an ideal we must develop and use. Second, these beliefs about women's use of research methods confuse *women's* and *feminists'* beliefs. Although there is no evidence that either women or feminists might conduct research in this way, it is certainly more likely that feminists, rather than women in general, would do this, since it is consistent with feminist values. To hold essentialist views about all women is to stereotype all women as feminists. It is too easy to forget that most women researchers (including feminist researchers) are primarily trained and socialized as traditional quantitative methodologists and, despite any interest in alternative procedures, it is far more likely than not that they will carry out their research largely using traditional methods and methodologies.

There is one additional belief concerning women's approach to science which is sometimes a focus for discussion not only among feminists, but in the public media as well. This is the stereotype of women as math anxious or as avoiding the acquisition of advanced math skills. Evidence indicates that females, beginning in high school, express more negative attitudes toward math than males, although the sex difference does not appear to be large (Eccles, 1984). Moreover, examination of average sex differences obscures equally important intra-sex differences among women. Nevertheless, Eccles suggests that anxiety may ultimately influence some women's academic choices. It can handicap women in their entrance to numerous professions, including the social sciences. Despite the evidence to support this view, it is not necessarily the case that those women who do enter social science professions and who may not therefore by 'typical' of 'all' women in a number of ways—with their current reliance on quantitative methods—are seriously handicapped by math anxiety. However, if women scientists *are* more suspicious or uncomfortable with mathematical analyses, they may be disadvantaged professionally. [. . .]

Although all women need not learn advanced mathematical or statistical skills, such skills are advantageous to feminist researchers for a number of reasons. First, although these skills are more or less appropriate for use in various disciplines,[2] in research in the social sciences they are used consistently and effectively as research tools. Furthermore, whether or not one intends to use these skills in one's own research, it is important that feminist researchers obtain adequate statistical or mathematical knowledge in order to evaluate and critique research which does use such tools. Given the abundance of research with an antifeminist message, it is absolutely critical that feminist researchers understand the methods behind such research, so that their critiques will be cogent.

A second reason for feminist researchers to have knowledge of statistical and mathematical principles is in their application to both qualitative and quantitative research. Without a basic understanding of the functioning of these principles in research procedures such as design, sample selection, data interpretation, and generalization, both qualitative and quantitative research can result in erroneous and misleading findings. However, more damaging than inaccurate results is the potential for others to generalize from one example of inferior research motivated by feminist values and to stereotype all feminist research as being politically motivated and biased, exactly the charge feminists make of traditional research. When feminist research is poorly done, it is not only difficult to defend the charge of bias, but it makes it increasingly difficult to defend quality feminist research as well.

Perhaps the clearest example of research claiming to be 'qualitative' which has been problematic for feminists is Hite's study on women's sexuality and love relationships, which resulted in two well-publicized books (Hite, 1976, 1987). Her work has been prominently identified as feminist both by her and by some of the media; it thereby reflects on all research by feminists. One difficulty with this work is that, while it strongly supports the feminist call for more qualitative, in-depth study of women's lives, it violates some very basic methodological principles, thus jeopardizing the validity of its conclusions. Although there are numerous examples which could be targeted for criticism, one stands out in particular. In *Women and Love* (Hite, 1987) Hite distributed approximately 100,000 questionnaires, 4,500 being returned. In spite of her attempt to justify the representativeness of her sample, it is clear that it is a highly self-selected sample[3] and not representative of the US female population, which she implies it is. Because of the unknown nature of the sample, it is inaccurate to draw *any* conclusions about what US women in general may believe. Nevertheless, such conclusions are intended in this volume. [. . .]

Despite the strength of this criticism, it is not a single methodological flaw which most concerns us, but rather the contribution which this research makes to the stereotype of feminists as biased researchers. The negative press which this type of research received, primarily for its shoddy methodology (see, for example, Tavris, 1987; Ferguson, 1987), detracts from its message and contributes to the stereotype of feminists as incapable of sophisticated and valid research. If Hite had used proper methodological procedures (even just better sampling methods), and the book were still attacked for its feminist message (which undoubtedly it would have been), at least it could have been defended. Instead, we are faced with guilt by association. [. . .]

It is important to note here that there are many examples of careful, rigorous qualitative research to set against the Hite studies. Unfortunately, none of them is likely to attract the level of media attention that her research did. Detailed consideration of the signs which distinguish excellent qualitative research may help make this point clearer. Gerson (1985) conducted a qualitative study of different patterns of work and family life among contemporary young women. In a thoughtful appendix to the monograph describing her findings, Gerson explained that 'the research questions called for an exploratory study' (p. 240), which was based on 'open-ended, in-depth interviews with a carefully targeted sample of women' (p. 241). She explained her sampling procedure in detail, spelling out the biases and limitations of the sample (pp. 241–5). She concluded that 'the insights and conclusions of this analysis can and, I hope will be applied to and tested among other groups of women in different social environments and of other races and age cohorts' (p. 243). Perhaps most important, in the body of the text itself, Gerson pointed to the proper use of her findings: 'They should be considered in the context of corroborative findings from larger, more representative samples' (p. 217). Research like this does indeed stand

> the best chance of avoiding the Scylla of qualitative research that is descriptively rich, but lacks analytic precision, and the Charybdis of quantitative research that is causally precise, but lacks the data necessary to uncover processes or answer the critical questions.
>
> (Gerson, 1985, p. 241)

The issue of objectivity

What is the issue? A frequent theme in feminist criticism of social science research is the negative consequences of professional obsessiveness with 'scientific objectivity,' which is in turn associated (historically, though not logically) with quantification. Feminist criticisms have focused on several important points: (1) apparently 'objective' science has often been sexist (hence, not 'objective') in its purposes and/or its effects (see, for example, Du Bois, 1983); (2) glorification of 'objectivity' has imposed a hierarchical and controlling relationship upon the researcher–researched dyad (Keller, 1978); and (3) idealization of objectivity has excluded from science significant personal subjectively based knowledge and has left that knowledge outside of 'science' (Unger, 1983; Wallston, 1981). This last point makes it clear that leaving the subjective outside of science also leaves it unexamined. [...]

It may be, then, that an important source of the sexist (and racist and classist) bias in traditional 'objective' research is the fact that the personal and subjective—which inevitably influences many aspects of the research process—were exempt from analysis (see Hubbard, 1978; Unger, 1983).

For some feminists a 'truly feminist social science' originates 'from women's experience of women's reality' (Smith, 1987). Some believe that this perspective implies the exclusion of the concept of objectivity in the research process. It is clear, nevertheless, that most contemporary feminists reject any notion that objectivity should be renounced as a goal altogether. Although absolute objectivity is not possible (even if it were desirable), the pursuit of some types of objectivity, as a goal, does have potential to protect against several forms of bias. For example, a researcher who has an investment in a particular theory may tend to use methods that are likely to produce supportive findings. However, the use of certain research procedures generally accepted in the social sciences mitigate against such biased results. An illustration of this safeguard is representative sampling techniques. Such techniques do not permit a researcher to generalize from a sample of selected respondents who are likely to exhibit the researcher's pet hypothesis. Thus, while many feminists wish to incorporate subjective elements into the research process, they also reject the notion that the process must be entirely subjective. As Rose (1982, p. 368) states, 'feminist methodology seeks to bring together subjective and objective ways of knowing the world' (p. 368). Furthermore, Birke (1986) notes that

> the association of objectivity with masculinity has sometimes led feminists to reject objectivity and to glorify subjectivity in opposition to it. While it is necessary to revalue the subjective ... we do ourselves a disservice if we remove ourselves from objectivity and rationality; we then simply leave the terrain of rational thought ... to men, thus perpetuating the system which excluded us in the first place (p. 157).

There is, then, increasing recognition that the use of particular methods and procedures does not automatically confer objectivity, just as inclusion of analysis of one's personal subjective experience does not preclude it. With no necessary connection between (qualitative and quantitative) methods and (objective versus subjective) outcomes, there is no substitute for a reflexive social science conducted by reflective social scientists (Harding, 1987).

Dangers of apparent objectivity   Despite our recognition of the legitimate use of objective methods, there are realistic dangers of poor-quality antifeminist research disguised as good, quantitative and, thus, 'objective' research. An example of such research which required a strong feminist critique and reinterpretation is work by Benbow and Stanley (1980, 1983) on math achievement. This study, which made headlines in major newspapers[4] throughout the country, supported the view that girls were innately less capable of math achievement than boys. A study assessing the negative impact of this research (Jacobs and Eccles, 1985) concluded that

> one of the major effects of popular media coverage of the research report was that it changed the 'social desirability' climate. Before the media coverage, it was popular to espouse a belief in equal math abilities of males and females. After the media coverage it was 'okay' to say that males are better than females in math. (Jacobs and Eccles, 1985, p. 24)

Numerous problems with this research have been pointed out and many are violations of basic principles for conducting quantitative research. Most important, the research failed adequately to examine the roles of values and attitudes in girls' math performance, which resonably may have explained the sex difference in performance. Although these critiques did not receive as much press coverage as the original Benbow and Stanley article, such critical analysis of traditional objective research is essential in the feminist and academic community and requires a thorough knowledge of basic research and statistical procedures. [. . .]

Benefits and uses of traditional research methods Although this example illustrates the damage which this kind of research can do, as feminists we must also consider any potential benefits which our own use of 'objectivity' can bring. The greatest benefit of apparent objectivity lies in its power to change political opinion. Thus, traditional research methods can be used to our advantage to change sexist belief systems or to support progressive legislation. For example, as noted in Jayaratne (1983), prior to the court decision of *Griggs v. Duke Power Company* (1971), which was argued under Title VII of the Civil Rights Act of 1964, sex discrimination could be substantiated in court only if one could prove intent on the part of the defendant. The decision resulting from this case, however, was that discrimination could be demonstrated by presenting statistics which show a different and unfair impact on a racial, sex, or other group covered by Title VII. This decision set a new course for discrimination suits. [. . .]

An additional benefit derived from the use of 'objective' methods in research lies in their ability to provide tests of theories. Thus, statistics can be a practical tool in the evaluation of feminist theories, since such analysis can identify the most effective strategies for implementing feminist goals. This remains an imperative task if feminists are going to correctly target problem areas for change or effectively direct our energies towards change.

A FEMINIST PERSPECTIVE ON METHODOLOGY

In much of the feminist methodology literature the critical questions ask for the definition of the 'feminist perspective' on research. We believe that there is now some consensus on the answer to this question. Thus, there is general concurrence in recent writing on feminist methodology that there can be no single, prescribed method or set of research methods consistent with feminist values, although there are methods antithetical to such values. [...] There is no substitute for each researcher making independent assessments about the appropriateness of a given method for a given research question and purpose, as well as about the competence of the execution of the research method used. Feminist researchers must be critical of both quantitative and qualitative research which is used against women and must be able to marshal the richest and most persuasive evidence in the service of women.

We believe that the focus of feminist dialogue on 'methods,' and particularly on qualitative versus quantitative methods, obscures the more fundamental challenge of feminism to the traditional 'scientific method'. That challenge really questions the epistemology, or theory of knowledge, underlying traditional science and social science, including the notion that science is, or can be, value free. It is appropriate and timely now to move the focus of the feminist methodology dialogue from definition to implementation. With such an enormous task ahead of us, as feminist researchers attempting to undo decades of sexist and elitist research, to continue the debate between quantitative and qualitative research at this point in the dialogue wastes our valuable time and effort.

STRATEGIES FOR PRACTICAL IMPLEMENTATION OF A FEMINIST PERSPECTIVE IN SOCIAL SCIENCE RESEARCH

Many significant contributions to the literature on feminist methodology are so abstract that the solutions they propose cannot easily or practically be implemented, let alone understood by those without knowledge of epistemology. Feminist researchers must develop realistic and pragmatic strategies which allow for implementation of the feminist perspective. We would like to emphasize, parenthetically, the importance of researchers selecting or developing other procedures which they can effectively implement. Thus, researchers need to consider practical issues such as the time, effort, money and other resources available to the research staff. It is our belief that *any*, even a limited, attempt at increasing the feminist value of research is worthwhile.

1. *When selecting a research topic or problem, we should ask how that research has potential to help women's lives and what information is necessary to have such impact.* The desire to conduct research can either stem from a general theoretical interest in a subject matter (e.g. beliefs about rape), or from a specific political perspective (e.g. how can research help to decrease the incidence of rape). Although ultimately the goal should always be political, theoretical research can also be important to feminists (Jayaratne, 1983). Whatever the

origins of the research topic, it is important to determine, specifically, the kind of information which will be most useful and will have the most positive impact on women's lives. One research goal is not always better or more appropriate for a given problem. For example, if a researcher is interested in helping battered women, legitimate research goals might vary from increasing public understanding of their plight to influencing legislation.

2. *When designing the study, we should propose methods that are both appropriate for the kind of question asked and the information needed and which permit answers persuasive to a particular audience.* Once a researcher knows the research goal or question and what information is necessary, the types of methods needed in the research should be clear. [...] As a general guideline, if the research goal is descriptive of individual lives and designed to promote understanding of a particular viewpoint of the subjects, more qualitative methods may be appropriate. If the goal is to document the operation of particular relationships between variables (e.g. how a government policy affects women), more quantitative methods may be useful. [...]

3. *In every instance of use of either qualitative and quantitative methods or both, we should address the problems associated with each approach.* Thus, if using qualitative methods, we must be aware of methodological problems of poor representation and overgeneralization. Alternatively, if using quantitative methods, we must consciously and actively incorporate feminist values into the procedures. Because quantitative methods have historically exploited women and excluded feminist values, those using such methods should be particularly aware of these problems.

4. *Whenever possible, we should use research designs which combine quantitative and qualitative methods.* This approach, termed a 'mixed method,' has been advocated by numerous authors as a way to offset the disadvantages of one method with the strengths of the other (Denzin, 1978). This strategy suggests the value of acquiring knowledge of both methods. Although this combination of methods is not always possible or even practical, it should result in a more powerful research product, that is, one which not only effectively tests theory but also is convincing.

5. *Whether the research methods are quantitative or qualitative, it is critical that procedures be bias-free or sex-fair.* Not only will such research better test theory or more accurately communicate the research goal, but such research should be more influential on policymakers and the public. [...]

6. *We should take the time and effort to do quality research.* This means learning and using a variety of appropriate research skills, rather than taking short cuts which are more expedient.

7. *When interpreting results, we should ask what different interpretations, always consistent with the findings, might imply for change in women's lives.* We should consider interpretations that imply the most effective interventions for improving women's lives. For example, victim-blaming interpretations tend to

result in individual intervention strategies, whereas situational/environmental interpretations can often yield more effective political strategies for change.

8. *We should always attempt some political analysis of the findings.* We should make an effort to explore how policy change suggested by research results might positively affect women's lives. This goal is not always clear from the findings and must be made explicit, when possible.

9. *Finally, as much as possible (given a realistic assessment of the frantic pace of academic life), we should actively participate in the dissemination of research results.* The importance of dissemination cannot be overstressed, since it is the goal of feminist research to make a difference in women's lives. If research is not 'advertised' it will not have an impact, either on policymakers or on the public.

In conclusion, we would like to reemphasize that we view these strategies, combined with others discussed in the feminist literature, as a contribution to a dialogue focusing on the practical application of feminist theory in social research. Such dialogue can best advance feminist goals by producing research which not only positively affects women's lives, but also makes the research endeavour itself an exciting, relevant, and profitable experience for the researcher.

Notes

1. It should be pointed out that criticism of quantitative methods has a long history which extends beyond the feminist community (Healy and Stewart, 1991).
2. See Hacker (1983) for an example of a discipline where mathematics is overemphasized.
3. Not only is her return rate profoundly low, but the highly personal and lengthy nature of the questionnaire would result in a sample of women to whom this subject is unusually salient, such as women who are unhappy in their love relationships.
4. Popular media coverage of this research, included headlines such as 'Do males have a math gene?' in *Newsweek* (Williams and King, 1980) and 'The gender factor in math: A new study says males may be naturally abler than females' in *Time* (The Gender Factor, 1980, Dec. 15, p. 57).

References

Benbow, C.P. and Stanley, J. (1980) Sex differences in mathematical ability: Fact or artifact? *Science* 210, 1262–4.

— (1983) Sex differences in mathematical reasoning ability: More facts. *Science* 222, 1029–31.

Birke, L. (1986) *Women, Feminism and Biology.* New York: Methuen.

Bleier, R. (1984) *Science and Gender.* New York: Pergamon.

Bronfenbrenner, U. (1977) Toward an experimental ecology of human development. *American Psychologist* 32, 513–29.

Cook, J.A. and Fonow, M.M. (1984) Am I my sister's gatekeeper? Cautionary tales from the academic hierarchy. *Humanity and Society* 8, 442–52.

Denzin, N.K. (1978) *The Research Act.* New York: McGraw Hill.

Du Bois, B. (1983) Passionate scholarship: Notes on values, knowing and method in social science. In G. Bowles and R. Duelli-Klein (eds) *Theories of Women's Studies* (pp. 105–16). Boston: Routledge and Kegan Paul.

Eccles, J. (1984) Sex differences in mathematics participation. In M. Steinkam and M. Maehr (eds) *Advances in Motivation and Achievement*, vol. 2 (pp. 93–137). Greenwich, CT: JAI Press.

Eccles, J.S. and Jacobs, J.E. (1986) Social forces shape math attitudes and performance. *Signs* 11, 367–89.

Ferguson, A. (1987) She says it's a dog's life in a man's world. *Wall Street Journal* Nov. 18, p. 13.

Finkelhor, D. and Yllo, K. (1985) *License to Rape: Sexual Abuse of Wives.* New York: Free Press.

Gerson, K. (1985) *Hard Choices.* Berkeley: University of California Press.

Gilligan, C. (1982) *In a Different Voice.* Cambridge, MA.: Harvard University Press.

Grady, K.E. (1981). Sex bias in research design. *Psychology of Women Quarterly* 628–36.

Griggs v. Duke Power Company (1971), 401 US 424.

Hacker, S. (1983). Mathematization of engineering: Limits on women and the field. In J. Rothschild *Machina ex dea: Feminist Perspectives on Technology.* New York: Pergamon.

Harding, S. (1987) Introduction. Is there a feminist method? In S. Harding (ed.) *Feminism and Methodology* (pp. 1–14). Bloomington: Indiana University Press.

Healy, J.M., Jr., and Stewart, A.J. (1991) On the compatibility of quantitative and qualitative methods for studying individual lives. In A.J. Stewart, J.M. Healy, Jr. and D. Ozer (eds) *Perspectives on Personality. Theory, Research, and Interpersonal Dynamics*, vol. 3. (pp. 35–57). London: Jessica Kingsley.

Hite, S. (1976) *The Hite Report.* New York: Macmillan.

— (1987) *Women and Love.* New York: Alfred Knopf.

Hornstein, G.A. (1988) Quantifying psychological phenomena: Debates, dilemmas, and implications. In J.G. Morawski (ed.) *The Rise of Experimentation in American Psychology.* New Haven: Yale University Press.

— (1991) Painting a portrait of experience: The phenomenological approach to the study of lives. In A.J. Stewart, J.M. Healy, Jr. and D.J. Ozer (eds) *Perspectives in Personality: Approaches to Studying Lives.* London: Jessica Kingsley.

Hubbard, R. (1978). Have only men evolved? In R. Hubbard, M.S. Henifin and B. Fried (eds) *Women Look at Biology Looking at Women.* Cambridge, MA: Schenkman.

Jacobs, J. and Eccles, J.S. (1985) Gender differences in math ability: The impact of media reports on parents. *Educational Researcher* 14, 20–5.

Jayaratne, T.E. (1983) The value of quantitative methodology for feminist research. In G. Bowles and R. Duelli Klein (eds) *Theories of Women's Studies* (pp. 140–61). Boston: Routledge and Kegan Paul.

Jayaratne, T.E. and Kaczala, C.M. (1983) Social responsibility in sex difference research. *Journal of Educational Equity and Leadership* 3, 305–16.

Jick, T.D. (1979) Mixing qualitative and quantitative methods: Triangulation in action. *Administrative Science Quarterly* 24, 602–10.

Keller, E.F. (1985) *Reflections on Gender and Science.* New Haven, CT: Yale University Press.

Lykes, M.B., and Stewart, A.J. (1986) Evaluating the feminist challenge to research in personality and social psychology: 1963–1983. *Psychology of Women Quarterly* 10, 393–412.

Mies, M. (1983) Towards a methodology for feminist research. In G. Bowles and R. Duelli Klein (eds) *Theories of Women's Studies* (pp. 117–39). Boston: Routledge and Kegan Paul.

Milgram, S. (1974) *Obedience to Authority.* New York: Harper.

Oakley, A. (1981). Interviewing women: A contradiction in terms. In H. Roberts (ed.) *Doing Feminist Research* (pp. 30—61). Boston: Routledge and Kegan Paul.

Parlee, M.B. (1975). Psychology: Review essay. *Signs* 1, 119—38.

Reinharz, S. (1979) *On Becoming a Social Scientist.* San Francisco: Jossey-Bass.

Roberts, H. (ed.) (1981) *Doing Feminist Research.* Boston. Routledge and Kegan Paul.

Rose, H. (1982) Making science feminist. In E. Whitelegg *et al.* (eds) *The Changing Experience of Women.* Oxford: Martin Robinson.

Scheuneman, J.D. (1986) The female perspective on methodology and statistics. *Educational Researcher* 15, 22—3.

Smith, D.E. (1987) Women's perspective as a radical critique of sociology. In S. Harding (ed.) *Feminism and Methodology* (pp. 84—96). Bloomington: Indiana University Press. (Reprinted from *Sociological Inquiry*, 1974, 44, 7—13.)

Stanley, L., and Wise, S. (1983) *Breaking Out. Feminist Consciousness and Feminist Research.* London: Routledge and Kegan Paul.

Tangri, S.S. and Strasburg, G.L. (1979) Can research on women be more effective in shaping policy? *Psychology of Women Quarterly* 3, 321—43.

Tavris, C. (1987) Method is all but lost in the imagery of social-science fiction. *Los Angeles Times* Nov. 1, p. V5.

Unger, R.K. (1983) Through the looking glass: No wonderland yet! (The reciprocal relationship between methodology and models of reality). *Psychology of Women Quarterly* 8, 9—32.

Wallston, B. (1981) What are the questions in psychology of women? A feminist approach to research. *Psychology of Women Quarterly* 5, 507—617.

Weisstein, N. (1977) How can a little girl like you teach a great big class of men? the chairman said, and other adventures of a woman in science. In S. Ruddick and P. Daniels (eds) *Working it Out* (pp. 241—50). New York: Pantheon.

Westkott, M. (1979) Feminist criticism of the social sciences. *Harvard Educational Review* 49, 422—30.

Williams, D.A. and King, P. (1980) Do males have a math gene? *Newsweek* Dec. 15, p. 73.

Wittig, M. (1985) Metatheoretical dilemmas in the psychology of gender. *American Psychologist* 40, 800—12.

Yllo, K. (1988) Political and methodological debates in wife abuse research. In K. Yllo (ed.) *Feminist Perspectives on Wife Abuse* (pp. 28—50). Newbury Park, NJ: Sage.

13 DEFENDING THE INDEFENSIBLE? QUANTITATIVE METHODS AND FEMINIST RESEARCH

LIZ KELLY, LINDA REGAN AND SHEILA BURTON

This article addresses what has become something of an orthodoxy, especially in sociology: that feminist methodology and, therefore, feminist research, draw on the qualitative tradition and involve women. In the terms set out by many writers the research project we have recently completed would not count: apart from the fact that it involved young women and young men, we used traditional survey research methods. Our questioning of the view which defines this methodology as antithetical to the feminist project is not a defence of that research, but a reflection on the challenges and issues that our work has produced. Whilst other individual feminist researchers have also used survey methodology, and at least one recent text (Stanley, 1990) has argued for a more open definition of feminist research/methodology, this is not yet reflected in the majority of discussions, either in writing or teaching, on feminist research. Here we record our changing perspectives, and reflect on similar shifts taking place elsewhere.

Our original intention was to construct a dialogue between writing on feminist epistemology and the mundanity and messiness of everyday research practice. The difficulties we encountered confirmed the increasing gap that is developing between theory and practice even within academia. When extended to the connection, or more accurately lack of connection, with practice and activism 'beyond the institution', this separation raises uncomfortable questions.

THE CONSTRUCTION OF 'FEMINIST METHOD'

Our central theme is that whilst recent feminist theory has questioned binary oppositions and accompanying value hierarchies in Western patriarchal thought (see Harding, 1986), many discussions of feminist methodology have reproduced them, albeit reversing the value hierarchy. In suggesting that an 'orthodoxy' has developed we refer to definitions of feminist research which specify that studies investigate women's lives (Klein, 1983) using forms which are 'non-hierarchical, non-authoritarian and non-manipulative' (Reinharz, 1983, p. 181). Qualitative methods, particularly the face-to-face in-

Source: Hinds, H., Phoenix, A. and Stacey, J. (eds) (1992) *Working Out: New Directions for Women's Studies* (pp. 149–60). London: Falmer.

depth interview, have become the definitive feminist approach, marginalizing if not excluding work which is indeed feminist but the participants men, or the focus on institutions and/or written texts. In many of these discussions 'experience' is privileged as unmediated access to women's reality. Thus far where experience has been problematized the discussions have tended to focus either on one's own experience (Stanley and Wise, 1983) or more recently on the construction of experience through discourses/texts.

Whilst most discussions of method refer to Ann Oakley's (1981) classic paper on interviewing women, few explore the implications of the fact that many of the charges made in relation to quantitative methods also informed traditional views on the conduct of the research interview: being distanced, objective, keeping to the researcher's agenda—i.e. not seeing oneself as a participant in an interaction. This suggests that what makes research feminist is less the method used, and more how it is used and what it is used for.

One of the fundamental premises of feminist research has been that we locate ourselves within the questions that we ask, and the process of conducting the research. Maureen Cain (1990) argues that there is a difference between personal and theoretical reflexivity, the former being seen as the unique thoughts, feelings and experiences of the researcher, the latter a theoretical understanding of the site from which one is working, which creates the standpoint from which one works. We will use both in this article. It is not easy to separate them unless we take theoretical reflexivity as informing the initial design stages and personal reflexivity as reflections on the 'doing' of research.

THE RESEARCH PROJECT

Each of us comes to research through a non-traditional route: taking first degrees as 'mature' students with a prior, and continuing, involvement in activism and no clear ambition or intention to become academics/researchers. Janice Raymond (1986) has described the position of feminists in academic institutions as 'inside/outsiders'. Her discussion focuses on the areas of choice we have about our location and the necessity of connection to feminism outside the institution. The extent to which women feel, and are, 'outside' involves more than choice, being amplified by identity and biography: class, race and sexuality have also functioned to exclude or marginalize, as has active political involvement. Differences in status, career prospects and visibility between full-time researchers and lecturers who also do research, amplify the 'outsider' location and have not been addressed by feminists, nor have the hierarchies that exist, or develop, within groups of feminist researchers.

The project on which our reflections are based was a study of the prevalence of sexual abuse, funded by the Economic and Social Research Council. The application resulted from discussions within the Child Abuse Studies Unit, which was established in 1987 to develop feminist theory and practice on child abuse. The context was a lack of a British knowledge base and growing debates around gender in terms of both victimization and offending. Policy and practice were developing rapidly, but in a reactive and ad hoc way, drawing on contested theoretical perspectives and generalizations drawn from small clinical samples.

The original application proposed to compare what young people chose to tell in a self-report questionnaire and what they revealed in face-to-face interviews. We wanted to explore the contention, based on US research, that face-to-face interviews encourage reporting of sexual victimization. No study has yet directly compared the two methods. Our original application to do so was turned down, as was a subsequent one. The research eventually funded limited us to the self-report questionnaire. To have refused this restriction would not only have prompted a major crisis around the future of the Unit, but would have left the knowledge gap in place.

The structure of the rest of this article is an engagement with the binary oppositions which construct the counterposing of quantitative/qualitative, traditional/feminist research methods. To organize the discussion we have used a table from Shulamit Reinharz's paper 'Experiential analysis: A contribution to feminist research' (1983, pp. 170–2). This article is not a critique of that piece, but draws on it as an explicit and systematic outline of a position which defines quantitative methods as antithetical to feminist work. The table as it appears in that paper is reproduced as Table 13.1.

UNITS OF STUDY

No feminist would suggest studying sexual abuse (or a range of other issues) as 'natural' events occurring within an ongoing context. We saw our project as an exploration of both method and issue. We did not know whether young people would complete the questionnaire, or tell us about experiences of abuse, and we experimented with ways of encouraging them to tell us. What counts as 'sexual abuse', both from the point of view of the young people and within analytic definitions, was part of the study. Hypothesis testing is an epistemological issue, linked to particular constructions of science. It is a use to which questionnaires and large-scale surveys have been put, but not an inherent feature of the method.

SHARPNESS OF FOCUS

Our original intention was to adapt a questionnaire used in an American study, but it was constructed within the limited and specific parameters of survey research, with ease of coding a primary concern. It placed huge limitations on what participants could say and the structure was extremely complex. In our questionnaire ease of coding was subordinated to encouraging responses, using open-ended questions where it was inappropriate to offer only pre-defined options, and placing experiences in context. The forms of questions were as inclusive as possible, particularly not using pre-defined concepts of what counts as abuse.

TABLE 13.1 Research models in contemporary sociology

	Conventional or patriarchal	Alternative or feminist
Units of study	Predefined, operationalized concepts stated as hypotheses.	Natural events encased in their ongoing contexts.
Sharpness of focus	Limited, specialized, specific, exclusive.	Broad, inclusive.
Data type	Reports of attitudes and actions as in questionnaires, interviews and archives.	Feelings, behavior, thoughts, insights, actions as witnessed or experienced.
Topic of study	Manageable issue derived from scholarly literature, selected for potential scholarly contribution, sometimes socially significant.	Socially significant problem sometimes related to issues discussed in scholarly literature.
Role of Research: in relation to environment	Control of environment is desired, attempt to manage research conditions.	Openness to environment, immersion, being subject to and shaped by it.
in relation to subjects	Detached.	Involved, sense of commitment, participation, sharing of fate.
as a person	Irrelevant.	Relevant, expected to change during process.
impact on researcher	Irrelevant.	Anticipated, recorded, reported, valued.
Implementation of method	As per design, decided a priori.	Method determined by unique characteristics of field setting.
Validity criteria	Proof, evidence, statistical significance: study must be replicable and yield same results to have valid findings.	Completeness, plausibility, illustrative, understanding, responsiveness to readers, or subjects' experience; study cannot, however, be replicated.
The role of theory	Crucial as determinant of research design.	Emerges from research implementation.
Data analysis	Arranged in advance relying on deductive logic, done when all data are 'in'.	Done during the study, relying on inductive logic.
Manipulation of data	Utilization of statistical analyses.	Creation of gestalts and meaningful patterns.
Research objectives	Testing hypotheses.	Development of understanding through grounded concepts and descriptions.
Presentation format	Research report form; report of conclusions with regard to hypotheses stated in advance, or presentation of data obtained from instruments.	Story, description with emergent concepts; including documentation of process of discovery.
Failure	Statistically insignificant variance.	Pitfalls of process illustrates the subject.
Values	Researchers' attitudes not revealed, recognized or analysed, attempts to be value free, objective.	Rsearchers' attitudes described and discussed, values acknowledged, revealed, labelled.
Role of reader	Scholarly community addressed; evaluation of research design, management and findings.	Scholarly and user community addressed and engaged; evaluate usefulness and responsiveness to perceived needs.

Source: Reinharz (1983), pp. 170–2.

DATA TYPE

Here interviews are located with questionnaires, and the limitations on what can be researched, and how, within the feminist band probably excludes the majority of published work by feminists. It is true that most survey research concentrates on closed questions and attitude scales, as these are most amenable to the hypothesis testing approach. However, just as researchers have changed interview practice it is possible to change the structure and content of questionnaires. There were no attitude-scaled questions in ours, and where we gave options about, for example, the impact of abuse or on policy issues, space was left for alternatives and/or comments. We also included questions about emotional responses.

Nor is our data restricted to the questionnaires. We kept detailed notes of the process of negotiating access, field notes for each session and notes of questions/insights that arose during coding. As a rider to this, some patterns which we noted during coding turned out to be less marked within the complete data set.

We are not disputing the breadth and depth of understanding that research which adopts Reinharz's suggested approach to data can bring. But we would argue that by only using small-scale studies we can be misled into believing that we have baseline knowledge which has not actually been collected. For example, most work on all areas of sexual violence draws on women who have in some way made their experiences public, and most work on domestic violence draws on women from refuges. The different experiences and needs of women who have not sought help, and why they haven't, have hardly been explored. Where they have, critical issues about how services for women are organized and perceived emerge (McGibbon, Cooper and Kelly, 1989; Schecter, 1989). Survey research is one way of expanding our understanding of the dimensions and complexities of the issues that concern us.

TOPIC OF STUDY

This raises the vexed question about what is a 'socially significant' problem. It would be unusual to find someone who did not agree that sexual abuse is a socially significant issue about which there is also a scholarly literature. One of our motivations in doing the study was to develop a stronger knowledge base from which to take issue with some of what we have called the 'new mythology'. In developing feminist understandings as researchers we are constantly engaged in re-evaluating prior constructions of knowledge, and usually have direct connection, albeit a critical one, to scholarly literature.

ROLE OF RESEARCH

In relation to environment/implementation of method

Our practice here is definitely a compromise between Reinharz's two positions. We did construct a protocol which we hoped to follow in each of the colleges we visited. Apart from some forms of participant observation there are practical arrangements that are necessary for research to take place; the issues must surely be how rigid one is about them. If researchers routinely provided detailed descriptions of how large-scale projects are actually conducted, we suspect that a more complex model would emerge which involves negotiation and adaptation in particular settings and circumstances. The 'management and control' model is reinforced through a silence about the realities of fieldwork on larger projects.

Our 'ideal' was to have students in combined class groups of 40–50, meaning we could do four groups on day one, and pick up on any problems during the next two days. We wanted to do the introductions ourselves, to ensure confidentiality for the students, and so that we could observe the process. The reality was that the research environment changed from one college to the next.

We suggested exam-type conditions because it could provide some privacy and decrease the likelihood of group responses. However, many students resisted our suggestion that they spread out and treat it like an exam. Rather than imposing our model, we only intervened where discussion and comments were disturbing others. Where we suspected that students had discussed their responses we marked the questionnaires and looked at this when coding.

As to immersion, again our position was a compromise. Whilst not 'hit and run', our presence for three days in each college was not immersion in the physical environment, but our study was not about the colleges. Our observations of the general atmosphere and interactions did aid our understanding of some responses. More interesting was the response of the students to our presence, some greeted or acknowledged us each time we saw them, others chose to act as if we were strangers. Amongst those who made a point of greeting us were individuals who had reported extremely painful experiences.

In relation to subjects

The concept and meaning of 'sharing of fate' is problematic given the increasing recognition of differences between women—unless we are to be limited to studying other (white) women sociologists/researchers! It also rules out the possibility of feminists studying men, or those more powerful than themselves. We were however not detached. One of our major concerns was whether participation might distress students. We produced resource sheets listing support services in college, in each local area and nationally for each college and one was placed in each questionnaire. We produced guidelines for staff on how to handle students telling about abuse, and conducted training with staff in three colleges.

Our field notes are full of references to behaviour and responses of students whilst they completed the questionnaires, and our own reactions and perceptions. For example:

> Strange sound of paper turning, turning ... does it inhibit those who are writing, concentrating?
> Three boys finish first—insist on chatting to women who cover their questionnaires with their bodies.
> Why is it taking degree-level students longer to fill in than CPVE class? Literacy and ability far more complex—is it something about thinking/reflecting and the connection to learning? Cannot tell from time taken to complete those who are answering the detailed sections—has this got something to do with how 'in control' of their experiences they feel?
> Three women holding their heads in their hands.
> Long line of young women next to one another—interesting how some feel fine close to others and some choose more privacy—doesn't seem to affect how much they say.
> Lots of questions but group appears very relaxed, comfortable. Able to spread out. Space in non-traditional settings far more conducive than formal teaching settings.

We adopted a stance of unobtrusive monitoring, shifting between reading and watching, taking note of any students who showed signs of distress/difficulty; some young people looked for reassurance and we responded through smiles and 'thank-yous' as they left.

It was impossible to be detached when we coded, and we learnt very quickly to pick up on each other's distress—tears, rage and despair were seldom far away. Sharing the accounts which distressed us was one strategy we developed. Including questions about resistance and coping, and about wider aspects of their lives, meant that we had a sense of the young people beyond their experiences of victimization.

Our concern about the issue and connection to the young people resulted in contradictory responses to students' accounts. Where there were no reports of unwanted sexual experiences, especially by young women, our initial reaction was one of disbelief and even irritation. Whilst the issues of willingness to tell, defining and remembering abuse could have affected these young women, we were resisting the possibility that they may have escaped sexual victimization. We denied ourselves the possibility of responding positively to that potential. The flip side of this was that when abuse was reported our initial response was relief, followed fairly rapidly by distress. The complexity of our reactions to the research process, and our uncomfortableness with some of them, were a source of tension and confusion, which have echoes in theoretical debates between feminists concerning sexuality and sexual violence.

As a person

Our relationships with each other, as well as our perspective on both sexual abuse and methodology, were transformed over a two-year period. We, like many feminists, had paid relatively little attention to abuse of boys or abuse by women. Both became essential to address if we were to do justice to what we had been told. The empathy we felt for some of the boys surprised us.

We were also surprised by how much some students chose to, or felt able to tell us. We began to ponder on whether they would have been so revealing in a face-to-face interview, and are fairly certain that some of them would not have told so much, if anything at all. Young people completing the question-naire were given the choice to complete combined with control over what and how much they told. Young people share with adults difficulties in talking about sexual experiences but we believe that the control they were given combined with our explicit permission to tell as much as they felt able gave them the security they needed. Those women who have taken part in in-depth interview studies are usually self-selected—this was a far more random group of young people. The confidentiality, not having to verbalize their experiences to someone, and the control over how much is said may enable some to tell about sexual abuse, especially those who have not told anyone thus far. It is this possibility which has led us to reassess survey research.

Impact on researcher

We had anticipated that we would be affected by the research process, but had confidence in our ability to 'handle' the topic. However, the fact that we hired a television during the most intense period of coding which coincided with Wimbledon and the World Cup, that our humour became increasingly barbed and full of 'in jokes' tells a rather different story, as does the fact that we often seemed to spend weekends in a haze. The intensity of that period is hard to put into words, as is documenting our individual and collective coping strategies. We have attempted in different ways and at different times to write about the project, but none of us has put a word on paper until now. Whilst we talked of keeping research diaries, the fact that we did not suggests that making ourselves consciously reflect on what we were doing daily threatened the fragile balance we were maintaining.

The impacts extended into our family and friendship networks, not only in terms of our needs and actions, but also how we were 'seen' by others. We became 'safe' to tell, and for us sexual abuse was indeed everywhere. In virtually any situation, no matter how unlikely, women and men would begin telling us about their experiences. The fact that we were being paid to work on this issue, that it was in most of the rest of our lives, made it hard to maintain boundaries.

VALIDITY CRITERIA

Here too our position is a compromise between these two positions, especially since what 'completeness' might mean is unclear and contested. The coding and punching of data has been meticulously checked, and mistakes or inconsistencies explored. Contradictions within detailed accounts or observed behaviour are not considered problematic, but they are within numeric data sets. Where coding is conducted as a routine task inconsistent responses are ignored, since they 'even out' in the data. Since we coded for meaning and were building a sense of each young person in the process contradictions were a source of concern. Did we leave them in, thus faithfully keeping to what was in each questionnaire, or did we attempt to create some kind of coherence and consistency? How should you code where individuals answer 'no' to the first question in a section and then proceed as if they had said 'yes'? Can you presume that the first response was a mistake, or is something more complex being communicated?

The idea that all studies must be not only replicable but produce the same results derives from a simplistic model of the physical sciences. Even experiments in the most controlled environments do not necessarily produce the same findings. It is extremely unlikely that any study in social science could be replicated in this way, even if it was desired. What does, and should, occur is that we build upon, adapt and extend previous work.

THE ROLE OF THEORY

As feminists we cannot argue that theory emerges from research, since we start from a theoretical perspective that takes gender as a fundamental organizer of social life. Moreover, any piece of research refers to what has gone before either by adding in levels of complexity or challenging previous perspectives. What research should produce is modifications, re-workings, extensions and/or critiques of existing theory, and the creation of new concepts.

DATA ANALYSIS AND MANIPULATION OF DATA

Analysis was not determined beforehand, indeed if it had been we would have saved ourselves a great deal of work. By structuring the questionnaire in order to encourage telling, not imposing our definition of abuse, giving students the option to tell very little or much more, analysis was extremely complex. There were eight places on the questionnaire where students could tell us about their experiences of abuse. There is no question that this resulted in experiences being reported, but it also created the danger of double counting. The only way of preventing this was to recode every questionnaire.

We have already pointed to the danger of relying solely on subjective perceptions of meaningful patterns. It is clear that the logic and meaning of an individual account cannot be translated into large-scale numeric data sets. But what we have are coexisting forms of information, and each can add meaning to the other. It is possible to recontextualize from numeric data—to move between quantitative statistics and the complexity and immediacy of individual experience. In working with two women film-makers for a feature on the research, we began with the figures. They decided which areas they wanted to focus on and we constructed young people's stories from their questionnaires as illustrative examples.

RESEARCH OBJECTIVES

Our aim was not to test hypotheses but to build a knowledge base on sexual abuse. The concepts we developed through coding and recoding did not simply emerge from the accounts of the young people, but drew on previous work. Since one of our concerns was to enable 'telling' and to limit any distress, we abandoned the most useful quantitative way of asking about forms of abuse—providing an explicit list of sexual acts. Our pilot groups said the list was too 'stark' and 'terrifying'. This meant that whilst we gave control to the young people in terms of what level of detail they gave us, in some circumstances we do not know what forms the abuse took—in others we have to work with responses such as 'interfered with'. We face the critical issues of whether we use less detailed information from more individuals or more detailed from fewer. That is one of the difficulties of attempting to balance researchers' desire for particular information with giving participants control over their responses.

PRESENTATION FORMAT

Our research report does present the data, but is not a technical description of statistical methods or hypothesis testing. We attempted to make it accessible to a non-academic audience and included a shortened summary for practitioners. We are also publishing short pieces in practitioner journals, using our work in training, and writing a book where the words of the young people will be integrated with quantitative analysis.

FAILURE

The notion of failure is in many ways inappropriate in relation to social research. The issue is not simply use of variant analysis or illustrating the pitfalls but rather what methods and projects enable and limit and what is learnt both about the topic and about research.

VALUES

Our values informed our choice of topic, our research design and the ways we interpret, conceptualize and extrapolate from it. Our research was about being committed to reflecting, and attempting to explain/account for what participants say, including allowing for findings which don't 'fit', and have not been addressed thus far by feminist perspectives. Both research and feminism are about discovery which requires being open to surprises, contradiction and challenge.

ROLE OF READER

Clearly this study has a number of overlapping audiences—academics, practitioners, feminists. One of the challenges is finding ways to speak simultaneously to different knowledges and interests. We hope that our work will be useful within current debates, but as researchers we cannot assess the usefulness of our work to others; that will emerge only in time and through feedback.

One of the core features of much large-scale survey research is that it is not the same individual who designs the study, conducts it, codes and punches the data, does the analysis, makes sense of the data and writes up the project. The fieldwork is usually done either by research assistants or by contract research companies. In a very real sense what they deal with are decontextualize numeric values and the relationships between them. This is not an inevitable part of the method, however. Immersion in the data is possible, as other researchers have found and as the many months we spent coding are testimony to. Our practice was one of creating numeric values for complex responses and then once we began analysis needing to recontextualize, to check for data errors and to explore specific areas. Each new piece of work we do involves going back to the questionnaires. This has far more in common with the ways sociologists work with qualitative data.

RELATIONSHIPS IN RESEARCH TEAMS

There are key areas that Reinharz's conceptualization of feminist method does not include, and the most critical for us are the relationships between researchers in terms of hierarchies of status and division of labour. We came to this project with different skills and statuses. Our skills were complementary, but the status division structural. The funding provided for two research fellows, in order that there be no structural inequality between the two full-time workers, and a part-time administrator. Whilst our aim was to co-operate collectively, the pressure of work meant that it was impossible to develop the skill-sharing we had hoped. However, a strong sense of collective responsibility for our work developed during the project.

A major factor affecting our working relationships is that one of us had a history and status as a feminist researcher. For the other two this was their first job after graduating. Deference to experience, knowledge and status has been something we have struggled with from our different positions. 'Doing different', though, requires more than our individual and collective commitment. The existing differences and confidences were reinforced by external responses, even from other feminists. At times what we managed to create internally was undermined by these interactions. Exploring these issues explicity and systematically also threatened the collectivity we managed to maintain most of the time. This echoes with our experiences in women's groups, where issues of power and responsibility remains major area of conflict, division and uncertainty, and where attempts to address them directly are fraught and frequently resisted.

CONCLUSIONS

We are suggesting that reworking an unhelpful system of polarities reproduces confusions between epistemology, method and methodology. We regard methods as ways of doing research, asking questions, collecting and collating information and making sense of it. It is epistemology which defines what counts as valid knowledge and why. If we begin from this position then it is possible to bring a feminist standpoint to a range of methods; we do not have to accept the 'scientistic' model of surveys or reject surveys as necessarily 'non-feminist'.

As Catharine MacKinnon says:

> Objectivity, as the epistemological stance of which objectification is the social process, creates the reality it apprehends ... feminist method has a distinctive theory of the relation between method and truth, the individual and her social surroundings, the presence and place of the natural and the spiritual in culture and society, social being and causality itself. Having been objectified as sexual beings while stigmatized as ruled by subjective passion, women reject the distinction between knowing subject and known object—the division between subjective and objective postures—as the means to comprehend social life ... women's interest lies in overthrowing *the distinction itself.*   (MacKinnon, 1989, pp. 114, 120–1)

References

Cain, M. (1990) Realist philosophy and standpoint epistemologies OR feminist criminology as a successor science. In L. Gelsthorpe and A. Morris (eds) *Feminist Perspectives in Criminology*. Milton Keynes: Open University Press.

Harding, S. (ed.) (1986) *The Science Question in Feminism*. Milton Keynes: Open University Press.

Klein, R.D. (1983) How to do what we want to do: Thoughts about feminist methodology. In G. Bowles and R.D. Klein (eds) *Theories of Women's Studies*. London: Routledge and Kegan Paul.

McGibbon, A., Cooper, L. and Kelly, L. (1989) 'What support?' An exploratory study of council policy and practice and local support services in the area of domestic violence within Hammersmith and Fulham. Final Report. Council Community and Police Unit, London Borough of Hammersmith and Fulham.

MacKinnon, C. (1989) *Towards a Feminist Theory of the State*. Cambridge, MA: Harvard University Press.

Oakley, A. (1981) Interviewing women. In H. Roberts (ed.) *Doing Feminist Research*. London: Routledge and Kegan Paul.

Raymond, J. (1986) *A Passion for Friends: Towards a Philosophy of Female Affection.* London: Women's Press.

Reinharz, S. (1983) Experiential analysis: A contribution to feminist research. In G. Bowles and R.D. Klein (eds) *Theories of Women's Studies.* London: Routledge and Kegan Paul.

Schecter, S. (1989) Why battered women don't use women's services. Unpublished paper.

Stanley, L. (ed.) (1990) *Feminist Praxis: Research Theory and Epistemology in Feminist Sociology.* London: Routledge.

Stanley, L. and Wise, S. (1983) *Breaking Out: Feminist Consciousness and Feminist Research.* London: Routledge and Kegan Paul.

14 'RACE', CLASS AND GENDER IN SCHOOL RESEARCH

MAUD BLAIR

'Race'-related research in Britain and in the USA (Stanfield, 1993) has tradi-tionally been dominated by White (usually male) researchers (Lawrence, 1982; Parekh, 1986), prompting allegations of careerism, paternalism and racism. Such studies were criticized for their ethnocentrism and for defining research problems, framing research questions and interpreting research findings in ways which distorted and pathologized the experiences of minority ethnic groups. There was a growing focus in the 1980s on the epistomological and methodological dilemmas facing White researchers who researched issues of 'race', and debates raged over who should carry out such research, the role of the researcher and the nature and purpose of research which related to subordinated groups. Like feminists who were increasingly questioning the dominant research paradigms within the social sciences, and were rewriting sociological modes of inquiry to take account of power within research (see Stanley and Wise, 1990), anti-racist White researchers reflected on the rela-tionships of power between White researchers and Black[1] and ethnic minority respondents, and on the policy implications of such studies (Troyna and Carrington, 1989; Ball, 1990; Connolly, 1993). What was seldom, if ever, addressed, was the question of continued White dominance in the field and what could be done about Black researchers who were generally invisible, often because of hegemonic processes within the research community, the funding organizations and academic journals. The alleged dearth of Black researchers was strongly disputed by those who continued to experience marginalization, discrimination and unemployment (Black Women in Social Research, 1993). The literature in the meantime continued to address the problems faced by White researchers and perpetuated both the invisibility of Black researchers and the idea of the White researcher as the authoritative voice on issues of 'race' and ethnicity.

In this article I address questions of identity and power in the research process, and illustrate the need for a complex understanding and analysis of 'race' and racism and of the experiences of Black pupils in schools. The intention is specifically to present these issues from the perspective of a Black researcher, drawing on the researcher's personal experience of researching in education. Feminists in particular have debated and written

Source: This article is based upon a paper first presented at a conference on ethnographic research in education in Barcelona, October 1993.

about the importance of rejecting the dichotomous subject/object relationship of positivist research and of acknowledging one's identity and subjectivity in influencing research processes and analyses. I describe the shifting nature of the Black researcher's identity in different contexts. There have also been debates amongst feminists and anti-racists about the need to match the sex and 'race' of the researcher with the researched for the sake of reliability and validity (Oakley, 1981; Finch, 1984; Davies, 1985). I argue that 'race' matching may not necessarily produce more reliable data, but that the willingness of a respondent to give (reliable) information is influenced at times by political considerations as well as by questions of self-interest. Stanfield, for example, states that

> The dilemma of outsiders studying 'the Others' does not stop at the threshold of research projects involving the racially dominant attempting to pierce the cultural and social veil of the racially subordinate. It also involves the perplexing fact that, given their credentials and the norms of professional community membership, researchers of color who study their own communities are also outsiders, owing to the class divide.
>
> (Stanfield, 1993, p. 9)

I also provide examples of the unpredictability of power in the research context arguing that the assumed hierarchical relationship of power between the researcher and the research participants (or 'objects') is often confused by other factors when researching 'race' in schools. Researching racialized, classed and gendered institutions is itself a complex activity and the researcher can become unwittingly embroiled in the intricate web of relationships in the school. Furthermore, the politics of 'race' and education are complex social arenas where the political agendas of different interest groups are often hidden. The feminist project, for example, to conduct research which is directed at the emancipation of women, assumes that women share a common political standpoint and that women are therefore able to make straightforward political decisions which are in the interest of women. Such a politics can in fact come into conflict with an anti-racist politics in specific circumstances. Finally, I contend that for the Black and anti-racist researcher, respondent accounts of racism can be a deeply emotional experience and it is important not to allow this to obscure an analysis of other processes which may be vital to an understanding of the complexity of people's lives. I provide an example from the experiences of two young Black students to illustrate this.

THE RESEARCH

In recent years, the number of pupils excluded[2] from schools in Britain has risen dramatically (National Union of Teachers, 1992). It seems clear from the literature and from teachers' accounts that this rise in school exclusions can be linked in part to the rapid changes that have been imposed on schools by the 1988 Education Reform Act. These changes have increased the amount of pressure faced by teachers whilst at the same time reducing the resources that schools depended upon to provide effective pastoral support and care for their pupils and also to manage and organize schools in a manner which was flexible and able to take account of pupils' different educational and social needs. Within the overall numbers of excluded pupils, the Department For Education's report showed that 8.1% of all exclusions was of Black pupils of African-Caribbean origin and yet pupils of African-Caribbean origin represent only 2% of the total school population (DFE, 1992). The vast majority of this 8.1% are boys. How can this disproportionate number of exclusions of Black pupils be explained? Why are boys so much more likely to be excluded than girls?

The research was carried out in three schools, one in a predominantly white shire county in the south-east of England and two inner-city London schools with higher proportions of black students. Despite the controversial nature of the research, negotiating entry into the schools was relatively straight-forward. The head of the shire school was cautiously welcoming, though this was not a feeling shared by all members of staff. In the two London schools, teachers were concerned about the increasingly worrying phenomenon of Black student exclusions and were interested in having the phenomenon investigated anyway. However, my attempts to include a primary school in the research were more problematic and served to highlight the sensitivity of 'race' as an area of research. None of the primary schools I approached were willing to be involved, giving as their reasons that they did not exclude children from their schools (despite local authority evidence to the contrary), or the numbers were too small, that they treated all their children the same, or, more often than not, *that they did not have a problem*—a problem, here, referring to the number of Black pupils in the school. In one school, a Black teacher accompanied me to the gate and said confidentially: 'The problem [of exclusions] is so big in this school that you'll never get them to agree to be researched. You just have to be in the school on any day and count the numbers of Black children who spend their time standing in the corridors to realize that exclusion of Black children is a big problem.'

The purpose of the study was to develop an understanding of the complex ways in which such inequalities are produced with specific reference to the *visible and invisible* processes of 'exclusion' as well as the actual physical removal of the pupil from school. The methods I chose were classroom obser-vation and in-depth interviewing with key players in the life of schools such as headteachers, deputy heads, heads of years, teachers, school governors, educational psychologists and education welfare officers. I also interviewed 15 Black pupils who had been excluded from the three schools between 1990 and 1993, and their parents, and other groups of pupils (Black and White) who were still in school. Interviews were also secured with six individuals who were members of off-site school support services, and from voluntary organizations such as Race Equality Councils, the Family Services Unit, and Legal Advice Centres.

RESEARCH AND THE POLITICS OF IDENTITY

'One of Them' and sometimes 'One of Us'

There were times when 'race' was the central defining factor in my interactions with teachers, in particular White teachers. White teachers are of course as diverse a group as any other so that examples of particular individual behaviours cannot be taken as representative of the group. These examples are given in order to make visible the kinds of experiences faced by Black researchers and to illustrate the role of 'race' in providing different insights into the research process.

I had been observing a lesson in which I noted that two boys, one White and one Black, who sat several places apart had been the most talkative in the class and had rightly been reprimanded most often. I had also noted, however, that the White boy had chatted, laughed, walked about and thrown things at least twice as much as the Black boy, yet the Black boy had had his name called out twelve times in the course of a one-hour lesson and the White boy's had been called out five times. On a number of occasions the Black boy had protested (and I had seen) that he was engaged in what might be termed 'legitimate' activity—borrowing a ruler, and then returning it, or throwing paper into the wastepaper basket—activities in which a lot of other pupils were taking part. I discussed these events with the teacher at the end of the lesson.

MB: I just wondered if you were conscious of doing that [picking on the Black student]?

Teacher: I do notice Dean[3] more than I do others I suppose because there are so few Black children in the class. But I confess I hadn't realized that I called him out that often. He's just so physical you see. The Black kids in the school are very physical. You notice it in sport. I mean, do you think *they* have to be so physical just to survive? I mean, the world over Blacks excel in the very physical sports. Do you think *they* need to, you know, make *their* mark on the world just to survive as a species?

The teacher's Darwinian views require no further analysis here. I would agree with Phoenix (1992) that this is interesting as data, rather than upsetting. What was interesting in terms of my experience as a researcher was that I was expected to adopt the stance of the research 'Orientalist' and explain *Them* to teachers for the purpose of more efficient teaching. I was expected to stand back from my 'racial' identity and adopt the cold, 'objective' stance of the 'scientific' researcher even though *I* was one of the 'species' under discussion!

The second example was similar to the first except that on this occasion I was definitely 'One of Them' and not 'One of Us'. I was talking to a Head of Year in her room when another teacher burst in and declared: 'I just don't know what to do about Sean. I am literally tearing my hair out.' Then turning to me she said, 'You tell me what I ought to do. You must know what makes *them* tick!'

In her address to the head of year she talked exclusively about Sean. She did not know what to do about *him*. But in her address to me, Sean suddenly took on a multiple identity to become *them* of whom I was clearly one, and hence must know (biologically or perhaps instinctively) 'what made them tick'. She had been teaching this boy for two terms; apart from observing him in two lessons, I had not exchanged a single word with him! I had interviewed this teacher previously, and on checking my research notes, found that I had written, 'Mrs X—a caring, committed teacher, very concerned about racism and the "underachievement" of black pupils'! It was clearly possible for this teacher to care and yet at the same time to interact with Black pupils on the basis of stereotypes. For her, skin colour determined (and therefore presumably held the secret to the 'cure') of Black pupils and by extension, of all Black people (see also Gillborn, 1990).

Neither 'One of Them' nor 'One of Us'

Perceptions of racial identity are not, however, confined to White respondents alone as was shown by one Black respondent, Mrs Jameson. When she opened the door to me on my first visit, her face fell and with what I felt was an element of hostility in her voice, she invited me in. Although I had explained fully on the telephone my reasons for wanting to talk to her, her opening remark was. 'So what's all this about then?' Somewhat taken aback, I explained again my concern about the disproportionate number of Black pupils who were being excluded from schools and my wish to understand the reasons so that the issues could be raised more publicly. Her next question was even more of a surprise to me. She asked, 'So what are you? Are you Black or half-caste, or what?'

I had gone about my research boldly assuming that 'race' for most people was a matter of Black and White and that both my politics and my identity were self-evident, whereas a major product of colonial power relations had been to create hierarchies on the basis of different shades of skin colour. There were people of 'mixed race' who through their attitudes and behaviour perpetuated this colonial legacy so that this woman's experiences undermined any notion of an essential 'Black' subject. As Hall states:

> What is at issue here is the recognition of the extraordinary diversity of subject positions, social experiences and cultural identities which compose the category 'Black', that is, the recognition that 'Black' is essentially a politically and culturally constructed category, which cannot be grounded in a set of fixed transcultural or transcendental racial categories and which therefore has no guarantees in nature.   (Hall, 1992, p. 254)

This experience was certainly one for which the literature on research methods had not prepared me! The theory of the 'objective' scientific researcher implies the power to shape and control the research process itself. The interview with

Mrs Jameson had shown that it was not an either/or situation as the debates amongst research theorists implies, but that how individuals are located in power relationship shifts and changes depending on context. But whilst in such situations the researcher might be in a position to ensure that the power s/he holds is minimized, for example by creating space for the respondent to ask the researcher questions about him/herself, in other situations it is the researcher who is rendered powerless and in ways which can damage the whole research project.

POWER AND THE RESEARCHER

The unprecedented rise in the number of permanent exclusions of black pupils has led to a crisis of confidence in the education system amongst Black communities. Numerous conferences and community meetings have been taking place all over the country to discuss the problem and people have drawn parallels with the 1960s and early 1970s when Black children were indiscriminately placed in what were then known as ESN or schools for the Educationally Sub-normal (see Coard, 1971). Some children stay out of school for as long as a year creating emotional and financial difficulties for Black families (Cohen et al., 1994). Parents are naturally anxious to find solutions to this problem and have been very willing to talk about their experiences in order to bring what they feel are gross injustices to public attention. But most want, understandably, to talk to those people they feel can do something to change their situation. Black people, whether or not they are professionals are not always associated with power. One Black parent who was talking about the Black social worker who had been assigned to her family declared,

> 'I had to tell her that it was nothing personal, you know, nothing personal. But I know that if I want things to happen for me I have to get a White social worker. This poor woman had been trying to get things done for us for a long time and just not getting anywhere. As soon as I got a White social worker, I got what I wanted.'

There are, of course, a number of unknowables in this statement. But what is interesting is that the parent did not assume the social worker's lack of competence but her lack of power, a situation which reflected her own failed struggles when dealing with teachers. It is in interactions with White teachers that Black parents are more likely to seek the assistance of Black professionals. This was the case for Mrs Paul whose 15-year-old son, Damian was permanently excluded from his school.

Before a pupil is excluded permanently from a school, a case conference or 'hearing' is held to which school governors, the headteacher, a representative of the local education authority (LEA), the pupil and her/his parents, are invited. The head puts forward her/his justification for excluding the pupils, and the pupils and their parents put forward their defence, all of which are taken into account by the governors who make the final decision to support or turn down the head's decision. The LEA officer remains an impartial observer. At the outset of my research in the school which Damian attended, I had established with the headteacher that, subject to parents' approval, I could sit in on exclusion hearings and that I would interview the parents and the excluded pupils in order to get their version of events.

After the hearing and before I had had a chance to arrange an interview with Damian or his mother, Mrs Paul telephoned me sounding very distressed. She was turning to me for help, she said, 'because I was a black woman and knew about the education system'. She was afraid that her son would be forced to attend the Education Support Unit where excluded pupils were sent pending a placement in another school. She was of the view that attendance at such a unit would destroy her son's character as well as his chances of getting back into a 'normal' school. She needed advice about the options available for her son's continued schooling. Contrary to her belief, I was not in fact familiar at that stage with procedures for placing excluded pupils into other schools or units. I suggested that she telephone her local education office and get their advice, to which she responded that it was precisely because she had not been able to get the kind of advice she wanted that she had decided to turn to me. The education officer, she said, had not wanted to listen to her and had been patronizing in his dealings with her. Would I telephone on her behalf? She was sure that I could explain things better.

Mrs Paul certainly recognized that even if I did not possess knowledge of the inner workings of the local education department, I had the 'cultural capital' to be able to find out and she assumed that I would, out of a sense of racial solidarity, help her with her problem. Although I was one of 'Us', a black woman, I was clearly also one of 'Them', the educated classes, and had greater access to the centres of power than most working-class Black women.

The shifting boundaries of power were, however, illustrated by the outcome of my relationship with Mrs Paul. In the course of my discussion with her, Mrs Paul had talked about the difficulties of trying, as a single parent, to keep up with her adolescent son's whereabouts and his educational progress and, at the same time, to hold down a full-time job. I suggested that perhaps a Black male mentor might be a good idea. The only Black male professional outside the school that she could think of was in the education support service, but she did not know him well enough to ask him. I agreed to telephone the education office in her area and get advice about the educational options available to her son, and also ask about mentors and specifically about this man in the education service. I later returned her call outlining all her options as presented to me by the education officer.

A few days later I was called to a meeting with David Cox, head of the school from which Damian had been excluded. I was not to conduct any further research in the school, he said, as I had broken my promise of confidentiality by advising Mrs Paul that she should appeal against the school's decision to exclude Damian and should try to get the (Black) education support officer (ESO) to act as advocate for her. He had been given this information by the ESO. Despite the clear inaccuracy of the ESO's report, the head would not back down, and I had to end my research in that school.

This event highlighted a number of issues for me. The first was that being Black was no guarantee of political solidarity. When I explained to one of the Black women teachers my reasons for cutting short my research in the school, she recounted an event in which the same ESO had totally misconstrued a situation and had gone to 'report' her to the head. She then explained that she had regretted the showdown she had had with this officer in the presence of the headteacher whom, she said, 'enjoyed the spectacle of Black people beating the hell out of each other'. Whatever its truth, the symbolic significance of this statement was not lost on me. I decided that just as I did not fully understand the conscious or unconscious processes that made this man target women for his inaccurate and damaging 'reports', neither did I understand sufficiently the headteacher's motives to dismiss my informant's explanation. I was caught between my feminism and not wanting to be bullied by two men without putting up some resistance, and my anti-racism and not wanting to provide racialized entertainment for the headteacher. I took what seemed like the easier option and withdrew without a fight. So much for standpoint theory!

This event also illustrated the interaction of 'race', class and gender in the experiences of the Black female researcher. Whilst 'race' and gender provided boundaries of solidarity and identification for Mrs Paul, these lines were clearly redrawn along gender lines in relation to the ESO.

Finally, it must be said that, although the ability to record and interpret these events is an indication of the researcher's ultimate power, the sudden end of the research in the school was potentially damaging to more than two years of work.

THE POLITICS OF SCHOOLING

The question of parents' and excluded pupils' rights was another issue that arose out of the incident I have described. Schools are sites of struggle where individuals and groups compete over meanings, identities, space and resources within a wider social, economic and political context (Sarup, 1986). Education generally and schools in particular are also sites where (racial) inequalities are reproduced (McCarthy, 1990).

There were two things which puzzled me. First, why should the mere act of advising families of their legal rights to appeal against an exclusion (advice which I had not in any case given), have been considered such an offence when it was incumbent on schools to provide that advice themselves? Second, why did the education officer dealing with the case, in the letter advising the school of Mrs Paul's decision to appeal, find it necessary as I discovered, to mention that Mrs Paul had talked to me about Damian's future, thus confirming the head's belief that I was taking sides in the case? The answer to these questions lay in the complex relationships between schools, the local state and government policy. In other words, you could not separate the life of the school from the political and economic life of society (McCarthy, 1990, p. 33).

Pupils formally excluded from school become the responsibility of the LEA. LEA's naturally want to prevent exclusions from occurring and try to keep pupils in the same school wherever possible. Although a representative of the local authority has to be present at an exclusion hearing when the school governors make the final decision about the pupil, she or he does not have voting rights and cannot be involved in the school governors' decision, which, in my experience, nearly always goes in favour of the headteacher and against the pupil. But LEAs have been squeezed of resources by the recent changes in education. These changes are seen by education analysts as a political ploy by the Conservative government to be rid of local authorities altogether (Troyna, 1992). There have been many redundancies and resultant staff shortages. Many off-site support units for excluded students have been forced to close for lack of money. Furthermore, excluded pupils are difficult to place into other schools especially when news of their exclusion and previous reputation precedes them along the headteacher grapevine. It is therefore in the interests of the local authority for a pupil to remain in the same school even though it is not always in the interests of the pupil. In Damian Paul's case, he did not want to return to the school which had excluded him as he was sure that the teachers did not want him and he (rightly or wrongly) feared victimization. The appeal was only useful to him to clear his name as he was in his last year of compulsory education. But it is also important that the local education office maintains good relations with the schools in its area. The role of the local education office in trying to reinstate pupils into schools through the appeals system can be a source of tension and disagreement with these schools. As a Black woman from whom Mrs Paul had sought help, I proved to be the right person in the right place and therefore a convenient peg upon which the local education officer could hang responsibility for Damian's appeal.

Damian's exclusion also exposed another aspect of the school's relations with the social and political world outside its boundaries and the delicate and sensitive nature of some of the decisions that headteachers have to make. In a school that serves diverse communities of ethnic groups, it is likely that any (political) rivalries/antagonisms between different groups will spill over into the life of the school itself. According to two teachers, the headteacher in this situation was anxious to mollify the Kurdish community which was made up, largely, of recent arrivals in an area with an established Turkish group. Damian and two White friends who were also excluded were said to have *racially* attacked three Kurdish boys in the school. In a conversation with me, and in the letters to the parents of the three boys, the head stressed the 'racial' element of the 'attack' and the seriousness with which this was regarded by the school. However, during the governors' hearing, when challenged by Mrs Paul and one of the other parents about the alleged racism, he retracted and stated that the boys were being excluded for fighting with the Kurdish boys but that it was the Kurdish community which was feeling vulnerable as it thought the 'attack' had been motivated by racism. The allegation of racism against the three boys clearly put the head in a difficult position. As Mrs Paul said later,

'For years Black children have been the victims of racism inside and outside the school and nothing has ever been done about it. Now a Black child is involved in a fight with a Kurdish child and suddenly it's called racism and becomes the biggest offence.'

The diversity of ethnic groups served by a school complicates further the already complex politics of schooling. Decision-making becomes a delicate balancing act in order not to upset any one group and risk inflaming and getting drawn into ethnic antagonisms which exist outside the school boundary. When this is placed within the context of the education system and the rhetoric of parental choice, the importance of strong leadership and a commitment to social justice within the school becomes apparent. As one teacher said:

'David [Cox] is basically a nice bloke but weak, and this kind of job has been made very difficult for blokes like him. You've got to be pleasing the parents all the time because your funding depends on parents choosing to send their children to your school. At the same time you've got to be pushing for good exam results so that your school looks good on the league tables. Now in a mixed area like this, you can't please everybody. So who do you prioritize? Those kids who are seen to be good academically and to behave themselves. Black kids are not seen to fit into that category, so once again, their needs are pushed to the bottom of the list.'

In a situation such as this, 'race' is not necessarily the active ingredient but the terrain upon which other political intrigues are played out.

ANALYSING THE EXPERIENCES OF BLACK PUPILS

The negative effects and deeply emotional impact that racism has on the lives of Black pupils has often obscured a more complex understanding of 'race' in schools. A number of writers have discussed the poor relations that exist between White teachers and Black pupils (Wright, 1987; Mac an Ghaill, 1988; Gillborn, 1990). They have also underlined the salience of racism as a structuring feature of teacher/pupil interactions. However, such relations are more complex than many sociologists allow. The focus on racism as an autonomous feature of White teacher relations with Black pupils obscures other interactive forces which influence teacher attitudes and black pupils' experiences of school. The students I interviewed placed a great deal of importance on the racism of individual teachers, but they also linked their experiences of school to external factors such as unemployment and relations with the police (Mac an Ghaill, 1988). The following conversation highlights the complexity of relations within schools and the importance of a different analysis which enables us to take account of this complexity in relation to the experiences of Black students.

Clive: ... My older brother was in trouble with the police once, and it wasn't serious but they just wouldn't leave him alone and every time something happened in the area, they would come looking for him. Then one day I was walking to school with my friend and this police car came up and this policeman says to me, 'So if it isn't Sean's brother. Where did you get that bag then? You haven't been out nicking bags have you?' Just because I had this new bag, he thinks I stole it. I was feeling so churned up inside I didn't want to talk to no White people that day and I was in a bad mood all day, and the teachers just think you're being cheeky to them.

MB: Why did you think it had anything to do with White people as a whole when it was only one White policeman who did that to you?

Clive: Because the police treat Black people worse, especially in my area, they just treat Black people really bad. So you *know* they are doing that to you because you're Black. And then you go to school and some teachers behave just like the police, they want to put you down, make you feel small.

MB: You said 'some teachers' do that and yet you find it difficult to speak to any White people.

Clive: Yeah, well you can't talk to the teachers about it because they think you must have done something bad because a policeman doesn't just come up to you and say things like that. It's never happened to them so they won't understand that it cuts really deep when someone does something to you just because of your colour. And they don't listen to you anyway, they would think it's got nothing to do with the school. So you sit there feeling resentful and you feel like taking it out on them.

MB: And do you?

Clive: If no teacher messes with me then I'm OK. It's just that they don't want me to have my own opinion. They don't respect you as a person. They want to do whatever they want to do without me having a say in it. That's just like the police. I would say it usually starts with one teacher, like Mr Adams.

Stephen: Yeah, Mr Adams, everyone hates him. He has no respect for the kids, especially the Black kids. You can tell by the way he talks to you and looks at you.

MB: Do you mean that he doesn't treat the White pupils like that?
Stephen: He treats everybody bad, but he mainly goes for the Black kids,
           especially the boys. He can't stand the way we dress and we have
           our own styles and he's always telling us to hurry up even if we're
           not late.
MB: You don't wear a school uniform so why should your style
           bother him?
Clive: Because it makes us popular with the girls ...
Stephen: Yeah, he's jealous [*laughs*].
Clive: He finds us threatening. He's frightened that we'll bring our
           street culture into the school and then all the White kids will
           start copying us and he won't have no control. That's what it's
           about ain't it—control. When we're in school we have to be like
           them, you know—middle class.

The above conversation with two 16-year-old boys reveals that 'race' intersects
with different ideologies to undermine relations within school and influence
the educational experiences of Black young people. They show how relations
with the police and the 'street cultures' which occur outside the school infil-
trate and impact on the activities of the school itself. Mr Adams was not
only a racist in his dealings with Black young people. His authoritarian and
unpleasant personality affected his dealings with everybody, but combined
with his racism to have a special effect on Black pupils. Racism thus tipped
the probability of exclusion higher for Black pupils and added a dimension
to their experiences which was absent for White pupils. To the Black pupils,
Mr Adams and teachers like him resembled the police in their behaviour, so
these pupils felt unfairly policed both inside and outside the school.
   But there were other elements of Mr Adams' character that coalesced with
his racism. The boys thought that he was jealous of their sexuality which was
manifested through their class and street styles. In a separate discussion which
I had with him, Mr Adams admitted that schools were middle-class institutions
and if working-class children wanted to get on, they had to 'leave the council
estate and the street behind'. This thinking formed an integral part of his
middle-class values—values which the school was trying to foster and which
were seen to be threatened by the unique styles of the Black boys. Any
understanding of teachers' relations with (Black) pupils, therefore, needs to
acknowledge the different frameworks within which teachers make sense of
their social world and to take into account their concepts of their professional
identities. Mr Adams' personal and professional identities were a volatile
combination in his relations with Black pupils.

CONCLUSION

In this article I have tried to show that whilst being a Black woman researcher
entailed a specific set of experiences, at the same time 'Black' as a mode

of identification is neither stable nor self-evident. The complex ways in which 'race', class and gender interact and complicate the research process is seldom addressed in the research literature. It was not always possible to be the 'detached', 'objective' observer propounded by certain theoretical approaches to research, not only because the researcher perceives and interprets situations in particular ways, but because s/he can at times be a pawn in the political games that form the complex web of interactions and decisions within schools. Racism, sometimes in benign and sometimes in virulent forms, is an ever-present feature of the experiences of Black people in British schools, whether as researchers, employees, parents or pupils. But 'race' is neither the sole nor at times the primary determinant of these experiences. For a proper understanding of the experiences of Black pupils, racism needs to be analysed in the context of different forms of subordination, identification and boundary formation that are part and parcel of the politics of schooling.

Acknowledgements

My thanks to Janet Holland and Caroline Ramazanoglu for their helpful comments on an earlier draft of this article.

Notes

1. For the purpose of this article, the term 'Black' is used to refer to people who are wholly or partly of African and Caribbean descent.
2. The term 'exclusion' was introduced by the then DES (Department of Education and Science in the 1986 (No. 2) Education Act). It provided a new definition for pupils who were either temporarily suspended or permanently expelled from school.
3. All names of individuals have been changed in order to preserve their anonymity.

References

Ball, W. (1990) A critique of methods and ideologies in research on race and education. Paper presented to the World Congress of Sociology, July 1990.

Black Women in Social Research (1993) Workshop held in London.

Coard, B. (1971) *How the West Indian Child is Made Educationally Sub-normal in the British School System*. London: New Beacon Books.

Cohen, R., Hughes, M. with Ashworth, L. and Blair, M. (1994) *Schools Out: The Family Perspective on School Exclusion*. Barnardos and Family Service Units.

Connolly, P. (1993) Doing feminist and antiracist research as a white male—a contradiction in terms? Paper presented to the British Sociological Association Annual Conference, 1993.

Davies, L. (1985) Ethnography and status: Focusing on gender in educational research. In R. Burgess (ed.) *Field Methods in the Study of Education*. Lewes: Falmer Press.

DFE (Department For Education) (1992) Exclusion. Discussion paper.

Finch, (1984) 'It's great to have someone to talk to': The ethics and politics of interviewing women. In C. Bell and H. Roberts (eds) *Social Researching: Politics, Problems, Practice*. London: Routledge and Kegan Paul.

Gillborn, D. (1990) *'Race', Ethnicity and Education: Teaching and Learning in Multiethnic Schools*. London: Unwin Hyman.

Hall, S. (1992) New ethnicities. In J. Donald and A. Rattansi (eds) 'Race', Culture and Difference. London: Sage.

Lawrence, E. (1992) 'In the abundance of water, the fool is thirsty': Sociology and black 'pathology'. In Centre for Contemporary Cultural Studies (ed.) The Empire Strikes Back. London: Hutchinson.

Mac an Ghaill, M. (1988) Young, Gifted and Black. Milton Keynes: Open University Press.

McCarthy, C. (1990) Race and Curriculum. London: Falmer Press.

National Union of Teachers (1992) Survey of pupil exclusions.

Oakley, A. (1981) Interviewing women: A contradiction in terms. In H. Roberts (ed.) Doing Feminist Research. London: Routledge and Kegan Paul.

Parekh, B. (1986) Britain's step-citizens. New Society August, 24–5.

Phoenix, A. (1992) Practising feminist research: The intersection of gender and 'race' in the research process. In H. Hinds, A. Phoenix and J. Stacey (eds) Working Out New Directions For Women's Studies. London: Falmer Press.

Sarup, M. (1986) The Politics of Multi-racial Education. London: Routledge and Kegan Paul.

Stanfield, J. H. (1993) Methodological reflections: An introduction. In J.H. Stanfield and R. M. Dennis (eds) Race and Ethnicity in Research Methods. Newbury Park: Sage.

Stanley, L. and Wise, S. (1990) Method, methodology and epistomology in feminist research processes. In L. Stanley (ed.) Feminist Praxis: Research, Theory and Epistemology in Feminist Sociology. London: Routledge.

Troyna, B. (1992) Local management of schools and racial equality in Britain: Divide and fool? Conference paper, Canada.

Troyna, B. and Carrington, B. (1989) 'Whose side are we on?': Ethical dilemmas in research on 'race' and education. In R. Burgess (ed.) The Ethics of Educational Research. Lewes: Falmer Press.

Wright, C. (1987) Black students—white teachers. In B. Troyna (ed.) Racial Inequality in Education. London: Tavistock.

15 PERSONAL AND POLITICAL: A FEMINIST PERSPECTIVE ON RESEARCHING PHYSICAL DISABILITY

JENNY MORRIS

This article is not really about gender and disability, except to point out that research which only includes disabled men is not ungendered research. Thus such research should be called a study of disabled men and not a study of disabled people; similarly, research which only includes White disabled people should be called a study of White disabled people.

Neither am I interested in talking about whether disabled women experience a 'double disadvantage'—for reasons which will become clear. Instead, I want to look at what a feminist perspective can offer to the analysis and study of disability.

In the proposal for a series of seminars on researching disability, funded by the Joseph Rowntree Foundation, the proposers identified that disability research has, in the main, been part of the problem rather than part of the solution from the point of view of disabled people. Such research, they said, has been severely criticized by disabled people because 'it has been seen as a violation of their experience, irrelevant to their needs and as failing to improve their material circumstances and quality of life'. In his seminar paper, Mike Oliver identified that disabled people experience disability research as alienation—in the sense of alienation from the product of research, from the research process, from other research subjects, and from one's self.

In that paper—and in other writings—he argued for the development of a new paradigm of research—emancipatory research. This must be based on empowerment and reciprocity; changing the social relations of research production; changing the focus of attention away from disabled individuals and on to disablist society.

As a disabled researcher, seeking to incorporate a feminist and a disability rights perspective into my research, what can I contribute to these aims?

WHAT CHARACTERIZES A FEMINIST PERSPECTIVE AND WHAT MAKES IT RELEVANT TO RESEARCHING PHYSICAL DISABILITY?

My life as a feminist began with my recognition that women are excluded from the public sphere, ghettoized into the private world of the family, our

Source: Disability, Handicap and Society (1992), 7 (2), 157–66.

standpoint excluded from cultural representations. When I became disabled I also realized that the public world does not take individual, particular, physical needs into account. Just as it assumes that children are reared, workers are serviced somewhere else, i.e. in the private world of the family, so people whose physical characteristics mean that they require help of some kind (whether this need is actually created by the physical environment or not) have no place in the public world.

As a feminist I recognized that men's standpoint is represented as universal and neutral. Simone de Beauvoir wrote: ' . . . the relation of the two sexes is not quite like that of two electrical poles for man represents both the positive and the neutral . . . whereas woman represents only the negative, defined by limiting criteria, without reciprocity.' Women have thus been excluded from a full share in the making of what becomes treated as our culture. When I became disabled I realized that, although disability is part of human experience, it does not appear within the different forms that culture takes—except in terms defined by the non-disabled (just as the cultural representation of women was/is defined by men). A lack of disability is treated as both the positive and the universal experience; while the experience of disability 'represents only the negative, defined by limiting criteria, without reciprocity'.

Patricia Hill Collins's statement (in her book *Black Feminist Thought*) has a doubly powerful meaning for me: 'Groups unequal in power are correspondingly unequal in their ability to make their standpoint known to themselves and others' (Hill Collins, 1990, p. 26). Making our standpoint known to both ourselves and to others is a central part of the feminist research agenda, as it must also be of a disability rights agenda.

WHAT IS MEANT BY THE TERM 'FEMINIST RESEARCH'?

Women have previously experienced research as alienation. 'Objectivity', as Liz Stanley says, 'is a set of intellectual practices for separating people from knowledge of their own subjectivity' (Stanley, 1990, p. 11)—or as Adrienne Rich once said: 'Objectivity is a word men use to describe their own subjectivity.'

Building on this recognition of research as alienated knowledge, feminist research is characterized by a method which, as Dorothy Smith says, 'at the outset of inquiry, creates the space for an absent subject, and an absent experience, that is to be filled with the presence and spoken experience of actual women speaking of and in the actualities of their everyday worlds' (Smith, 1988, p. 107).

Does disability research do this for disabled people? Most of it clearly does not which is one reason why disabled people experience such research as alienation.

This quote from Dorothy Smith also reminds me of one of the reasons why

I am uneasy about the use of medical and social models in disability research. Such models are problematic because they do not easily allow the space within the research for the absent subject. The use of models as an analytical tool comes from theory and research which treats us as objects. Is it possible to adapt such an analytical tool for the production of unalienated research?

As Dorothy Smith says in the context of feminist research on women: 'The problem ... is how to do a sociology that is for women and takes women as its subjects and its knowers when the methods of thinking, which we have learned as sociologists as the methods of producing recognizably sociological texts, reconstruct us as objects' (Smith, 1988, p. 109). This is the task for disability research also and, again, I am wary of the use of models for they come from a form of thinking which has treated disabled people as objects.

According to Liz Stanley (1990, p. 12), three things distinguish 'unalienated knowledge' in feminist terms:

- the researcher/theorist is grounded as an actual person in a concrete setting
- understanding and theorizing are located and treated as material activities and not as unanalysable metaphysical 'transcendent' ones different in kind from those of 'mere people'
- the 'act of knowing' is examined as the crucial determiner of 'what is known'.

HOW HAVE FEMINIST RESEARCH AND THEORY FAILED TO APPLY THEIR BASIC PRINCIPLES TO DISABILITY?

If we apply the above principles to feminist research concerning disability, however, we see that such research is in fact alienated knowledge as far as disabled people are concerned. This is because the researcher/theorist has not grounded herself as a non-disabled person holding certain cultural assumptions about disability; because the understanding and theorizing have not been treated as taking place in the context of an unequal relationship between non-disabled people and disabled people; and because the 'act of knowing', which in this case is predicated on the social meaning of disability, has not been examined as the crucial determiner of 'what is known'.

The feminist research on informal carers is a prime example of the production of alienated research from the point of view of disabled people—as Lois Keith's (1990) paper shows.

However, it is not just the way that feminists have treated disabled people within their research which is problematic, it is also how they have left disabled women out. This is clear if we look at the development of research over the last 20 years.

There were two stages to the development of feminist research. The first was that of 'adding women in' to the previously male-dominated view of the world. This produced some revealing studies in a number of different disciplines, but it was the second stage that was more revolutionary. Feminists found that, rather than just adding women to the subject matter of research, theories and methodologies had to be fundamentally challenged for existing models and paradigms were inadequate to explain women's (or men's) realities.

In so doing, feminists not only asserted that the personal, subjective experience of women was a legitimate area of research but that how this research was done had to be revolutionized. They went on to develop new paradigms, theories and, finally a new philosophy which illustrated that feminism is not just about the study of women but about an entirely new way of looking at the world.

The most recent developments in feminist thought have focused on a recognition of the experiences of different groups of women and the relationship between gender and other forms of oppression. Elizabeth Spelman, amongst others, has argued that feminism's assertion of what women have in common has almost always been a description of White middle-class women and that when other groups of women are considered they tend to be 'added on' as subjects of research and theorizing. White middle-class women's experiences have been taken as the norm and other women's experiences have been treated as 'different', as the subject of particular study and analysis. Thus, White middle-class women's reality is the basis of general theory and analysis (in the same way that men's reality was), and the reality of other groups of women is treated as particular, as separate from the general.

Spelman writes, for example:

> Most philosophical accounts of 'man's nature' are not about women at all. But neither are most feminist accounts of "woman's nature", "women's experiences" about all women. There are startling parallels between what feminists find disappointing and insulting in Western philosophical thought and what many women have found troubling in much of Western feminism.   (Spelman, 1990, p. 6).

Such a recognition has (potentially) as radical an effect on feminist thought as feminism itself has had on world-views dominated by men and men's experiences.

Yet there are two groups of women who are missing from Spelman's analysis. In identifying that 'working class women, lesbian women, Jewish women and women of colour' have been considered as 'inessential' within feminist philosophy, Spelman has—in common with most non-disabled feminists—left out two important groups, namely older women and disabled women. Disability and old age are aspects of identity with which gender is very much entwined but they are identities which have been almost entirely ignored by feminists.

Feminist theory has been broadened, and refined, by the placing of the issues of class and race at the heart of feminism as a philosophy and as explanation. But the issues of disability and old age are either not considered at all, or dismissed in the way that Caroline Ramazanoglu does when she justifies her failure to incorporate disabled and older women into her analysis. She writes: 'While these are crucial areas of oppression for many women, they take different forms in different cultures, and so are difficult to generalize about. They are also forms of difference which could be transformed by changes in consciousness' (Ramazanoglu, 1989, p. 95). These are really flimsy arguments. Racism also takes different forms in different cultures yet recent feminist analysis has, quite rightly, argued that black women's experiences and interests must be placed at the heart of feminist research and theory. Her second statement is an extraordinary denial of the socio-economic base of the oppression which older people and disabled people experience—we might as well say that racism can be eradicated by compulsory anti-racism training.

The fact that disability has not been integrated into feminist theory arises from one of the most significant problems with feminism's premise that 'the personal is political'. As Charlotte Bunch acknowledges:

> In looking at diversity among women, we see one of the weaknesses of the feminist concept that the personal is political. It is valid that each woman begins from her personal experiences and it is important to see how these are political. But we must also recognize that our personal experiences are shaped by the culture with all its prejudices. We cannot therefore depend on our perceptions alone as the basis for political analysis and action—much less for coalition. Feminists must stretch beyond, challenging the limits of our own personal experiences by learning from the diversity of women's lives.
>
> (Bunch, 1988, p. 290).

Disabled people—men and women—have little opportunity to portray our own experiences within the general culture—or within radical political movements. Our experience is isolated, individualized; the definitions which society places on us centre on judgements of individual capacities and personalities. This lack of a voice, of the representation of our subjective reality, means that it is difficult for non-disabled feminists to incorporate our reality into their research, their theories, unless it is in terms of the way the non-disabled world sees us.

This does not mean that the experience of disability and old age should be 'added on' to existing feminist theory. Integrating these two aspects of identity into feminist thought will be just as revolutionary as feminism's political and theoretical challenge to the way that the experience of the white male was taken as representative of general human experience. Indeed feminism's challenge must remain incomplete while it excludes two such important aspects of human experience and modes of social and economic oppression.

So where does this leave me as a disabled feminist? It means that I want to both challenge feminism to incorporate the subjective reality of disabled women, but I also want disability research to incorporate feminist research methods.

TWO CHALLENGES FOR FEMINISM

First, disability is an important issue for women but the subject of 'disabled women' should not be tacked on as a 'free-standing' research subject bearing no relationship to other research areas in which feminists are engaged.

In my own research, I have recently come across three examples of oppression experienced by disabled individuals where gender issues intermesh with disability, although in different ways:

- The rape of a young disabled woman by an ambulance attendant while she was being taken home from a residential college with a broken arm.
- The recording, by a male social worker, in the case notes of a disabled client that he thought he had discovered her masturbating and the conclusions that he drew from this about her personality.
- A policeman and social worker waiting in a hospital corridor for a disabled woman to give birth at which point they removed her baby from her under a Place of Safety Order on the grounds that her physical disability prevented her from looking after the child.

These incidents are all concerned with violation of one kind or another and they all take place in the context of both unequal power relationships and oppressive ideologies. My challenge to feminists is that they need to ask themselves whether these experiences of oppression are only of interest to disabled women.

The three examples illustrate different ways in which the oppression experienced by women and by disabled people intermesh. However, it is something of a red herring to spend much time analysing the relationship between sexism and disablism. What is more interesting to me is whether the experience of the women described above appears on the main agenda of non-disabled feminist researchers—or is it, at best, tacked on as a supplementary issue, on the assumption that disabled women's experience is separate from that of non-disabled women.

Secondly, I would also argue that it is not very helpful to talk about disabled women experiencing a 'double disadvantage'.

Images of disadvantage are such an important part of the experience of oppression that emancipatory research (research which seeks to further the interests of 'the researched') must consistently challenge them. Therein lies one of the problems with examining the relationship between gender and disability, race and disability in terms of 'double disadvantage'. The research can itself be part of the images of disadvantage.

If disability research is to be emancipatory research then it must be part of disabled people's struggle to take over ownership of the definition of oppression, of the translation of their subjective reality.

As Alice Walker writes, 'In my own work I write not only what I want to read ... I write all the things I should have been able to read'. I do not think that I, or many other disabled women, want to read non-disabled researchers analysing how awful our lives are because we 'suffer from' two modes of oppression.

WHAT KIND OF DISABILITY RESEARCH DO I WANT TO SEE?

I am interested in identifying the relevance of feminist theory and methodology for developing disability research which will empower disabled people. There are four main points which I would make in this respect.

(1) The role of research in personal liberation

For women like me, as Liz Stanley and Sue Wise write, feminism is a way of living our lives:

> It occurs as and when women, individually and together, hesitantly and rampantly, joyously and with deep sorrow, come to see our lives differently and to reject externally imposed frames of reference for understanding these lives, instead beginning the slow process of constructing our own ways of seeing them, understanding them, and living them. For us, the insistence on the deeply political nature of everyday life and on seeing political change as personal change, is quite simply, 'feminism'.
>
> (Stanley and Wise, 1983, p. 192)

In a similar fashion, a disability rights perspective—which identifies that it is the non-disabled world which disables and oppresses me—enables me to understand my experience, and to reject the oppressive ideologies which are applied to me as a disabled woman.

I look to disability research to validate this perspective (in the same way that feminist research has validated a feminist consciousness).

> Susan Griffin identified the way in which during the 1970s, women asserted that our lives, as well as men's lives, were worthy of contemplation; that what we suffered in our lives was not always natural, but was instead the consequences of a political distribution of power. And finally, by these words, we said that the feelings we had of discomfort, dissatisfaction, grief, anger and rage were not madness, but sanity.
>
> (Griffin, 1982, p. 6)

I look to disability research to confirm the relevance of these words to disabled people—our anger is not about having 'a chip on your shoulder', our grief is not 'a failure to come to terms with disability'. Our dissatisfaction with our lives is not a personality defect but a sane response to the oppression which were experience.

Unfortunately very little disability research does anything other than confirm the oppressive images of disability.

(2) The personal experience of disability

Researchers such as Vic Finkelstein (e.g. 1980) and Mike Oliver have been arguing for years against the medical model of disability and in so doing they have been making the personal political in the sense that they have insisted that what appears to be an individual experience of disability is in fact socially constructed. However, we also need to hang on to the other sense of making the personal political and that is owning, taking control of, the representation of the personal experience of disability—including the negative parts to the experience.

Unfortunately, in our attempts to challenge the medical and the 'personal tragedy' models of disability, we have sometimes tended to deny the personal experience of disability. Disability *is* associated with illness, and with old age (two-thirds of disabled people are over the age of 60), and with conditions which are inevitably painful. The Liberation Network of People with Disabilities, an organization which made an explicit attempt to incorporate the politics of the personal, recognized this in their policy statement. This statement included the point that, unlike other forms of oppression, being disabled is 'often an additional drain on the resources of the individual, i.e. it is not inherently distressing to be black, whilst it may be to suffer from painful arthritis' (*In From the Cold*, June 1981). To experience disability is to experience the frailty of the human body. If we deny this we will find that our personal experience of disability will remain an isolated one; we will experience our differences as something peculiar to us as individuals—and we will commonly feel a sense of personal blame and responsibility.

When illness and physical difficulties—and old age—are so associated with personal inadequacies and are so painful to confront, it is also easy for us, in our attempts to assert control over our lives, to insist that we are young, fit, competent. The truth of the matter is that most disabled people are not young, are not fit, and have great difficulty in developing the competence to control our lives.

The experience of ageing, of being ill, of being in pain, of physical and intellectual limitations, are all part of the experience of living. Fear of all of these things, however, means that there is little cultural representation which creates an understanding of their subjective reality. The disability movement needs to take on the feminist principle of the personal is political, and in giving voice to such subjective experiences, assert the value of our lives. Disability research, if it is emancipatory research (in the way that Mike Oliver defines it), can play a key role in this.

(3) Non-disabled researchers as allies

All oppressed groups need allies. Non-disabled researchers have two roles as allies.

First, non-disabled academics and researchers should ask themselves where are the disabled researchers? students? academics? They should recognize and challenge both direct and indirect discrimination. Unfortunately, most non-disabled people don't even recognize the way that discrimination against disabled people operates within their workplace. Getting disabled people into the positions where we play a full role in carrying out research and disseminating it is as important for disabled people as the same process was and is for women. As Audre Lourde says, 'It is axiomatic that if we do not define ourselves for ourselves, we will be defined by others—for their use and to our detriment' (quoted by Hill Collins, 1990, p. 26).

Second, non-disabled people, if they make their living from being involved in the field of disability, should ask themselves whether/how they can do research which empowers disabled people.

Non-disabled researchers have to start by questioning their own attitudes to disability. For example, why does Caroline Ramazanoglu dismiss disability and old age in the way that she does? She cannot see either as a source of strength, celebration or liberation in the way that race, class and gender can become through a process of struggle. Non-disabled people need to examine why not.

Feminist research places women's subjective reality (i.e. experience defined in the subject's own terms) at its core. However, when researchers (feminist or not) approach disabled people as a research subject, they have few tools with which to understand our subjective reality because our own definitions of the experience of disability are missing from the general culture.

If non-disabled people are to carry on doing research on disability—as they undoubtedly will—what kind of research should they be doing?

(a) Turning the spotlight on the oppressors. Non-disabled people's behaviour towards disabled people is a social problem—it is a social problem because it is an expression of prejudice. Such expressions of prejudice take place within personal relationships as well as through social, economic and political institutions and, for example, a study of a caring relationship therefore needs to concern itself with prejudice, in the same way that studies of relationships between men and women concern themselves with sexism.

(b) Our personal experience of prejudice must be made political—and space must be created for the absent subject. This point is illustrated by an example of research which needs to be done—namely, research concerning the experience of abuse within institutions. Such research would have three aims: (1) naming the experience as abuse, (2) giving expression to the anger, pain and hurt resulting from such experiences, and (3) focusing on the perpetrators of such abuse, examining how and why it comes about.

The disability movement has started to identify the different forms of abuse that disabled people experience. One example is what has been called 'public stripping'. This is experienced by many disabled people in a hospital setting. For example a woman with spina bifida described her experience throughout her childhood when she was required by an orthopaedic consultant to be examined once a year. These examinations took place in a large room, with 20 or more doctors and physiotherapists looking on. After the hospital acquired videotaping equipment the examinations were videotaped. She described how, when she was 12, she tried to keep on her bra which she had just started to wear. I quote from the article which described her experience: 'The doctor, in order to explain something about her back, took it off without saying anything to her, but with noticeable irritation. A nurse quickly apologized—not to Anne but to the doctor' (*Disability Rag*, Jan./Feb., 1990). Anne knew that this kind of humiliation was inflicted on her because she was, as one doctor called her, 'significantly deformed and handicapped'.

The prejudice and the unequal power relationships which are an integral part of disabled people's experience of health services has led, in this type of situation, to both abuse and exploitation: abuse because privacy and personal autonomy have been violated, leading to long-lasting psychological consequences for many who have experienced this kind of public stripping; exploitation because, rather than being provided with a medical service (which is why people go to doctors and hospitals) people like Anne are actually providing a service to the medical profession.

(4) Disability research and disability politics are of general relevance to all social groups

This is not just because disability is found amongst all social groups but also because the experience of disability is part of the wider and fundamental issues of prejudice and economic inequality.

Black people's experience of racism cannot be compartmentalized and studied separately from the underlying social structure; women's experience of sexism cannot be separated from the society in which it takes place; and neither can disabled people's experience of disablism and inequality be divorced from the society in which we all live.

Feminists ask how and why the public world assumes that responsibilities and tasks which take place within the private world will not impinge on the responsibilities and tasks of the workplace. Disability research must ask how and why the public world of work assumes a lack of disability and illness. It is such a focus which takes both women and disabled people out of a research ghetto for these are fundamental questions about the very nature of social and economic organizations. Our society is characterized by fundamental inequalities and by ideologies which divide people against each other—the experience of disability is an integral part of this.

References

Bunch, C. (1988) Making common cause: Diversity and coalitions. In C. McEwen and S. O'Sullivan (eds) *Out the Other Side*. London: Virago.

Collins, P.H. (1990) *Black Feminist Thought: Knowledge Consciousness, and the Politics of Empowerment*. London: Unwin Hyman.

Finkelstein, V. (1980) *Attitudes and Disabled People: Issues for Discussion*. New York: World Rehabilitation Fund.

Griffin, S. (1982) *Made from This Earth*. London: Women's Press.

Keith, L. (1990) Caring partnership. *Community Care* 22 (February), v–vi.

Morris, J. (1991) *Pride against Prejudice: Transforming Attitudes to Disability*. London: Women's Press.

Ramazanoglu, C. (1989) *Feminism and the Contradictions of Oppression*. London: Routledge.

Smith, D. (1988) *The Everyday World as Problematic: A Feminist Sociology*. Milton Keynes: Open University Press.

Spelman, E (1990) *Inessential Woman*. London: Women's Press.

Stanley, L. (1990) *Feminist Praxis: Research, Theory and Epistemology in Feminist Sociology*. London: Routledge.

Stanley, L. and Wise, S. (1983) Back into the personal or: Our attempt to construct 'feminist research'. In G. Bowles and R.D. Klein (eds) *Theories of Women's Studies*. London: Routledge and Kegan Paul.

16 ACCOUNTING FOR SEXUALITY, LIVING SEXUAL POLITICS: CAN FEMINIST RESEARCH BE VALID?

JANET HOLLAND AND CAROLINE RAMAZANOGLU

Our questions about validity come from our experience as sociologists and feminist researchers. In this article we draw on work, carried out with colleagues in the Women, Risk and AIDS Project (WRAP) and the Men, Risk and AIDS Project (MRAP), on interpreting young people's accounts of their sexuality.[1]

[...]

In these studies we have tried to make it as clear as possible to ourselves what we are doing when we do research: what we are taking for granted and why; what 'findings' we disagree over, and generally what we do to the interview transcripts and field notes that comprise our primary data. To do this we must locate ourselves as researchers and as fallible, subjective people within the research process (Ramazanoglu, 1989). More than this, we have to make explicit what the young people who agreed to be interviewed contributed to the research, and what we have made of these contributions.

Since no researcher can gain more than a glimpse of other people's lives through accounts given in an interview, much of the 'skill' of interview-based research lies in what sense we make of the interview after the subject is gone—how we interpret our interview texts. The many possible ways of interpreting interview transcripts face feminists, like other researchers, with a problem of validity. We cannot read meaning *in* texts, allowing them to propose their own meanings, without also reading meaning *into* them, as we make sense of their meanings.

Dorothy Smith (1989, pp. 35–6) has warned that feminists face the danger that in turning talk into texts and texts into sociology, we can be drawn into incorporating people's accounts into existing sociological frameworks.

> ... a moment comes after talk has been inscribed as texts and become data when it must be worked up as sociology. ... as long as we work within the objectifying frame that organizes the discursive consciousness, we will find ourselves reinscribing the moment of discovery of women's experiences as women talk with women, into the conceptual order that locate the reader's and writer's consciousness outside the experience of that talk. (Smith, 1989, p. 35)

Source: Abridged from a paper given at the British Sociological Association Annual Conference (1993) 'Research Imaginations'.

Smith argues that sociological discourse embodies a standpoint from 'the relations of ruling' (p. 36) in which relationships of gender, class and race are 'seen'
from the standpoint of those in dominant positions, notably White men. When
we attempt to write sociology from the standpoint of women's experience 'we
are returned to just that way of looking we have tried to avoid' (p. 36). Patricia
H. Collins notes that even if we incorporate women's experience into our ways
of knowing, decisions about:

> . . . who to trust, what to believe and why something is true are not benign
> academic issues. Instead these concerns tap the fundamental question of
> which versions of truth will prevail and shape thought and action.
>   (Collins, 1990, pp. 202–3)

Struggles over interpretation can be political struggles between women or
between men as well as between masculinist and feminist knowledge.

The WRAP team has not resolved the problems of inheriting both the
patriarchal sociological discourses recognized by Smith, and the racist and
Eurocentric categories identified by Collins. But we have tried to be conscious
and critical of this problem and to avoid the exclusions that are inherent in
unacknowledged relations of ruling. This has meant an emphasis on the
salience of power relations throughout the research.

Starting from a feminist standpoint, however, we may end by producing
sociology that is little different from other sociologies in making objects of
the subjects of research. In the language of ethnomethodology, Smith (1989,
p. 57) notes that sociology's 'objectifications are always at odds with the lived
actuality in which they are accomplished'. Even if the researcher identifies
politically *with* women, this does not necessarily give us the methodological
tools with which to avoid the conceptual distancing of women from their
experiences.

Smith comments that this is not an epistemological issue—it is not one of
realism. Interpreting interview transcripts, however, does raise questions about
whether we should believe feminist conclusions. Feminists are divided over
whether there is some essential or material reality in people's lives of which
they may be unaware, or whether the only level of reality accessible to us is
the multiple accounts of plural realities given by different informants, all of
which may be true in their own terms. This contrast between feminist realism
and feminist empiricism (overlapping with various postmodern versions of
relativism) divides feminist researchers (Harding and Hintikka, 1983; Hekman,
1990; Stanley and Wise, 1990).

These issues were not resolved within our own experience of the research
process. Although the project team was constituted as an explicitly feminist
and collective effort, we sensed the dangers of exploring too openly the extent
of our feminist differences. We embarked upon research without an open
exploration of everything that we were taking for granted. Differences have

emerged in the course of coming to conclusions, and in adding a male researcher to the team. We have tried to meet these, however imperfectly, through retrospective reflexivity in handling our selection and interpretation of data, in developing different areas of feminist theory, and in thinking about the policy implications of the research.

The WRAP research on young people and sexuality was intended to be of practical use to policy makers concerned with sex education, the promotion of safer sex and the transmission of HIV; specific efforts were made by our original funding body (the ESRC), and ourselves, to communicate our conclusions to policy makers and practitioners.[2] Our conclusions, which we believe to be valid, mattered in terms of their possible effects on people's lives: for example, our claim that the pursuit of conventional femininity by young women encourages unsafe sexual practices. Our interpretations of interview data were available for incorporation into various processes of decision-making.

In this article we locate analysis of transcripts in the research process to show interpretation as a political, contested and unstable process between the lives of the researchers and of the researched. Interpretation needs somehow to unite a passion for 'truth' with explicit rules of research method that can make some conclusions stronger than others. Our lived experience as women does not simply create us as feminists: feminist methodology requires critical theory and critical reflection on people's accounts of their experiences. The different possible ways of knowing what sexuality is like, link theory, experience and our openness to hearing and conceptualizing the diversity of the voices of different women. By treating interviews as social events, we were able to see them as a learning process both for the research team and for our informants. Rules of method are made explicit by clarifying our epistemological position and recognizing our parts in the research process.

The WRAP research team aimed [...] to build up a detailed picture of the sexual practices, beliefs and understanding of young people in order to interpret their understanding of HIV and sexually transmitted diseases; their conceptions of risk and danger in sexual activity; their approaches to relationships and responsibility, and their ability to communicate effectively their ideas on safety within sexual relationships. We intended to contribute to the development of the theory of the social construction of sexuality, by identifying some of the complexity of the processes and mechanisms through which young people construct, experience and define their sexuality and sexual practices. Interpretation of interview transcripts was central to our data analysis.

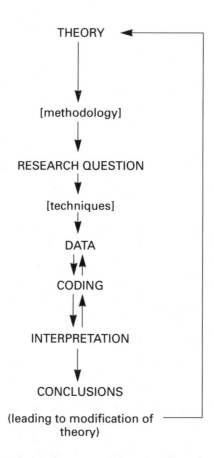

FIGURE 16.1 The research process

THE PLACE OF INTERPRETATION IN THE RESEARCH PROCESS

In order to make sense of interviews the feminist researcher, like any other, has to have some conception of the research process. Conventionally sociologists say very little about exactly what happened during the course of their research (there are exceptions, e.g. Bell and Newby, 1977; Bell and Roberts, 1984). The conventions of field research place interviewing at a particular point in a complex research process. Figure 16.1 represents the research process as starting from theory—in our case feminist theories of the social construction of sexuality—and proceeding through the collection and interpretation of data to a logical conclusion.[3]

The model in Figure 16.1 assumes that the production of generally valid conclusions is based on the ability of the researcher to control his or her own subjectivity through the rigour of the research method. Objective, or at least generalizable, knowledge is assumed to be separable from subjectivity. Feminists have challenged this dualism extensively and effectively (e.g. Harding, 1987; Smith, 1988; Cain and Finch, 1981). The simple claim that the personal is poltical undermines the validity of knowledge that excludes women's experiences. Feminists have shown the power that can be exercised over women, and their 'subjugated knowledges', through defining objective knowledge as superior to personal experience. It is the assertion of women's experience as valid that has powerfully demonstrated the subordination of women to men in every area of social life. Women's accounts of what their lives are like have forced reconceptualizations of social relationships and the nature of power; experience challenges the validity of 'objective' masculinist knowledge.

This challenge, however, does not make all feminist knowledge necessarily equally valid. The validity of experience is in constant tension with the limitations of experience which social sciences try to transcend. Women's account of other women's power over them (through, for example, racism, class, sexual orientation, physical ability) have shown clear, painful and persistent social divisions between them, and so problems in how to validate feminist knowledge of what the social world is like. It is an uncomfortable conclusion for feminism that women can put considerable effort into achieving their own subordination to men, or into subordinating other women.

Feminism is then faced with a dilemma. Feminists want to make political and moral judgements about the illegitimacy of men's power over women, or of women's power over each other. But such judgements rest on general statements about the nature of social life—about, for example, the extent of male control of women's bodies. We cannot develop strategies for changing power relations if we do not understand power. Like other researchers, we need ways of knowing social life that give us more or less valid knowledge. Feminist innovation in methodology has been through trying to grasp the parts that experience, emotion and subjectivity play in the research process, rather than seeing these as weaknesses to be controlled.

Figure 16.2 suggests additional factors that impinge on what can be known through the research process.

If we locate the researcher as an actor in the research process, we open the way to recognition of the power relations within which the researcher is located. Each researcher brings particular values and particular self-identities to the research and has lived through particular experiences. While these values, identities and experiences do not rigidly determine particular points of view,

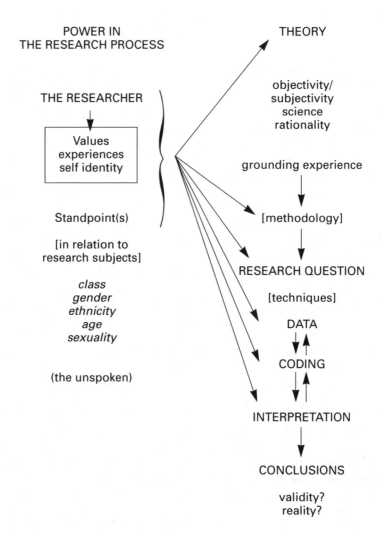

POWER IN
THE RESEARCH PROCESS

THEORY

THE RESEARCHER

objectivity/
subjectivity
science
rationality

Values
experiences
self identity

grounding experience

Standpoint(s)

[methodology]

[in relation to
research subjects]

RESEARCH QUESTION

*class
gender
ethnicity
age
sexuality*

[techniques]

DATA

CODING

(the unspoken)

INTERPRETATION

CONCLUSIONS

validity?
reality?

FIGURE 16.2 The research process: The subjectivity of the researchers

they do give researchers variable standpoints in relation to subjects of research (Hartsock, 1983; Cain, 1990). Since differences may be more apparent to the subjects of research than to the researcher, they constrain what it is possible to know about, and affect our emotional sensitivities.

The point here is not that we know the ways in which particular stances may systematically affect research, but that we do *not* know. The masculinist methodologies and rules of validation that have been developed to control subjectivity do not fully recognize the unpredictability, variability and complexity of the human interactions in ways which take account of power in the research process. We can never be sure that we know what is unspoken or unthought (Cain, 1993).

Postmodern methodologies that attempt to deconstruct texts, discover subjugated knowledges and analyse discourses, tend to be even less explicit than modern methodologies about the place of the researcher in the research. Feminist researchers have been very successful in, for example, recovering women's history, and giving voice to women's experiences which have previously been silenced. But this does not necessarily entail sensitivity to where the 'knower' is situated. While the work of Michel Foucault, for example, has been particularly influential in allowing women to see power relations in the social construction of sexuality and the body, his own gender-blindness allowed him to ignore the ways women experience men's power over them (Bartky, 1990; Braidotti, 1991; Ramazanoglu and Holland, 1993).

The conception of the research process shown in Figure 16.2 is fairly far removed from an orderly and logical progression of rules of validation. In drawing on theory the researcher has to make a series of decisions about epistemology—about what theory of knowledge they subscribe to. In particular researchers have to decide how far their theory is grounded in experience, and in whose experience, and how they understand the nature of 'reality'. It is the *different decisions* taken at this stage that account for the considerable variations within feminist methodology and between feminist researchers.

The process of interpretation can now be seen as a site of struggle at a critical point of the research, and one on which the presence of the researcher in the research process has a profound effect. Research based on interviews, however, also brings in the subjects of research, which makes interviews social events and research more clearly a social process (Thomson, 1989). In Figure 16.3 the place of interviews and of those who are researched is suggested.

By taking interviews to be social events, we can envisage interview research as a learning process for both researchers and those who are researched. A number of feminists have written on the problems of how to take account of social relationships in the research process. Figure 16.3 serves to indicate relevant relationships:

(1) Inside the research team, where conventionally in the UK, and elsewhere, relationships are hierarchical and very generally male-dominated, even though most contract researchers are women (Kay, 1990; Bell, 1977).

(2) Between the researcher and the researched as they interact in the stylized social events that constitute interviews (Brannen, 1988).

(3) Between researchers, researched and wider social connections. The standpoints of both researchers and researched situate them socially in ways which may or may not be apparent or salient to them in the

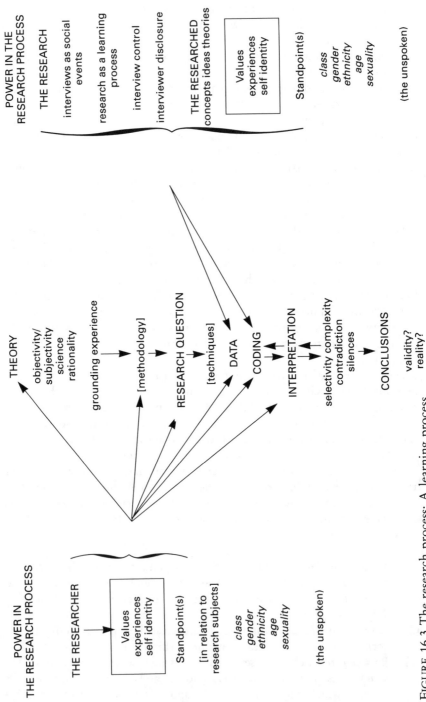

FIGURE 16.3 The research process: A learning process

same ways. Power relations in the research process can be recognized and made overt, but differences such as age, class, gender, ethnicity, religion, impinge on the possibilities of interaction and interpretation, and so on how the social world is known.

(Cain and Finch, 1981; Hartsock, 1983).

Feminists have had to accept that there is no technique of analysis or methodological logic that can neutralize the social nature of interpretation. Feminist researchers can only try to explain the grounds on which selective interpretations have been made by making explicit the process of decision-making which produces the interpretation, and the logic of method on which these decisions are based. This entails acknowledging complexity and contradiction which may be beyond the interpreters' experience, and recognizing the possibility of silences and absences in the data.

Feminists can aim at reflexivity, in the sense of continuous critical reflection on the research processes we use to produce knowledge. These aims, however, are not necessarily (or ever?) realized as we might wish. As systematic self-knowledge is not easily available, we cannot break out of the social constraints on our ways of knowing simply by wanting to. A continuous critique of research conclusions is required from those whose standpoints differ from our own.

In Figure 16.4 we show that by taking the place of the researched into account, we can also raise questions about what the research is for. Introducing policy implications into our conclusions opens up new problems about claims to valid knowledge. The differing conclusions to which researchers come are based on the interaction of their various standpoints with their interpretations of their data. The same interview transcripts are then open to different interpretations, and so different conclusions on policy. This is not to say that all interpretations are equally valid. Distinguishing between policies is always a matter both of values and of the power of the theory used.

By asking 'for whom' policies are intended, we recognize variability in the research process. The initial conclusions of the WRAP team value the autonomy of young women, so our policy recommendations are aimed at empowering young women to take more control of their sexual safety. Forming our conclusions then demands that we make explicit what concepts and values we draw on in thinking about such issues as agency and empowerment, and reflecting on what affects constraints on sexual safety. This process of reflection reveals the extent to which young women can collude in their own subordination, and the tremendous efforts they make to produce themselves as successfully feminine. Our values do not simply inform our conclusions in any determinist way, but interact with the knowledge we have produced: our conclusions favour feminist policies that empower young women, over masculinist policies that reaffirm sexuality as an area to be controlled and policed. While policy recommendations are consistent with

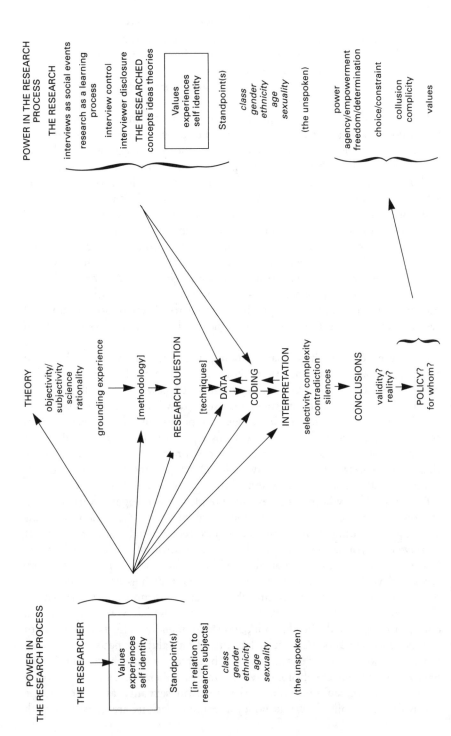

FIGURE 16.4 The research process: Interpretation in its place

our value position, we also claim that we have valid grounds for coming to these conclusions.

The process of interpretation that is so central to this claim of validity remains problematic and contested. But this does not mean that feminists should lack confidence in their conclusions. In the next section we consider some implications of this claim.

LOCATING RESEARCHER AND RESEARCHED IN THE RESEARCH PROCESS

The interview as a social event: An interactive learning process

The unstructured interview is modelled on the conversation and, like the conversation, is a social event with, in this instance, two participants. As a social event it has its own set of interactional rules which may be more or less explicit, more or less recognized by the participants.

In addition to its generally social character, there are several ways in which the interview constitutes a learning process. At the level of this process, participants can discover, uncover or generate the rules by which they are playing this particular game. The interviewer can become more adept at interviewing, in general, in terms of the strategies which are appropriate for eliciting responses, and in particular, in our case, in enabling people to talk about the sensitive topic of sexuality, and thus to disclose more about themselves.

Often neither young women nor men in our studies had had the opportunity to talk about the issues in the terms in which they were raised, or to think about sexuality and sexual experience in relation to themselves in the ways invited by the interview. The interviewee then could learn more about themselves in both the process and content of the interview, as indeed could the interviewer.

In this context issues of control and power in the research and interview context become crucial in shaping the production of data for interpretation. There is a conflict between the requirements made of a researcher through their membership of an academic or disciplinary community, and the needs and interests of the women they research. Measor identifies the problem precisely in the context of the interview. The interview she says:

> . . . involves entering another person's social world and their perspective, but remaining alert to its configurations at the same time . . . There is a contradiction in aiming for ultimate rapport and yet treating the person's account both critically and sociologically. (Measor, 1985)

The researcher has the power to define the research situation and to reconstitute the content of the interview, the statements of the researched, in her own terms. Her 'standpoint' in relation to the researched in terms of a number of social categories may vary in ways which enhance the possibilities for control. An aware, feminist researcher may be older, more educated, from a different social class and ethnic background than the woman she interviews, who may in turn defer to her, or feel relatively powerless on one or other of those grounds. It is true too that those same 'standpoint' factors which mark differences between women, may give the researched the power to control what information they are prepared to disclose to the researcher, and possibly (probably?) inhibit disclosure.

Feminists have identified some of the problems of exploitation of women as subjects of research, and of women interviewing women. The 'naturalistic' interview, conducted with empathy by a woman might lead women into considerable revelation. Despite different standpoint factors, identification could operate, particularly if the researcher uses shared experience to facilitate rapport. Women can be easy targets for women interviewers, as Finch points out. 'I have also emerged from interviews with the feeling that my interviewees need to know how to protect themselves from people like me' (Finch 1984, p. 90). Interpretation is always structured at least in part by how the researched enter into the research process set up by the researchers.

[...]

LANGUAGE AND MEANING

The essence of the naturalistic interview is flexibility, and responsiveness, although it is clear that the researcher and, indeed, the researched come to the situation with an agenda. In the WRAP studies we had a series of topics which we wished to explore, but there was no set way in which they were to be covered. The intention was to be very responsive to the concerns of the respondent, if necessary letting them talk their way into what was important for them in an interview lasting on average one and a half hours. We also had to stay open to the meanings which the accounts of sexuality had for the young people themselves, and to possible different meanings in the way we understood and responded to what they were saying.

[...]

It can be very difficult for respondents to talk about sensitive issues with an interviewer. In our case, quite often young people did not have an appropriate language with which to discuss sexual matters. But beyond the limitations of the descriptive vocabulary for bodily parts and sexual acts, lies the absence of a language to describe the ambiguities and uncertainties about sexuality and sexual behaviour which many of them did communicate, and particularly to describe female sexuality and desire in positive terms. Since there is no language to describe a woman's desire to both have and not to have sex, or indeed the pressures on her to do both, we have had to make these meanings explicit through a further level of interpretation.

[...]

From the feminist perspective of the WRAP studies, the difficulties which the young women in particular have in talking about issues related to sexuality, and the hesitations, silences and contradictions which abound in their responses, are interpreted as reflecting the contradictory nature of the social construction of feminine sexuality. Our interpretation connects the experience of the interviews to feminist theories.

There were instances where, in making such connections, the interviewer spoke the silence, voiced the unvoiced. In the following example a young woman is describing a situation where she has asked a man to use a condom because she was worried about HIV and AIDS, but could not tell him so. She has difficulty in the interview in saying what it was that she said, just as she had difficulty in saying what she wanted in the sexual situation:

Q: What counts in that situation is how it feels.
A: Yes. You don't, you don't. I wouldn't swear he was safe. He hadn't got anything. But you just don't know. But I said, listen, don't, don't . . .
Q: Don't come inside you . . .
A: Don't come inside me. I've never talked like this . . .
Q: These things are important to talk to people about.
A: That's what I said, yeah.

In two other examples, the interviewer felt strongly that some crucial meaning, or explanatory factor, lay behind the entire narrative provided in the interview, but did not voice it since she also felt that it was the interviewee's to reveal, or perhaps to own.

In each case the interviewee did make explicit this meaning. One young man revealed at the end of a very long interview that it was his religious conviction which kept him a virgin at 21, prefacing his explanation with the statement, 'Don't you want to know why?' The interviewer interpreted this comment as a criticism of the fact that she had not asked the question, or made the suggestion.

This failure to voice the unvoiced was made explicit in the second instance, where again a 21-year-old virgin, this time a woman, after the long interview was over and the tape turned off, revealed that it was 'race' and the way that it situated her which made it impossible for her to become sexually active . . . When the interviewer revealed that she had sensed that something like this was the case but had felt inhibited from expressing it, the interviewee responded: 'Why didn't you just say?!' The unvoiced can never be fully grasped in an interview, and we can only negotiate recognition of what may be hinted at (see also Opie, 1992).

[. . .]

While interviewees may give interviewers information on their actions, they can present other meanings too. One young woman, who was not sexually active at the time of the interview, gave an analysis of the meanings of condom use, through her reflections on the experiences of others. She asserted that she would use a condom in a sexual relationship, and tried to describe why some people would not. In doing so she seems to cover most of the problems and issues involved in condom use—opening an interpretation to the interviewer:

A: Most of them [her friends] do say if they were to have sex they would use a condom, and they say they wouldn't—I mean they say we'd probably feel embarrassed, you know, saying 'do you mind using a condom?' and stuff, but most of them say that—like if I was to have sex it would probably be because we like foreplay, you know, sort of getting into it, and then afterwards it would kind of ruin it if you was to say, excuse me, could you go and get a condom please. I don't know, it just seems an offputting idea. That's the only bit I'm sort of—that's why I'd say that the sort of carried-away situation where you wouldn't use a condom and like that, that's the only way we wouldn't use one. Other than that we would. But most of us would feel embarrassed at asking a boy, I don't know why.

In interpreting this passage we want to go beyond the text to 'see' embarrassment as a 'real experience'. We validate this conclusion through our theory of the social construction of femininity, and our own experience as women. We can also 'find' in the text a notion of the essential spontaneity of the sexual event, and the desire to protect herself against infection. These meanings struggle for ascendancy; a struggle complicated by the slippage between what she sees as her own position on the issue and what she is trying to describe as that of her friends (Holland, 1993).

In another interview, a young woman returned to the topic of pleasure, raised earlier by the researcher, which she did not pursue at the time, revealing the pressure on her to engage in sexual activities in which she was not particularly interested, in order to meet male needs:

A: Actually, seeing as you asked me earlier, 'did you find it enjoyable or pleasurable?' I find everything enjoyable and pleasurable except for the actual penetration, so I mean, why bother? I think really if you're with a guy and you are going to do everything but, it's obviously a big tease.

In this extract the researcher can 'find' a clear reference to experience—a preference for non-penetrative sex—which can be compared with accounts given by other interviewees. We have here one statement which 'fits' with other sources of information about the 'realities' of sexual encounters. But the next statement does not inform us about 'teasing' behaviour. Rather it suggests that this young woman conceives non-penetrative sex as problematic in view of her assumptions about men's needs.

[. . .]

In coding and analysing the complexities of different levels of information, hints, images and meanings in these interview transcripts, we draw on the interaction of three levels of conceptualization: the terms and meanings offered by the young women and explicit in the data; the interviewer's fieldnotes made after the interview, which entail some reflection on meanings in the interview; and team members' discussion, interpretation and coding of these data in the light of feminist and sociological theory.

The sense we make of interviews, in the light of the complications suggested above, interacts with our sense of appropriate policy strategies. Drawing policies from confused and contested meanings can never be an orderly or value-free process. Feminism plays methodological, moral and political roles in struggling to ensure that as much of women's experience as possible can be grasped, and that appropriate policy recommendations can be drawn from this experience.

THROUGH A GLASS, DARKLY?

In discussing something of the difficulties of interviewing on sensitive subjects we have tried to problematize the central place of interpretation in the research process. As researchers we need to be continuously aware of how problematic interpretation is and will remain.

[. . .]

If we cut through the complexities of epistemological differences, we can show, rather crudely, three possible positions that feminists can take in producing conclusions from interviews. (There are roughly three positions current in social research, but these are overlaid by multiple variations and qualifications which we do not consider here.)

First, the data produced by researchers can be regarded as in some way directly reflecting an unproblematic reality. Truth is then connected to reality through set procedures of interpretation. Interpretation can be seen as a process which can be contaminated by failure to control the subjective, political, personal. . . . The overt problem in this view is not how to interpret the text, but how to avoid contaminating the connection between truth and reality. This methodology is then very concerned with the minutiae of interview techniques, control of bias, sampling accuracy, and generally with the mechanisms of reliability and validity. It assumes that reality can be accessed through correct technique. Human subjectivity is acknowledged as a problem but is controlled through the sophistication of sampling and the research instruments. While some feminists may operate with these as implicit assumptions, feminism has made this approach problematic because the 'truths' produced are overwhelmingly the 'truths' of patriarchal societies which render women's experience marginal, deviant or trivial. Feminism then seems to rule out the possibility of a direct relation between the texts we produce in research and an agreed, shared social reality. Transcripts cannot mirror social life.

Second, and at the other extreme, the assumption that there is a reality which is knowable through interviews is rejected. In this view, interview transcripts and comparable texts cannot reflect reality since we have no way of knowing the relationships between truth and the interview text. An interview is a specific account given to a particular interviewer at a particular moment. An interview with the same person would have produced a different text in any other circumstances. We cannot then take these singular texts as in any way accessing reality, or recording past actions. They are accounts in which people present themselves to specific audiences. We can only allow diverse accounts to speak for themselves through multiple possible readings of transcripts as texts.

This approach, and the influence of ethnomethodology, has had an appeal to some feminists in privileging the validity of women's accounts of their experience, and in allowing the experience of the silenced to be heard and shared. The growing influence of poststructuralism and postmodernism on feminism has given a new respectability to the view that women's lives are contradictory and so feminism itself should be fragmented, plural, multiplex. We can only analyse unstable, fragile, shifting social constructions.

This relativist view of women's lives producing many truths does not fully acknowledge the factors influencing researchers' interpretations of women's lives and diversity. Feminist researchers who interview others to produce feminist knowledge can never simply allow the experience of the other to speak for itself. To treat what people say to interviewers simply as textual, leaves us unable to show how we have come to any conclusions. It does not expose interpretation as a social process in deciding between possible notions of what is there.

The third position, and the one the WRAP team, along with most feminists, adopted is the middle way between the extremes. The great attention paid to method and methodology in recent years by feminists indicates both the central importance of clarifying how we come to conclusions, and the difficulty of doing so—difficulties which have provoked considerable methodological variation within feminism (Harding, 1992).

If we assume that there is some material reality in people's lives—such as the reality of gendered relationships between women and men—this does not ensure a means of accessing it. Any understanding of the nature of 'real' relationships involves a degree of conceptualization, and so some process of interpretation of our 'evidence' for the existence of relationships.

The middle way is then first to claim that there is some level of reality which can be accessed through people's accounts, but also to accept that there is no precise solution as to exactly *how* this can be done. Ultimately we do not know whether or not we have done it.

Over the years, feminists have made a convincing case that women 'really' are dominated by men in many respects and many situations. The claim rests heavily on women's own accounts of their experiences, which have forced a reconceptualization of violence, sexuality, marriage, domestic labour and so on. Women's accounts have not simply spoken for themselves; they have been interpreted and conceptualized by feminists.

The process of interpretation we have tried to show here, is both positive and creative, but also flawed in that we can never be sure that we have got it right. There are no general rules of validation that can impose an abstract order on the confusion and complexity of daily life. This flaw does not lie specifically in feminism, but in the tension between the vulnerability and the power of any social researcher who tries to read through their data to some version of social reality behind it.

Sociologists, like other social scientists have responded to this problem by diversifying into schools of thought each with their own methodological *solution* to the problem of knowing (or not knowing) what is 'really' the case. Feminists are continually showing that this problem is not solved, but rather is with us at the start of every research project and must be resolved at the point of interpretation in that project. Some form of openly reflexive interpretation then seems essential if we are to claim any validity for our conclusions.

[. . .]

In any research project the quest for valid knowledge is at odds with a desire for order, stability and certainty in our methodology. We 'know', however, that feminism is not just chasing shadows, because experience tells us so. We recognize domestic violence, male power, gender socialization, when these are identified as public political issues (although all women do not necessarily recognize or experience them in the same ways). But this is not to privilege experience, subjectivity or emotion as general means of validation—there are always limits to experience, as painful struggles around difference show. New 'cultural creations' give us new ways of knowing sexuality, but no stable rules of validation which can ensure that feminists always know best. Feminist struggles to assert the centrality of gender relationships in women's lives are also struggles to rework the unstable politics of daily life. In these struggles, the validity of our interpretations depends on the integrity of the interaction of our personal experiences with the power of feminist theory and the power, or lack of power, of the researched. Our conclusions should always be open to criticism.

Notes

1. The Women, Risk and AIDS Project (WRAP) study of young women was staffed by the authors and Sue Scott, Sue Sharpe, and Rachel Thomson, working collectively. The project was funded by ESRC and supplementary support from the Department of Health, Goldsmiths' College, and the Institute of Education. The WRAP team interviewed 150 young women in depth between 1988 and 1990. A pre-selection questionnaire (completed by 500 young women) provided a statistical profile of a large (non-random) sample from which we generated two purposive samples

(one in London, one in Manchester). The defining variables were age (16–21), social class, power (based on level of educational attainment and/or type of work experience), ethnic origin and type of sexual experience. The Men, Risk and AIDS Project (MRAP) was a comparative study of 46 young men in London between 1991 and 1992. A pre-selection questionnaire was also used in this project that gave additional statistical data on 250 young men. Tim Rhodes was a team member on this project, which was funded by the Leverhulme Trust with supplementary support from the Department of Health and Goldsmiths' College. In both studies the main technique used was an unstructured interview, tape-recorded, transcribed and computerized. The interviews were informal and intensive, covering sensitive areas about sexual experience.

2. More detailed results of this research are available as WRAP Papers from the Tufnell Press, 47 Dalmeny Rd, London N7 0DY.

3. Figure 16.1 may appear to represent an hypothetico-deductive model of research, in which an hypothesis or research question is derived from theory and tested against data produced by the researcher, as opposed to an analytical inductive model in which the researcher collects data and generalizes from them. Our purpose is to show that feminist methodology disrupts both these positions, since they do not take account of research as a social process.

References

Bartky, S.L. (1990) *Femininity and Domination*. London: Routledge.

Bell, C. (1977) Reflections on the Banbury restudy. In C. Bell and H. Newby (eds) *Doing Sociological Research*. London: Allen and Unwin.

Bell, C. and Newby, H. (eds) (1977) *Doing Sociological Research*. London: Allen and Unwin.

Bell, C. and Roberts, H. (eds) (1984) *Social Researching: Politics, Problems, Practice*. London: Routledge and Kegan Paul.

Braidotti, R. (1991) *Patterns of Dissonance*. Cambridge: Polity.

Brannen, J. (1988) Research note: The study of sensitive subjects. *Sociological Review* 36 (3), 552–63.

Cain, M. (1990) Realist philosophy and standpoint epistemologies *or* feminist criminology as a successor science. In L. Gelsthorpe and A. Morris (eds) *Feminist Perspectives in Criminology*. Milton Keynes: Open University Press.

—(1993) Foucault, feminism and feeling: What Foucault can and cannot contribute to feminist epistemology. In C. Ramazanoglu (ed.) *Up against Foucault: Explorations of Some Tensions Between Foucault and Feminism*. London: Routledge.

Cain, M. and Finch, J. (1981) Towards a rehabilitation of data. In P. Abrams *et al.* (eds) *Practice and Progress: British Sociology 1950–1980*. London: Allen and Unwin.

Collins, P.H. (1990) *Black Feminist Thought: Knowledge, Consciousness and the Politics of Empowerment*. Boston: Unwin Hyman.

Finch, J. (1984) It's great to have someone to talk to: The ethics and politics of interviewing women. In C. Bell and H. Roberts (eds) *Social Researching: Politics, Problems, Practice*. London: Routledge and Kegan Paul.

Harding, S. (ed.) (1987) *Feminist Methodology*. Milton Keynes: Open University Press.

—(1992) The instability of the analytic categories of Feminist Theory. In H. Crowley and S. Himmelweit (eds) *Knowing Women: Feminism and Knowledge*. Cambridge: Open University Press in association with Polity Press.

Harding, S. and Hintikka, M. B. (1983) *Discovering Reality: Feminist Perspectives on Epistemology, Metaphysics, Methodology and Philosophy of Science*. London: Reidel.

Hartsock, N. E. M. (1983) The feminist standpoint. In S. Harding and M.B. Hintikka (eds) *Discovering Reality: Feminist Perspectives on Epistemology, Metaphysics, Methodology and Philosophy of Science*. London: Reidel.

Hekman, S. (1990) *Gender and Knowledge*. Cambridge: Polity Press.

Holland, J. (1993) *Sexuality and Ethnicity: Variations in Young Women's Sexual Knowledge and Practice*. WRAP Paper 8. London: The Tufnell Press.

Kay, H. (1990) Research note: Constructing the epistemological gap: Gender divisions in sociological research. *Sociological Review* 38 (2), 344–51.

Measor, L. (1985) Interviewing: A strategy in qualitative research. In R. Burgess (ed.) *Strategies of Qualitative Research: Qualitative Methods*. Lewes: Falmer Press.

Opie, A. (1992) Qualitative research, appropriation of the 'other' and empowerment. *Feminist Review* 40, 52–69.

Ramazanoglu, C. (1989) Improving on sociology: Problems in taking a feminist standpoint. *Sociology* 23 (3), 427–42.

Ramazanoglu, C. and Holland, J. (1993) Women's sexuality and men's appropriation of desire. In C. Ramazanoglu (ed.) *Up Against Foucault: Explorations of Some Tensions Between Foucault and Feminism*. London: Routledge.

Smith, D. (1988) *The Everyday World as Problematic: A Feminist Sociology*. Milton Keynes: Open University Press.

—(1989) Sociological theory: Methods of writing patriarchy. In R. Wallace (ed.) *Feminism and Sociological Theory*. London: Sage.

Stanley, L. and Wise, S. (1990) Method, methodology and epistemology in feminist research processes. In L. Stanley (ed.) *Feminist Praxis: Research, Theory and Epistemology in Feminist Sociology*. London: Routledge.

Thomson, R. 91989) Interviewing as a process: Dilemmas and delights. Unpublished essay.

17 FEMINIST PERSPECTIVES ON EMPOWERING RESEARCH METHODOLOGIES

PATTI LATHER

By way of introduction, let me briefly state the many strands of this article. One is my present research into student resistance to liberatory curricula. As one cannot talk of students learning without talk of teachers teaching, I also look at empowering pedagogy. A second strand is my exploration of what it means to do empirical research in a postpositivist/postmodern era,[1] an era premised on the essential indeterminancy of human experiencing, 'the irreducible disparity between the world and the knowledge we might have of it' (White, 1973). A final strand of this article is my effort to unlearn the language I picked up through my interactions with Marxism as I was trying to define what kind of feminist I was and am and am becoming. I now call myself a 'materialist feminist', thanks largely to French social theorist, Christine Delphy (1984); but I have also, finally, grasped the essence of the 'new French feminists': that I am a constantly moving subjectivity.[2]

A few years ago I wrote of women's studies as counter-hegemonic work, work designed to create and sustain opposition to the present maldistribution of power and resources (Lather, 1983, 1984). Women's studies, I have argued, creates spaces where debate over power and the production of knowledge could be held 'through its cogent argument that the exclusion of women from the knowledge base brings into question that which has passed for wisdom' (Lather, 1984, p. 54). C. A. Bowers (1984, p. vii) terms such spaces 'liminal cultural space that allows for the negotiation of new meanings' as traditional forms of cultural authority are relativized. [. . .]

Bowers writes in his chapter, 'Understanding the power of the teacher': Teachers need to problematize 'areas of consensus belief, grounded in the habitual thinking of the past' (p. 58); but the danger is substituting our own reifications for those of the dominant culture. This leaves the student without the conceptual tools necessary for genuine participation in the culture. Bowers goes on to argue that issues need to be explored in settings free of slogans and predetermined answers. Reproducing the conceptual map of the teacher in the mind of the student disempowers through reification and recipe approaches to knowledge. Unlike Freire (1973), says Bowers, he does not believe that 'the dialectical relationship of student to teacher can transcend the problem

Source: Abridged from *Women's Studies International Forum* (1988), 11 (6), 569–81.

of cultural invasion' (p. 96). Issues of imposition, hence, become of prime importance in understanding what happens in our classrooms in the name of empowering, liberatory education.

In addition to this substantive focus, I have spent the last few years wrestling with what it means to do empirical research in an unjust world (Lather, 1986a, c). This article continues that dialogue by focusing on my ongoing efforts, begun in September 1985, to study student resistance to the introductory women's studies course my colleagues and I teach at Mankato State University.[3] It is as an example of feminist efforts to create empowering and self-reflexive research designs.

My exploration is guided by three key assumptions. The first is that we live in a postpositivist/postmodern era, an era termed by Lecourt (1975, p. 49) 'the decline of the absolutes', as foundational views of knowledge are increasingly under attack (Bernstein, 1983; Haraway, 1985; Harding, 1986). It is the end of the quest for a 'God's Eye' perspective (Smith and Heshusius, 1986) and the confrontation of what Bernstein (1983) calls 'the Cartesian Anxiety', the lust for absolutes, for certainty in our ways of knowing.

We live in a period of dramatic shift in our understanding of scientific inquiry, an age which has learned much about the nature of science and its limitations. It is a time of demystification, of discourse which disrupts 'the smooth passage of "regimes of truth"' (Foucault quoted in Smart, 1983, p. 135). Within empirical research grounded in such a world-view, the search is for different ways of making sense of human life, for different ways of knowing which do justice to the complexity, tenuity, and indeterminancy of most of human experience (Mishler, 1979). My first basic assumption is that a definitive critique of positivism has been established and that our challenge is to pursue the possibilities offered by a postpositivist/postmodern era.

My second assumption is that ways of knowing are inherently culture-bound and perspectival. Harding (1986) distinguishes between 'coercive values—racism, classism, sexism—that deteriorate objectivity' and 'participatory values—antiracism, anticlassism, antisexism—that decrease distortions and mystifications in our culture's explanations and understandings' (p. 249). This second assumption, then, argues that change-enhancing, advocacy approaches to inquiry based on what Bernstein (1983, p. 128) terms 'enabling' versus 'blinding' prejudices on the part of the researcher have much to offer as we begin to grasp the possibilities offered by the new era. As we come to see how knowledge production and legitimation are historically situated and structurally located, 'scholarship that makes its biases part of its argument'[4] arises as a new contender for legitimacy (Peters and Robinson, 1984).

My third assumption is that an emancipatory social science must be premised upon the development of research approaches which both empower the researched and contribute to the generation of change enhancing social theory. Shulamit Reinharz (1979, p. 95) uses the term 'rape research' to

name the norm in the social sciences: career advancement of researchers
built on their use of alienating and exploitative inquiry methods. In contrast, for those wishing to use research to change as well as to understand
the world, conscious empowerment is built into the research design.

While feminist empirical efforts are by no means a monolith, with some
operating out of a conventional, positivist paradigm and some out of an
interpretive/phenomenological paradigm, an increasing amount operates out
of a critical, praxis-oriented paradigm concerned with both producing emancipatory knowledge and empowering the researched. I turn now to feminist
efforts to empower through empirical research designs which maximize a dialogic, dialectically educative encounter between researcher and researched so
that both become, in the words of feminist poet-singer, Cris Williamson, 'the
changer and the changed.'

POSTPOSITIVIST FEMINIST EMPIRICAL PRACTICE

This assertion of the priority of moral and political over scientific and epistemological theory and activity makes science and epistemology less important, less
central, than they are within the Enlightenment world-view. Here again, feminism makes its own important contribution to postmodernism—in this case,
to our understanding that epistemology-centred philosophy—and, we may add,
science-centered rationality—are only a three-century episode in the history of
Western thinking.

When we began theorizing our experiences during the second women's
movement a mere decade and a half ago, we knew our task would be
a difficult though exciting one. But I doubt that in our wildest dreams
we ever imagined we would have to reinvent both science and theorizing
itself in order to make sense of women's social experience (Harding, 1986,
p. 251).

The heart of this article addresses three questions: What does it mean to
do feminist research? What can be learned about research as praxis and practices of self-reflexivity from looking at feminist efforts to create empowering
research designs? And, finally, what are the challenges of postmodernism to
feminist empirical work?

WHAT IS FEMINIST RESEARCH?

Very simply, to do feminist research is to put the social construction of gender
at the center of one's inquiry. Whether looking at 'math genes' (Sherman, 1983)
or false dualisms in the patriarchal construction of 'rationality' (Harding, 1982),
feminist researchers see gender as a basic organizing principle which profoundly
shapes/mediates the concrete conditions of our lives. Feminism is, among other
things, 'a form of attention, a lens that brings into focus particular questions'
(Fox Keller, 1985, p. 6). Through the questions that feminism poses and the
absences it locates, feminism argues the centrality of gender in the shaping

of our consciousness, skills, and institutions as well as in the distribution of power and privilege.

The overt ideological goal of feminist research in the human sciences is to correct both the *invisibility* and the *distortion* of female experience in ways relevant to ending women's unequal social position. This entails the substantive task of making gender a fundamental category for our understanding of the social order, 'to see the world, from women's place in it' (Callaway, 1981, p. 460). While the first wave of feminist research operated largely within the conventional paradigm (Westkott, 1979), the second wave is more self-consciously methodologically innovative (Bowles and Duelli-Klein, 1983; Eichler, 1980; Roberts, 1981; Stanley and Wise, 1983). For many of those second wave feminist researchers, the methodological task has become generating and refining more interactive, contextualized methods in the search for pattern and meaning rather than for prediction and control (Acker, Barry and Esseveld, 1983).

Hence, feminist empirical work is multiparadigmatic. Those who work within the positivist paradigm see their contribution as adhering to established canons in order to add to the body of cumulative knowledge which will eventually help to eliminate sex-based inequality. Some, like Carol Gilligan (1982), start out to address methodological problems within an essentially conventional paradigm and end with creating knowledge which profoundly challenges the substance and, to a less dramatic degree, the processes of mainstream knowledge production (Lather, 1986b). But it is to those who maximize the research process as a change-enhancing, reciprocally educative encounter that I now turn.

RESEARCH AS PRAXIS

[...]

Research as praxis is a phrase designed to respond to Gramsci's call to intellectuals to develop a 'praxis of the present' by aiding developing progressive groups to become increasingly conscious of their situations in the world (quoted in Salamini, 1981, p. 73). At the center of an emancipatory social science is the dialectical, reciprocal shaping of both the practice and praxis-oriented research and the development of emancipatory theory. In praxis-oriented inquiry, reciprocally educative process is more important than product as empowering methods contribute to consciousness-raising and transformative social action. Through dialogue and reflexivity, design, data, and theory emerge, with data being recognized as generated from people in a relationship.

In another paper, I look at three interwoven issues in the quest for empowering approaches to inquiry: the need for reciprocity, dialectical theory building versus theoretical imposition, and issues of validity in praxis-oriented, advocacy research (Lather, 1986a). My task here is to look at some feminist efforts toward empowering research designs, focusing mostly on my own empirical efforts to study student resistance to liberatory curriculum, but briefly highlighting four other examples.

Mies (1984) field-tested seven methodological guidelines for doing feminist research in an action research project in Cologne, Germany, designed to respond to violence against women in the family. A high visibility street action drew people who were then interviewed regarding their experiences with and views on wife beating. The resulting publicity led to the creation of a Women's House to aid victims of domestic abuse. A desire for trans-formative action and egalitarian participation guided consciousness-raising in considering the sociological and historical roots of male violence in the home through the development of life histories of the battered women who came to the Women's House. The purpose was to empower the oppressed to come to understand and change their own oppressive realities.

Hanmer and Saunders (1984) studied the various forms of violence to women through community-based, at-home interviewing with the purpose of feeding the information gained back to the community in order to 'develop new forms of self-help and mutual aid among women' (p. 14). Research involvement led to an attempt to form a support group for survivors of violence and make referrals to women's crisis and safety services. Like Oakley (1981) dis-covered in her interview study of the effects of motherhood on women's lives, Hanmer and Saunders found that, 'Women interviewing women is a two-way process' (1984, p. 20) as research participants insisted on inter-active, reciprocal self-disclosure.

Acker *et al.* (1983), in a laudatory effort to 'not impose our definitions of reality on those researched' (p. 425), studied women entering the paid labor force after years in a homemaking role in order to shed light on the rela-tionship between social structure and individual consciousness. A series of unstructured interviews began with 65 women and followed 30 for five years. Data was used as a filter through which the researchers engaged in

> an ongoing process of reformulating our ideas, examining the validity of our assumptions about the change process, about how to conceptualize consciousness, the connections between changing life circumstances and changing views of self, others and the larger world, and how to link ana-lytically these individual lives with the structure of industrial capitalism in the USA in the 1970s.   (Acker, Barry and Esseveld, 1983, p. 427)

Like Hanmer and Saunders, the work of Acker *et al.* notes the insistence of the researched on reciprocal dialogue and is especially noteworthy for its attention to methodological discussion. Both studies do what Polkinghorne (1983) says is so important: 'for practitioners to experiment with the new designs and to submit their attempts and results to examination by other participants in the debate' (p. xi). The methodological self-reflections of Acker *et al.* are especially provocative as they wrestle with issues of false consciousness versus researcher imposition: 'The question becomes how to produce an analysis which goes beyond the experience of the researched while still granting them full subjectivity. How do we explain the lives of others without violating their reality?' (p. 429).

A final example before turning to my own work is that a group called Women's Economic Development Project (WEDP), part of the Institute for Community Education and Training in Hilton Head, South Carolina.[6] Funded by the Ford Foundation, low-income women were trained to research their own economic circumstances in order to understand and change them. The participatory research design involved 11 low-income and underemployed women working as community researchers on a one-year study of the economic circumstances of 3,000 low-income women in 13 South Carolina counties. Information was gathered to do the following:

(1) raise the consciousness of women regarding the sources of their economic circumstances;
(2) promote community-based leadership within the state;
(3) set up an active network of rural low-income women in SC;
(4) support new and pending state legislation centering on women and work, and on educational issues.

With the culmination of our research process, the mechanism to effect changes in the status of low-income women is in place. Women from across the state have come together through the project, and are stronger for it. The project, thus, has stimulated a process of consciousness-raising and action-taking that will continue to grow for a broad spectrum of SC low-income women in the years to come.

(January, 1987, research update)

[...]

The project's success depends on the degree to which low-income and underemployed women are at the center of this process of identifying and acting upon issues. At the time of writing 150 of the women originally interviewed continue to participate in the project's ongoing efforts of 'building self-confidence, developing a support network for getting and sharing information, and empowering underemployed women ... building a statewide coalition of low-income women,' developing leadership training and funding sourcebooks, and planning annual Statewide Women's Symposiums (1987 project pamphlet). As an example of praxis-oriented research, this project illustrates the possibilities for what Comstock (1982) regards as the goal of emancipatory research: stimulating 'a self-sustaining process of critical analysis and enlightened action' (p. 387) by participating with the researched in a theoretically guided program of action over an extended period of time. The WEDP is especially interesting for how the research process itself serves to engage people in the project's ongoing activities, activities designed to help people understand and change the material conditions of their lives.

Student resistance to liberatory curriculum

Theoretically, my own empirical work is grounded in a desire to use and expand upon the concept of 'resistance' as it has developed in recent neo-Marxist sociology of education[7] in order to learn lessons from student resistance in the building of what Giroux (1983b) calls 'a pedagogy of the opposition.' Rather than dismiss student resistance to our classroom practices as false consciousness,[8] I want to explore what these resistances have to teach us about our own impositional tendencies. The theoretical objective is an understanding of resistance which honors the complexity of the interplay between the empowering and the impositional at work in the liberatory classroom. As a taste of where we are heading, one of my graduate students came up with our research team's working definition of resistance:

> A word for the fear, dislike, hesitance most people have about turning their entire lives upside down and watching everything they have ever learned disintegrate into lies. 'Empowerment' may be liberating, but it is also a lot of hard work and new responsibility to sort through one's life and rebuild according to one's own values and choices.
>
> (Kathy Kea, Feminist Scholarship class, October, 1985).

This is far different from the standard usage: those acts of challenge that agents intentionally direct against power relations operating widely in society (Bernstein, 1977, p. 62). There is something which tells me that the difference is rooted in what feminist and postmodern ways of knowing have to offer toward the development of a less patriarchal, dogmatic Marxism. But I jump ahead of myself. I want now to simply describe what I attempted with the research design that evolved throughout our three-year study of student resistance to liberatory curriculum.

In the fall of 1985, the study began with the intention of studying 20% of the 150 students who take our introduction to women's studies course each quarter. Within that approximately 30 students, I expected to find some who would not like the course. It is them I found of particular interest, given my theoretical concern with the processes of 'ideological consent' (Kellner, 1978, p. 46), especially the processes by which false consciousness is maintained. What I had not anticipated was the combination of generally positive student response to the course with the way the experience of participating in the research project shifted in a more positive direction the reactions of even the few who did develop a critical stance toward aspects of the course.

Working with the ten researchers-in-training from my Feminist Scholarship class, we interviewed 22 students three times, at the beginning, middle and end of the course, regarding their attitudes toward and knowledge gained from the course, a course designed to opposed dominant meaning systems. The second interview included collaborative group work on designing a survey to eventually be used as a pre/post-measure for purposes of on-going formative course evaluation. In groups of five or six, the students were first asked to articulate changes they perceived going on inside themselves as a result of the course and then asked to critique the questions the research team designed based on students' own words and sense of the issues. The third interview included collaborative group response to the preliminary report which summarized interviews one and two, the results of field-testing the survey, and findings from phone interviews with ten former students of the course. We also asked them to comment on what they saw as the impact of participating in the research process on their experience of the class.

What did I learn in a very hurried quarter of data gathering?

- Sequential interviews conducted in an interactive, dialogic manner that entails self-disclosure on the part of the researcher foster a sense of collaboration.

- Group interviews provide tremendous potential for deeper probing and reciprocally educative encounter.

- Negotiation of meaning did not play as large a role as I anticipated. Students felt that the preliminary report accurately captured their sense of the situation. 'Member checks' (Guba and Lincoln, 1981) seemed to have the major effect of contributing to a growing sense of collaboration as opposed to a negotiated validation of the descriptive level. Negotiation never even attempted either the collaborative validation of interpretation or, moving even closer to a fully participatory research design (see Lather, 1986a), the collective development of empirically grounded theory.

- Issues of false consciousness and the dangers of conceptual overdeterminism in theoretically guided empirical work are every bit as complex as I had anticipated (see Lather, 1986a). Regarding false consciousness, for example, as I look for how students incorporate new oppositional or alternative concepts[9] into old ideological formations, I do not see the distortion of evidence that contradicts prior belief for which social psychologists argue (Unger *et al.*, 1986). Instead, the overwhelming response is, 'My eyes are opened'; 'Why didn't I see that before?' 'It's like I'm just waking up;' or, my favorite, 'The point is, I didn't know I didn't know.' All involved became much more sensitive to the 'psychological vertigo' that occurs in many students as a result of the course. One, for example, said, 'I'm highly impressionable as I search for meaning. Can you be a feminist and do what's right for yourself and still have a husband and family? I don't want to lose my family in the finding of myself.' And one of my favorites: 'When you asked us where we stood on feminism at mid-term, it was the first time I became upset in the class. I didn't feel it was right to let myself change so much in such a short time.'

Regarding the dangers of imposing researcher definitions on the inquiry, I know I had a preconceived notion of a 'resister': someone so saturated with false consciousness that she could not see the 'light' being offered her in our classrooms. The work of Ann Berlak (1983) began to focus my attention on the sins of imposition we commit in the name of liberatory pedagogy. An emergent focus began to take shape: to turn the definition of resistance inside out somehow so that it could be used to shed light on efforts toward praxis in the classrooms of those of us who do our teaching in the name of empowerment and emancipation. As I designed the continuation of research over the next two years, I focused increasingly on the conditions which enhance the likelihood that students will begin to look at their own knowledge problematically and those that limit this process (Berlak, 1986). I especially attempted to probe the enabling conditions which open people up to oppositional knowledge.

The survey was field-tested and then, beginning fall quarter, 1986, we began to collect survey data for each of the 15 sections of the course taught yearly. The survey grew out of dialogue with students taking the course and was, hence, couched in their own language and understanding of key experiences in taking the course. My colleague, Dr Janet Lee (1988), has written about the results of the survey data.

The fall of 1986, along with students in the Feminist Scholarship class, I worked with 20 of the students in the introductory course in a *participatory research design* to interview their peers regarding their reactions to course readings. We held nonstructured interviews to co-develop the questions for the peer interviews. We then conducted group mini-training in interviewing skills prior to their interviewing four or five of their peers regarding their reactions to course readings. Finally, we held meetings with five or six student co-researchers where they reported their data and we began to wrestle with what the data meant.

The fall of 1987, I and the Feminist Scholarship students interviewed students ($N = 22$) who had taken the course one to two years ago in order to provide some grasp of the longitudinal effects of the course. Interviews were conducted in both structured and unstructured ways in an effort to ground the interview questions. [...]

By addressing a series of methodological questions raised by poststructuralism, I want to use the data amassed in this study to explore the parameters of what might be called deconstructivist empirical work where questions of interpretive strategy, narrative authority, and critical perspective go far toward blurring the lines between 'the humanities' and 'the social sciences'. As I work with the data, I feel keenly how self-reflexivity becomes increasingly central as I attempt to make meaning of my interaction with the data and the politics of creating meaning.

REFLEXIVITY

> Can an approach that is based on the critique of ideology itself become
> ideological? The answer is that of course it can ... What can save critical
> theory from being used in this way is the insistence on reflectivity, the
> insistence that this theory of knowledge be applied to those propounding
> or using the theory. (Bredo and Feinberg, 1982, p. 439)

C. A. Bowers argues that *reflexivity* and *critique* are the two essential skills we
want our students to develop in their journey toward cultural demystification.
I argue that the same is true for those of us who teach and do scholarly work
in the name of feminism. As feminist teachers and scholars, we have obviously
developed critical skills as evidenced by a body of scholarship which critiques
partriarchal misshapings in all areas of knowledge (e.g. Schmitz, 1985). But
developing the skills of self-critique, of a reflexivity which will keep us from
becoming impositional and reifiers ourselves remains to be done.

As Acker *et al.* (1983) so aptly states, 'An emancipatory intent is no guarantee
of an emancipatory outcome' (p. 431). Too often, we who do empirical research
in the name of emancipatory politics fail to connect how we do research to our
theoretical and political commitments. Yet if critical inquirers are to develop
a 'praxis of the present,' we must practice in our empirical endeavors what
we preach in our theoretical formulations. Research which encourages self
and social understanding and change-enhancing action on the part of 'developing progressive groups' (Gramsci, 1971) requires research designs that allow
us as researchers to reflect on how our value commitments insert themselves
into our empirical work. Our own frameworks of understanding need to be
critically examined as we look for the tensions and contradictions they might
entail. Given such self-flexivity, what Du Bois (1983) calls 'passionate scholarship' can lead us toward the development of a self-reflexive paradigm that
no longer reduces issues of bias to a canonized method of establishing scientific knowledge.

In my own research, the question that interests me most is the relationship
of theory to data in praxis-oriented research programs. Gebhardt (1982), for
example, writes:

> what we want to collect data *for* decides what data we collect; if we
> collect them under the hypothesis that a different reality is possible, we
> will focus on the changeable, marginal, deviant aspects—anything not
> integrated which might suggest fermentation, resistance, protest, alterna-
> tives— all the 'facts' unfit to fit. (Gebhardt, 1982, p. 405).

Given my combination of feminism and neo-Marxism I have some strong
attachments to particular ways of looking at the world. [...] I see gender
as a central explanatory concept everywhere I look, including why male neo-
Marxist deny its centrality through what Mary O'Brien (1984) terms the
'commatization of women' phenomenon.[10] A question I want to explore

in my future empricial work is how such a priori concepts shape the data I gather and the ways in which that data is interpreted.

THE CHALLENGE OF POSTMODERNISM TO FEMINIST EMPIRICAL WORK

> Translation was never possible.
> Instead there was always only
> conquest, the influx
> of the language of metal,
> the language of either/or,
> the one language that has eaten all the others.
> (Margaret Atwood, 1986)

> this is the oppressor's language
> yet I need it to talk to you
> (Adrienne Rich, 1975)

> The demise of the Subject, of the Dialectic, and of Truth has left thinkers in modernity with a *void* which they are vaguely aware must be spoken differently and strangely. (Jardine, 1982, p. 61)

I conclude with a note regarding the implications of postmodernism for the ways we go about doing emancipatory research.

Those of us interested in the role of 'transformative intellectual' (Aronowitz and Giroux, 1985) work within a time Foucault argues is noteworthy for its disturbing of the formerly secure foundations of our knowledge and under-standing, 'not to substitute an alternative and more secure foundation, but to produce an awareness of the complexity, contingency and fragility of historical forms and events' (Smart, 1983, p. 76). Within this postmodern context, 'what we know is but a partial and incomplete representation of a more complex reality' (Morgan, 1983, p. 389). The postmodern argument is that the dualisms which continue to dominate Western thought are inadequate for understanding a world of multiple causes and effects interacting in complex and nonlinear ways, all of which are rooted in a limitless array of historical and cultural specificities. The fundamental tensions between the Enlightenment and postmodernist projects provide a fertile instability in the most foundational tenets of how we regard the processes of knowledge production and legitimation. And, as Harding (1986, p. 245) writes, 'the categories of Western thought need destabilization.'

Harding's critique of feminist critiques of science explores 'the problem of the problematic' (p. 238) as she opposes *objectifying* versus *relational* world-views (p. 185) and argues that feminism must run counter to 'the psychic motor of Western science—the longing for "one true story"' (p. 193). To avoid the 'master's position' of formulating a totalizing discourse, feminism must see itself as 'permanently partial' (p. 193) but 'less false' (p. 195) than androcentic, male-centered knowledge. Harding argues that we find ourselves in a puzzling situation where the search for a 'successor science' 'epistemologically robust and politically powerful enough to unseat the Enlightenment version' (p. 150) is in tension with a postmodernism which struggles against claims of totality, certainty, and methodological orthodoxy.

This article has attempted to explore both Harding's conundrum and the territory opened up by Irigaray's (1985) recommendation of a detour into *technique* as we struggle toward vision, self-knowledge, self-possession, even in one's decenteredness' (p. 136). What it means to decenter the self within the context of a feminism devoted to women's self-knowledge and self-possession continues to confuse me. Although I understand Longino's (1986) and Harding's (1986) caution against a 'suspect universalization' produced by a failure to decenter the self, I stand suspicious of what Meese (1986) warns as 'a premature de-privileging of women as the political or feminist force within feminist criticism itself' (p. 79). While postmodernism makes clear that the supplanting of androcentric with gynocentric arguments so typical of North American feminism is no longer sufficient, Derrida argues for a necessary stage of 'deconstructive reversal,' 'Affirmations of equality will not disrupt the hierarchy. Only if it includes an inversion or reversal does a deconstruction have a chance of dislocating the hierarchical structure' (Culler, 1982, quoted in Meese, 1986, p. 85).

Exchanging positions, however, does not disrupt hierarchy and, 'What feminism and deconstruction call for is the displacement of hierarchicization as an ordering principle' (Meese, 1986, p. 85). The goal is difference without opposition and a shift from a romantic view of the self as unchanging, authentic essence to self as a conjunction of diverse social practices produced and positioned, socially, without an underlying essence. [. . .] While all this decentering and de-stabilizing of fundamental categories gets dizzying, such a relational, non-reductionist way of making sense of the world asks us to 'think constantly against [ourselves]' (Jardine, 1985, p. 19) as we struggle toward ways of knowing which engage us in the pressing need to turn critical thought into emancipatory action.

CONCLUSION

> The most rigorous reading . . . is one that holds itself provisionally open to further deconstruction of its own operative concepts.
>
> (Norris, 1982, p. 48)

In the quest for less distorting ways of knowing, the ideas presented in this article need to be viewed as pieces of a transitory epistemology which can, given broad self-reflexivity, help make Harding's (1986) hope come true: that 'feminist empiricism has a radical future' (p. 162). Those of us interested in the development of a praxis-oriented approach to inquiry, however, need to wrestle with the postmodern questioning of the lust for authoritative accounts if we are not to remain as much a part of the problem as of the solution ourselves.

Notes

1. Postpositivism: the era of possibilities that has opened up in the human sciences given the critique that has amassed over the last 20 years or so regarding the inadequacies of positivist assumptions in the face of human complexity (see Lather, 1986a, b).

   Postmodernism (or modernity, as the French prefer): a term much argued about but generally referring to the need for a different mode of thinking, a relational versus an objectifying or dialectical world view. [...]

2. For background on and representatives of 'new French feminisms' (as opposed to the 'old French feminism' of Simone de Beauvoir), see Delphy (1984), Irigaray (1985), Jardine (1985), Moi (1985) and Marks and de Courtivon (1980). See, also, *Signs* 3 (4), 1978 (entire issue) and *Ideology and Consciousness*, 4, 1978 (entire issue). Jardine (1982) makes clear that the term feminist is problematic given that many of these women define themselves as beyond a feminism which is seen as 'hopelessly anachronistic, grounded in a (male) metaphysical logic which modernity has already begun to overthrow' (p. 64).

3. This work was started under the auspices of a Bush Curriculum Development Grant, supplemented by Mankato State University Faculty Research Grants, 1986–1988. I especially thank my colleagues who also teach the introductory course for opening up their classrooms for purposes of this research. The data gathering was a collective effort that included my Feminist Scholarship classes of 1985, 1986, 1987 [names listed].

4. Phrase used by Jean Anyon in a session of the American Educational Research Association annual meeting, Montreal, 1984.

5. Morgan (1983) distinguishes between positivist, phenomenological and critical/praxis-oriented research paradigms. While my earlier work used the term 'openly ideological,' I find 'praxis-oriented' better describes the emergent paradigm I have been tracking over the last few years (Lather, 1986a, b, c). 'Praxis-oriented' clarifies the critical and empowering roots of a research paradigm openly committed to critiquing the status quo and building a more just society.

6. I read of this project in *Participatory Research Newsletter* September 1985 (229 College St., Toronto, Ontario, Canada M5T 1R4, tel. 416–977–8118).

7. See Giroux's (1983a) review of neo-Marxist theories of resistance.

8. Brian Fay (1977) argues that we must develop criteria/theory to distinguish between reasoned rejections by research participants of researcher interpretations and theoretical arguments and false consciousness.

9. Raymond Williams (1977, p. 114) makes a very helpful distinction between alternative and oppositional, with the former being one of the many legitimate perspectives and the latter a clear intention of critique and transformation.

10. This argument is developed much more fully in Lather (1987) where I look at how male neo-Marxist discourse on schooling largely obscures male privilege and the social construction of gender as central issues in the shaping of public school teaching. In contrast, it is worth noting the *theoretical* and *strategical* centrality given to the politics of gender in the work of some male postmodernists.

References

Acker, J., Barry, K. and Esseveld, J. (1983) Objectivity and truth: Problems in doing feminist research. *Women's Studies International Forum* 6, 423–35.
Atwood, M. (1986) *The Greenfield Review* 13 (3/4), 5.

Aronwitz, S. and Giroux, H. (1985) Radical education and transformative intellectuals, *Canadian Journal of Political and Social Theory* 9 (3), 48–63.

Berlak, A. (1993) The critical pedagogy of skilled post-secondary teachers: How the experts do it. Paper delivered to annual conference of the American Educational Research Association, New Orleans, LA, April.

—(1986) Teaching for liberation and empowerment in the liberal arts: Towards the development of a pedagogy that overcomes resistance. Paper delivered at the eighth annual Curriculum Theorizing Conference, Dayton, Ohio, October,

Bernstein, B. (1977) *Class, Codes and Control*. London: Routledge and Kegan Paul.

Bernstein, R. (1983) *Beyond Objectivism and Relativism: Science, Hermeneutics, and Praxis*. Philadelphia: University of Pennsylvania Press.

Bowers, C.A. (1984) *The Promise of Theory: Education and the Politics of Cultural Change*. New York: Longman.

Bowles, G. and Duelli-Klein, R. (1983) *Theories of Women's Studies*. Boston, MA: Routledge and Kegan Paul.

Bredo, E. and Feinberg, W. (eds) (1982) *Knowledge and Values in Social and Educational Research*. Philadelphia: Temple University Press.

Callaway, H. (1981) Women's perspectives: Research as re-vision. In P. Reason and J. Rowan (eds) *Human Inquiry* (pp. 457–72). New York: John Wiley.

Comstock, D. (1982) A method for critical research. In E. Bredo and W. Feinberg (eds) *Knowledge and Values in Social and Educational Research* (pp. 370–90). Philadelphia: Temple University Press

Culler, J. (1982) *On Deconstruction: Theory and Criticism After Structuralism*. Ithaca, NY: Cornell University Press.

Delphy, C. (1984) *Close to Home: A Materialist Analysis of Women's Oppression*. Amherst: University of Massachusetts Press.

Du Bois, B. (1983) Passionate scholarship: Notes on values, knowing and method in feminist social science. In G. Bowles and R. Duelli-Klein (eds) *Theories of Women's Studies*. Boston, MA: Routledge and Kegan Paul.

Eichler, M. (1980) *The Double Standard*. New York: St. Martin's Press.

Fay, B. (1977) How people change themselves: The relationship between critical theory and its audience. In T. Ball (ed.) *Political Theory and Praxis* (pp. 200–33). Minneapolis: University of Minnesota Press.

Fox Keller, E. (1985) *Reflections on Gender and Science*. New Haven, CT: Yale University Press.

Freire, P. (1973) *Pedagogy of the Oppressed*. New York: Seabury Press.

Gebhardt, E. (1982) Introduction to Part III: A critique of methodology. In A. Arato and E. Gebhardt (eds) *The Essential Frankfurt School Reader* (pp. 371–406). New York: Continuum.

Gilligan, C. (1982) *In a Different Voice*. Cambridge, MA: Harvard University Press.

Giroux, H. (1983a) Theories of reproduction and resistance in the new sociology of education: A critical analysis. *Harvard Educational Review* 53 (3), 257–92.

— (1983b) *Theories of Resistance in Education: A Pedagogy for the Opposition*. South Hadley, MA: Bergin and Garvey.

Gramsci, A. (1971) *Selections from the Prison Notebooks of Antonio Gramsci (1929–1935)*. (Q. Hoare and G. Smith, eds. and trans.) New York: International Publishers.

Guba, E. and Lincoln, Y. (1981) *Effective Evaluation*. San Francisco: Jossey-Bass.

Hanmer, J. and Saunders, S. (1984) *Well-Founded Fear: A Community Study of Violence to Women*. London: Hutchinson.

Haraway, D. (1985) A manifesto for cyborgs: Science, technology and socialist feminism in the 1980s. *Socialist Review* 80, 65–107.

Harding, S. (1982) Is gender a variable in conceptions of rationality? *Dialectica* 36, 225–42.

—(1986) *The Science Question in Feminisim.* Ithaca, NY: Cornell University Press.

Irigaray, L. (1985) *Speculum of the Other Woman.* Translated by Gilian Gill. Ithaca, NY: Cornell University Press.

Jardine, A. (1982) Gynesis. *Diacritics* 12, 54–65.

—(1985) *Gynesis: Configurations of Women and Modernity.* Ithaca, NY: Cornell University Press.

Kellner, D. (1978) Ideology, marxism, and advanced capitalism. *Socialist Review* 42, 37–65.

Lather, P. (1983) Women's studies as counter-hegemonic work: The case of teacher education. Unpublished doctoral dissertation, Indiana University.

—(1984) Critical theory, curricular transformation and feminist mainstreaming. *Journal of Education* 166 (1), 49–62.

—(1986a) Research as praxis. *Harvard Educational Review* 56 (3), 257–77.

—(1986b) Issues of validity in openly ideological research: Between a rock and a soft place. *Interchange* 17 (4), 63–84.

—(1986c) Issues of data trustworthiness in openly ideological research. Paper presented at annual meeting of the American Educational Research Association, San Franscisco, April.

—(1987) Patriarchy, capitalism and the nature of teacher work. *Teacher Education Quarterly* 14 (2), 25–38.

—(1988) Educational research and practice in a postmodern era. Paper delivered at the American Educational Research Association annual conference, New Orleans, LA, April.

Lecourt, D. (1975) *Marxism and Epistemology.* London: National Labour Board.

Lee, J. (1988) The effects of feminist education on student values. Paper delivered to the National Women's Studies Association annual conference, June.

Longino, H. (1986) Can there be a feminist science? Working paper 163, Wellesley Center for Research on Women, Wellesley, MA, 02181, USA.

Marks, E. and de Courtivon, I. (eds) (1980) *New French Feminists.* Amherst: University of Massachusettes Press.

Meese, E. (1986) *Crossing the Double-Cross: The Practice of Feminist Criticism.* Chapel Hill: University of North Carolina Press.

Mies, M. (1984) Towards a methodology for feminist research. In E. Hoshino Altbach, J. Clausen, D. Schultz and N. Stephan (eds) *German Feminism: Readings in Politics and Literature* (pp. 357–66). Albany: State University of New York Press.

Mishler, E. (1979) Meaning in context: Is there any other kind? *Harvard Educational Review* 49 (1), 1–19.

Moi, T. (1985) *Sexual/Textual Politics: Feminist Literary Theory.* New York: Methuen.

Morgan, G. (ed.) (1983) *Beyond Method: Strategies for Social Research.* Beverly Hills, CA: Sage.

Norris, C. (1982) *Deconstruction Theory and Practice.* London: Methuen.

Oakley, A. (1981) Interviewing women: A contradiction in terms. In H. Roberts (ed.) *Doing Feminist Research* (pp. 30–61). Boston, MA: Routledge and Kegan Paul.

O'Brien, M. (1984) The commatization of women: Patriarchal fetishism in the sociology of education. *Interchange* 15 (2), 43–60.

Peters, M. and Robinson, V. (1984) The origins and status of action research. *The Journal of Applied Behavioural Sciences* 20 (2), 113–24.

Polkinghorne, D. (1983) *Methodology for the Human Sciences: Systems of Inquiry.* Albany: State University of New York Press.

Reinharz, S. (1979) *On Becoming a Social Scientist*. San Francisco: Jossey-Bass. (Reissued in paperback by New Brunswick NJ: Transaction.)

Rich, A. (1975) The burning of paper instead of children. *Poems: Selected and New, 1950–1974*. New York: W.W. Norton.

Roberts, H. (1981) *Doing Feminist Research*. London: Routledge and Kegan Paul.

Salamini, L. (1981) *The Sociology of Political Praxis: An Introduction to Gramsci's Theory*. London: Routledge and Kegan Paul.

Schmitz, B. (1985) *Integrating Women's Studies into the Curriculum: A Guide and a Bibliography*. Old Westbury, NY: The Feminist Press.

Sherman, J. (1983) Girls talk about mathematics and their future: A partial replication. *Psychology of Women Quarterly* 7, 338–42.

Smart, B. (1983) *Foucault, Marxism and Critique*. London: Routledge and Kegan Paul.

Smith, J.K. and Heshusius, L. (1986) Closing down the conversation: The end of the quantitative—qualitative debate among educational inquirers. *Educational Researcher* 15(1), 4–12.

Stanley, L. and Wise, S. (1983) *Breaking Out: Feminist Consciousness and Feminist Research*. Boston, MA: Routledge and Kegan Paul.

Unger, R. K., Draper, R.D. and Prendergrass, M.L. (1986) Personal epistemology and personal experience. *Journal of Social Issues* 42 (2), 67–79.

Westkott, M. (1979) Feminist criticism of the social sciences. *Harvard Educational Review* 49 (4), 422–30.

White, H. (1973) Foucault decoded: Notes from underground. *History and Theory* 12, 23–54.

Williams, R. (1977) *Marxism and Literature*. Oxford: Oxford University Press.

INDEX

abuse
— of disabled people 271
— sexual 182, 222, 236-46
Acker, Joan *et al.* 296-7, 301
action, political 29, 30, 35, 37
— and research 235, 236
— and teaching of English 157
action research, on curriculum 15-16, 296
adolescence
— and menstruation 196-212
— and physical development 94
— and subcultures 8-10
age, and feminism 265-6, 270
agency, and desire 5, 47, 48, 49-56, 61, 68
alienation
— from body 101, 103
— and research 262, 263-4
anti-racism 118-20, 124
— and infant chidren 190
— and research 248
anti-sexism
— and English teaching 158, 160-1
— and home economics 136, 138, 139
— and infant children 190
— literature 19
— in physical education 98-9
Anyon, Jean 304 n.4
appearance, and construction of femininity 7-8, 94, 96, 100, 104
Askew, Sue 138
assertiveness
— and gender domains 148-9
— in physical education 100, 103
— seen as male 53-4
— and women in science 85
— and women teachers 160
Attar, Dena 129-41
Atwood, Margaret 302
authority
— in feminist pedagogy 32-5, 39

— parental/adult 47, 49, 50-1, 53, 54-5, 57, 67
autobiography, in teaching English 158

Banks, Chas 45-68
Bateson, Gregory 198, 201
Benbow, C. P. 228
Berlak, Ann 300
Bernstein, Richard 293
biology
— and body 196, 200-1, 211
— and gender 70, 72-3, 79-80, 86-7, 91-3
— ideology of 91, 93
Birke, Linda 72
Black, as cultural construct 252
Blair, Maud 248-60
Bleier, Ruth 72, 85
body, female
— and biology 198-200, 211-12
— as gendered 4
— and menstruation 196, 201-12
— as object 94-5, 100, 101, 103, 104, 206
  see also physicality
Bourdieu, Pierre 169
Bowers, C. A. 292-3, 301
boys
— and constructional toys 143, 145-51, 155
— and masculine identities 169-92
— peer group relations 174-7
— and physical education 90, 92, 105
— and school exclusions 250, 252-9
— and science 152-4
— treatment of menstruating girls 203-4, 206, 209
  see also masculinity
Brackenridge, Celia 102
Bredo, Eric 301
Browne, Naima 143-56
Bunch, C. 34, 266
Burton, Leone 84
Burton, Sheila 235-46
Butler, Judith 211